The New Left Revisited

In the series

CRITICAL PERSPECTIVES ON THE PAST

edited by Susan Porter Benson, Stephen Brier, and Roy Rosenzweig

The New Left
R E V I S I T E D

EDITED BY

John McMillian and Paul Buhle

TEMPLE UNIVERSITY PRESS

PHILADELPHIA

Temple University Press, Philadelphia 19122
Copyright © 2003 by Temple University
All rights reserved
Published 2003
Printed in the United States of America

♾ The paper used in this publication meets the requirements
of the American National Standard for Information Sciences—Permanence
of Paper for Printed Library Materials, ANSI Z39.48-1984

Library of Congress Cataloging-in-Publication Data

The new left revisited / edited by John McMillian and Paul Buhle.
    p. cm. — (Critical perspectives on the past)
  Includes bibiographical references.
   ISBN 1-56639-975-0 (cloth : alk. paper) — ISBN 1-56639-976-9 (pbk. : alk. paper)
    1. New Left—United States. 2. Radicalism—United States. 3. United States—
Social conditions—1960–1980. I. McMillian, John Campbell. II. Buhle, Paul, 1944–.
III. Series.

HN90.R3 N49 2003
303.48′4—dc21

                                               2002071462

Contents

INTRODUCTION

"You Didn't Have to Be There": Revisiting the New Left Consensus

John McMillian

Look carefully enough, and you'll find that nearly each day's newspaper bears some further testimony to the enduring power of the Culture War. It's happening everywhere, and the debates on abortion, homosexuality, multiculturalism, public schools, and gun control are only the most obvious fronts. Moreover, it is commonly accepted that behind the conservative position on all of these issues is a deeply rooted animus against the 1960s. Indeed, the majority of today's social conservatives hold as a central article of their faith that most of our pressing problems have their origins in the Great Society, the New Left, and the hippie counterculture—all of which are conflated in their understanding of "the sixties."[1]

Conservatives are surely correct to argue that something momentous happened during the 1960s. But at the same time, we can scarcely afford to rely on pundits or politicians for judicious historical perspective. Years from now, when social historians begin to examine the *Kulturkampf* of the 1990s, they may well conclude that the ruthless right-wing parody of the 1960s was largely shaped by their anxiety over a changing social order. Increased religious tolerance and secular humanism, the changing roles of women, the rising social status of homosexuals, the institutionalization of multicultural ideals, and the exploration of cultural taboos in the arts and media are all (in their own fashion) promoting new systems of moral understanding.

Perhaps this helps explain why the "sixties-as-catastrophe" critique is almost always sloppily argued. As Thomas Frank has noted, the conservatives' historical vision "is undermined by their insistence on understanding 'the sixties' as a causal force in and of itself and their curious blurring of the lines between various historical actors: counterculture equals Great Society equals new left equals 'the sixties generation,' all of them driven by some mysterious impulse to tear down Western Civilization."[2] Put another way, the conservatives have taken the New Left both too seriously and not seriously enough. Too seriously, it seems, by attributing virtually all of today's social problems to the excesses of student radicals, and not seriously enough to acknowledge the real gains the movement accomplished. Listening only to the fusillade of anti-1960s rhetoric from Republican politicians and their hacks on cable television and AM radio, one might never know that the 1960s was also a time when students stood up for civil rights and interracial solidarity, achieved reforms in badly outdated college curricula, protested a war now commonly regarded as a mistake, demonstrated civic initiative and democratic participation, and liberalized American culture in countless salutary ways.

Much of the scholarship on the 1960s offers little more understanding than do the mainstream media. In spite of what conservatives believe about "tenured radicals" running roughshod over the academy, the ivory towers are hardly an asylum for 1960s sympathizers. In fact, as Bruce Schulman has demonstrated, a careful survey of popular college textbooks suggests that the New Left and the counterculture "receive almost no sympathetic treatment" in the classroom. Instead, campus protestors are frequently cast as childish and starry-eyed, and the New Left is depicted as a short-lived episode of white protest, a mere intermediary between the civil rights movement and "the emerging movements for women's liberation, gay rights, and multiculturalism." Although the *Port Huron Statement* and the 1964 Free Speech Movement at Berkeley typically receive a few paragraphs, many other key events in the New Left's history are ignored. Likewise, the political implications of the counterculture cosmology and West Coast hippiedom receive such superficial treatment that even the most charitable accounts, "which credit the counterculture with lasting innovations in sexual mores, cuisine, and popular culture, focus entirely on sex, drugs, and rock 'n' roll."[3]

Not surprisingly, many of the leading monographs on the New Left were written by those who participated in the student movement, especially in its early, formative stage. Building on Kirkpatrick Sale's impressive *SDS* (1973), in the late 1980s—just in time for a predictable wave of *It Was Twenty Years Ago Today* nostalgia—the most influential body of writing on the 1960s suddenly appeared on the scene: Allen Matusow's *The Unraveling of America* (1984), Todd Gitlin's *The Sixties: Years of Hope, Days of Rage* (1987), James Miller's *"Democracy Is in the Streets": From Port Huron to the Siege of Chicago* (1987), and Maurice Isserman's *If I Had a Hammer . . . : The Death of the Old Left and the Birth of the New Left* (1987).[4] These landmark studies are generally considered "authoritative" and remain staples of graduate student reading lists. By some coincidence, these authors are all first-rate stylists as well. But, as they say, "each generation must rewrite the history of its predecessors."[5]

In recent years, a critique of these books has steadily been growing among younger historians, who feel that the reigning narrative of the New Left too closely reflects the idiosyncratic experiences and perspectives of its architects. Some writers—including 1960s historian David Farber—also believe that scholarship on the 1960s has been hindered by "generational politics" within the academy, where "too many professional gatekeepers . . . have resisted letting young scholars challenge their memories, criticize their generation, or simply explain their experiences in unfamiliar contexts."[6] Seeking a greater degree of critical detachment and a more nuanced and comprehensive under-standing of the New Left, these younger writers have already begun to plow through a mountain of primary source material relating to the 1960s, including oral history ar-chives, manuscript collections, municipal and federal government documents, leaflets, underground newspapers, and FBI records. To make sense of this material, they have also begun employing new interpretative paradigms. According to Farber, "the New Left . . . has captured the interest of some of the best young scholars."[7] This still devel-oping work suggests that the insider accounts published in the 1980s represent only the first fruits, not the final word, on the student movements of the 1960s.

Allowing for a few variations and shifts of emphasis, the reigning narrative of the 1960s —we can safely call it the "New Left consensus"—proceeds accordingly: In 1962, with Kennedyesque optimism and youthful enthusiasm, a cadre of student activists began the New Left when they gathered at Port Huron under the somewhat impertinent notion that they might set forth "an agenda for a generation." They were influenced by a wide array of sources, including the critical sociology of C. Wright Mills, French existential-ism, and theories of participatory democracy derived from the civil rights movement, as well as less obviously political sources—*Mad* magazine, Beat poetry, the hipster ethos of the "White Negro," and left-wing folk music. Although they were not communist sympathizers, they refused to declare themselves *anti*communist, thereby distinguishing themselves from parts of the Old Left. Precocious intellects like Tom Hayden, Al Haber, and others led lives of "principled nonconformity," devoted themselves to "secular ideals of social justice," and (like all good liberal reformers) exhibited great faith in the trans-forming potential of marches, meetings, and mimeograph machines.

But even at its vigorous origins, a serious of "unavoidable dilemmas" threatened the New Left's project. As Todd Gitlin put it, "the internal frailties that were to undo [Stu-dents for a Democratic Society] were already built in at the moment of its greatest growth and vigor."[8] Rather than seeing themselves as radical agents, student activists were constantly on the lookout for another "revolutionary vanguard" that would facil-itate meaningful social change. The concept of "participatory democracy," the leading theoretical light for the New Left, proved to be a "stick of conceptual dynamite" that degenerated into a "catchword" and a "cliché" as the student movement developed.[9] In addition, activists underestimated the dangers of provoking opposition from the Right. They were unprepared for the sudden growth of Students for a Democratic So-ciety (SDS) in the wake of their successful protests against the Vietnam War, and they never found a way to reconcile the divergence, by the mid-1960s, between one wing of the movement, which emphasized "militancy" and immediate "action," and another that valued "critical reflection" and long-term strategy. The New Left suffered the dif-ficulty of wanting to "be both strategic and expressive, political and cultural: to change the world (end the war, win civil rights) while freeing life in the here and now."[10]

Having already sown the seeds of its destruction, the movement's decline was pre-dictable: Activists were ill prepared to cope with the intransigence of the war, govern-ment repression, internal differences, unresolved cultural contradictions, and a political

backlash from the established culture. By the end of the decade, some students were using outlandish revolutionary rhetoric that bore little relation to reality, while others retreated into hedonism and drug abuse, fell prey to sectarian arrogance, and, at the extreme, descended into violence. Then—to make absolutely sure that everyone
understood the movement was *over*—they sounded its death knell at a series of symbolic end-points: the 1968 Democratic National Convention, the "Days of Rage," the
Rolling Stones concert at Altamont, the Manson Gang murders, or the Manhattan
townhouse explosion that killed three members of the ultra-militant Weather Underground. With all this, the movement that had promised to change society "collapsed,
plummeting into cultural oblivion as if it had been some kind of political Hula-
Hoop."[11]

Although the 1960s are often associated with a scholarly view which holds that our
understanding of the world can be enriched from a "bottom-up" perspective, most
chroniclers of the New Left have been disappointingly "top-down" in their approach.
Far too many historians dwell on the institutional history of SDS and the powerful personalities of (admittedly fascinating) movement leaders. Although the activities of New
Left luminaries were surely important, the New Left was clearly a broad-based, grassroots movement. Ironically, even during the 1960s, some activists anticipated that future scholars might do damage to their history by looking at the wrong types of sources.
As Jesse Lemisch observed in 1967, "We need hardly contend that the peace movement
is on the brink of power today to note that a future historian who studies it from the
top down ... will seriously underestimate its numbers and diversity of activities."[12]
Wini Breines has likewise noted that "there were many centers of action in the movement, many interpretations, many visions, many experiences."[13] Even if we allow that
the student movement of the 1960s is a large subject, not easily suited to comprehensive description, we still need to ask what the New Left consensus leaves out, and why?

These are the questions that the contributors to this volume attempt to answer. The essays are divided into two sections. Those in Part I, *Local Studies, Local Stories,* fill in
some of the gaps created by the participant-observer studies of the late 1980s. The essays in Part II, *Reconsiderations,* suggest new ways of thinking about well-worn issues.
But readers should be advised that none of these essays conforms rigidly to either of
these categories; rather, each displays some measure of cross-pollinization. Just as the
authors of the local studies underscore the larger significance of their findings, those in
Part II have grounded their studies in archival research, often at the local level.

The essays do, however, share a few traits in common. First (with the exception of
Paul Buhle's afterword), they are all written by scholars too young to have had any firsthand engagement with the social movements of the 1960s. Our reason for structuring
the book this way is simple: library shelves already groan with textbooks, monographs,
document collections, memoirs, and biographies that tell us about the 1960s from the
perspectives of those who lived through them. We felt it was time to showcase the tal-
ents of a younger generation that is already beginning to reconfigure the landscape of
New Left historiography.

Second, each of these essays could be fairly described as iconoclastic. None in itself poses a sweeping new paradigm or hypothesis that might completely transform our understanding of the New Left. But taken as a whole they offer testimony in support of Andrew Hunt's proclamation that "the Sixties—and the early Seventies—were full of surprises. Much happened outside the cramped SDS National Office, and the myriad layers of Sixties history still beg for research."[14] Although New Left historiography is still in its infancy, the writers of this volume are keenly aware of the shortcomings in the existing literature, and each of them challenges or revises the current orthodoxy of historical writing on the 1960s. Furthermore, these essays collectively describe a "New Left" that is considerably more diverse, inclusive, nuanced, complicated, fractious, fluid, and (dare I say) *interesting* that that which has been constructed by the architects of the New Left consensus.

A few more themes run through this book. One is the affinity that many of these young scholars have for social history. Although some of them draw on intellectual history, sociology, and cultural criticism, many also seem to agree with Maurice Isserman's trenchant 1989 *American Historical Review* essay, "The Not-So-Dark and Bloody Ground," which suggested that "The history of the 1960s . . . must move beyond the boundaries of organizational history and leadership biography toward something like the 'history from the bottom up' that an earlier generation of New Left historians demanded in other fields."[15]

These writers have also highlighted the striking regional differences that marked the New Left, and have recovered the voices of compelling local personalities that contributed to these variations. Until recently most historians of the 1960s have focused on the San Francisco Bay, New York City, and a few hip enclaves in between. Accordingly, they have drawn their conclusions from a fairly homogeneous cross-section of activists and, collectively, have painted canonical portraits of "typical" 1960s radicals. By contrast, we offer a mélange. This book features politicized hippies on Hollywood's Sunset Strip, party-going protestors in Illinois, African American community activists in Maryland, white students clearing space for dissent in the "harsh, repressive atmosphere" of the South, radicalized welfare mothers in Cleveland and Chicago, and more—all part of a larger "movement to change America."

In addition, the writers in this collection tend toward a somewhat less circumscribed definition of the New Left than many other scholars have. However useful it may be to disentangle the different protest tendencies of the 1960s in order to hold them up for examination, revisionist historians are addressing the astonishing level of fluidity between the civil rights movement and the college-based protestors of SDS, between New Left "politicos" and countercultural hippie types, and even between the New Left and the Old Left. Yet, at the same time, we think it is important to draw a distinction—for the sake of both clarity and accuracy—between the New Left and what is sometimes called "the movement."

Briefly, the New Left can be defined as a loosely organized, mostly white student movement that promoted participatory democracy, crusaded for civil rights and various types of university reforms, and protested against the Vietnam War. It first began to crystallize in the early 1960s and then picked up steam toward the middle of the decade, following the Free Speech Movement and the escalating U.S. invasion of Vietnam, only to dwindle away in the early 1970s—several years after the evaporation of SDS. "The movement," on the other hand, was a much larger constellation of social protest activity that either grew out of the New Left (e.g., gay liberation, radical feminism, and the hippie counterculture), or influenced and inspired the New Left (e.g., the civil rights and black power movements.) Indeed, throughout the 1960s New Left radicals often made this distinction themselves, defining their movement as mostly white and concerned with pragmatic political goals. Although it would certainly be worthwhile to publish a collection with greater breadth, addressing feminism and gay liberation, the counterculture, black power, and Latino and Native American activism, we have chosen a more limited focus on the white New Left; nevertheless we do not treat the activity of white radicals as hermetically sealed off from other types of protest activity.

The New Left's relation to the feminist and multicultural revolutions demands special comment here. These essays leave no doubt that activists of color were potent sources of inspiration for the New Left, and that combating racism was a central component of New Left politics. However, the United States in the 1960s was (and it still is) culturally and politically segregated to an enormous degree. As the 1960s unfolded, black and white radicals operated more on parallel tracks than on the same track. Whites acknowledged and at times lamented the exclusivity of their activism, and they sometimes expressed frustration over their inability to win the trust of activists of color. And although radical feminism was one of the most important protest traditions to emerge from the 1960s, strictly speaking, it was not part of the New Left. Very few male radicals developed progressive gender politics in the 1960s; as a result, the women's liberation movement emerged largely as a *response* to sexism within SDS and the civil rights movement. That is, women deliberately seceded from the male-dominated New Left to launch their own social and intellectual revolution. The challenge for historians, then, is to present the New Left accurately, as a mostly white and largely patriarchal movement, without writing women and African Americans out of this history and reinforcing the forms of segregation that plagued the New Left. We think we have succeeded in this.

As wide-ranging as these essays are, it is not too difficult to see where the new scholarship is headed. Previous studies have told the history of the New Left as a tragic rise-and-fall story; from "Port Huron" to the "Siege of Chicago," from "Years of Hope" to "Days of Rage," it was the "Unraveling of America." Even though writers like Sale, Gitlin, Miller, and Matusow have tried to show that the New Left was vital, serious, and world-historical, their works ultimately marginalize the movement as a faddish aberration—a *dernier cri* that left the scene as quickly as it came. This is a tidy, convenient framework, and there are elements of it that ring true. (Indeed, the rightward-looking countermovement that emerged in response to the New Left, and that continues to be a dominant force in politics, should serve as a reminder of this.)

But in their own way the historians of the New Left consensus inadvertently fueled the sober, jaundiced critiques of the 1960s we have seen in such films as *Forrest Gump*, in books like *The Closing of the American Mind*, and in the intolerant rhetoric of the far Right. In painting a more panoramic portrait of the movement, even as they pay attention to the fine details, the revisionist historians of the New Left have made a vital contribution to an already mammoth body of literature.

And think how much more there is still to do! So action-packed were the 1960s that, as Geoffrey O'Brien recalled, in 1966 two writers wearily suggested in *Esquire* magazine that someone should just *cancel the rest of the decade* because enough had happened already.[16] (One can only imagine what they might have been howling by the end of 1968!) Although we need to keep in mind just how new the field of 1960s scholarship is, it is clear enough that the New Left consensus is on its way out. Just as surely as historians of previous generations have been influenced by the social and political milieus in which they wrote, the standard works on the New Left owe much—indeed, too much—to the particular experiences of their authors, to the values and assumptions that fueled their activism, and to the intemperate climate of the Culture War.

Notes

Acknowledgments: The author would like to thank Eric Foner, Kim Phillips-Fein, Doug Rossinow, Jeremy Varon, and Ken Waltzer for their comments on an earlier version of this essay.

1. I write this on Tuesday, 18 September 2001—one week after the terrorist attacks in New York and Washington. In today's *New York Times* is a story reporting that "The Rev. Jerry Falwell apologized last night for saying that last week's terrorist attacks reflected God's judgment on a nation spiritually weakened by the American Civil Liberties Union, providers of abortion, supporters of gay rights and federal court rulings on school prayer" ("Falwell Apologizes for Saying An Angry God Allowed Attacks," *New York Times,* 2 Sept. 2001, B4). I also received by E-mail an article by David Horowitz titled "Allies in War," in which Horowitz draws a demented parallel between 1960s radicals and Al Qaeda. According to Horowitz, Bill Ayers's recent memoir of the 1960s, *Fugitive Days,* is "a text that the bombers of the World Trade Center could have packed in their flight bags alongside the Koran, as they embarked on their sinister mission." Left-wing academics and politicos, he continues, "have been busy at work for the last two decades seeding our educational culture with anti-American poisons that could one day destroy us" (David Horowitz, "Allies in War," <http://www.frontpagemag.com/Articles/ReadArticle.asp?ID=1021>.

2. Thomas Frank, *The Conquest of Cool: Business Culture, Counterculture, and the Rise of Hip Consumerism* (Chicago: University of Chicago Press, 1997), 3.

3. Bruce J. Schulman, "Out of the Streets and into the Classroom? The New Left and the Counterculture in United States History Textbooks," *Journal of American History* 85 (1999): 1529, 1531.

4. Derek Taylor, *It Was Twenty Years Ago Today* (New York: Bantam Books, 1987); Kirkpatrick Sale, *SDS* (New York: Random House, 1973); Allen Matusow, *The Unraveling of America: A History of Liberalism in the 1960s* (New York: Basic Books, 1984); Todd Gitlin, *The Six-*

ties: Years of Hope, Days of Rage (New York: Bantam Books, 1987); James Miller, *"Democracy Is in the Streets": From Port Huron to the Siege of Chicago* (New York: Simon and Schuster, 1987); Maurice Isserman, *"If I Had a Hammer . . .": The Death of the Old Left and the Birth of the New Left* (New York: Basic Books, 1987). Isserman's book, as the title indicates, discusses only the early history of the New Left.

5. Peter Gay, *Style in History* (New York: McGraw-Hill, 1974), 212.

6. David Farber, "The 60s: Myth and Reality," *Chronicle of Higher Education* (7 Dec. 1994), B2. Also see Rick Perlstein's splendid article, "Who Owns the Sixties? The Opening of a Scholarly Generation Gap," *Lingua Franca* (May–June 1996): 30–37.

7. David Farber, "New Wave Sixties Historiography," *Reviews in American History* 27 (1999): 298.

8. Todd Gitlin, *The Whole World Is Watching: Mass Media and the Unmaking of the New Left* (Berkeley: University of California Press, 1980), 31.

9. Miller, *"Democracy Is in the Streets,"* 152.

10. Gitlin, *The Sixties*, 5–6.

11. Miller, *"Democracy Is in the Streets,"* 311.

12. Jesse Lemisch, "New Left Elitism: A Rejoinder," *Radical America* 1 (1967): 37.

13. Wini Breines, "Whose New Left?" *Journal of American History* 75 (1988): 543.

14. Andrew Hunt, "When Did the Sixties Happen? Searching for New Directions," *Journal of Social History* 33 (Sept. 1999): 157.

15. Maurice Isserman, "The Not-So-Dark and Bloody Ground: New Works on the 1960s," *American Historical Review* 94 (1989): 991, 999.

16. Geoffrey O'Brien, *Dream Time: Chapters from the Sixties* (New York: Viking, 1988).

Part I

**Local Studies,
Local Stories**

CHAPTER 1

"It Seemed a Very Local Affair": The Student Movement at Southern Illinois University at Carbondale

Robbie Lieberman and David Cochran

In late February 1970, Southern Illinois University's Carbondale campus was in an uproar. More than a thousand students were engaged in a campaign of civil disobedience, and the dean of students responded by suspending six leaders of the student government, including Dwight Campbell, the first African American president of the student body in SIU's history, and student body vice president Richard Wallace. Student leaders reacted by calling for a boycott of classes, while Campbell proclaimed, "Students are niggers and it's time to break the chains."[1]

On the surface, these events appear fairly typical of the student movement of the late sixties and early seventies in terms of tactics and rhetoric. But a closer look reveals a much more complicated and paradoxical picture. In the first place, we have a black leader defining himself as a "nigger"—not because he is African American but because he's a student.[2] Second, the issue that provoked such upheaval concerned the university's *in loco parentis* policies, specifically restrictions on the hours that men and women could study together in women's dormitories. Led by Campbell and Wallace's Unity Party, the student senate had passed a bill extending these hours from 9:00 P.M. to 11:00 P.M. on weeknights and from 11:00 P.M. to 1:00 A.M. on weekends. When the bill was vetoed by the board of trustees, students began defying the administration *en masse*.[3]

Finally, the strategy of nonviolent civil disobedience over the issue of dorm hours stands out when placed against the backdrop of increasing violence nationally and events at SIU over the previous two years. In 1968 SIU had witnessed numerous bomb threats and several bombings, including one in May that caused $50,000 worth of damage to the Agriculture Building. In June 1969 the Old Main Building—the campus's most recognizable landmark—burned to the ground. All such acts were attributed to anti–Vietnam War radicals.[4] In the first two months of 1970, antiwar students had engaged in a series of demonstrations against the Center for Vietnamese Studies on campus, including an occupation of the center that had been forcibly put down by campus and city police.[5] Student leaders had responded to police violence with an explicit rejection of nonviolence. Terming the event a "police riot," Campbell said, "there is a crisis on this campus and this is just the beginning. Going up against a club with a flower will never work."[6] It thus seems jarring that a few weeks after defending the occupation of buildings and urging self-defense in antiwar activities, Campbell would be engaged in leading something so quaintly anachronistic as an integrated, nonviolent protest over dorm hours.

The rapid growth of the student movement in places like Carbondale created these kinds of juxtapositions. Nationally the movement had evolved, as ideologies and tactics developed and adapted to changing situations. Integration gave way to "black power," Gandhi to Fanon, civil disobedience to revolution, the *Port Huron Statement* to the Weathermen. But in places like Carbondale this development was telescoped into a brief period. We see then, coexisting simultaneously, rhetoric and strategies that had developed over several years nationwide. For instance, at least at the leadership level, the movement at SIU was still largely integrated, long after the national movement had fractured along racial lines.[7]

The contradictions in the Carbondale student movement largely grew out of the fact that it was composed of three separate strains that that gradually came together in the late sixties. The first can be described as a student party culture, which developed with the rapid increase in university enrollments during the sixties. The second was the student rights movement, which began in earnest in the mid-sixties, drawing together politically active students from across the spectrum. The third student culture, and numerically the smallest, was the New Left, which had been a presence on campus since the civil rights movement of the early sixties and had developed through such organizations as the Student Non-Violent Freedom Committee (SNFC) and Students for a Democratic Society (SDS). These strains alternately converged and separated until, by the spring of 1970, a combination of local and national events brought them together for a series of mass demonstrations that culminated in a student strike and riot that closed the university.

In many ways, Carbondale is an unlikely place for a major university. Located on the boundary where the prosperous farmland that makes up most of Illinois gives way to rugged, forested hills, the area around Carbondale and southward differs from the rest of the state both economically and culturally. The economy of southern Illinois historically has been based on mining, and the region is marked by many small towns and a history of violent labor struggles and frequent depressions.[8] The nearest metropolitan area, St. Louis, lies more than a hundred miles away, while Chicago is more than three hundred miles north.[9] As SIU professor and novelist John Gardner wrote in 1973, "nobody arrives at and nobody escapes from Southern Illinois University at Carbondale by accident."[10]

The transformation of SIU from a small teachers' college to a major multiversity occurred between the end of World War II and 1970, thanks largely to the efforts of one man, SIU president Delyte Morris. A visionary, Morris undertook a massive building campaign to accompany the expansion of the university's mission. Under his leadership, SIU attracted such luminaries as Buckminster Fuller and pioneered in a variety of fields, from handicap accessibility to the creation of the first U.S. program in ecology. Enrollment exploded, increasing from nine thousand in 1960 to eighteen thousand in 1968 to almost twenty-four thousand in 1970.[11] The result was an environment characterized by flux and experimentation. As one former student recalls, "When I first came to SIU in '64, the campus was raw, unfinished. . . . Temporary barracks, cheap buildings were being used, with a great many important functions—things you would think of as important in a university—carried on in these buildings which were essentially shacks."[12]

As SIU alumnus Dick Gregory remembers, Morris "was not just the head of the university, he was the father. . . . Delyte Morris was the first white man I knew who had both power and compassion."[13] He was in most respects a staunch liberal. From the beginning he strongly supported civil rights and sought to increase the black enrollment at SIU.[14] He was also deeply committed to using the university to combat the region's poverty and to keeping costs and admission standards low enough to ensure accessibility for the area's population.[15] At times Morris's liberal principles caused him to put students' right of free speech above the university's prestige. In 1962, for instance, he defended the rights of SIU students to participate in the civil rights movement in nearby Cairo, and in 1965 he allowed the campus SDS and Socialist Discussion Group to invite Communist Herbert Aptheker to speak on campus. Both actions provoked strong criticism outside the university.[16]

At the same time, as Dick Gregory implies, Morris was a paternalistic ruler over his domain. He tried to run the university he had created as if it were still a small teachers' college where he knew the students and faculty and they deferred to his benevolent authority.[17] He dealt with challenges through a combination of strength of character and diversionary tactics. In 1952 he successfully faced down a crowd of one thousand male students on a panty raid with the words, "It's been fun. Now let's all go home and go to bed."[18] In 1965, when the student rights organization, the Rational Action Movement, presented a petition calling for greater student participation in university policy making, Morris defused the challenge by appointing a commission of students to begin meeting the following fall and issue recommendations nearly a full year later.[19]

Morris's leadership style grew increasingly untenable throughout the decade. SIU students were in the position, then as now, of being part of a large university in a small town in the middle of nowhere, with limited sources of entertainment. With the rapid increase in enrollment in the sixties, SIU developed a reputation as a "party school," which often placed students in opposition to university administrators and city officials. The first major confrontation occurred during finals week in June 1966 and became known as the "Moo and Cackle riots" after Carbondale's first fast-food restaurant, the Moo and Cackle, outside which much of the action took place.

The events began on Sunday, 5 June, when students engaged in a late-night water fight that was broken up by police. The next night a large crowd of male students took

part in a panty raid at two women's dorms. "Eye-witnesses said many of the coeds encouraged the men in the demonstrations and threw various 'unmentionables' out of
dormitory windows," according to the local paper.[20] Again police broke up the festivi-
ties, using, students complained, excessive force. The third night students returned,
spreading into downtown Carbondale. State police dressed in riot gear joined local and
campus cops, firing tear gas into the crowd as students built a bonfire in the street,
threw rocks at police cars, and chanted, "cops eat shit." When police arrested thirteen
students, the crowd marched to the police station and held a sit-in on Main Street. On
the fourth night police arrested twenty-three more rioters, and President Morris ex-
pelled all students who had been arrested, the first mass expulsion in SIU's history.[21]

The Moo and Cackle riots were merely the first in Carbondale's long history of impromptu street demonstrations that frequently turned into clashes with the police.[22]
Placed in context, the event is characteristic of the development of SIU's student movement in several ways. In the first place, the origins of the riots were completely apolitical. But overreaction by the police created resentment on the part of students, which
then became the issue. A reporter on the fourth night of the riot commented, "Students
who were present could give no clear idea of why they were there, except that 'they
didn't want to be pushed around by police' or 'we have a right to be out here.'"[23] Once
the demonstrations gained a focus, however, students began imitating tactics from
the civil rights movement, engaging in a mass sit-in. In spite of such tactics, the overall
atmosphere was anything but nonviolent, as students enjoyed engaging the police in
violent confrontations. As one participant recalled, "There were a bunch of people running up and down the street, because once you know the police are after you, it's fun
time."[24]

Even as this party culture developed at SIU, it increasingly came to be dominated by
the counterculture of the late sixties. As southern Illinois native Larry Vaughn, who entered SIU as a freshman in 1968, remembers:

> When I first got here, y'know, I hung out in West Frankfort with beer-drinking, fast-car-
> driving kids, so I started hanging out with the same type in Carbondale in the dorms. And
> over Christmas I went home for the holidays and a friend of mine had gone to Stanford Uni-
> versity and he brought some pot home. So we got in the car and drove out into the country.
> Instead of drinking we started smoking pot and by the time the holidays were over it was
> like my whole perspective on how to have a good time had changed. So I came back to the
> dorms and I started hanging out with an entirely different crowd of people.[25]

The counterculture was not just about drug use, however. It was also about exploring alternative ideas and ways of life, all of which created a strong sense of community.
Jim Hanson, a graduate student at SIU in the late sixties, described the scene: "There
was a lot of socializing in those days. Most of the houses around Carbondale, you didn't
even knock on the door, you just walked in. People laid down real cool, 'hey man.' . . .
It was a neat time, especially this kind of public part of living in Carbondale."[26]

The student rights movement developed contemporaneously with the party culture,
but at first there were few direct connections between the two.[27] The development of
student rights as a significant movement on campus began in the spring of 1965 with

the founding of the Rational Action Movement (RAM). In late April and early May, RAM gathered twenty-five hundred signatures and held a mass rally focusing on student control of the student center, the administration's decision to shorten spring break, and its censorship of the editorial page of the student newspaper.[28] One member warned that "unless our demands are met along the way, the movement may end up in a riot."[29] Another supporter, though, stated that the movement "is not going to be another Berkeley."[30] RAM drew the support of a broad cross-section of students; its twenty-member coordinating committee included Mike Harty of the Student Peace Union as well as representatives from the Young Republicans and the Young Americans for Freedom.[31] RAM also led to the creation of a student party, the Action Party, which consistently fought for student rights issues for the rest of the decade. But President Morris increasingly dug in his heels, refusing to abolish women's dorm hours and, in 1967, banning *KA,* a student-edited insert in the campus newspaper, after it published an anonymous article encouraging students to violate dorm visitation rules.[32]

The third student culture in the mix grew out of the Student Non-Violent Freedom Committee, a local chapter of the Student Nonviolent Coordinating Committee, which was formed in 1962. The SNFC engaged in regional actions (in Cairo, for instance) as well as in picketing local businesses that practiced racial discrimination.[33] In the words of student activist Jim Hanson:

> There was always that group of people [who] got their first baptism as radicals working in Cairo for civil rights in about '62 or, at the latest, '63. And there were probably . . . fifteen to twenty people who were down there who got shot at, who were SIU students . . . and that was the core. Most of them operated out of a Marxist-Maoist understanding of how the world worked and how the United States was conducting itself, how the university was conducting itself, and, of course, how the Department of Defense was conducting its foreign policy in Vietnam.[34]

A small group of students active in local civil rights activities but seeking to expand the scope of the movement formed the Socialist Discussion Club in 1965 because, as founding member Mike Harty put it, "it occurred to us . . . if you were a recognized student organization you could get a room at the student center for a meeting or if you wanted to pass out pamphlets—not that we had any—if you wanted to and you were a recognized student organization, you could have a table there." The group soon began to focus on the war, handing out antiwar literature next to military recruiters in the student center.

Within a fairly short time, the Socialist Discussion Club developed into a chapter of SDS. As Harty explains, SDS was

> never a large organization, but it was always kind of a front organization and it, the membership of that old Socialist Discussion group, pretty much became SDS. Some one of us got a hold of the *Port Huron Statement.* We all read it, we all pretty much agreed with it and felt, well hell, here's something we can affiliate with and still have fun, which is pretty much what it was. . . . The irony was that from '65 through '68, SDS was in technical terms quite conservative. We were sort of serious, we weren't interested in game playing, we weren't interested in drugs.[35]

The local SDS chapter was also totally autonomous and separate from the national office, though not necessarily by choice. As Harty says, "We tried to have contact, but nobody ever wrote back."[36] Jim Hanson echoes Harty:

> It seemed a very local affair. . . . I didn't see any coordinated national leadership. . . . As far as national SDS people coming in holding rap conferences with us—"Here's what we're doing here, what are you guys doing here? We'll assist you, we'll send you money, we'll help you get out posters, we'll do this, we'll do that at Carbondale, we'll help you if you'll help us"—I never heard [of or] attended a meeting like that. It was all local insofar as I knew.[37]

In addition to SDS, there were other small leftist political organizations forming on campus in the late sixties. One of the most important was the Southern Illinois Peace Committee (SIPC), founded in 1967 and led by Bill Moffett, a black Trotskyite and pacifist.[38] One SIPC member says that Moffett played a major role in holding the group to a philosophy of nonsectarianism and nonviolence. "We had a lot of debates about . . . ideology, did we stand for a certain ideology? Moffett always succeeded in telling us, no, we're an issue-related social movement—that is, we're going to stop the war—and any political statements or any acts of violence in the end would be counterproductive."[39] Moffett and the SIPC would maintain this philosophy throughout the period. Following a violent antiwar riot in February 1970, the SIPC went into the streets and cleaned up the debris before leading a peaceful march of twenty-five hundred.[40] And during the May 1970 riot, Moffett entered occupied buildings to plead with students not to engage in vandalism.[41] But the SIPC remained relatively small, and while Moffett was a visible leader at virtually every antiwar rally of the period, he never gained a large following.[42]

From the beginning, organizations such as SDS served as the left wing of the student rights movement. In Harty's view, the Left viewed *in loco parentis* issues as valuable for educating students about the nature of their powerlessness. Even apolitical students resented the administration's paternalistic actions and SDS believed that such resentment could be used to "show people what the university was all about. . . . We also saw it as a way of forming alliances with people you wouldn't necessarily go to for an alliance with. People who you didn't even know, student government, fraternity and sorority people."[43]

Despite the efforts of SDS to pull the student rights movement leftward, RAM continued to represent a broad cross-section of the political spectrum for several years. It was not until the 1967–68 school year that the three strains—party culture, student rights, and New Left—began to come together, especially under the leadership of student government president Ray Lenzi. A candidate for the Action Party, Lenzi had been elected with his running mate and fraternity brother Richard Karr on a straight student rights platform. But during the fall term Lenzi hesitantly began to speak out against the war, a stance that created tension between him and the conservative and pro-war Karr.[44]

During the winter and spring quarters of 1968, Lenzi consciously began to try to pull the three strains of the movement together. He was aware that the politicization of many students grew out of their participation in the party culture. "Everybody was getting turned on. . . . They were smoking pot, they were dropping acid. . . . That increased their sense of negativity toward the government. 'What do you mean, they put you in jail for doing *this*?' That was just another reason to assume there was something evil about the authorities and the government system."[45] In April Lenzi introduced a bill in the student senate titled "Legalization of Marijuana: Pot is Groovy," which stated that "marijuana is too popular to be denied the public" and called on SIU police to "take the most relaxed attitude toward enforcement of this law" and "preferably exercise no enforcement whatsoever."[46] During the same period Lenzi also became one of the featured speakers at the growing antiwar demonstrations.[47]

Although Lenzi and Karr found themselves more and more at odds on political and cultural matters, they still cooperated on student rights issues. In April they published an open letter in the campus paper criticizing the administration for ignoring a student senate bill calling for the reform of women's dorm hours. The letter called on students to engage in mass civil disobedience by ignoring university rules and "determin[ing] their own hours."[48]

Student rights issues continued to provide the glue that held the three student cultures together, though frequently in odd ways. In April 1969, for example, three hundred women staged an after-hours walkout from their dorm, chanting "hour power" and "we shall overcome." But as the politicized women exited the dorm, they were greeted with the old-fashioned party culture in the form of a crowd of men chanting, "We want pants [sic]."[49]

The most self-conscious attempt to pull together the student rights, party, and New Left cultures came with the Unity Party campaign in the spring of 1969. The party crossed racial lines, running the black Campbell for president and the white Wallace for vice president. Ray Lenzi wrote optimistically in the underground paper *Big Muddy Gazette*, "The forces for change on this campus are no longer disparate. Blacks, new left radicals, freaks, hippies, workers, and all other progressive people can stand together supporting the candidacy of Dwight Campbell and the Unity Party. The pieces of a truly *mass radical movement for social change* have fallen together in Southern Illinois. This spring we shall capture the initiative and change will come."[50] Campbell also emphasized bringing different kinds of people together. "We've got to realize that we are all students and all our problems are intertwined. . . . To unify the campus the Party has to have people who dig people, and this is the first thing I do."[51]

The party platform that united the various student groups focused primarily on student rights issues; of the twelve-point program the party put forth, eight involved student rights. Other points included hiring more black faculty members and increasing the university's involvement in Carbondale's poorest neighborhoods. Significantly, no mention was made of the war.[52] This effort to build a coalition of left-liberal forces proved successful, as the Unity Party gained the endorsement of the Action Party and won the election in a landslide.[53]

While the Unity Party sought to avoid the issue, other groups were anxious to focus on the war, especially since U.S. policies in Vietnam now had a tangible symbol on campus. In July 1969 Morris and the board of trustees had approved the creation of the

Center for Vietnamese Studies and Programs. Widely believed to be a CIA front, the center was financed by the Agency for International Development (AID), which would provide $200,000 a year for five years to study ways to reconstruct Vietnam after the war.[54] Appointed as the center's distinguished visiting professor was Wesley Fishel, who had been part of a similar program at Michigan State, well known for antiwar activist Robert Scheer's 1966 exposé in *Ramparts* of the connections between the CIA and the Michigan State program.[55]

SDS attacked the center in its *Big Muddy Gazette*, denouncing it as an example of American imperialism and running a drawing of a nude Delyte Morris on the front page. University officials responded by withdrawing the permit that allowed the *BMG* to be sold on campus.[56] In the resulting furor, many people spoke out in defense of the *BMG*'s free speech rights, including those who did not necessarily share the paper's politics, putting university administrators on the defensive.[57]

By the fall of 1969 the convergence of the student rights movement, the New Left, and the party culture, along the increasing intransigence of the administration, created palpable tension on campus. As one person recalled, "everyone kind of knew something was going to happen in the fall [before the spring riots]. It was just like all anybody could talk about at every party."[58] Under Campbell's leadership the Unity Party not only led the fight for student rights but also sought to involve itself in the broader community. The party inaugurated a campaign called "Serve the People," which sent student volunteers into Carbondale and surrounding towns to offer a free extermination service and trash cleanup projects.[59]

But the war was the elephant in the room, and it was increasingly difficult to ignore. The reasons for student concern were as much personal as ideological. In the words of one African American student, "for me, the two big issues [were] the civil rights movement and the Vietnam War, although I felt more involved in protesting the Vietnam War. That had more of a direct impact on me because I knew people who were dying."[60] Larry Vaughn agreed: "The war in Vietnam affected me directly from high school. I actually had older friends, brothers of friends, sons of my parents' friends, that had already died in Vietnam. For me it was a real thing. That was one of the most important aspects, we knew that we could die, that we could be killed. Y'know, it wasn't a joke, it wasn't something on TV."[61]

As protests against the Vietnam Studies Center mounted, Campbell and Wallace offered the resources of student government to the antiwar movement. In late January 1970 violence broke out in demonstrations against the center that lasted two days and resulted in fifteen arrests. As tension escalated, so did student rhetoric. Both Campbell and Wallace denounced "the pig power structure," and Wallace declared, "We fear that the brutal and reprehensible tactics used by police may be the beginning of a total police state at SIU."[62] Students responded with the creation of a coalition to "Off Viet Studies" and on 20 February two hundred protesters entered a meeting of the board of trustees and demanded the removal of the Vietnam Studies Center. In an exchange with board member E. T. Simonds, Wallace echoed Malcolm X: "If we're beaten again, we'll have to resort to self-defense in any form necessary." When Simonds asked, "Is that a threat, partner?" Wallace responded, "If we're attacked, we'll defend ourselves. We haven't threatened anybody."[63] That night demonstrators engaged police in a series of disturbances that resulted in two arrests and $15,000 in damage to university buildings and Carbondale stores.[64]

Four days later Campbell and Wallace were suspended for their participation in the protest over dorm hours. Student rights, then, remained a central issue, and dorm hours, especially, provided a locus for all strains of the movement. For the student rights group, the curfew issue represented the university's paternalism; for the New Left, it symbolized the broader issue of powerlessness; and for the party culture, it ruined many an evening plan. As for the war, despite its resonance for so many students, it would probably have remained a peripheral issue had it not been for the Vietnam Studies Center.

But all that changed in May 1970. On the evening of 1 May fifty people gathered in a parking lot just off campus to protest President Nixon's announcement, the day before, that the U.S. military had invaded neutral Cambodia. When the small crowd started a fire in the street, police arrived and arrested eight people. The same night, someone threw a firebomb into the Vietnam Studies Center.[65]

On Monday, 4 May, Ohio National Guard troops killed four students at Kent State University. That night SIU's student government held an emergency meeting and voted unanimously to join a national student strike, with a boycott of classes to begin at noon on Wednesday. On Tuesday two thousand students gathered at a rally in front of Morris Library, and the administration announced that classes would be canceled on Thursday for a day of mourning.

The next day another rally in front of the library drew three thousand people. After listening to several speakers, a crowd marched through nearby buildings, calling students to leave classes and join the strike. About fifteen hundred strong by this time, the crowd moved to Wheeler Hall, where the air force ROTC offices were located. Using bricks from the remains of Old Main, protesters broke windows and then occupied the building.[66] While Bill Moffett urged students inside Wheeler to refrain from vandalism, others chanted, "burn it down." Shortly after 5:00 P.M., about a thousand people marched through downtown Carbondale before returning to campus, where they reoccupied Wheeler Hall until they were forcibly cleared by police. In the meantime, at the request of the sheriff, 650 National Guard troops had been sent to Carbondale, a number that would swell to twelve hundred over the next several days.[67]

On the evening of Thursday, 7 May, another rally attracted two thousand people to the front of the library. At 9:00 P.M. demonstrators marched up Illinois Avenue and sat in at Main and Illinois, the town's major intersection. City and university officials informed the demonstrators that they could remain and that traffic would be rerouted. At this time, according to H. B. Koplowitz, the crowd was "low-key, somewhat festive but benign."[68] Speakers addressed the gathering as wine bottles circulated and marijuana smoke wafted through the air. Monitors wandered through the crowd, urging calm.

At around 10:00 P.M. about seventy-five people attempted to block the nearby railroad tracks. Carbondale's mayor and several march leaders pleaded with them to keep the tracks clear, while most of those sitting at Main and Illinois remained oblivious to the controversy. At this point national guardsmen and state police decided to move the entire crowd and began firing tear gas into the group of demonstrators. Panic ensued as police forcibly removed the crowd; many protesters responded by throwing bricks and smashing windows. By the end of the night there had been seventy-nine arrests, fifty-nine injuries, and $100,000 in damage done to seventy-eight businesses. The mayor declared a state of civil emergency and a sundown-to-sunrise curfew.

Violent confrontations continued for several days as students held ever larger rallies demanding that SIU be shut down. Finally, on Tuesday, 12 May, SIU chancellor Robert MacVicar announced to a crowd of four thousand outside the president's office that the university would be closed "indefinitely." The next morning President Morris met with a crowd of three thousand students who encouraged him to keep the school open; Morris announced a referendum to be held the next day to determine whether the university would remain closed. On 14 May students voted decisively (8,224 to 3,675) to keep the university closed.[69]

During this chaotic two-week period, a complex relationship developed between the movement's leaders and the rank and file, each group interpreting events differently. From the leaders' perspective the events were not so much a riot as a student strike. In Ray Lenzi's words, "it was a very conscious, planned activity that was organized. The goal was to shut down the university as a statement to the state and the nation against the war in Vietnam and even though definitely things got out of hand and got a little disorganized at times . . . there were leaders with a conscious strategy who wanted to shut SIU down."[70]

But the question of leadership in SIU's student movement was problematic. For one thing, New Left organizations like SDS distrusted the very idea of leadership.[71] Even the most hard-core politicos at SIU neither provided nor saw any significant leadership of the student movement. Bennett recalls, "There were no charismatic leaders . . . who could stand up and rally the troops around [them]. This was pretty much a leaderless movement and I just don't think there were any substantial leaders. There were functional leaders, people who, if a meeting needed to occur, got it organized. In a sense, it was a mob, a leaderless mob."[72] While leaders like Ray Lenzi kept in mind the goal of a student strike and tried to move things in that direction, events seemed much more spontaneous to the rank and file. As one participant recalls, "there were a couple of leaders, so to speak, people who got to make speeches. I thought it was pretty much issue-run. I'm sure there was somebody who said we're going to get that together here and have this demonstration and pass out these things, but I never got the feeling that someone was manipulating us."[73] Even some of the speakers saw events in a similar light. Jim Hanson remembers that "people took to the streets kind of spontaneously. From that point on, there really wasn't any organizing to speak of. Not to say we weren't happy to jump in front of a crowd [and] tell them what we wanted them to hear, but it was all very short-term planning, like hours prior to organizing something."[74]

Doug Allen, an assistant professor in the philosophy department who was "right in the middle of things," was also struck by the spontaneity of events. "Things really escalated and it got to the point that it couldn't be controlled."[75] In the end the movement's rank and file, imbued with the party culture ethic, was in no mood to listen to voices of reason encouraging restraint. Larry Vaughn recalls, "What we did is we divided up into groups and we would roam around the streets and we would take bricks and we would pound police cars with all these bricks. The police cars looked like junk cars on wheels, completely torn up. . . . We were just out there doing what [we] thought [we] had to do."[76]

While the events culminating in the student strike brought together the various strains of SIU's student movement, the decision to close the university revealed the movement's rifts. When the university shut down, thousands of students reacted predictably. As Bill Bojanowski put it, "It was the original street party at SIU. People were smoking dope on the street. . . . We had our makeshift parades going down the street. Some guy with a Nixon mask on, it was a circus atmosphere. It was a lot of fun, nobody got hurt. . . . It was pretty peaceful, everybody was everybody's friend."[77]

But for the more politically conscious within the movement, the closing of the university dissipated the movement's strength and destroyed further opportunities for organizing. Doug Allen, for one, says he felt let down when the school closed and everyone went home:

> There was a lot of potential, we were even talking about educational things, priorities, and what kind of university did we want this to be. It was exciting, sitting all day in rap sessions, exploring different things like non-violent resistance. . . . Normally, you'd have a small group of people, but here [was] a huge number of people. There was a sense of excitement building up [and then] the whole thing toppled.[78]

Similarly, SDS activist Larry Bennett believes that the growing influence of the party faction drowned out the influence of the more serious politicos and proved counterproductive for the creation of a long-term mass movement. According to Bennett:

> None of the *Big Muddy Gazette* collective or the SDS types wanted this university closed. I think the pressure from the riots became more of a party and it sucked in a lot of people who weren't politically on board and it just became like a happening, a way to be part of something that felt like a national movement. But it sucked up a lot of extra people and I think those people did want the university closed and had they been in Moo and Cackle in 1966, it would have been a panty raid. . . . I don't think the serious movement people thought that was the thing to do because we understood that people were employed at the university. Close the university, you jeopardize people's jobs. And we were also concerned about the way the working-class people in the surrounding communities would actually regard the movement. We wanted to be popular, we didn't want to be elitist college students. . . . We didn't want to alienate the working class.[79]

The student movement did not die out altogether after the riots, but its character did seem fixed by the events of May 1970. Two years later, when Nixon announced the mining of Haiphong harbor, Carbondale again erupted in riot, as more than one thousand people participated in several days of both nonviolent and violent protests. Once again rank-and-file protesters often overruled the reasoned voices of leaders. On 10 May, when a crowd of about a thousand marched to the Vietnam Studies Center and began hurling rocks at windows, Bill Moffett confronted the demonstrators and urged non-violence, saying, "We cannot trash [this place] because we are going to lose and alien-ate a lot of students who are against the war." Believing his call for restraint had worked, Moffett then asked, "Do you want to trash?" and the crowd resoundingly an-swered "yes!"[80]

In his address at the 6 May rally in front of Morris Library, Dwight Campbell drew a comparison between Kent State and SIU. "We need to understand that what happened at Kent State is something we should've expected a long time ago." Referring to a Jan-uary confrontation between students and campus security forces outside the Vietnam Studies Center at Woody Hall, Campbell said, "The only difference between what hap-pened here at Woody Hall and what happened at Kent State is a matter of degree." In conclusion Campbell urged people to honor the dead by continuing the movement against the war. "Them cats don't want flowers. They want you to carry on the strug-gle where they left off. Don't just have a memorial service—have a struggle service."[81]

In echoing Wobbly martyr Joe Hill's last words, "Don't mourn, organize," Camp-bell's speech placed events at SIU in the context of the long-term history of the Ameri-can Left, the national mass movement against the war in Vietnam, and the escalating tensions between SIU students and administrators over local issues. The convergence of national and international issues with those of purely local significance, in Carbondale and similar places across the country, complicates our view of the development of the New Left and the student antiwar movement in the late sixties and early seventies.

On the most obvious level, our study of SIU reflects the diversity of the movement; the "prairie power" protesters of the late sixties had different backgrounds and sen-sibilities from the founders of the New Left.[82] In less elite institutions, where students often lacked ties to the Old Left and where protesting meant a larger break from fam-ily and community than it did for students from professional, middle-class families, there was little sectarianism and a less distinct boundary between New Left and coun-terculture. Clearly, in parts of the country where the movement was too small and iso-lated to be able to afford the luxury of arguing over fine points of doctrine, people learned to work with others whose politics they did not share. And, always, the issues were as much personal as they were political.

Our conclusions about SIU point to the need for more studies at the grassroots level, as it becomes clear that formal organizations such as SDS were relatively unimportant on many campuses. The story of the student movement is not synonymous with SDS. Such studies must also address the different components, or cultures, of the movement on various college campuses. Surely SIU was not the only campus where a political movement developed as an overlay of the party culture that already existed. It was not so much that people joined the movement simply to be "cool" or to save themselves from the draft—to mention two of the more popular explanations for student activism. It was, at least in part, because the protest movement was, for a time, a way to have fun. As students became swept up in something bigger than themselves, they discovered the joy of feeling part of a community and taking control over the decisions that affected their lives (living out SDS's vision of "participatory democracy"). Having fun was an important part of that story.

In the wake of Kent State many young people dropped out of the movement, as the stakes seemed too high.[83] But activists did more than mourn—and they did not flock to Wall Street. Instead they struggled in new and different ways to live out the values of the movement. In the meantime universities such as SIU tried to deny, and sometimes to suppress actively, their own New Left, student rights, and party traditions.

As for the historiography of the student movement, the evidence suggests that there is no dominant narrative that fits every case; what local stories tell us is that the supposed anomalies *are* the story.[84] While the May 1970 riots at SIU appear in retrospect as a small piece of a large national story in which hundreds of campuses shut down, they were experienced at the time and at the grassroots as "a very local affair." For a brief moment, the party culture became politicized enough to go beyond fighting for student rights and, in its own way, join a larger battle for the soul of the university.

Notes

1. Campbell is quoted in Bob Carr, "Slaves No More," *Daily Egyptian* [Southern Illinois University at Carbondale], 27 Feb. 1970, 4. See also P. J. Heller and Marty Francis, "Coed Study Hours Started at SIU," *Daily Egyptian*, 25 Feb. 1970, 1; "Campbell, Five Others Are Suspended by Moulton," *Daily Egyptian*, 26 Feb. 1970, 1; "Student Boycott Today," *Daily Egyptian*, 27 Feb. 1970, 1.

2. This is even more interesting when understood as an allusion to Jerry Farber's classic essay, "The Student as Nigger," an attempt by white radicals to assert their oppressed status as students (Jerry Farber, "The Student as Nigger," in *The Student as Nigger: Essays and Stories* [New York: Pocket Books, 1969], 90–100). The essay first appeared in 1965 in the *Los Angeles Free Press* and was widely reprinted.

3. Details of the bill can be found in Marty Francis, "Campbell Urges All Students to Reject Hours Compromise," *Daily Egyptian*, 21 Jan. 1970, 1.

4. Betty Mitchell, *Delyte Morris of SIU* (Carbondale: Southern Illinois University Press, 1988), 168–69, 183; H. B. Koplowitz, *Carbondale after Dark and Other Stories* (Carbondale: Dome Publications, 1982), 19–20. Robert A. Harper points out that, despite popular mythology, "the cause of the Old Main fire has never been determined" (Robert A. Harper, *The University That Shouldn't Have Happened, But Did!* (Carbondale: Devil's Kitchen Press, 1998), 259.

5. Win Holden and Nathan Jones, "Six Arrested in Fracas at Center; Trial Set Feb. 26," *Daily Egyptian*, 30 Jan. 1970, 1; "Police, Students Clash at Woody," *Daily Egyptian*, 31 Jan. 1970, 1; "Campus Melee Evokes Varying Reactions," *Daily Egyptian*, 31 Jan. 1970, 9; Bob Carr, "Rally Voices Opposition to Viet Center, AID," *Daily Egyptian*, 21 Feb. 1970, 9; "Protesters Interrupt Trustees Meeting," *Daily Egyptian*, 21 Feb. 1970, 11; P. J. Heller and Bob Carr, "Weekend Results; Peaceful March, $15,000 Damage," *Daily Egyptian*, 24 Feb. 1970, 1.

6. P. J. Heller and Win Holden, "Coalition Stresses Themes," *Daily Egyptian*, 3 Feb. 1970, 8.

7. In interviews with Jim Hanson (20 July 1997, Collinsville, Ill.) and Mike Harty (24 Nov. 1997, Carbondale, Ill.), both offered impressionistic evidence that this integration did not filter

down to the grassroots level. M. Browning Carrot, who came to SIU in 1967 as an assistant professor of history, concurs, saying he never saw any African Americans at antiwar rallies (interview with M. Browning Carrot, 21 May 1999, Carbondale, Ill.). Other observers recall the movement as being integrated at all levels but as predominantly white.

8. For an example of the bitter labor wars in southern Illinois's mining region, see Paul M. Angle, *Bloody Williamson: A Chapter in American Lawlessness* (New York: Knopf, 1952).

9. See Harper, *The University That Shouldn't Have Happened*, 6–11. Even today, the nearest interstate is fifteen miles outside town.

10. John Gardner, "Southern Illinois University: 'We Teach and Study and Raise All the Hell We Can,'" *Change*, June 1973, 43.

11. Harper, *The University That Shouldn't Have Happened*, 161, 209; the 1970 enrollment figure was 23,846. Cited in *The Southern Illinoisan*, 22 Aug. 1999, 33.

12. Harty, interview.

13. Dick Gregory, foreword to Mitchell, *Delyte Morris* ix.

14. On Morris's early commitment to civil rights, see Harper, *The University That Shouldn't Have Happened*, 39, 132.

15. Ibid., 34–38.

16. As reported in the *Southern Illinoisan* (Carbondale), 26 Feb. 1965. See, for example, Delyte W. Morris to Reverend Lockard, 2 Aug. 1962, SIU Archives, Student Affairs Division, 1951–69, Box 12. Thanks to E. Jan Jacobs for making known to us this archival material.

17. See Harper, *The University That Shouldn't Have Happened*, 38.

18. Koplowitz, *Carbondale after Dark*, 10–11.

19. "Background Information about SIU, RAM and the Commission," Nov. 1966, SIU Archives, Student Affairs Division, 1951–69.

20. According to the local paper, "Estimates of the number of students involved varied from 500 to 3,000" ("Students Romp through Streets until 3 A.M.," *Southern Illinoisan*, 7 June 1966, 1.

21. Ibid.; Richard Carter, "Police Stop New Student Uproar," *Southern Illinoisan*, 8 June 1966, 1; D. G. Schumaker, "SIU Expels Students Arrested During Riot," *Southern Illinoisan*, 9 June 1966, 1; Koplowitz, *Carbondale after Dark*, 14–15; interview with Ray Lenzi, 20 March 1997, Carbondale.

22. For a history of the many confrontations on Carbondale's strip, see Koplowitz, *Carbondale after Dark*, 9–51.

23. Ben Gelman, "Few Riot, Many Cheer," *Southern Illinoisan*, 9 June 1966, 3.

24. Larry Bennett, telephone interview by authors, 14 April 1999. Bennett went on to be active in Carbondale's chapter of SDS and worked for the underground student newspaper, the *Big Muddy Gazette*.

25. Larry Vaughn, "'I'm on the Pavement, Thinkin' about the Government: Vietnam, Carbondale, and the May 1970 Riot"(panel discussion at SIU-Carbondale, 16 April 1997). Bill Bojanowski, who arrived at SIU in the summer of 1969, remembers how completely the counterculture seemed to dominate the Carbondale scene by that time.

26. Hanson, interview.

27. In 1960 Bill Morin ran for student body president, pledging to "stand up for student rights for everything from segregation to cars." Morin had no problem with students demonstrating to express their feelings—which they did on the issue of having automobiles—as long as there was no violence or mob action. *Daily Egyptian*, 6 May 1960, 1.

28. Frank Messersmith, "Student Protest Group Distributing Petitions," *Daily Egyptian,* 1 May 1965, 1.

29. Ric Cox, "Dissatisfactions Stirred Rational Action Move," *Daily Egyptian,* 1 May 1965, 1.

30. "Students at SIU Seek Policy Voice," *St. Louis Globe-Democrat,* 4 May 1965.

31. Cox, "Dissatisfactions," 1. By 1965 Harty was also a member of the Socialist Discussion Group and would soon help start SIU's chapter of SDS.

32. Koplowitz, *Carbondale after Dark,* 16. Morris also temporarily refused to allow *KA*'s editors to reenroll.

33. Ibid., 12, 14.

34. Hanson, interview.

35. Harty, interview.

36. Ibid. Harty also states, "I think it's important to note that there were no red diaper babies at SIU, or if there were, I never knew them."

37. Hanson, interview.

38. Koplowitz, *Carbondale after Dark,* 16.

39. Hanson, interview.

40. Heller and Carr, "Weekend Results."

41. "Police, Students Clash; Several Hurt," *Daily Egyptian,* 7 May 1970, 1.

42. Harty claims that Moffett "was one of these self-appointed leaders. You could find him on the front line of any demonstration, but that was only because he put himself there. . . . I mean, he was a Trotskyist cell of one." Harty, interview.

43. Ibid.

44. Lenzi, interview.

45. Ibid.

46. "Senate to Consider Marijuana Bill," *Daily Egyptian,* 30 April 1968, 2.

47. John Durbin, "700 Persons March in Saturday's Rally," *Daily Egyptian,* 30 April 1968, 1.

48. Ray Lenzi and Richard Karr, "Senate Writes Students," *Daily Egyptian,* 5 April 1968, 1, 9.

49. Dan Van Atta, "300 Coeds Stage 'Walkout' in Protest of Women's Hours," *Daily Egyptian,* 16 April 1969, 2.

50. Ray Lenzi, "Unity," *Big Muddy Gazette,* 9 April 1969, 12. Emphasis in original.

51. Norris Jones, "Dwight Campbell's Idea—'Unity is Strength,'" *Daily Egyptian,* 11 April 1969, 12.

52. Ibid. Another issue was the abolition of the loyalty oath for student workers and faculty.

53. "Unity Party Slate Receives Backing of Action Party," *Daily Egyptian,* 23 April 1969, 9. According to Roger Leisner, the student government representative to the Carbondale city council, Campbell's leadership style played a crucial role in the building of this coalition.

54. On the Center for Vietnamese Studies, see Harper, *The University That Shouldn't Have Happened,* 256–59, 279–86; and *Center for Vietnamese Studies and Programs Newsletter,* 15 Sept. 1969, Tom Busch papers, Box 3, Special Collections, Morris Library, Southern Illinois University, Carbondale. For a history of the development of an opposition movement at SIU focusing on the Center, see Douglas Allen, "Universities and the Vietnam War: A Case Study of a Successful Struggle," *Bulletin of Concerned Asian Scholars* (Oct.–Dec. 1976): 2–16.

55. On the Michigan State program, see "The University on the Make," *Ramparts* 4 (April 1966): 11–22; Robert Scheer, *How the United States Got Involved in Vietnam* (Santa Barbara: Report to the Center for the Study of Democratic Institutions, 1965); Stanley K. Sheinbaum, "The

Michigan State–CIA Experience in Vietnam," *Bulletin of Concerned Asian Scholars* (spring 1971): 71–75.

56. Dan Van Atta, "Big Muddy Gazette Loses Permit to Sell on Campus," *Daily Egyptian*, 11 April 1969, 11.

57. For instance, on 16 April the *Daily Egyptian* ran an editorial defending the *BMG*'s first amendment rights next to a virulently anti-*BMG* cartoon showing a group of hippies making such comments as "How's the editorial coming?" "I don't know. Fidel hasn't pulled our strings yet."

58. Vaughn, "I'm on the Pavement," panel discussion.

59. Marty Francis, "'Serve the People' Does 'Crazy Things' in Community," *Daily Egyptian*, 20 Nov. 1969, 9. Though neither Dwight Campbell nor Delyte Morris would probably have appreciated the irony, "Serve the People" stood firmly within Morris's mission of using SIU to combat the region's economic deprivation. See Harper, *The University That Shouldn't Have Happened*, 34–38.

60. Patty Miller (pseud.), interview by authors, 7 July 1998, Carbondale.

61. Vaughn, "I'm on the Pavement," panel discussion.

62. "Campus Melee Evokes Varying Reactions," *Daily Egyptian*, 31 Jan. 1970, 9. Heller and Holden, "Coalition Stresses Themes," 8.

63. "Protesters Interrupt Trustees Meeting," *Daily Egyptian*, 21 Feb. 1970, 11.

64. Heller and Carr, "Weekend Results."

65. "Eight Demonstrators Arrested," *Daily Egyptian*, 5 May 1970, 1. In addition to reports in the *Daily Egyptian*, this description of the events of May 1970 is drawn from a detailed chronology of events entitled "Chronology of Events Related to Closing of Southern Illinois University," prepared by Max Turner, Government Department, for President's Office, with comments by Roy Miller, Government Department, Tom Busch papers, Box 2, Special Collections, Morris Library, Southern Illinois University, Carbondale. For narrative accounts, see Koplowitz, *Carbondale after Dark*, 52–63, and Harper, *The University That Shouldn't Have Happened*, 290–96. Of the two, Koplowitz's is much more sympathetic to the demonstrators.

66. In an interesting instance of student-worker solidarity, the campus paper reported, "Several workers at Old Main were observed passing bricks over the construction fence to students." "Police, Students Clash: Several Hurt," *Daily Egyptian*, 7 May 1970, 1.

67. Ibid., 1, 10.

68. Koplowitz, *Carbondale after Dark*, 57.

69. Another 608 students voted for free choice. The faculty vote was 603 to 341 in favor of keeping the university open, with 62 voting for free choice. Staff voted 1,131 to remain open, 447 to close, and 49 for free choice. See Turner, "Chronology of Events."

70. Ray Lenzi, "I'm on the Pavement," panel discussion.

71. Harty, interview; Bennett, interview.

72. Bennett, interview.

73. Bill Bojanowski, interview by authors, 29 June 1998, Carbondale.

74. Jim Hanson, "I'm on the Pavement," panel discussion.

75. Doug Allen, telephone interview by authors, 26 April 1999. Allen was later denied tenure at SIU because of his leadership in the movement opposing the Vietnam Studies Center.

76. Vaughn, "I'm on the Pavement," panel discussion.

77. Bojanowski, interview.

78. Allen, interview.

79. Bennett, interview.

80. Koplowitz, *Carbondale after Dark*, 26–28.

81. "Kent State, Vietnam protest draws 3,000," *Daily Egyptian*, 7 May 1970, 10.

82. Despite the lack of contact with the national SDS, the student movement at SIU lived out in many ways the notion of "prairie power," a tendency that dominated SDS from 1966 to 1968. According to Carl Davidson, New Left theorist and national leader of SDS during this period, prairie power centered around students from large state universities, not the elite schools that had produced SDS's founders. These were young people without connections to the Old Left or, for that matter, to liberalism. They were homegrown radicals, more activist and less ideological than the SDS old guard. Fueled by the civil rights movement, they were fighting battles for themselves on college campuses on issues that ranged from dorm hours to university complicity with the war machine. They were not controlled from a center. They symbolized the spirit of alienated youth, and, for a brief time, their adolescent rebellion was politicized. Carl Davidson, interview by authors, 17 Sept 1997, Carbondale.

83. Doug Rossinow, *The Politics of Authenticity: Liberalism, Christianity, and the New Left in America* (New York: Columbia University Press, 1998), 16.

84. Thanks to James Farrell for this insight.

CHAPTER 2

Between Despair and Hope: Revisiting *Studies on the Left*

Kevin Mattson

At best a New Left may only be able to define a new intellectual creed at home which permits honest men to save their consciences and integrity even when they cannot save or transform politics.

—Gabriel Kolko, *Studies on the Left*

Historians traditionally study the New Left as a succession of movements that combated a variety of injustices during the tumultuous decade of the 1960s, but rarely as an episode in intellectual history, even though it clearly was this. Many New Left leaders thought of themselves as intellectuals. They did politics largely in the realm of ideas, where we can best see what legacy they have left for those who came after them.[1]

They were, of course, indebted to some "big-name" intellectuals, who provided much of the scaffolding for their ideas, for example, C. Wright Mills, Paul Goodman, William Appleman Williams, and Arnold Kaufman, whose writings throughout the 1950s and 1960s formulated some of the fundamental questions and assumptions that fueled political movements. Mills criticized the "labor metaphysic" (the Marxist tradition of placing of all radical hope in the hands of the working class), and called for young intellectuals to lead in the formation of a new Left; Goodman renewed the political ideal of decentralization and argued that work and education within a bureaucratic corporate economy had become inhumane; Williams dissected American foreign policy and its imperialist tendencies; and Kaufman, who directly inspired Tom Hayden, explained how participatory democracy related to the history of political thought.[2]

There were also younger, less well known leftist intellectuals who struck out on their own, forming small magazines during the late 1950s and early 1960s. In this they inherited a rich legacy; the small magazine has always played a central role in the history of the intellectual Left. Among these was *The Masses,* published during the early-twentieth-century explosion of Greenwich Village bohemianism; *Partisan Review,* with its quirky combination of modernism and Trotskyism during the Great Depression; *politics,* with its explorations of anarchism and nonviolence at the dawn of the Cold War in the 1940s; and *Dissent,* which held on to democratic socialism during the 1950s, an era that its editor, Irving Howe, labeled an "age of conformity." All of these publications provided a forum in which writers thought through the pressing issues of the day and advocated creative political change.[3]

During the late 1950s and early 1960s, several small magazines helped define the New Left. *New University Thought, Root and Branch,* and *Studies on the Left,* like their predecessors, confronted an increasingly prosperous corporate economy, a consumer culture that was beginning to spread to the working classes, the decline of the older (Marxist) Left, and the rise of new protest movements like those for civil rights and peace. Perhaps just as important, they saw the GI Bill and the expansion of the military industrial complex move the research university to the center of the modern economy. Academia became a much more viable setting for young intellectuals. The editors of *Studies on the Left*—the publication I will focus on here—faced up to this new context and set out to examine the future of radicalism in the United States.

Because *Studies on the Left* endured for almost ten years and dealt with numerous issues, I will not attempt an overarching study of the journal in this essay but will focus on key themes within its pages that illuminate the intellectual orientation of politically motivated intellectuals during the late 1950s and 1960s. My interest is in the tension in *Studies* between a certain type of optimism and a pervasive fear of co-optation that developed out of theories of "corporate liberalism" and the twentieth-century welfare state. This focus, admittedly, brackets certain issues and ideas developed in the journal—namely, debates about black power and the civil rights movement, Marxist theory, European socialism, and avant-garde art and theater. Nonetheless, it helps illuminate what was clearly a central question for these thinkers: What could social movements actually accomplish in late-twentieth-century American politics?

Forming a Journal and Keeping It Together (Sometimes)

Studies on the Left formed at the University of Wisconsin in 1959 through the efforts of the Wisconsin Socialist Club. Although some of its editors had once associated with the Communist Party, they had rejected it by the mid- to late 1950s and were searching for an alternative to the Old Left. While most of them were originally from New York City—a hotbed of sectarian Marxism—they were able to leave behind such antiquated debates as Trotskyism vs. Stalinism and pursue fresh ideas in Madison. The first managing editor, Eleanor Hakim, explained to a friend: "A journal like *Studies* could never have originated on either the east or west coast where there are so many splits and factions—most of which are at least 25 years behind the times." Or as the editors stated in the magazine's third year: "The isolation from the large metropolitan centers pro-

vided the opportunity to develop our own conceptions of the necessity for radical scholarship." The word "scholarship" says a great deal, for the editors found themselves not
just in the Midwest but in a capital town that was home to a major research university.
Madison had escaped the general stultifying atmosphere of Cold War America, thanks
in part to the Progressive Era legacy of its university and some independent-minded
scholars there. Most importantly, the editors of *Studies* were influenced and helped by
University of Wisconsin professor William Appleman Williams, a scholar who was already writing about the history of American foreign policy and radical politics during
the 1950s. Some of Williams's students were among the founding editors of the magazine, and it always drew upon the energy of his graduate students.[4]

Williams offered the editors of *Studies* many intellectual tools. First, he showed how
historical inquiry could inform political and social criticism. Building on the legacy of
Charles Beard, Williams rejuvenated the idea of a "useable past," the conviction that
understanding the past shows us who "we are as well as the way we would like to be."
Williams also showed his students how modern liberalism relied on an "open-door"
policy that maintained domestic peace and prosperity through constant foreign expansion. He argued that modern liberalism could never be divorced from overseas empire,
a particularly pertinent lesson as America moved toward Cold War entanglements in
Cuba and eventually Vietnam.[5]

Perhaps most important of all, the editors of *Studies* found in Williams's work hope
for radical alternatives to corporate capitalism in America, even though Williams remained pessimistic about the possibility of radical political change. In *The Tragedy of
American Diplomacy,* published in 1959, the year that *Studies* first appeared, Williams
ended on a bleak note. Although he hoped for a "radical but noncommunist reconstruction of American society," he saw "at the present time no radicalism in the United States
strong enough to win power, or even a very significant influence, through the processes
of representative government—and this essay rests on the axiom of representative government." Writing on Williams's work years later, Michael Harrington commented that
his arguments led more to quietism and pessimism than to radical exuberance. This
view of predestined defeat would mark the pages of *Studies* in years to come.[6]

The editors of the new magazine formed a small, informal circle. James Weinstein
(who left Columbia University and New York City for Madison), Martin Sklar (a student of Williams), Saul Landau, Lloyd Gardner (who would eventually edit a collection
of essays on Williams), Joan Bromberg, Steven Scheinberg, and a few others formed the
primary cadre. They appeared to be as much drinking buddies, gathering in bars off
campus for lively discussion, as editors of a magazine for public consumption. They acknowledged a conflict between their academic training and their political goals. As they
explained in their first editorial, "As graduate students anticipating academic careers,
we feel a very personal stake in academic life, and we feel that, as radicals, we are ham-
pered in our work by the intrusion of prevailing standards of scholarship." The "objectivity" that academia encouraged, and its concomitant careerism, left a bad taste in
their mouths. At the same time, they were clearly attracted to the analytical approach
of academic life, and they devoted themselves to what Eleanor Hakim described as

"high level scholarly and speculative analyses and think pieces." Their goal was to publish a radical, committed, but scholarly journal.[7]

With the help of some foundation money and the energy of its devoted editors, *Studies on the Left* braved the seemingly quiescent and conformist years of the Cold War. But already there had emerged the civil rights movement of the mid-1950s, which became radicalized when young people took the reins during the sit-ins of 1960. California protests against the House Un-American Activities Committee (HUAC) had challenged the dogmatic anticommunism that ruled American political debate. And there was early opposition to the nuclear arms buildup and some small support for the Cuban revolution—two movements that signified a serious challenge to American foreign policy during the Cold War. The editors at *Studies on the Left* took note of these developments and hoped that something more cohesive would grow out of them.[8]

As Eleanor Hakim wrote to Martin Sklar in the early 1960s, "The big student movements; the sit-ins; the anti-capital punishment; anti-HUAC; pro-Cuba's right to make her own revolution . . . the disarmament and peace movements are, it seems to me, not political movements per se. Rather, they are issue-oriented protest movements. . . . The people protesting today are idealistic young 'liberals' who do not have any over-all left wing orientation." Partly in response to this letter, Sklar wrote "Some Notes on the 'New American Left': American, All Too American," in which he expressed a bit more hope than Hakim would, while recognizing the New Left's limitations. He explained in November 1960 that "what we are witnessing in the student and Negro movements, then, is a process that contains the seeds of a new American left capable of becoming a politically viable movement nationally, a process in which the new left is learning those forms of struggle which will make a radical movement relevant to the American body politic." Sklar agreed with Hakim and other editors that the New Left would need a great deal of intellectual guidance if it was to become more than just a string of disjointed protest movements.[9]

With its early interest in new calls for political change, *Studies* appealed to a new audience. Its first issue sold three thousand copies; by the mid-1960s—when the New Left was really on the move—the magazine's circulation was ten thousand. The editors were never entirely clear about their mission, and they vacillated between wanting more scholarly articles—often publishing esoteric pieces on Marxist theory—to featuring articles on current political issues. Less than a year into the journal's existence, the editors began to give precedence to new developments, such as student-led initiatives in the civil rights movement or the Cuban revolution; but they wanted critical scholarly writing, not simply a journalistic account of events.

The journal's focus began to shift more decisively in 1963. Hakim left over personal conflicts with other editors. In the same year the publication uprooted itself and moved from the placid setting of the Midwest to the loud, sectarian world of New York City. James Weinstein explained the transition in a letter to a reader in 1965. He reviewed the journal's early stages, from 1959 to 1964, when it "was read primarily [*sic*] by graduate students and young faculty members in the social sciences." The editors had hoped to "lay the theoretical basis for the emergence of a new radical politics." "The movements have blossomed," Weinstein wrote, and the editors "have been reorienting the journal toward a more active and immediate concern with existing practice." Weinstein was carrying over some of the enthusiasm he had felt when attending the 1964 convention of Students for a Democratic Society (SDS), but his enthusiasm did not inspire all of the other editors. Helen Kramer, for instance, complained that this sort of immediate reportage on movements would create an "editorial line" and "restrict the scope and freshness of discussion in our pages." The debate between Weinstein and Kramer about the purpose of intellectual work continued to haunt the publication as it did the New Left in general, which always found itself torn between immediate struggle and long-range analysis. But under Weinstein's leadership, reportage on the political movement increased in 1964.[10]

This reportage was successful, in part, because *Studies* recruited three key New Left intellectuals—Tom Hayden, Norm Fruchter, and Staughton Lynd. These men were sympathetic not just to SDS, which Hayden had helped to organize, but to new forms of community organizing and the ideal of "participatory democracy." Having taken part in SDS's Economic Research and Action Project (ERAP)—an attempt to organize poor people that looked a lot like Saul Alinksy's previous work—these writers celebrated grassroots activism. Perhaps most importantly, Hayden always expressed discomfort with the word "socialism" as a description of New Left politics, feeling that it would alienate potential supporters. And even though Lynd wrote an early article for *Studies* that was provocatively entitled "Socialism: The Forbidden Word," what he meant by the term was really participatory democracy and economic populism, not economic planning. Fruchter was content to espouse the new gospel of community organizing and the important work done by the SNCC. In short, these three thinkers challenged James Weinstein's vision of *Studies* as a socialist journal and began to articulate a different kind of orthodoxy for the New Left.[11]

Studies proved unable to keep these three new voices, however, when a split emerged among the editorial board in 1965. Lynd, Hayden, and Fruchter butted heads with Weinstein and two of the other editors, Eugene Genovese and Stanley Aronowitz. As is often the case with intellectual feuds, it was unclear how much of the animosity centered on substantive differences. In a 1965 letter Weinstein called Hayden a chameleon who did not take political debate seriously. "The problem with Tom has nothing to do with where he stands (that changes constantly in any case) but with his refusal to participate honestly in theoretical discussion. To Tom, theory is something you use to rationalize where you're at." Staughton Lynd defended Hayden and suggested that Weinstein envied Hayden's fast-growing celebrity. "In Tom you have encountered the only representative of the new generation of student leaders who has taken a major part in the magazine, and have not merely failed to enlist his energies permanently but have contributed (for surely it cannot all be Tom's fault) to the present bitterness," Lynd wrote Weinstein.

Hayden, Fruchter, and Lynd left the publication for good in 1965, leaving behind a journal that focused less on grassroots political movements than on socialism and electoral politics. Two years later, even before SDS itself began to splinter into factions,

Studies on the Left collapsed. Weinstein said that it had run its course, but others believed that personal squabbles had done it in.[12]

Between Co-optation and Hope

Central among the tensions and conflicts that marked *Studies on the Left* was the editors' vacillation between hope for political change in America and despair over the "genius for co-optation" that quashed protest. In maintaining a tension between hope and despair, the writers at *Studies* believed that they were doing their duty as engaged public intellectuals. They formulated possibilities for radical change while also pointing to the historical limits of political movements. Their work shows that the New Left was not made up solely of naive, idealistic revolutionaries, but of worried (and sometimes fatalistic) intellectuals who understood the limits to radical possibilities.[13]

Their attitude became more fatalistic as SDS—the arm of the New Left with which *Studies* most clearly identified—disintegrated into squabbling factions in 1967, foreshadowing its collapse, which began the next year. But it was visible much earlier—for instance, in the editors' attempts to solicit contributions from Herbert Marcuse, the famed Frankfurt School theorist who inspired the New Left in later years. (In the end, Marcuse never contributed to the journal.) Weinstein regarded Marcuse's most important work of the 1960s, *One-Dimensional Man* (1964), as very much in line with his own concerns about co-optation. In a letter to Marcuse in 1965, Weinstein wrote, "The area that interests me most is that which deals with the possibilities for social change (that is, a change in the power relationships between classes) in our one dimensional society. Put another way, the topic could be what is the potential for revolutionary politics in the New Left."[14]

In his classic work on "one-dimensional society," Marcuse used Hegelian philosophy and "dialectical thinking" to show how social systems became resistant to social change and critical thought. Marcuse's work was unlike that of orthodox Marxists; instead, he followed his Frankfurt School brethren, Theodor Adorno and Max Horkheimer, who did not see the origin of social and economic injustice in capitalism but in science and Western rationality itself. The source of repression, as Marcuse saw it, was *technical rationality*—the first steps made by Western science to produce labor-saving instruments, a form of rationality that Adorno and Horkheimer traced back to the ancient Greeks. As Marcuse explained, "In the medium of technology, culture, politics, and the economy merge into an omnipresent system which swallows up or repulses all alternatives."[15]

If technical rationality went all the way back to the Greeks, it would be difficult to overthrow. Worse yet, capitalism offered pseudo forms of liberation—most notably, marketed forms of sexual excitement and release. Marcuse analyzed what he called "repressive desublimation," best symbolized in how the "culture industry" marketed sexual imagery and sexual freedom to masses of consumers. He believed that advanced capitalism allowed for certain freedoms that appeared revolutionary on their face but in fact upheld the status quo. Marcuse coined the oxymoronic term "repressive tolerance" to describe advanced industrial societies. These societies could allow for anything, since nothing really mattered except profit. Marcuse's term "repressive tolerance" resonated with the editors of *Studies,* who used the term "flexible totalitarianism" to suggest the same thing.[16]

In fact, the editors of *Studies* had formulated theories of co-optation long before they cracked open their copies of *One-Dimensional Society.* In 1962, for instance, Eleanor Hakim argued that "the double-think and totalitarianism by dissent of corporate capitalist liberalism is much more subtle and smooth than the bludgeoning techniques of fascism! And then there is the added advantage of neutralizing and making impotant [*sic*] any protest movement—radicals and dissenters need not be persecuted too much since they are made harmless." Anticipating what Marcuse would write three years later, Hakim argued, "Thus the illusion of tolerance and democracy can be maintained. Such techniques are much more effective than out and out fascism, and in fact, render it superfluous."[17]

Hakim's suspicion of corporate capitalism drew on the work done by the historians at *Studies,* who analyzed what they called "corporate liberalism." Martin Sklar (and later William Appleman Williams and James Weinstein) argued that the birth of modern liberalism in the Progressive Era (a move away from nineteenth-century individualism toward twentieth-century welfare-state policies and economic regulation), could best be interpreted as a means of keeping the new corporate economy intact, both by regulating its excesses at home and expanding its markets abroad. Grouping many reform movements under one rubric, Martin Sklar explained Progressive Era reforms in a 1960 essay on Woodrow Wilson this way: "The Progressive reform movements . . . were led by and [consisted] of large corporate interests and political and intellectual leaders affirming the large corporate industrial capitalist system." Liberalism, though it might at first appear humanitarian and reform-minded, had become, for the editors of *Studies on the Left,* a means of social control. In 1962 they wrote, "Twentieth-century liberalism, insofar as it is not merely rhetorical, is a system of political ideas consciously developed to strengthen the system of large-scale corporate capitalism." Hence radicals had to beware the system's capacity to co-opt their vision and turn it into something tame, controlled, and capable of affirming an inhumane system. According to Weinstein, "'Victories' for reform within the system have never been more than partial and almost invariably have been intended to blunt the effect of, or break up, movements for serious social change."[18]

Though the work done to explicate corporate liberalism was predominantly historical, it undoubtedly reflected the viewpoints and biases of the editors' own historical circumstances. No modern president embodied corporate liberalism and technocratic managerialism better than John F. Kennedy, who was in office during *Studies*'s most formative years. Kennedy's "New Frontier," once applied to the economy, became little more than a tax cut and mild corporate regulation. His foreign policy was aggressively anticommunist, especially since he felt personally belittled in his personal meetings with Khrushchev, whom he called "that son of a bitch." Oliver Stone's interpretation notwithstanding, Kennedy risked nuclear war over Cuba and pushed the country toward a ground war in Vietnam. To accentuate this mixture of tame corporate policy at home and aggressive foreign policy, Kennedy sought the advice of intellectuals like Arthur Schlesinger, an arch-nemesis of William Appleman Williams. The editors of *Studies,* therefore, were merited in characterizing liberalism as a political philosophy that had come to protect the status quo of large corporations and aggressive foreign policy.[19]

It is unclear whether the editors accepted the necessity of compromise in modern politics. On this point Weinstein, especially, waffled. In debating Staughton Lynd (who had a predilection for conspiracy theories) in 1964, Weinstein seemed to suggest that all reform would inevitably be absorbed into the system. "We have a liberal administration that is capable of moving in whatever direction conditions demand. They will do whatever is deemed best by the wisest and most powerful of our financial and corporation leaders." He expressed little hope for the newly formed Johnson administration: "At present, it appears they see the advantage in moving 'left'—that is, espousing a program against poverty, supporting 'disarmament,' condemning segregation as morally wrong —all considered steps in the direction of liberalism. . . . Of course, none of these programs are designed to solve the problems . . . but they are a good pose, and they must take token steps." Seen from this perspective, every reform initiative was suspect, or, in Weinstein's words, could "blunt the effect of, or break up, movements for serious social change." Reform and co-optation were synonymous.[20]

But in Weinstein's debates with other editors, he changed his tone somewhat. It is not surprising to find him defending the (pre-1919) Socialist Party against interpretations of co-optation. He wrote to Saul Landau, "I don't think the SP played into TR's hand by advocating reform. . . . To say so is to say that any demands other than socialism now! is reformism." Or, as Weinstein explained to a reviewer of Charles Forcey's classic work on progressive intellectuals, *The Crossroads of Liberalism,* Theodore Roosevelt's and Woodrow Wilson's reform planks were "genuinely progressive within the context of the large scale corporate system." Apparently, then, reform *could* resist co-optation and actually amount to something. It could at least hope to accomplish some social change, and at best it could achieve social justice and be "genuinely progressive." Weinstein seemed to want to have it both ways.[21]

The tension in Weinstein's thought about co-optation showed up in the journal in other ways—for instance, in writing on the labor movement. As Peter Levy has shown in *The New Left and Labor,* young radicals were both critical—following C. Wright Mills's lambasting of the labor metaphysic—and hopeful about the radical potential of labor. So it was with certain pieces on the labor movement within *Studies.* Ronald Radosh, in an essay brazenly entitled "The Corporate Ideology of American Labor," applied the corporate liberalism thesis to labor unions. As Radosh saw it, industrial leaders accepted labor unions because they believed labor held "an equal stake with management in developing efficient industrial production." Presaging the famous conflict between "hardhats" and "peaceniks," Radosh argued that "the labor movement and its leadership chose to align itself with American business and its path of foreign expansion." In Radosh's view, labor could never be a force for radical social change because it was too closely allied with, and invested in, the status quo.[22]

But others maintained faith that the rank-and-file membership of labor unions might become more radical under the right circumstances. Sidney Peck argued that the "political consciousness of the rank and file labor leaders" was much more progressive than many people thought. Robert Wolfe criticized C. Wright Mills's dismissal of labor as a radical force in American politics, as did Martin Glaberman in an article entitled "Marxism, the Working Class, and the Trade Unions." Stanley Aronowitz, foreshadowing his later work, interviewed rank-and-file members of more radical unions and published the interviews in *Studies*. Radosh held the minority view of the labor movement at *Studies,* but given the divergent opinions published in its pages it was unclear whether the editors saw labor as a source of co-optation or hope—or both.[23]

The journal reflected plenty of ambiguity, even inconsistency, on the question of co-optation. In response to Paul Goodman's famous dismissal of the Beats in *Growing Up Absurd,* Paul Breslow blasted hipsters as apolitical conformists who mirrored the passivity of the new middle classes. Breslow argued that the "public to which the term 'beat' is most appropriately applied" was "the moderately educated middle class." "In the contemporary cesspool of American political life the beat middle class is unpleasantly confined to a petty and confusing consolation for its social anxieties in a search for an undefinable, unsatisfying, irrelevant, mystical salvation," he wrote. The coolness and passivity of so-called rebels such as Kerouac and Ginsberg actually helped prop up the status quo, Breslow argued. But this critique concerned cultural matters, where the stakes were lower than in political protest movements, where the editors of *Studies* most feared co-optation.[24]

During the famous "National Teach-In" Arnold Kaufman organized in 1965, when professors publicly debated representatives from the U.S. State Department, the editors saw only co-optation. Joan Scott thought the teach-in organizers had solicited a group of rarefied academics with little power to change things; she dismissed them as the "Loyal Opposition." Peter Lathrop agreed that "the powerful and their representatives cannot be expected to submit themselves to the test of Reason." Lathrop's critique of co-optation was extreme: What was he suggesting should replace reasonable debate? Why shouldn't State Department officials be recruited—forcibly—into a dialogue on the principles of the Vietnam War? Was this not the essence of radical democracy, making public officials stand before the court of public opinion? Lathrop and Scott seemed to suggest that a rational public could control dissent, but they never made clear (perhaps because the alternatives were too frightening) what could take its place.[25]

On Liberalism, the New Left, and Other Possibilities

The editors of *Studies* were quick to apply their theory of co-optation to modern liberalism. Their critique of liberalism, in fact, united the New Left faction (Lynd, Hayden, Fruchter) and the editors who were more sympathetic to traditional socialism (Weinstein, Aronowitz, Genovese). Both camps were hostile to the welfare state that was emerging from Great Society programs. In one issue of the journal, Hayden and Lynd criticized welfare policies for creating passive "clients." Weinstein restated his corporate liberalism thesis in the same issue. The New Left faction and the socialist faction agrees on at least this much even after their split. Long after Hayden and Lynd had left the journal, an editorial echoed them in charging Great Society programs with "coopt[ing] potential leaders and reduc[ing] the rest to the status of clients."[26]

In their unrelenting critique of liberalism, the editors of *Studies* ignored the inconvenient fact that "liberalism" was not a monolith. There were plenty of liberals, for example, who opposed the Vietnam War and wanted something more than mild regulatory politics. In fact it was John Roche, the president of Americans for Democratic Action (an independent liberal organization started by Arthur Schlesinger and other intellectuals), who argued that "JFK is totally dedicated to managerial politics . . . the end point of which is to beautify cities by replacing Negroes with trees. The choice is between efficiency and justice . . . examples of that are to desegregate the armed forces, not because it is inefficient to have a segregated army but because it is wrong. The same is true with education. Good education is right, not just a device to beat the Soviets to the moon." Many liberals believed that the moral dimension of their political philosophy was ignored by politicians like Kennedy. But the editors of *Studies* rarely acknowledged this or saw the prudence of allying radical politics with mainstream liberalism. Most of them felt that the focus of radicals should be to push liberals to the left or, better yet, overthrow them with a radical alternative. Martin Sklar and James Weinstein expressed this position in an editorial on "Socialism and the New Left," in which they "assum[ed] that liberalism will remain the dominant political ideology of the large corporations . . . and the socially disruptive programs of the ultra-right will continue to be rejected." This was a big assumption. But as they had put it in an earlier editorial, "If the left hopes to begin to play a meaningful role in American life it must cut itself off from the stifling framework of liberal rhetoric and recognize that at heart the leaders of the United States are committed to the warfare state as the last defense of the large-scale corporate system." The power of liberalism to co-opt radical views had to be opposed.[27]

In this the editors at *Studies* were of one mind with the leaders of SDS. SDS president Carl Oglesby, for example, used the term "corporate liberalism" in major speeches during the mid-1960s. Agreement on this issue enabled Hayden, Lynd, and Fruchter to work with Weinstein, Genovese, and Aronowitz for the time being. They reported on the movements that constituted the New Left and acknowledged with approval the politics of the civil rights movement as it moved north. The community-organizing initiatives of SDS were amply covered. When the student movement—especially the Free Speech Movement at Berkeley—emerged, the editors were ecstatic, and for the brief period of 1964 to 1965 it seemed that *Studies on the Left* would become the intellectual organ of the New Left.[28]

But the center did not hold. Besides the aforementioned clash between Hayden and Weinstein, these intellectuals differed on how realistic the New Left really was. While Hayden, Lynd, and Fruchter placed their faith in protest, community organizing, and theories of participatory democracy, Weinstein, Aronowitz, and Genovese believed that socialism, electoral politics, and coalition building should come first. Up until 1965 Weinstein and Aronowitz expressed hope for the antiwar protest movements; and the editors all seemed to agree that the civil rights movement could become radicalized when it turned north. But once the split between the two camps emerged and turned hostile, *Studies* pronounced the New Left as good as dead. After the departure of Hayden, Fruchter, and Lynd, hopes dimmed that the movement could amount to more than a disjointed series of protests. Though Weinstein praised SDS's attempt to form a Radical Education Project (REP)—an initiative through which SDS hoped to combat the anti-intellectualism that *Studies* despised—he and his allies believed that the New Left was based on a faulty premise. As they saw it, the protesters assumed that once "the hypocrisy of liberal rhetoric had been exposed, the corporate establishment would move to repair its shattered image by making real concessions and real reforms." But Sklar and Weinstein had already rejected this assumption.[29]

Weinstein, a historian, looked to the past for an alternative to the politics of protest and participatory democracy. He, and apparently Aronowitz and Genovese as well, saw the Socialist Party (SP) of the Progressive Era as a model for radical political change. Before Bolshevism was imported into the United States, Weinstein argued, the SP had successfully won political power through electoral politics, joined immigrants together in a cohesive force, forged alliances between the educated and working classes, and stayed true to socialist ideals. Weinstein admitted that once the Bolshevik model was imported, the SP and all future leftist parties became irrelevant and out of touch. He wrote in a letter to Gabriel Kolko, whose article on the history of American radicalism echoed Weinstein's thesis, "1919 marks a genuine dividing line, after which the entire socialist movement becomes concerned with extraneous and irrelevant questions." But Weinstein believed the SP was stronger than most historians thought, and that it could serve as a model for the New Left. Replying with Aronowitz and Genovese to an editorial by Hayden and Fruchter, Weinstein argued that the pre-1919 SP provided a model for current struggles, one that was "democratic and decentralized" but committed to something more than protest or community organizing.[30]

Of course it was a big jump from 1919 to the 1960s; and Weinstein admitted that the Communist and Socialist Parties, during that period, were fairly useless. But he still believed that activists could renew the vision of the pre-1919 SP by committing themselves to electoral politics. Along with Aronowitz and Genovese, he formed the Committee on Independent Political Action (CIPA). When Aronowitz and Genovese ducked out of running for office, Weinstein decided to run for City Council himself on the Upper West Side of Manhattan (he lost, and the CIPA collapsed a few years later). During his campaign Weinstein talked openly about socialism and told Saul Landau that he "used the old Debs party as [a] loose model" while talking "about the failures of the Communists and Socialists from 1920 to 1960." Caught up in the excitement of a political campaign, he expressed more hope than usual, even expressing the view that a "national movement of a socialist character" might emerge in the near future. Weinstein also wanted to form a coalition like the one Bayard Rustin had called for after the civil rights legislative victories of 1964 and 1965. Rustin wanted a poor people's movement that could push for more social democratic politics. But while Weinstein liked the idea of a coalition, he rejected the "Rustin approach," which was based on "the assumption that independent radical politics is meaningless and that 'coalition' must mean hooking up with the existing political power structure." Weinstein seemed to prefer some sort of coalition politics coupled with a radical third party modeled on the pre-1919 Socialist Party.[31]

The Role of Intellectuals in Political Change

If the editors of *Studies on the Left* had a clear political vision, they were not necessarily clear about how to implement it. Organizing a third party was a momentous task, as was forging a coalition at a time when black power and feminism were first emerging (it should be noted that *Studies* had made an early showing of support for black nationalism—not exactly an ideology conducive to coalition building—in publishing the early work of Harold Cruse). More importantly, it was never clear what role the editors *themselves* should play in generating political change. As some historians have pointed out, SDS housed large numbers of intellectuals and academics. C. Wright Mills had argued that the future agency for the New Left would come less from labor and more from students. As he asked in his famous 1960 essay "Letter to the New Left," "Who is it that is getting fed up? Who is it that is getting disgusted with what Marx called 'all the old crap'?" For Mills the answer was clear: "It is the young intelligentsia."[32]

In 1944, however, Mills had defined intellectuals as "the powerless people," and this despairing view seemed to capture the early sentiment of *Studies*'s editors. In 1961 Eleanor Hakim made an apt comparison between the editors of *Studies on the Left* and those of the British *New Left Review,* who included E. P. Thompson, Raymond Williams, and others who worked closely with the Labor Party while defining what the New Left meant. She argued that "The *New Left Review* people have a student movement and a political party [the Labor Party] to work within. We have no such institutions." Hence, their work would be more "scholarly" than "directly programmatic." This pessimism soon gave way to a more hopeful attitude. The shift in Mills's thinking—from seeing intellectuals as powerless to seeing them as agents of radical change—carried over into the pages of *Studies,* especially as New Left movements heated up. The journal began publishing a section called "On the Movements" in which the editors analyzed community organizing, the student movement, and antiwar protests for peace; in this way they saw themselves in direct dialogue with activists. As we have seen, the editors wanted intellectuals to help protest movements adopt a wider vision of political change, which was difficult not only because activists often refused to listen but because the editorial board was not unified. In 1965 Evan Stark echoed Helen Kramer when he wrote that reports on the movement were increasingly full of "mundane 'comments' from members of the new 'rub your nose in grime' school of middle-class engagement." Stark called on *Studies* to return to more scholarly, theoretical work.[33]

This debate reflected not only an editorial division but a lack of clarity on the part of *Studies*'s editors about how intellectual work related to political movements. The editors never explained how activists were supposed to use what they read in *Studies on the Left.* At the same time they felt maligned by charges of "anti-intellectualism" in the New Left. Years later James Weinstein lamented that the journal never really had much impact on activists. Saul Landau had likewise once complained, "You know what everyone thinks about Studies? (By everyone I mean four or five people). They think it is very professional and dull." Landau's choice of words was significant. The editors of *Studies* did write from a "professional" and academic point of view; they thought of themselves as graduate students and future professors. But this desire for academic credibility did not square with trying to change the world, as Staughton Lynd's experience testified (he was fired from Yale for being too overtly political). During the 1960s academic professions were becoming increasingly insular. When the *Studies* editors explained why they were organizing "Socialist Scholars' Conferences," they called for radical scholars to "to draw into [their scholarship] the peripheral scholarly work being done now in various fields." How this really differed from scholarship as it was then constituted was never made clear. Radical scholarship risked becoming just another subdivision (perhaps called "labor history" or "social history" or "women's studies" or "queer studies") among the other specialized areas in the academy.[34]

Though the editors of *Studies* intended to reach beyond the walls of academia, they were hamstrung by their desire for academic standing, as their critics pointed out. Richard Chase, a liberal who wrote for *Harper's,* argued, "The academicism one finds in [*Studies on the Left*]—the long articles on Senator Borah, Woodrow Wilson, chapters extracted from Ph.D. dissertations, and so on—must be attributed in part to the uncertainty of young rebels about themselves and their place in society." Interestingly enough, Eleanor Hakim agreed, even if she chafed at Chase's liberalism. Robert Scheer made a similar assessment from a more radical standpoint. Writing in *Root and Branch,* Scheer pointed out that *Studies* "holds out to young academics the possibility that they can pursue a successful academic career by making a radical political contribution." As Scheer saw it, the safe haven of the academy trapped young intellectuals by cutting them off from public life. "The University is 'home'; this is the world we understand, and the other one frightens the hell out of us." Scheer contrasted the editors of *Studies,* who wrote only for other academics, with C. Wright Mills, who had written popular books, not academic articles. The editors at *Studies* understood that the academic virtue of "objectivity" might conflict with their radical predilections. But they failed to ask whether the university was the best place for a radical intellectual committed to social and political change.[35]

What's Left?

It is clear that the editors of *Studies on the Left* hungered for a role in radical politics and hoped for more from the New Left than just a string of protest movements. As they put it in a late editorial, they wanted to move "Beyond Protest," and here, once again, they echoed Bayard Rustin's call to move from "protest to politics." So what sort of legacy did they leave? How well did they articulate a political vision that could affect the future of America? Did their ideas help guide movements committed to achieving social justice?

Perhaps *Studies on the Left* should be remembered for the thing it hoped for: a progressive coalition of poor and working-class people organized around issues of redistribution and a more humane economy. The editors saw such a coalition focusing on "basic, widespread inequalities of wealth, privilege, and power; intensification of elite decision making; increasing physical and psychic damage to millions of underprivileged and privileged Americans; institutionalization of corruption, waste, and cynicism." Of course the editors of *Studies* were not alone in dreaming of such a coalition. There were plenty of liberals who wanted to see this kind of coalition emerge *within* the Democratic Party during the mid- to late 1960s. Bayard Rustin was one of the first to imagine such a coalition; unfortunately, as the editors of *Studies* knew all too well, Rustin had compromised so thoroughly with the Johnson administration that he could not see how the Vietnam War had damaged his hopes (he criticized Martin Luther King for trying to link the civil rights and peace movements in 1967, an attempt that may have been the best hope for coalition politics). The tragedy of Vietnam destroyed the hope of a progressive coalition in America just as it destroyed the lives of young American soldiers. But there were other liberals, such as Arnold Kaufman, who opposed the war and still argued for a coalition within the Democratic Party. Arthur Waskow, along with other editors at *New University Thought,* argued with Weinstein precisely over the meaning of coalitions and the desire for a third party. The editors of *Studies* were not alone in their hopes, but they were alone in their belief that a third party could mobilize such a coalition.[36]

That said, the *hope* for coalition politics remains a legacy of the New Left, and *Studies* deserves credit for bequeathing one version of this hope. In reaction to "identity politics," many leftists today are rediscovering coalition politics, and Weinstein himself has steadfastly argued the importance of coalition building up to the present. One of the tragedies of the American Left historically is its inability to form lasting, effective coalitions, and the result is that there exists in this country no viable radical alternative to mainstream politics. That the editors of *Studies* articulated a vision of coalition politics that could bridge different identities should help us remember that the New Left amounted to something more than protest politics or cultural liberalism.[37]

This vision never materialized, of course, and the editors at *Studies on the Left* were the first to admit it. As they saw it in the mid-1960s, the New Left was not moving beyond single-issue protests against racial oppression, poverty, and the Vietnam War. In the end, it seems that the New Left bequeathed to future generations exactly what the editors feared it would—a mere succession of protest movements and a vague ideal of participatory democracy that was never realized. On this point Weinstein and his fellow editors had hit the mark, but it is impossible to conclude that their own vision of a socialist movement was any more viable. As their liberal antagonists never ceased pointing out, socialism was a bad word in the American lexicon. Victor Rabinowitz noted that "It is a conservative estimate that 90% of the people in the Civil Rights Movement neither know nor care what Socialism is and the percentage is almost as high in the rest of 'The Movement.'" And even if more people had heard of socialism, it was never clear how an equivalent to the pre-1919 Socialist Party could be re-created during the 1960s. Weinstein, Aronowitz, and Genovese were historians. They knew that certain historical conditions—the brutality of a new industrial order and extremely high levels of political participation among the working class—explained the success of the Socialist Party. How could those conditions be reinvented? And perhaps most important of all, how would the editors prevent the sort of factionalism that had overcome the Left after 1919? Need it be said that, in the end, a new form of factionalism killed SDS? Why did they have such confidence that this obvious danger could be overcome when the past forty years argued just the reverse? When, by James Weinstein's own admission, socialist parties of all stripes, from the 1920s to the present, had left so little to build upon?[38]

Though they were often pessimistic about co-optation, the editors could also show signs of radical exuberance. For instance, Weinstein's failure to win public office filled him with optimism. He wrote to Saul Landau in 1966, "Our perspective is to build a popular socialist movement, to develop a program that deals with the question of power, who exercises, who's [sic] interest programs serve, how they are controlled. This in a context of explanation that meaningful change can only come about through a national movement of a socialist character, active in politics. There is no such thing, of course, and we make it plain that there won't be for some years (5–20), but that all activity must build toward this or go play golf." The notion that a socialist majority could come about in twenty years was delusional, and not only in retrospect. After all, Weinstein *lost* the election for City Council in the Upper West Side of Manhattan—the most liberal district in the country during one of the most liberal eras in American history. His confidence seems startling in that light, and especially so in retrospect. Today the majoritarian politics Weinstein embraced is further from reality than ever. Of course some recognized the improbability of radical victory even in the midst of the era's exuberance. In 1971 Arnold Kaufman wrote, "Radical liberals are not and for the foreseeable future will not be a majority of the population or the voting public." Kaufman's realism seems more appropriate today than Weinstein's hope for majoritarian socialism. Both shared a *vision* of coalition politics, but they differed on its actual prospects.[39]

Realism also suggests the need for a more conciliatory attitude toward centrist liberals. When the editors of *Studies* argued that liberals should move left or clear out they helped liberalism push itself off the map. Liberals had made a Faustian pact with America's foreign policy during the Cold War. In response, the radicals at *Studies* emphasized the staying power of liberalism—a political set of ideas that started to disintegrate during the late 1960s—and downplayed the power of conservatism. They were right to criticize liberals for their expansionist tendencies and the imbroglio of Vietnam, but they also ignored the conservatives who were waiting in the wings or who were out on stage already, among them California governor Ronald Reagan. One year after *Studies on the Left* collapsed, Richard Nixon ran for president on his "silent majority" campaign. Although it was not until Reagan's reign that the welfare state began to be dismantled, Nixon's "silent majority" talk—much more than the frantic paranoia of Goldwater—foreshadowed the effectiveness of conservative ideology, his liberal domestic policies notwithstanding. That *Studies* ignored the conservative threat and assumed that liberalism would always be around as a whipping boy reveals a fundamental weakness in their analysis of American politics.[40]

Weaker still was their theory of co-optation. It goes without saying that intellectuals have a responsibility to point out where ideals are being manipulated by those in power; and the phony liberalism of John F. Kennedy deserved exposure. But Weinstein and thinkers like Martin Sklar and Gabriel Kolko never distinguished clearly between co-optation and effective change. Moreover, paranoia about co-optation could lead to the marginalization of the Left through sheer paralysis. The New Left's later pseudo-militance—captured in the absurd antics of the Weathermen—was certainly not indebted to *Studies on the Left*. Nonetheless, the rejection of compromise and reform for the sake of radical purity condemned the Left to an increasingly militant, and increasingly irrelevant, stance, even if only in the world of of ideas.

This criticism of the New Left may simply reflect my own historical context. As American politics has grown increasingly conservative over the past three decades, co-optation does not sound like such a bad thing. We could do with a little more co-optation of leftist values today. Reform itself seems like a goal worth supporting, especially in light of implosion of the New Left during the late 1960s. Though Weinstein was no revolutionary, his fear of the co-opting capacity of corporate liberalism showed repugnance for pragmatic, tentative, and piecemeal political reforms. Yet reform, with all its imperfections, frustrations, and compromises, is probably the only realistic approach to achieving political change, a lesson that the events of the 1960s should make clear.[41]

Perhaps the most we can hope for, as the twenty-first century dawns, is a rebirth of liberal and radical tendencies in American politics. There are reasons to hope. During the 1980s protests against U.S. intervention in Central America grew, and large segments of the American public took to the streets to demand a freeze on the growth of our nuclear arsenal. These were negative protests—like the single-issue protests that caused the editors of *Studies* so much consternation during the 1960s—but they did hold out an alternative vision of America. They showed that many Americans wanted their government to respect the lives of foreign people and to invest its resources not in arms buildup but in education and the alleviation of poverty and other humane pursuits. This is the vision that the New Left might have left behind—a vision that the editors of *Studies on the Left* did not think was enough.

In 1961 Herb Mills wrote an article for *New University Thought* about the "student movement," a term that became interchangeable with the New Left. Like the editors at *Studies*, he believed that student protests had limited effect, and he, like Eleanor Hakim, described most student activists as "liberals." Rather than castigate them for this or try to make them into socialists, he saw the virtue in their preoccupation with direct action, protest, and deliberation:

> The most basic desire and hope which lies behind the political action of both the liberal and "radical" student is that by raising and acting up certain basic issues he can do something to create an atmosphere where political debate is again possible. Reacting against a period during which political debate was suffocated by an all-pervasive McCarthyism and complacency, the student has an urgent desire to make politics—*almost any* kind of politics—legitimate once more.

The editors of *Studies on the Left* would have argued that Mills's sentiment only underlined the limits of the New Left—its inability to transcend single-issue protest politics. But Mills's comment, I believe, appeals to those who live in an era that has witnessed the collapse of state socialism and are not entirely comfortable with the self-congratulatory triumphalism of American capitalism and the accompanying decline of trust in public institutions. If the only thing the New Left bequeathed to us is an existential politics of protest, it is not such a bad legacy. And to the extent that the editors of *Studies on the Left* warned that there were limits to this political philosophy, they did not leave such a bad legacy either. Those who came after them can—if we try our best to embrace the humility taught by history's twists, turns, and contradictions—learn from both perspectives.[42]

Notes

Acknowledgments: I would like to thank Paul Buhle, John McMillian, and Stacy Sewell for very helpful comments and engaging debate. The epigraph comes from the anthology *For a New America: Essays in History and Politics from "Studies on the Left," 1959–1967,* ed. James Weinstein and David Eakins (New York: Vintage, 1970), 220. Kolko's piece was entitled "The Decline of American Radicalism in the Twentieth Century."

1. Perhaps one exception is James Miller's outstanding book on the 1960s, with its particular focus on Tom Hayden's intellectual development. See his *"Democracy Is in the Streets": From Port Huron to the Siege of Chicago* (New York: Simon and Schuster, 1987).

2. See Kevin Mattson, *Intellectuals in Action: The Origins of the New Left and Radical Liberalism, 1945–1970* (University Park, Pa.: Penn State University Press, 2002).

3. One of the best histories of small magazines, with a particular focus on *Partisan Review,* was written by an editor at *Studies on the Left.* See James Gilbert, *Writers and Partisans: A History of Literary Radicalism in America* (New York: John Wiley, 1968).

4. Eleanor Hakim to Helene Brewer (of the department of English, Queen's College), undated, Studies on the Left Archives, Wisconsin State Historical Society Archives, box 1; "A Note from the Editors," *Studies on the Left* 3 (1962): 3 (journal hereafter abbreviated SoL).

5. William Appleman Williams, *The Tragedy of American Diplomacy* (New York: Dell, 1959), 13. For Williams's influence on the New Left and history in general, I rely on Paul Buhle and Edward Rice-Maximin, *William Appleman Williams: The Tragedy of American Empire* (New York: Routledge, 1995), 116–19.

6. Williams, *The Tragedy of American Diplomacy,* 308. Harrington's comments can be found in "America II (A Symposium on William Appleman Williams)," *Partisan Review* 37 (1970): 504.

7. "The Radicalism of Disclosure: A Statement by the Editors," *Studies on the Left* 1 (1959): 3; Hakim in letter of 29 Nov. 1961, SoL Archives, box 1.

8. On the origins of the New Left in general, see Staughton Lynd, "Towards a History of the New Left," in *The New Left,* ed. Priscilla Long (Boston: Extending Horizons Books, 1969); George Vickers, *The Formation of the New Left* (Lexington: Lexington Books, 1978); Penina Migdal Glazer, "From the Old Left to the New: Radical Criticism in the 1940s," American Quarterly 24 (1972): 584–603; Maurice Isserman, *"If I Had a Hammer . . .": The Death of the Old Left and the Birth of the New Left* (New York: Basic Books, 1987).

9. Letter from Hakim to Sklar, undated, and Sklar in letter to board members, 19 Nov. 1960, both in SoL Archives, box 9. On the funding of *Studies,* see Hakim to Saul Landau, 20 Oct. 1961, which addresses a grant from the Rabinowitz Foundation. The journal also received some funding from a small, left-oriented foundation known as the Fund for Social Analysis.

10. James Weinstein to Mrs. Ann Farnsworth, 3 Aug. 1965, SoL Archives, box 3; Helen Kramer to Jim Weinstein, 13 June 1965, SoL Archives, box 5. For Weinstein's enthusiasm about the 1964 SDS convention, see his letter to Clark Kissinger, 15 June 1964, SoL Archives, box 5.

11. For Hayden, I rely on his autobiography, *Reunion: A Memoir* (New York: Random House, 1988), and Miller, *"Democracy Is in the Streets";* for Lynd's essay on socialism, see "Socialism, the Forbidden Word," *SoL* 3 (1963): 14–20.

12. Weinstein to Robin Brooks, 13 July 1965, SoL Archives, box 2; Weinstein reiterated this outlook when I interviewed him on 1 June 1999; Staughton Lynd to Weinstein, 9 May 1966 (in which Lynd asks to have his name taken off the editorial masthead), SoL archives, box 6. For a nice overview of the transitions within *Studies on the Left,* see the editorial by James Weinstein, "Socialist Intellectuals," *SoL* 6 (1966): 3. For Weinstein's explanation of the journal's collapse, see his *"Studies on the Left*: R.I.P." *Radical America* (Nov.–Dec. 1967): 1–6.

13. "After the Election," *SoL* 5 (1965): 4.

14. Weinstein to Herbert Marcuse, 22 Nov. 1965, SoL Archives, box 6.

15. Herbert Marcuse, *One-Dimensional Man: Studies in the Ideology of Advanced Industrial Society* (Boston: Beacon Press, 1964), xvi.

16. For "flexible tolerance," see "Up from Irrelevance," editorial in *SoL* 5 (1965): 3. For Marcuse's theories of "one-dimensional society," see Marcuse, *One-Dimensional Man,* and his "Repressive Tolerance" in Robert Paul Wolf, Barrington Moore, and Herbert Marcuse, *A Critique of Pure Tolerance* (Boston: Beacon Press, 1965). See also the historical work of Martin Jay, *The Dialectical Imagination* (Boston: Little, Brown, 1973).

17. Hakim to Bart Bernstein, 6 Dec. 1962, SoL Archives, box 1.

18. Martin Sklar, "Woodrow Wilson and the Political Economy of Modern United States Liberalism," in Weinstein and Eakins, *For a New America,* 86; "The Ultra-Right and Cold War Liberalism," *SoL* 3 (1962): 8; Weinstein in *SoL* 5 (1965): 138.

19. Kennedy on Khrushchev quoted in Richard Reeves, *President Kennedy: Profile of Power* (New York: Simon and Schuster, 1993), 199. On Kennedy, I rely on this work as well as on Bruce Miroff, *Pragmatic Illusions: The Presidential Politics of John F. Kennedy* (New York: McKay, 1976), and Alan Brinkley's historical analysis of modern liberalism's trajectory in "The Idea of the State," in *The Rise and Fall of the New Deal Order, 1930–1980,* ed. Steve Fraser and Gary Gerstle (Princeton: Princeton University Press, 1989).

20. Weinstein to Staughton Lynd, 29 April 1964, SoL Archives, box 6.

21. Weinstein to Saul Landau, 6 Dec. 1958, SoL Archives, box 5; Weinstein to Lawrence Goldman, 11 Oct. 1962, SoL Archives, box 4.

22. Ronald Radosh, "The Corporate Ideology of American Labor," in Weinstein and Eakins, *For a New America,* 126, 151.

23. Sidney Peck, "The Political Consciousness of Rank-And-File Labor Leaders," *SoL* 2 (1961): 43–51; Robert Wolfe, "Intellectuals and Social Change," *SoL* 2 (1961): 66–67; Martin Glaberman, "Marxism, The Working Class and the Trade Unions," *SoL* 4 (1964): 65–72; Stanley Aronowitz, "Against the Mainstream: Interview with James Mattes of the U.E.," *SoL* 5 (1964): 43–54.

24. Paul Breslow, "The Support of the Mysteries," *SoL* 1 (1959): 16. For an argument similar to Breslow's, see Lawrence La Fave, "Any Glory in the Beat Way to Satori?" *New University*

Thought 1 (1961). It should be noted that Breslow's attitude toward the Beats makes clear that, at least in its origins, the New Left had no sympathy for the counterculture.

25. Joan Wallach Scott, "The Teach-In: A National Movement or the End of an Affair?" *SoL* 5 (1965): 85; Peter Lathrop, "Teach-Ins: New Force or Isolated Phenomenon?" *SoL* 5 (1965): 52. For an argument in favor of the teach-ins, see Arnold Kaufman, "Teach-Ins: New Force for the Times," in *Teach-Ins: USA*, ed. Louis Menashe and Ronald Radosh (New York: Praeger, 1967).

26. Tom Hayden and Staughton Lynd in a response to Herbert Gans, "The New Radicalism," in *SoL* 5 (1965): 133; "Beyond Protest," *SoL* 7 (1967): 8. It is interesting to note the parallels between Hayden and Lynd's critique of the welfare state and the later critique launched by neoconservatives; see E. J. Dionne on the similarities between the New Left and the Right in *Why Americans Hate Politics* (New York: Simon and Schuster, 1992).

27. ADA president John Roche quoted in Reeves, *President Kennedy*, 655. "Socialism and the New Left," *SoL* 6 (1966): 70. One of the few defenses of liberalism came from James O'Connor in a reply to Weinstein; see *SoL* 3 (1962): 61.

28. On community organizing see, for instance, James Williams, "On Community Unions," *SoL* 4 (1964): 73–78; Jesse Allen, "Newark: Community Union," *SoL* 5 (1965): 80–85; Danny Schechter, "Reveille for Radicals, II," *SoL* 6 (1966): 20–27. On the Free Speech Movement, see Michael Nagler, "Berkeley: The Demonstrations," *SoL* 5 (1965): 55–62; Larry Spence, "Berkeley: What It Demonstrates," *SoL* 5 (1965): 63–68. On Oglesby, see Todd Gitlin, *The Sixties: Years of Hope, Days of Rage* (New York: Bantam Books, 1987), 185.

29. Editorial, "Beyond Protest," *SoL* 7 (1967): 3; for the optimism about the civil rights movement, see "After the Election," 4. On the peace movement, see Aronowitz and Weinstein, "The New Peace Movement," *SoL* 5 (1965): 9. For Aronowitz's personal account of this conflict, see his "When the New Left Was New," in *The Sixties without Apology*, ed. Sohna Sayres et al. (Minneapolis: University of Minnesota Press, 1984).

30. Editorial in *SoL* 5 (1965): 12; Weinstein to Gabriel Kolko, 3 Aug. 1966, SoL Archives, box 5. Weinstein spelled out his history of socialism out in *The Decline of Socialism in America, 1912–1925* (New York: Monthly Review Press, 1967).

31. Weinstein to Saul Landau, 3 May 1966, SoL Archives, box 5. Weinstein to Louis Goldeberg, 23 June 1965, SoL Archives, box 3.

32. C. Wright Mills, "The New Left," in *Power, Politics, and People*, ed. Irving Louis Horowitz (New York: Oxford University Press, 1963), 257. The essay was originally titled "Letter to the New Left."

33. C. Wright Mills, "The Powerless People: The Role of the Intellectual in Society," *politics* (April 1944): 68–72; Hakim to Richard Chase, 7 July 1961, SoL Archives, box 2; Evan Stark, "Theory on the Left," *SoL* 5 (1965): 82.

34. James Weinstein, interview by author, 1 June 1999; Saul Landau letter written sometime in 1961, SoL Archives, box 6. For a critique of the New Left for becoming overly academic, see Russell Jacoby, *The Last Intellectuals* (New York: Basic Books, 1987). See also Jon Wiener, "Radical Historians and the Crisis in American History, 1959–1980," *Journal of American History* 76 (1989): 399–434, and Christopher Lasch's response, "Consensus: An Academic Question?" in the same issue, 457–59.

35. Richard Chase, "The New Campus Magazines," *Harper's*, Oct. 1961, 169.

36. On Rustin, see Jervis Anderson, *Bayard Rustin: Troubles I've Seen* (New York: Harper Collins, 1997), 294, 301. See also Arnold Kaufman, "New Party or New Democratic Coalition?" *Dissent* (Jan.–Feb. 1969), 13–18. See also the debate between Waskow and Weinstein, SoL Archives, box 10.

37. "After the Election," 4. For the classic statement on coalition politics, see Bayard Rustin, "From Protest to Politics," *Commentary* (Feb. 1965). Doug Rossinow has most recently argued that the New Left's most important legacy is cultural liberalism. See Rossinow, *The Politics of Authenticity: Liberalism, Christianity, and the New Left in America* (New York: Columbia University Press, 1998), esp. 294.

38. Victor Rabinowitz, undated letter, SoL Archives, box 6.

39. Weinstein to Saul Landau, 3 May 1966, SoL Archives, box 5; Arnold Kaufman, "A Strategy for Radical Liberals," *Dissent* (Aug. 1971): 382.

40. See Alan Matusow, *The Unraveling of America: A History of Liberalism in the 1960s* (New York: Basic Books, 1984).

41. See Russell Jacoby, *The End of Utopia: Politics and Culture in an Age of Apathy* (New York: Basic Books, 1999) and my review, "The End of Declarative Statements," *Social Policy* (winter 1999).

42. Herb Mills, "In Defense of the Student Movement," *New University Thought* 1 (1961): 10.

CHAPTER 3

Building the New South: The Southern Student Organizing Committee

Gregg L. Michel

Speaking at the first conference of the Southern Student Organizing Committee (SSOC), historian Howard Zinn remarked, "This is an historic moment. Someday historians will write about it."[1] Zinn was only half right; while this was the first major conference of southern white student activists in the 1960s, neither the conference nor the sponsoring organization itself has received much attention from historians. This is both curious and unfortunate, since the SSOC was the most important organization of activist white students in the South during the decade. Born in Nashville in 1964, during the heyday of the civil rights movement, SSOC initially focused its work on the struggle for black equality. Before long, though, the group transformed itself into a multi-issue organization interested not only in civil rights but in a variety of other issues, from the Vietnam War to the persistence of rural poverty to the plight of working-class southerners. Throughout its five-year existence, SSOC was active at a broad cross-section of predominantly white southern colleges and universities—public and private, parochial and secular, large research institutions and small liberal arts colleges. The group appealed to liberal-leaning and progressive white southern students because it was less confrontational and less ideologically driven than either the Students for a Democratic Society (SDS) or the Student Nonviolent Coordinating Committee (SNCC), the most well known activist youth organizations of the day. Moreover, SSOC's regional orientation, well-developed southern identity, and belief that the South was unique helped attract young whites to the group and made it more popular on many campuses than either SDS or SNCC.

SSOC was the creation of a small but vocal group of white students committed to social change. These students were drawn to activist causes for a variety of reasons. Some were sensitized to the sufferings of others by deeply held religious beliefs. Others were motivated by specific experiences during their collegiate careers. For all of the white students, however, becoming an activist was not a decision made lightly. Stepping "outside the magic circle" and rejecting the dominant views of the white South required great courage, for these students knew that their activism could lead to the loss of friends, rejection by their families, and expulsion from school.[2] But SSOC activists were united by their belief that the white South was not monolithically opposed to progressive causes. In their view, other whites in the region would become involved in, or at least would support, movements for social change if approached in the right way by the right people—that is, by a nonthreatening organization of fellow southerners. Thus energized by the hope that they could create a New South free of poverty, racism, and oppression, the students of SSOC enlisted boldly in the progressive movements of the day.

Although SSOC engaged in both campus and community organizing, the group was most effective when it worked with white southern students. On many predominantly white campuses, SSOC activists were the first outspoken proponents for such causes as university reform and desegregation, and they played the key role in popularizing these issues with the student body and pressuring administrators to institute reforms. But while SSOC members formed this activist vanguard, the organization did not survive long enough to see the full effects of its efforts. Increased recruitment of black students, official university condemnation of the Vietnam War, the creation of black studies programs—all of these progressive reforms were the product of the post-SSOC world. Importantly, though, these developments were the direct result of student activism in the late 1960s and early 1970s, activism for which SSOC had paved the way by having earlier created the space for discussion of progressive issues. By the late 1960s other students, including moderates who had not previously identified with student activists, and other groups, including even student political parties, long the bastion of Greek conformity, moved into these spaces and became the champions of liberal reforms at southern colleges and universities. In short, SSOC helped to make dissent respectable on southern campuses.

SSOC was a force for change until 1969, when it went into rapid decline, collapsing altogether in June of that year. The organization's death resulted in part from the power struggle that was tearing SDS apart, as the competing factions within SDS, after first trying to control SSOC, worked to destroy it in an effort to enhance their position. But SSOC was not just a victim of SDS's factional warfare. Just as importantly, SSOC contributed to its own undoing, for the group was beset by serious internal difficulties that made it vulnerable to meddling by SDS. By 1969 many SSOC activists concluded that the group had come to place too much emphasis on the South's differences from the rest of the nation, thus obscuring similarities in the problems faced by northerners and southerners alike and inappropriately suggesting that SSOC should remain separate from the national progressive movement.

Especially problematic was that in making their case for southern distinctiveness, some activists drew on the images and rhetoric of the Old South and the Confederacy. Although they insisted that they infused such rhetoric and symbols with a new meaning

—for instance, they might speak of "seceding" from the Vietnam War—others in the group believed that linking SSOC to the ignoble and discredited parts of southern history, regardless of motive, was awkward and immoral. Differences over this issue helped to precipitate SSOC's disintegration into factions.

Equally debilitating in the context of the SDS attack was that SSOC lacked a sharp analytical focus. The group neither developed a coherent radical ideology nor relied on an overarching philosophy of social change to guide its actions. Instead, its activism was motivated by a general desire to create a more humane, non-racist, and peaceful society. To the more intellectually sophisticated members of SDS, with their position papers and formal ideologies, SSOC's broadly conceived vision of a better society contrasted sharply with their highly developed Marxist analysis of America, and they attacked SSOC's agenda as both too vague and as insufficiently radical. Moreover, by 1969 some SSOC activists advocated that the group adopt a more theoretical perspective and develop its own radical analysis—in short, that it become more like SDS. Disagreement on this question served to harden the emerging factions in the group, dividing the organization at a time when unity was vital. Thus weakened by internal problems, SSOC was unable to mount an effective defense against the SDS assault.

Although it was the preeminent group of white southern student activists in the 1960s, SSOC is largely absent from the historical literature on the era.[3] Historians who do mention it offer brief or inaccurate descriptions. Kirkpatrick Sale and Clayborne Carson, authors of the most thorough histories of SDS and SNCC, respectively, each suggest that SSOC's roots were in the organization they study, as do some subsequent writers.[4] That most academic work on the South and the social movements of the 1960s neglects SSOC reflects its general disregard for white student activists in the South. By ignoring or glossing over the activism of young whites in the region, the scholarship perpetuates the image of the white South as backward and benighted, unwilling to reform itself and ready to use violence to preserve the "southern way of life." White students in the South simply are not part of the story of the progressive movements of the 1960s. If they appear in histories of the era, they do so only as the enemies of change, as rabble-rousers and thugs whom the movement had to overcome. The story of the civil rights movement has been a narrative of southern black heroes and northern white missionaries who suffered the scorn and abuse of southern whites. And northern whites and, especially, southern blacks *were* the agents of change in the South. But by ignoring the contributions of white southern students to the civil rights struggle and lumping all southerners together as enemies of desegregation, this scholarship oversimplifies the history of the movement and leaves the erroneous impression that in the 1960s all southern whites were on the wrong side of history.[5]

White southern students were not uniformly opposed to the progressive movements of the 1960s, and they need to be reintegrated into the narrative of the era. For more than five years the SSOC defied stereotypes about southern whites through its work for racial reform, gender equality, an end to the Vietnam War, and other progressive causes. Yet because we know so little about the organization and the students who worked with it, Howard Zinn's charge to the participants at SSOC's first conference still resonates more than thirty-five years later: "Let us hear who you are, why you have come, and where you want to go."[6]

SSOC's roots were in the black student-led movement that developed after the 1960 Greensboro sit-ins and the subsequent creation of SNCC. In early 1961, with funding from the Southern Conference Educational Fund (SCEF), an interracial civil rights group, SNCC hired Bob Zellner, a white Alabama native and recent graduate of Huntingdon College in Montgomery, to recruit white student support for the group—what became known as the White Southern Student Project.[7] Although Zellner did not have much success, at least in part because he spent most of his time working in the black community with other SNCC staffers, he was succeeded in 1963 by another white Alabaman, Sam Shirah, who was more deeply committed to working among southern whites. Although he had participated in numerous black-led civil rights actions, Shirah had concluded in 1963 that "just offering my body in the Negro demonstrations was not enough. I began to feel that something had to be done to reach the great numbers of white people in the South who have felt that this movement is their enemy." By the fall of 1963 he believed that recent events, from the violent repression of the Birmingham demonstrations to the interracial harmony of the March on Washington, had made young whites increasingly receptive to calls for racial reform. Shirah thus began visiting predominantly white southern campuses to reach out to these students. In early 1964 Ed Hamlett, a native Tennessean and veteran of the civil rights movement at the state's flagship university in Knoxville, left graduate school to join Shirah in this work, and for the next several months the two men made contact with students across the region.[8]

At the same time, white students at Vanderbilt University, Peabody College, and Scarritt College, closely connected schools in Nashville, intensified their involvement in the local civil rights movement. Students from these institutions had participated in desegregation campaigns in Nashville since 1960, taking part in marches and promoting boycotts. In the fall of 1963 they stepped up their efforts by organizing a virtually all-white campaign to integrate the Campus Grill, an eatery near the schools. The drive's eventual success—the restaurant agreed to integrate—and the students' awareness of Shirah's and Hamlett's work elsewhere, convinced the Nashville activists that a southern white student organization was needed to keep white activists, scattered as they were throughout the region, in touch with one another. Moreover, these students were convinced that many white southern students were quietly sympathetic to civil rights goals but felt isolated and afraid of hostile reaction should they voice their opinions. An organization of like-minded white students could inspire such students to action. Working closely with Shirah and Hamlett, the Nashville group called a meeting on Easter weekend 1964 for the purpose of founding a new South-wide student organization.[9]

Their call resonated on southern campuses large and small, public and private, far removed from civil rights actions and already familiar with protest activity. Dan Harmeling and Rosemary Ezra came to Nashville representing two large state institutions—the University of Florida and the University of North Carolina at Chapel Hill—while Marjorie Henderson arrived from tiny Maryville College in Tennessee. The Students for

Integration at Tulane University sent Cathy Cade, and Marti Turnipseed came on behalf of the few interested students at Millsaps College in Mississippi. Soon after finishing his final exams at the University of Georgia, Nelson Blackstock headed for Nashville, as did Lynchburg (Virginia) College's Bob Richardson and Bruce Smith, who were invited because they had picketed the local newspaper after it red-baited a schoolteacher who opposed the Vietnam War. One African American student even participated in the conference — Marion Barry Jr., the former SNCC chairman who was then leading a civil rights group at the University of Tennessee, where he was pursuing postgraduate studies. In all, forty-five students from fifteen predominantly white schools in ten southern states responded to the invitation, and by the end of the meeting they had created the Southern Student Organizing Committee.[10]

For the white students involved, the decision to join SSOC was momentous. They knew that their participation in the group could alter their lives irreversibly, that they would be seen as "race traitors" by other whites, that their friends and families might reject them, that certain career opportunities would be closed to them. Dorothy Burlage, an SDS leader from Texas who maintained close ties with SSOC, remarked years later, "As you got deeper into the movement you, in fact, did burn your bridges. . . . We kept getting further and further from anything we knew about how to live a life." Most southern activists were keenly aware of the sacrifices social activism entailed and were thus extremely committed to the cause once they became involved. As Virginia activist Nan Grogan put it, "you think a long time [before deciding to participate] and when you make up your mind you really believe."[11]

Before they departed from Nashville, the student activists adopted an eight-hundred-word manifesto announcing the group's creation. Entitled "We'll Take Our Stand," its principal author was Robb Burlage, a University of Texas graduate and founding member of SDS then living with his wife, Dorothy, in Nashville. Burlage's emotional attachment to the South and his interest in the region's economic history prompted him to take the lead in writing SSOC's founding document.[12] Working at the kitchen table in their tiny apartment above a garage, Burlage crafted a document that expressed the new organization's values and outlined its goals. Inspired by the black-led freedom movement, the students of SSOC vowed to return to their colleges and their communities, in Burlage's words, "to create non-violent political and direct action movements dedicated to the sort of social change throughout the South and nation which is necessary to achieve our stated goals." These included the abolition of segregation, "an end to personal poverty and deprivation," and the transformation of the South into an idyllic "place where industries and large cities can blend into farms and natural rural splendor to provide meaningful work and leisure opportunities for all." Bringing the manifesto to its emotional peak, Burlage declared, "We as young Southerners hereby pledge to take *our* stand now together here to work for a new order, a new South, a place which embodies our ideals for all the world to emulate, not ridicule. We find our destiny as individuals in the South in our hopes and our work together as brothers."[13]

The title of Burlage's manifesto alluded to the famous 1930 book *I'll Take My Stand,* which condemned the expanding urban-industrial order and extolled the virtues of southern rural life, including segregation. Burlage saw the book's authors, twelve southern intellectuals who became known as the Nashville Agrarians, as backward-looking southerners who sought to "escape from the modern South and not deal with the racist implications of the old heritage." As he pointedly remarked in SSOC's founding document, the Agrarians "endorsed the old feudal agrarian aristocratic order of the south and opposed what they saw coming in the new order—widespread industrialization and urbanization with democracy and equality for all people." Burlage's twist on the title ingeniously cut both ways, rejecting the Agrarians' racial views while at the same time acknowledging that they had been radicals in their own way for opposing the industrialization of the South. Although Burlage and other SSOC founders may not have shared the Agrarians' contempt for modern industry, they did respect them for courageously standing up for their principles and resisting the dominant economic and social trends.[14]

Burlage and the SSOC students also shared with the Agrarians a sense of southern difference from the rest of the nation owing to the region's culture and history. The group understood that most white southerners felt that the South was unique and exceptional, and they hoped that evoking southern distinctiveness would enable them to reach white students who were otherwise indifferent or hostile to progressive activism. Emory University student Gene Guerrero, the organization's first chairman, later admitted that "all of us in SSOC were southern chauvinists for a while; we sort of bent over backwards to try and celebrate the South and southernness."[15] From its start, then, SSOC worked to build its reputation as a proudly southern group that whites could join without having to reject their culture and history. The activists thus initially entitled SSOC's newsletter *The New Rebel*. More controversial was the symbol a black SNCC worker created for the group: a picture of clasping black and white hands superimposed over the battle flag of the Confederacy. SSOC consciously adopted this symbol to suggest "a new way for the South." Though some activists did not like the flag, more believed that appropriating the preeminent symbol of previous century's rebellion could aid their attempt to initiate a very different type of uprising in the 1960s.[16]

Initially, civil rights dominated SSOC's agenda. For its first project, undertaken just two months after the group's founding, SSOC took on the daunting task of trying to build support for racial reform among whites in Biloxi, Gulfport, and Jackson, Mississippi. The White Folks Project, as it came to be known, was a component of Freedom Summer, the SNCC-led campaign to galvanize the movement in Mississippi. Twenty-five whites participated in the project. Seven worked in Jackson, primarily with middle-class whites, in hopes of demonstrating that white moderates could support civil rights.[17] The other workers traveled to Biloxi and Gulfport, where they tried to persuade working-class whites that it was in their self-interest to ally with blacks. Neither group had much success. Though most whites listened politely to the organizers, very few agreed to become involved in the movement. Sympathetic whites "didn't know what they could do," Guerrero concluded, "and were too scared to do it even if they knew what they could do." Less supportive whites charged that the organizers were outside agitators who only wanted to help blacks, not whites. In August the project collapsed, when white fears that the students were running an employment bureau for blacks led to the group's eviction from its Biloxi office. Within ten days all the activists left the state, and SSOC soon shifted its attention from the white community to white campuses.[18]

This was fine with the many SSOC activists who were more comfortable working on predominantly white campuses than in the wider white community. A majority of the group, in fact, came to prefer working with students to working with other whites. For the next two years, SSOC focused exclusively on predominantly white southern college campuses. During this time the organization led, helped organize, and supported numerous local civil rights campaigns. In Nashville SSOC activists were prominent among the Vanderbilt, Peabody, and Scarritt students who led a "sip-in" at the segregated Morrison's Cafeteria near the campuses.[19] At Auburn University and the University of Georgia, SSOC students were at the forefront of movements to promote civil rights on campus and in the broader community.[20] And at the University of Virginia, students associated with SSOC helped to found activist campus organizations that worked to desegregate the state's most prominent university.[21]

SSOC leaders were enthusiastic about this burgeoning local activism. But tying the organization so closely to local activists had the unintended effect of drawing SSOC away from civil rights issues. That is, while SSOC initially focused its work on black equality, the group began to spend more time on issues such as university reform and the Vietnam War because those were the issues animating white activists in the region. Though the black freedom struggle always received strong support from the group, by 1966 the broad-based activism of white students across the South helped transform SSOC into a multi-issue organization in which non–civil rights concerns became increasingly important.

One of these concerns was university reform, a term that reflected students' desire to transform their schools into more diverse and democratic institutions. University reform emerged as a critical item on the agenda of white student activists in the South thanks in large measure to the publicity attending the Free Speech Movement at the University of California at Berkeley in 1964 and the less well known but closer-to-home free speech demonstrations at the University of North Carolina in 1963.[22] Southern white activists came to consider university reform in the context of the larger struggle for social justice. For many, the desire for personal autonomy linked university reform to civil rights and even to the Vietnam War. University of Florida student Alan Levin spoke for many white southern activists when he demanded at one rally that "individuals be permitted to play a part in making decisions that effect [sic] their lives. We hold this for the people of Vietnam, Greece, Harlem, Selma, and the University of Florida."[23]

The connection between university reform and other progressive causes inspired student activism on a wide range of campus issues after 1965. At Duke University and the University of Virginia, white students worked for curricular reform and joined the few black students on campus in demanding the creation of black studies programs.[24] At the University of Florida and Marshall University in West Virginia, dissident students sought to win control of student government by organizing political parties with platforms calling for greater student power.[25] On campuses large and small, SSOC activists helped to foment student opposition to administrative efforts to restrict free speech. While SSOC students at Florida led protests against a policy prohibiting the distribution of certain publications on campus, activists at the University of Tennessee and Furman University in South Carolina organized campaigns that forced administrators to repeal "speaker bans" on prominent activists such as comedian Dick Gregory (at Tennessee) and Chicago Eight defendant Rennie Davis (at Furman).[26]

SSOC activists also targeted *in loco parentis* policies governing women's lives on campus, dictating everything from what they could wear to how late they could stay out in the evening. SSOC did not come quickly to the issue of women's rights, however. At first, both men and women in the group considered civil rights issues more important—many SSOC men dismissed women's concerns as irrelevant, trivial, or even imaginary. But by 1968 the women in the group, led by Lynn Wells, SSOC's most respected and effective activist and the author of "American Women: Their Use and Abuse," a seminal essay on women's rights, had prodded SSOC to adopt women's issues as part of its agenda. At the local level SSOC activists assumed leadership roles in protests against women's rules on campus. At the University of Georgia in 1968, SSOC activist David Simpson cofounded the Movement for Co-Ed Equality, a campus group that forced school officials to abolish women's rules.[27] Later that year the University of North Carolina SSOC chapter helped pressure the administration to scrap the rules governing visitation between the sexes in campus residences. And at the University of South Carolina the SSOC chapter initiated an ambitious drive in 1968 to eliminate curfew for women on campuses throughout the state.[28]

SSOC's opposition to the Vietnam War was another issue on which it followed the lead of local activists. Initially the organization took no stand on the war, as a number of its members supported American intervention in Southeast Asia or felt that the war was irrelevant to SSOC's work on campus. By the middle of 1966, however, SSOC had become a vigorous opponent of the war. The group's adoption of the antiwar position stemmed in part from the recognition that the issue resonated with southern students; large, well-attended teach-ins on the war at Vanderbilt, Florida, the University of Kentucky, and Emory in late 1965 had made this clear.[29] Moreover, SSOC members concluded that the group's work on civil rights and university reform required that it also oppose the war. Participation in the civil rights struggle had made some of them acutely sensitive to the war's pernicious effect on racial reform. As Ed Hamlett recalls, "You couldn't fight poverty, you couldn't fight racism, you couldn't do the kinds of things that we needed to do domestically 'cause everything was being poured into—emotionally, fiscally—everything was being poured into this damn war over in Vietnam." Others believed that the principle of self-determination linked the war to the civil rights movement. "It distresses me," Archie Allen, one of SSOC's founders, complained in early 1966, "when persons who, for a few days, risked their lives in voter registration projects in Mississippi cannot envision the pursuit of democracy and self-determination for the people in the Mekong Delta in Vietnam." By 1966 SSOC also had begun to attract support from students who, unlike Allen and his cohorts, had only recently become active in progressive causes. For these students the war was a more salient issue than civil rights; although they supported black equality, they felt that passage of federal civil rights legislation in 1964–65 enabled them to shift their focus to the more urgent matter of the war, which was escalating under Lyndon Johnson.[30]

At first SSOC manifested its opposition to the war by taking part in actions sponsored by other organizations. In 1966, for instance, it coordinated southern demonstrations against the national draft deferment exam as part of an antidraft campaign led by SDS.[31] In 1967 and 1968 SSOC became more active in its opposition to the war, organizing a series of Peace Tours, in which the group's leaders toured schools in six southern states.[32] The group also focused on the selective service system, offering draft counseling at numerous schools and organizing demonstrations to support those who refused induction.[33] Such actions heightened the group's visibility across the region. So too did its growing penchant for more militant actions. Like the broader antiwar movement, SSOC adopted more provocative and radical tactics as a response to the intensification of the war. From the perspective of many SSOC members, the escalation of hostilities in Southeast Asia required that they adopt more aggressive, confrontational tactics. For example, the group organized several demonstrations at which activists threatened to immolate dolls or even small animals to dramatize the horrors of napalm.[34] Several SSOC staffers in Nashville also tried to disrupt President Johnson's 1967 visit to Nashville; three of them were arrested after they tried to block Johnson's motorcade by sitting down in front of his limousine.[35]

Despite SSOC's success in organizing white college students in the South, some members felt increasingly that the organization should not confine its work to campuses. Although the White Folks Project in Mississippi had shown how difficult it could be to work with non-student whites, many believed they had to attempt this nevertheless, that it was essential to involve other segments of the white community if the South was truly to change. In 1966, the difficulties of the White Folks Project a dim memory, SSOC renewed its commitment to working in the white community.

The ascendancy of black power within SNCC also encouraged SSOC to focus on nonstudent whites. Stokely Carmichael, SNCC's new chairman and a passionate advocate of black separatism, conveyed this message at SSOC's annual meeting in April 1966. While Carmichael made clear that SNCC appreciated the white activists' commitment and contribution to civil rights for blacks, he told SSOC members that the time had come for them to go to work in their own communities, a job for which SSOC, not SNCC, was best suited. As one SNCC organizer from Mississippi put it, according to SSOC's Tom Gardner, "'What we're saying is that someone has got to organize those white guys hanging around the gas station. We can't do it, but you can.'"[36]

SSOC readily accepted Carmichael's challenge. Many agreed with Ed Hamlett that, as whites, SSOC activists needed to reach out to those whites "who do the dirty work of bombing and beating." It would be impossible to build a New South, Hamlett argued, "as long as the Klan is almost the only group now attempting to organize this large, sometimes hated, and often forgotten minority group."[37] SSOC acted quickly on its new commitment, developing the Atlanta Project to promote civil rights consciousness among middle-class whites in that city, and the North Nashville Project to try to organize poor whites there around deteriorating housing conditions and the lack of municipal services in their neighborhoods. It was through the Textile Workers Union of America (TWUA), however, that SSOC made its most concerted effort to reach out to nonstudent whites in the region.[38]

In 1967 SSOC worked with the TWUA on a series of unionization drives at North Carolina textile mills. The campaigns, at seven Cone Mills plants centered on Greensboro and the National Spinning Company mill in Whiteville, resulted in strikes over the companies' refusal to recognize the union as the workers' bargaining agent. SSOC activists, led by Gene Guerrero and Lynn Wells, traveled to campuses across the state to build support for the workers. Thanks to their efforts, more than three hundred students became involved in the campaigns, leafleting their campuses in support of the strikes, walking the picket line with workers, and joining mass demonstrations at company headquarters. At the outset, many workers worried that the students would hinder their efforts. They feared a bunch of longhaired, drug-abusing radicals who would offend their cultural sensibilities, alienate their supporters in the community, and undermine the entire campaign. To counter these anxieties, the SSOC activists coached the student organizers to obey all laws, speak politely, dress nicely, and shave, because, as one union organizer explained to students, "beards make people think of things like LSD."[39] Once the workers saw that the students would not threaten the campaigns and in fact could offer crucial support as the confrontation at the mills intensified, they welcomed their assistance and made a concerted effort to encourage student interest in the drives. In April workers from the Cone plants joined student activists in organizing a conference on textile workers' rights in Greensboro attended by nearly three hundred students. Shortly thereafter National Spinning workers traveled to the Chapel Hill campus to speak to students about their grievances and to encourage them to support the union.[40]

The student–worker alliance was particularly heartening to SSOC activists deeply involved in the labor drives, since it gave southern activists the chance to relate directly to working-class whites. The alliance between students and workers did not translate into a union victory, however. The refusal of the TWUA's national leaders to support a protracted walkout at the Cone plants and the Whiteville workers' inability to raise enough funds to sustain their strike led to the collapse of both campaigns by September 1967.[41]

Meanwhile, the role SSOC had played in these campaigns made white community organizing a source of conflict with the group. While many veterans of the union work thought the group should lavish more attention and resources on working-class organizing, other SSOC activists argued that it should focus its efforts on students and the issues that mattered most to them, such as the war and university reform. The latter camp saw the purpose of SSOC as the organizing of students by students; as they argued in one SSOC publication, "experience has taught us that we work best with those we know best, the group of which we are part."[42] Differences on this issue caused a serious rift in the group and contributed to its factionalization.

This disagreement reflected a larger and ultimately more debilitating problem for SSOC, namely, its lack of analytical focus. Throughout its existence SSOC gave primacy to action over analysis; as the group's leaders never tired of pointing out, SSOC was an organization of doers, not talkers. Eventually, though, SSOC's failure to develop an analytical framework to guide its actions caused tension within the organization and drove a wedge between SSOC and SDS. Much of the trouble stemmed from the group's privileging of a unique and distinctive South. Southern distinctiveness was a useful frame of reference for the young whites as they confronted the uniquely southern system of racial segregation, but it was not a broadly conceived ideology. As a result, two new fault lines emerged: one within SSOC between the proponents and detractors of the "southern distinctiveness" concept, the other between SSOC and SDS, as SDS grew increasingly disenchanted both with SSOC's regionalism and with its lack of analytical focus. While the division within SSOC fueled its degeneration into rival factions, the differences with SDS led the larger, northern group to distance itself from the organization, a development that accelerated SSOC's demise.

As the end of the decade neared, many members' sense of southern difference intensified. Drawing on the work of such scholars and writers as C. Vann Woodward, Kenneth Stampp, F. Ray Marshall, Henry Caudill, James Agee, and V. O. Key, the group argued that poverty, corruption, defeat, domination, and occupation defined the southern past and were the basis of the region's separateness in the present. As Woodward wrote, it was because of its history "that the South remains the most distinctive region of the country."[43] Despite the shameful stains of slavery and Jim Crow, these activists believed that white southerners could take pride in parts of the southern past, and that this pride could serve the group's current needs. By emphasizing the positive elements of the past, they hoped to encourage progressive activism in the present.

Not surprisingly, this group of SSOC members focused particular attention on the dissenters and radicals of the South's past. In late 1967 the group's monthly publication, the *New South Student,* inaugurated "The Roots of Southern Radicalism," a series of articles by prominent scholars and activists on radical moments and individuals in southern history. Over the course of the next year it published essays by Herbert Aptheker on slave revolts, Norman Pollock on Populism, Myles Horton on the Highlander Center, H. L. Mitchell on the Southern Tenant Farmers' Union, Don West on southern abolitionists, Clarence Jordan on Koinonia, and Anne Braden on the Southern Conference for Human Welfare.[44] The group also sponsored a 1969 conference on radical southern history to educate students about this past. "Radical southern history is our history," the group proclaimed in the conference's program notes. "We are that struggle alive today—fighting the same oppression and many of the same problems."[45]

SSOC also sought to discover and emphasize positive features of the most unsettling parts of the southern past. They did not promote a whitewashed version of the region's history, but they did believe that there were praiseworthy components in even the darkest moments of southern history. Such an understanding of the past accounted for the growing prominence of Confederate symbols and rhetoric within SSOC during its final years, most notably the readoption, in 1967, of its hand-over-flag symbol, which it had jettisoned during a short-lived attempt to attract black students in 1965. Although some SSIC members opposed the symbol's reappearance, the majority supported its return. As Lynn Wells put it, the symbol was meant to convey that "You didn't have to deny your identity and your heritage and your birthright to take a good stand on civil rights."[46]

Talk of rebellion and secession began to be heard within the group. In 1968 SSOC organized the Southern Days of Secession, a series of antiwar protests in which it called for southerners to "secede" from the war. "As young Southerners," read the protest flier, "we hereby SECEDE from: THE WAR AGAINST THE VIETNAMESE; THE RACISM AND EXPLOITATION OF THE POOR; THE SELECTIVE SERVICE SYSTEM. . . . By seceding from our country's oppression . . . we reaffirm our determination to work together to create a new South, free from racism and exploitation and a world in which people are free to determine their own destinies."[47] Lynn Wells and Tom Gardner explained, "We are calling for a kind of secession not in its more widely-accepted Confederate usage, but in the tradition of . . . other Southerners and Southern movements that have resisted Yankee imperialism, whether it is directed against South Vietnam or our own South."[48]

Such rhetoric infuriated some SSOC supporters, who believed it was wrong and immoral for the group to connect itself to the Confederacy in any way. It also prompted SDS to cut ties with SSOC in 1969. Although SDS had invited SSOC to become a fraternal organization in 1964, gradually it had grown unhappy with the southern group, considering it too liberal in its views and too timid in its tactics. SSOC's renewed emphasis on the distinctiveness of the South irreparably damaged relations between the groups. SDS had by now adopted an international perspective and considered SSOC's regionalism counterproductive for the building of a radical national movement.

The struggle within SDS itself only exacerbated its criticism of SSOC's regionalism. As the Revolutionary Youth Movement and the Progressive Labor Party battled for control of SDS, SSOC became a weapon that the factions used against each other. Initially, the two groups believed that winning the support of SSOC members or, if necessary, control of the organization, would give them leverage in SDS. By 1969, however, with SSOC reluctant to get involved in the SDS dispute, the two factions moved to break relations with the group as a means of demonstrating their own radical credentials. At the SDS National Council meeting in Austin, both factions condemned SSOC for its regional orientation and agreed that it was time to sever relations. At the end of the meeting, SDS voted to cut ties to SSOC and to urge the group to disband.[49]

Many SSOC activists were both humiliated by SDS's renunciation and outraged by its presumption that it knew what the South needed. As staffer Alex Hurder reflected shortly after the meeting, "I don't suspect what happened in Austin could have been avoided. The Yankees had made up their minds and didn't consider it a Rebel's place to contradict them." Others, however, led by Lynn Wells, showed sympathy for SDS's position and accepted the northerners' criticisms as valid. Although Wells and her followers had been the leading advocates of SSOC's regionalism, "we began to realize," they explained in a letter to the membership, that it "had backfired, causing the development of regional chauvinism instead of class consciousness." The remedy, they suggested, was to disband and allow SDS to become the primary movement organization in the South.[50]

This infighting sealed SSOC's fate. Widespread respect for Wells strengthened the emerging pro-SDS faction. In the weeks after the SDS meeting in Austin, SSOC loyalists found it increasingly difficult to hold the group together. Feeling attacked from without and betrayed from within, they were reduced to sniping at Wells and trying desperately to rally support from local activists, to no avail. At a membership meeting in early June at the Mt. Beulah Conference Center in Edwards, Mississippi, a small town near Jackson, SSOC members were joined by the competing factions in SDS to decide SSOC's fate. The dominant pro-SDS group introduced a resolution that SSOC should dissolve itself, on the grounds that "a regionally separate organization of white students in the South is an anachronism left over from an earlier state in our own development as radicals. Perpetuation of SSOC would encourage a localism which hinders political development of the movement in the South as a functioning and organic part of the national movement." This argument carried the day, and at the end of the meeting SSOC voted itself out of existence.[51]

SSOC loyalists blamed SDS for the meeting's outcome. In Ed Hamlett's view, SSOC "was sacrificed on the altar . . . of some faction or other of SDS. . . . I thought we were the sacrificial lamb."[52] But it is easy to overestimate SDS's role in SSOC's breakdown. SDS could never have caused the group to collapse had it not been beset by internal divisions. The SDS challenge merely exacerbated and exploited these divisions.

Southern distinctiveness was one primary cause of tension within SSOC. Another was the group's indifference to ideological matters and its disinclination to develop a radical analysis of the South. Although the vision of a more humane, peaceful, equitable, and integrated society motivated SSOC's actions, the activists found it difficult to articulate this vision in the face of the SDS challenge. Unlike the SDS factions' rigid ideologies, SSOC's dream of a better society was closer to a worldview or way of life that drew on the lived experiences of the South. While its vision consistently animated SSOC's work, it was no match for the demanding and dogmatic ideologues of SDS.

SSOC activists never made a priority of developing a sharper analytical or ideological focus. Ed Hamlett speculated this was because SSOC activists felt inferior to and intimidated by their peers in SDS. Contrasting the two groups, he suggested that "SSOC people generally saw themselves as activists, administrators, catalysts, servicers, 'Paul Reveeres' [sic] . . . but rarely as ideologues or intellectuals. Yankee SDSers, on the other hand, were thought of as theorists, analysts, intellectuals . . . though a bit lacking in soul, roots, and at times patronizing and paternalistic." SSOC members' sense of difference grew in part out of the awareness that their lives and experiences in the South did not lend themselves to abtraction. Howard Romaine, SSOC's chairman in 1965, later observed, "We weren't part of a historical tradition of critical left thinking in the way of [Tom] Hayden and those SDS people."[53] Many had grown up in traditional communities where their progressive sentiments isolated them from their friends and families. They deemed it vastly more important to win white support for desegregation, build opposition to the war, and induce southern schools to abolish *in loco parentis* regulations than to write theoretical papers on the alliance between the intelligentsia and the proletariat. "Being confronted with such a massive enemy," Romaine reflected in 1969, "left little time for the luxury of massive fights over minute (relatively speaking) theoretical and tactical differences."[54]

What SDS ideologues condemned as anti-intellectualism could be seen as a virtue from the ground, in the white southern communities and campuses where SSOC activists worked. Most SSOC members valued practice more highly than theory, action more highly than abstract analysis. However, criticism from SDS resonated with increasing numbers of SSOC activists, who were persuaded that maybe SDS was right, maybe their approach was insufficiently analytical. But attempts to develop an analytical approach proved too divisive to sustain. Those like Lynn Wells, who agreed with the SDS critique, faced off against others who repudiated northern presumption and interference. And even those who agreed that the group needed more analytical rigor refused to develop it quickly enough to satisfy SDS. As Tom Gardner angrily counseled his peers in April 1969, "We shouldn't try to whip together the scanty knowledge we have at this point into some instant analysis just because the grand tribunal of revolution, SDS, has told us to turn in our term paper by the end of the month or we just won't make the grade."[55]

By June 1969 the majority of SSOC members simply believed that it was not worth the energy to try to reinvigorate SSOC. They already felt the organization was more a part of their past than their future. They were ready to move on to new challenges, and they had little interest in fighting to save an organization in which they were feeling less and less invested with each passing day. And so, after 8 June 1969, SSOC ceased to exist, a victim of both SDS's factional struggles and its own internal divisions.

SSOC's demise does not diminish the significance of its existence; after all, many a worthy and fruitful effort has collapsed, finally, because of internal weaknesses. What is most remarkable about SSOC is not its eventual collapse but its healthy survival for more than five years in the harsh and repressive atmosphere of the South. What should impress us is not that it eventually succumbed to external and internal obstacles but that it surmounted them for so long. By the early 1970s forces similar to those which claimed SSOC's life had destroyed most of the other radical organizations of the 1960s —including SDS, just two weeks after it helped dissolve SSOC. In its five years SSOC accomplished something that no other civil rights or New Left organization had: It brought progressive activism into the white South, to people and places previously considered immune to progressive forms of change. SSOC's achievement, in the words of former member David Nolan, was "that it went from nothing to something, that it did create something, and it did it in a place where things otherwise would not have happened."[56]

Notes

1. *Southern Patriot*, Dec. 1964.

2. Longtime white civil rights activist Virginia Durr wrote poignantly in her autobiography about the consequences of stepping "outside the magic circle" of friends and family to support racial equality. See Hollinger F. Barnard, ed., *The Autobiography of Virginia Foster Durr* (Tuscaloosa: University of Alabama Press, 1985).

3. Works that fail to discuss or even mention SSOC include Terry H. Anderson, *The Movement and the Sixties: Protest in America from Greensboro to Wounded Knee* (New York: Oxford University Press, 1995); Kenneth J. Heineman, *Campus Wars: The Peace Movement at American State Universities in the Vietnam Era* (New York: New York University Press, 1993); David Goldfield, *Black, White, and Southern: Race Relations and Southern Culture, 1940 to the Present* (Baton Rouge: Louisiana State University Press, 1990); Alexander Bloom and Wini Breines, eds., *"Takin' It to the Streets": A Sixties Reader* (New York: Oxford University Press, 1995); Taylor Branch, *Pillar of Fire: America in the King Years, 1963–1965* (New York: Simon and Schuster, 1998).

4. Kirkpatrick Sale, *SDS* (New York: Random House, 1973), 537; Clayborne Carson, *In Struggle: SNCC and the Black Awakening of the 1960s* (Cambridge: Harvard University Press, 1981), 102; Alice Echols, *Daring to Be Bad: Radical Feminism in America, 1967–1975* (Minneapolis: University of Minnesota Press, 1989), 316 n. 52; William A. Link, *William Friday: Power, Purpose, and American Higher Education* (Chapel Hill: University of North Carolina Press, 1995), 142–43. Among the few scholars who actually have studied SSOC, Sara Evans's study of the origins of the women's liberation movement is concerned only with the women of SSOC. Bryant Simon provides a more thorough treatment of SSOC in an excellent primer on the organization's history. Harlon Joye and Christina Greene, in essays published twenty-four years apart, offer brief but thoughtful and informative overviews of SSOC's rise, short life, and collapse. See Sara Evans, *Personal Politics: The Roots of Women's Liberation in the Civil Rights Movement and the New Left* (New York: Knopf, 1979); Bryant Simon, "Southern Student Organizing Committee: A New Rebel Yell in Dixie" (honors essay, University of North Carolina at Chapel Hill, 1983); Harlon Joye, "Dixie's New Left," *Trans-action* 7 (1970): 50–56, 62; Christian Greene, "'We'll Take Our Stand': Race, Class, and Gender in the Southern Student Organizing Committee, 1964–1969," in *Hidden Histories of Women in the New South,* ed. Virginia Bernhard et al. (Columbia: University of Missouri Press, 1994), 173–203.

5. Among the works that virtually ignore progressive white students in the South are local studies and synthetic histories such as Doug McAdam, *Freedom Summer* (New York: Oxford University Press, 1988); Charles W. Eagles, *Outside Agitator: Jon Daniels and the Civil Rights Movement in Alabama* (Chapel Hill: University of North Carolina Press, 1993); John Dittmer, *Local People: The Struggle for Civil Rights in Mississippi* (Urbana: University of Illinois Press, 1994); Tom Wells, *The War Within: America's Battle over Vietnam* (Berkeley: University of California Press, 1994), and several others.

6. *Southern Patriot,* Dec. 1964.

7. SCEF started as the tax-exempt arm of the Southern Conference for Human Welfare (SCHW), a liberal organization founded in the 1930s to advocate economic reform and civil rights. The SCHW disbanded in 1948, but SCEF continued on.

8. Carson, *In Struggle,* 51–53; *Southern Patriot,* June 1963; Anne Braden, untitled essay (quotation), 1964, Carl and Anne Braden Papers, 1928–1972, State Historical Society of Wisconsin, Madison, Wisconsin, folder 4, box 62; Ed Hamlett, interview by author, 6 May 1993.

9. *Southern Patriot,* April 1962 and Jan. 1963; Fred Powledge, *Free At Last? The Civil Rights Movement and the People Who Made It* (Boston: Little, Brown, 1991), 449–51; Ron K. Parker, "The Southern Student Organizing Committee," 1–3, Edwin Hamlett Papers, Jean and Alexander Heard Library, Vanderbilt University, Nashville, Tenn.; David Kotelchuck, interview by author, 31 Aug. 1994; Sue Thrasher, interview by author, 1 Sept. 1994; *Southern Patriot,* Feb. 1964; Ron K. Parker, letter on Campus Grill to interested students, 14 Oct. 1963, Gregory T. Armstrong, "Dear Colleague," 7 Nov. 1963, "Please Do Not Patronize the CAMPUS GRILL," and

"Please Continue to Withhold Patronage from the CAMPUS GRILL," fliers, Nov. 1963, and *Vanderbilt Hustler,* 1, 8, and 15 Nov. 1963, all in David and Ronda Kotelchuck Papers, Alderman Library, University of Virginia, Charlottesville, folder 2; "Notes on the First SSOC Conference," Hamlett Papers.

10. "Mailing List of Students Attending the Nashville Conference, SSOC" and "Participants at Nashville Conference," Constance Curry Papers, Alderman Library, University of Virginia, Charlottesville, Va.; Nelson Blackstock, interview by author, 8 Aug. 1995; Bruce Smith, interview by author, 2 April 1995; Anne Braden, interview by author, 25 April 1993; Thrasher, interview. Also in attendance were students from Western Kentucky University in Bowling Green, the University of Texas at Austin, Duke University, Emory University, Georgia Tech University, Clemson University, the University of Louisville, and Martin College in Pulaski, Tenn.

11. Dorothy Burlage, interview by author, 4 Sept. 1994; *Southern Patriot,* Sept. 1964.

12. Robb Burlage, interview by author, 22 April 1993; Dorothy Burlage, interview. Robb Burlage had previously written about the South's economic history; see Robb Burlage, "For Dixie with Love and Squalor," prospectus and introduction for an SDS pamphlet, 1962, in the possession of Dorothy Burlage; Robb Burlage, "The South as an Underdeveloped Country," distributed by SDS, 1962, *Students for a Democratic Society Papers, 1958–1970* (Glen Rock, N.J.: Microfilm Corp. of America, 1977), 4B: 46, reel 36.

13. "We'll Take Our Stand," Hamlett Papers.

14. Robb Burlage, interview; "We'll Take Our Stand," Hamlett Papers; Twelve Southerners, *I'll Take My Stand: The South and the Agrarian Tradition* (New York: Harper and Bros., 1930).

15. Gene Guerrero, interview by author, 26 March 1993.

16. Steve Wise, interview by author, 18 March 1993; Joye, "Dixie's New Left," 52; "Second SSOC Conference," Curry Papers; Parker, "The Southern Student Organizing Committee," 10, Hamlett Papers; "Agents of Change," public seminar, 7 April 1994, Charlottesville, Va.

17. Ed Hamlett to John A. Strickland, 1964, Hamlett Papers; *Southern Patriot,* Oct. 1964.

18. Guerrero, interview; *New Rebel* 1 (Oct. 1964); "Mississippi Project," A: xv:157, reel 38, and Bruce Maxwell, "We Must Be Allies . . ." A: xv:225, reel 40, *Student Nonviolent Coordinating Committee Papers, 1959–1972* (Sanford, N.C.: Microfilm Corp. of America, 1982); Len Holt, *The Summer That Didn't End* (New York: William Morrow, 1965), 132–41; Irwin Klibaner, *Conscience of a Troubled South: The Southern Conference Educational Fund, 1946–1966* (Brooklyn: Carlson Publishing, 1989), 217–19; *Southern Patriot,* Oct. 1964.

19. Kotelchuck, interview; *Nashville Tennessean,* 4 May 1964; *Southern Patriot,* May 1964 (quotation); *New Rebel* 1 (27 May 1964); *Student Voice* 5 (5 May and 19 May 1964).

20. *Newsletter: Southern Student Organizing Committee* 2 (May 1965); *New South Student* 3 (Feb. 1966); "We Believe Segregation Is Wrong: Join Us to Fight It" and "Mass Protest Sunday," Nelson Blackstock Papers (uncatalogued), Alderman Library, University of Virginia, Charlottesville, Va.; *Red and Black,* 25 Feb. 1964; Blackstock, interview.

21. Bill Leary, interview by author, 2 April 1995; David Nolan, interview by author, 13–14 March 1995; *Newsletter: Southern Student Organizing Committee* 2 (Jan. 1965); *New South Student* 3 (Sept. 1966); Roger Hickey, speech at the University of Virginia, 20 Nov. 1990, in the author's possession.

22. On the Free Speech Movement, see W. J. Rorabaugh, *Berkeley at War: The 1960s* (New York: Oxford University Press, 1989). On the Chapel Hill protests, see William J. Billingley, *Communists on Campus: Race, Politics, and the Public University in Sixties North Carolina* (Athens: University of Georgia Press, 1999).

23. Levin quoted in *New Left Notes* 1 (19 Aug. 1966).

24. *Southern Patriot,* June 1968; *Phoenix* 1 (March 1969), "NC-SSOC Worklist #2," ca. April 1969, and North Carolina SSOC, "Worklist Mailing #1," 17 Feb. 1969, Steve Wise Papers, uncatalogued, Alderman Library, University of Virginia, Charlottesville; Bryan Kay, "The History of Desegregation at the University of Virginia, 1950–1969" (undergraduate honors essay, University of Virginia, 1979), 141–54; Lisa Anne Severson, "A Genteel Revolution: The Birth of Black Studies at the University of Virginia" (unpublished seminar paper, University of Virginia, 1995), in the author's possession.

25. *Southern Patriot,* March 1966; *Newsletter: Southern Student Organizing Committee* 2 (Jan., Feb., and April 1965); *New South Student* 3 (March 1966); "The History of the Freedom Party," Braden Papers, folder 4, box 61; "Freedom Party Proposal for Action, 1966," *Southern Student Organizing Committee Papers,* Archives and Library, Martin Luther King Jr. Center for Nonviolent Social Change, Atlanta, folder 37, box 2; *Florida Alligator,* 22, 26 and 29 Jan. and 3, 5, 8 Feb. 1965, 24 Jan. and 4 Feb. 1966; Marshall B. Jones, "Berkeley of the South: A History of the Student Movement at the University of Florida, 1963–1968" (unpublished manuscript), 42–44.

26. *Florida Alligator,* 16 Feb. 1966; *New South Student* 3 (March 1966); Alan Levin, interview by author, 26 Dec. 1994; Jones, "Berkeley of the South," 61–70; *Daily Beacon,* 18 April, 19, 26, 28 Sept., 15 Oct. 1968, 29 Jan., 4, 5, 7, 11, 12, 13, 21, 28 Feb., 7 March, 19 April, and 20 June 1969; "Worklist Mailing," 5 April 1968, and *Phoenix* 1 (Jan. 1969), Wise Papers; Jack Sullivan, interview by author, 31 Aug. 1994; John Duggan, interview by author, 16 March 1995; Alfred Sandlin Reid, *Furman University: Toward a New Identity, 1925–1975* (Durham: Duke University Press, 1976), 229–31, 247–48.

27. Press Release, 14 April 1968, and "A Report on the Demonstrations at the Administration Building," 15 April 1968, SDS Papers, 3:28, reel 22; "Worklist Mailing," 20 April 1968; *Phoenix* 1 (Aug. 1968), Wise Papers; *Southern Patriot,* June 1968; Thomas G. Dyer, *The University of Georgia: A Bicentennial History, 1785–1985* (Athens: University of Georgia Press, 1985), 347–49.

28. *Daily Tar Heel,* 1, 4, 18 Oct. 1968, 19 Nov. 1968, 12 Dec. 1968; David Littlejohn to all SSOC chapters [in South Carolina], 6 Feb. 1969, Papers of the Boyte Family, Special Collections Library, Duke University, Durham, N.C., box 17.

29. *New South Student* 2 (Oct., Nov., and Dec. 1965) and 3 (Jan. 1966); *Emory Wheel,* 1, 15, 29 Oct., 4 Nov. 1965; Jody Palmour, interview by author, 2 and 18 April 1995; Kotelchuck, interview.

30. Hamlett, interview; *New South Student* 3 (Feb. 1966).

31. *New South Student* 3 (April 1966); *Southern Patriot,* April and June 1966; *New Left Notes* 1 (3 June 1966); "If You Would," Worklist Mailing 1 (April 1966), Southern Student Organizing Committee and Thomas N. Gardner Papers, Alderman Library, University of Virginia, Charlottesville, Va.

32. Between February 1967 and December 1968 the Peace Tour traveled to campuses in Florida, Arkansas, Virginia, North Carolina, Tennessee, and South Carolina. The Florida Peace Tour was the most significant because it was the first and because the three tourers—Tom Gardner, David Nolan, and Nancy Hodes—were arrested when they tried to speak on the North Campus of Miami-Dade Junior College (Tom Gardner, Nancy Hodes, and David Nolan, "Florida Peace Tour, February 23–April 7, 1967," ca. May 1967, in author's possession; Tom Gardner, interview by author, 2 Sept. 1994; Nancy Hodes, interview by author, 3 Sept. 1994; Nolan, interview).

33. In late 1967, for example, SSOC organized demonstrations at induction centers in Gaines-ville and Atlanta. While protesters rallied outside, Alan Levin in Gainesville and Gene Guerrero in Atlanta refused induction inside. "Worklist Mailing," Sept. 1967, SSOC and Gardner Papers; "Worklist Mailing: Confront the Warmakers Oct. 21," 1 (11 Oct. 1967), in the possession of Dorothy Burlage; *Southern Patriot,* March 1968; "Press Release: 75 Picketers Support Atlanta Draft Refuser Gene Guerrero," 4 Dec. 1967, in the author's possession; Gene Guerrero, "Why I Must Refuse Induction," 4 Dec. 1967, SSOC and Gardner Papers, folder 8, box 1; *Phoenix* 1 (Dec. 1968); Levin, interview; Tom Gardner, interview by author, 5 May 1993; Guerrero, inter-view; Nan Grogan Orrock, interview by author, 14 Nov. 1994.

34. Bob McMahon, "Questionnaire," SSOC Thirtieth Reunion and Conference, April 1994, Charlottesville, Va., in the author's possession; Robert McMahon, interview by author, 30 Oct. 1994; Smith, interview; *Cavalier Daily,* 6 Dec. 1967; *Daily Progress,* 6 Dec. 1967.

35. "Executive Committee Minutes," 25–26 Feb. 1967, Wise Papers; Brian Heggen, "Appli-cation for Employment," 24 Feb. 1967, Bruce Smith Papers, Alderman Library, University of Vir-ginia, Charlottesville, Va.; *Nashville Tennessean,* 15, 16, 17 March 1967; "Press Release: Stop the Genocide in Vietnam," and Ronda Stilley to Nan and Gene Guerrero, 30 March 1967, both in Wise Papers; Shirley Newton Bliley, "The Sixties—A Personal Perspective," in the author's pos-session; interview with Earl Wilson, 11 Nov. 1994; Nolan, interview.

36. *Southern Patriot,* April 1966; SSOC, *Prospectus, 1967–68,* 2–3, in author's possession; Tom Gardner, "The Southern Student Organizing Committee, 1964–1970," 21–22; Tom Gard-ner to author, 26 April 1996, in the author's possession.

37. Hamlett quoted in *New South Student* 3 (May 1966); "Southern Student Organizing Committee: 1966–67 Proposal," "Southern Student Organizing Committee, November 1966," Field Foundation Archives, 1940–1990, Center for American History, University of Texas at Austin, file, box 2S427.

38. "Southern Student Organizing Committee: 1966–1967 Proposal," "Southern Student Or-ganizing Committee, November 1966," Field Foundation Archives, file, box 2S427; *New South Student* 3 (Feb. 1966); *Southern Patriot,* Aug. 1966; Ronda Stilley to Bruce Smith, ca. April 1966, Smith Papers.

39. *New South Student,* April 1967; Ann Schunior, "Student Support for Textile Workers' Rights," *Cone Workers' Union Voice* 2 (19 April 1967), "Press Release" (on Whiteville to Wilm-ington march), 27 July 1967, and *Our Union Speaks* (newsletter of the National Spinning Com-pany Union Members, TWUA, AFL-CIO), 22 June, 6 July, 3 Aug., and 10 Aug. 1967, all in Wise Papers; "Students and Labor," SSOC and Gardner Papers, 2, folder 9, box 4; *Daily Tar Heel,* 14 April 1967; *Southern Patriot,* June 1967; *Phoenix,* Nov. 1968; Guerrero, interview; Lynn Wells Rumley, interview by author, 16 Nov. 1994; Orrock, interview; Frank Goldsmith, interview by author, 17 March 1995; *National Observer,* 15 May 1967.

40. *Report on Students and Labor* 2 (April 1967), and *Our Union Speaks* (20 July 1967), both in Wise Papers.

41. *Southern Patriot,* May 1968; *Our Union Speaks* (7 and 15 Sept. 1967), Wise Papers; Guer-rero, interview; Orrock, interview.

42. Southern Students Organizing Committee, Prospectus, 1967–68, 5.

43. C. Vann Woodward, "The Search for Southern Identity," in C. Vann Woodward, *The Bur-den of Southern History* (Baton Rouge: Louisiana State University Press, 1960), 16.

44. David Nolan, who as editor of the *New South Student* was the SSOC official who had asked these individuals to contribute to the series, also had approached historians Eugene Gen-

ovese and C. Vann Woodward about writing for the magazine. Neither was able to do so. Woodward's rejection must have been a deep disappointment to Nolan, for in his letter he had written, "I realize we are not the *Journal of Southern History* or *Harper's,* but we do try hard, and for many of us your book on Tom Watson has become something of a bible." Indeed, no one shaped SSOC activists' view of the past more than Woodward, and his books, particularly *Tom Watson and Origins of the New South,* were frequent topics of conversation in the group. As a way of acknowledging his contribution, SSOC dedicated the March 1967 issue of the *New South Student,* which focused on southern identity and southern nationalism, to Woodward and Stokely Carmichael, since "each, in his own way, was an inspiration to us in the decision to undertake this edition." See David Nolan to C. Vann Woodward, 22 May 1967, and C. Vann Woodward to David Nolan, 31 May 1967, David Nolan Papers, State Historical Society of Wisconsin, Madison, folder 2, box 6; *New South Student* 4 (March 1967).

45. "Conference on Radical Southern History" (quotation), April 1969, Hamlett Papers.

46. Executive Committee Meeting Minutes, 12 April 1967, in "Get the Word Out, Membership Mailing Number Seven," 18 April 1967, SSOC and Gardner Papers, folder 2, box 1; "The New SSOC, Membership Mailing Number Eight," 17 May 1967, Papers of the U.S. National Student Association, 1955–1969, Archives and Library, Martin Luther King Jr. Center for Nonviolent Social Change, Atlanta, folder 28, box 38; Rumley, interview.

47. "We Secede," informational mailing, April 1968, in the author's possession.

48. Lyn Wells and Tom Gardner, "SSOC: The New Rebels Secede," 19 March 1968, SSOC and Gardner Papers, folder 1, box 4 (reprinted in *New Left Notes* 3 [25 March 1968]).

49. "Build SDS in The South," Blackstock Papers; *New Left Notes* 4 (4 April 1969); Ed Clark, "The South Must Be Won," *PL: Progressive Labor* 7 (Nov. 1969), 26–27; Howard Romaine, "Movement South," *Great Speckled Bird,* 28 April 1969; Rumley, interview; Sale, *SDS,* 538. Sale's work remains the most authoritative account of the factional divide within SDS.

50. Alex Hurder to Tom Gardner, 12 April 1969, SSOC and Gardner Papers, folder 4, box 3; David Simpson, Lynn Wells, and George Vlasits, "Dear Sisters and Brothers," letter to SSOC membership, 26 May 1969, Boyte Papers, box 17.

51. "Resolution: To Dissolve SSOC," 7 June 1969, Wise Papers. Among contemporary accounts of the final SSOC meeting are Ed Hamlett, "Southern Student Organizing Committee 1964–1969: R.I.P.," Hamlett Papers, box 9; Bob Goodman, "SSOC Dissolves," *Great Speckled Bird,* 16 June 1969; and Mike Eisenscher, "Memorandum on the SSOC Conference: June 5–8, 1969 in Edwards, Miss.," Nolan Papers, folder 19, box 5.

52. Hamlett, interview.

53. Hamlett, "Southern Student Organizing Committee 1964–1969," Hamlett Papers, box 9; interview with Howard Romaine, 17–18 March 1993.

54. Howard Romaine to M. Hayes Mizell, 6 May 1969, M. Hayes Mizell Papers, South Caroliniana Library, University of South Carolina, Columbia.

55. Tom Gardner, "A Political Criticism of the 'Political' Criticism," ca. April 1969, SSOC and Gardner Papers, folder 7, box 3.

56. Nolan, interview.

CHAPTER 4

The Black Freedom Struggle and White Resistance: A Case Study of the Civil Rights Movement in Cambridge, Maryland

Peter B. Levy

The Cambridge experience is not merely of local interest. On the contrary, the factors which created the crisis . . . are present in practically every place in the United States where there is a sizeable Negro population. It is only the convergence of a number of factors which have made the crisis come earlier and more intensely than in other areas.

—Cambridge Nonviolent Action Committee (1963)

Fresh from his triumphant trip to Europe, where he delivered his *Ich bin ein Berliner* speech, visited his ancestral homeland, and enjoyed an audience with the new pope, President John F. Kennedy held his first press conference in months on 13 July 1963. Addressing an audience of reporters and more than four hundred reverent students, JFK confidently answered a broad array of questions. Regarding relations with the Soviet Union and the domestic economy, Kennedy observed that both were in excellent shape. After responding to an inquiry about the Peace Corps, the president turned to the subject of civil rights. During the spring and early summer of 1963, civil rights protests had reached an all-time peak. Kennedy had responded with a more aggressive, pro–civil rights stance than he had followed during the first two years of his presidency. On the day before his departure to Europe, he met with the leaders of the civil rights movement and reaffirmed his commitment to civil rights reforms.[1]

"Do you think that the demonstrations which are taking place are a handicap to you?" one reporter asked. "No," Kennedy replied emphatically, adding, in reference to the upcoming March on Washington, "We want citizens to come to Washington if they feel that they are not having their rights expressed." Then the president contrasted his endorsement of the March on Washington with civil rights protests occurring in Cambridge, Maryland, a port town of about thirteen thousand on Maryland's eastern shore. The demonstrators in Cambridge, he asserted, had "almost lost sight" of what they were protesting for. "I think they go beyond . . . protest. They get into a very bad situation where you get violence, and I think the cause of advancing equal opportunity only loses."[2]

Why Kennedy singled out Cambridge, while at the same time reversing his earlier position on the March on Washington, remains a mystery. Nothing in his private records provides a clue. Nor have any historians explored the subject. It is true that Cambridge, as we shall see, had been the site of some of the most heated civil rights protests in the nation. As of 17 July it was occupied by the National Guard, who had been called in to restore law and order several weeks earlier. The 14 July Sunday edition of the *New York Times* contained a prominent story on the turmoil there, but it is not known whether the president read this story. Five days later, ironically, Robert Kennedy, the president's brother and the U.S. attorney general, posed for photographers with Gloria Richardson, the militant leader of the Cambridge Nonviolent Action Committee (CNAC) and state and local officials and announced that the federal government had negotiated an "agreement." Arguably, this accord met nearly all of the demonstrators' demands and represented the Kennedy administration's most direct intervention in the racial affairs of a single community.[3]

About a year later Alabama governor George C. Wallace, the most famous symbol of white resistance, traveled to Cambridge to deliver a well-publicized address to upwards of two thousand supporters at the arena of the all-white Volunteer Rescue and Fire Company. Wallace hoped that his stop in Cambridge would help him win the upcoming Democratic presidential primary in Maryland. He had already performed surprisingly well outside the old Confederacy. Although he did not repeat his blatantly racist signature slogan—"Segregation then, segregation now, segregation forever"—Wallace warned that the growing power of the federal government represented a threat to long-cherished American liberties. Pending civil rights legislation, he declared, threatened the right of association and trampled on the private property protections guaranteed by the Constitution. If Americans did not draw the line soon, they would lose all of their liberties.[4]

While Wallace spoke inside the arena, civil rights activists from up and down the eastern seaboard assembled outside to assert their opposition to the politics of white backlash. Following the address the protesters, led by Gloria Richardson, confronted a large force of national guardsmen on Race Street, the road that divided the all-black Second Ward from the rest of the city. For nearly a year the National Guard had enjoyed favorable relations with Richardson and CNAC, but on this occasion the Guard, under the command of J. Millard Tawes, the nephew of Maryland governor, ordered the demonstrators to disperse. Student Nonviolent Coordinating Committee (SNCC) stalwart Cleveland Sellers recalled, "It was a crucial moment, the kind that can make or break a movement. We all understood that Gloria was the only one who could decide its outcome. If she had told us to return to the [Elks] lodge, we would have done so. . . . 'I'm going through,' she said." No sooner had Richardson stepped forth than the Guard arrested her and whisked her away. Other demonstrators, including Stokely Carmichael, quickly rushed to take her place and went limp in the streets. Frustrated, Tawes ordered the Guard to spray the protestors with tear gas. Chaos followed. Those who did not flee were arrested. Later that night a two-year-old black boy who lived nearby died. Although a county coroner listed congenital heart failure as the cause of death, some activists insisted that blacks were being gassed to death.[5]

Among the civil rights activists who participated in this protest was H. Rap Brown, a Louisiana native and a member of the National Action Group (NAG), a Howard University branch of SNCC. In 1967, shortly after being elected SNCC's new chairman, he accepted an invitation to return to Cambridge to help rejuvenate the local movement, moribund since Richardson's departure. For about an hour Brown lambasted white "honkies" and exhorted the virtues and achievements of African Americans. He condemned the police, white landlords, and the federal government. "Like I said in the beginning, if this town don't come around, this town should be burned down."[6]

Later that night a fire erupted at the Pine Street Elementary School, across the street from where Brown had spoken. Fearing for its safety, the Volunteer Fire Company refused to enter the Second Ward to douse the blaze, and two square blocks of the Second Ward burned to the ground. At dawn, the embers of the fire still smoldering, Maryland governor Spiro T. Agnew rushed to Cambridge from his vacation home in nearby Ocean City. Visibly upset by the destruction, Agnew immediately called for Brown's arrest for inciting a riot and condemned black radicals nationwide for their incendiary language.

Heretofore a moderate "Rockefeller Republican" who had been elected governor in 1966 thanks in large part to overwhelming support from black voters, Agnew quickly became a symbol of the emerging new Right. Richard Nixon, for one, took note of Agnew's ability to voice the frustration of large segments of the white population and tapped him as his vice presidential running mate in 1968. Not even Nixon's rise to prominence in the late 1940s and early 1950s could match the rise of Agnew, who went from being an obscure manager of Baltimore County to vice president of the United States in less than four years.[7]

Although Cambridge was associated with all of these developments, it has received scant attention from historians. A dozen leading works on the civil rights movement, including Taylor Branch's exhaustive two-volume chronicle of the "civil rights years," devote no more than a paragraph to Cambridge. One encyclopedia even mistakes Cambridge, Maryland, for Cambridge, Massachusetts. *Portrait of a Decade,* written in 1964 by *New York Times* reporter Anthony Lewis, proves the exception to the rule, but Lewis focused on Cambridge largely to lambaste Gloria Richardson for betraying the principles of the movement.[8] Other works mention Cambridge only in passing, in broader discussions of black power and the urban riots of the late 1960s.[9] Perhaps this is so because Martin Luther King Jr. never visited the town, or because standard narratives treat SNCC as a southern-based group before it abandoned its commitment to nonviolence and integration after 1965. In fact, a more detailed consideration of the movement in Cambridge raises several questions about the accepted view.

Unlike historians, contemporaries paid a great deal of attention to Cambridge. Some even saw it as a microcosm of the nation that offered special insight into the nature and trajectory of the civil rights movement. Analyses by journalists Michael Durham and L. Brent Bozell that appeared in *Life* and *National Review,* respectively, epitomized the conflicting liberal and conservative interpretations of the social unrest of the 1960s that still persist today. Durham blamed Cambridge's white leaders for the town's troubles. Unlike black and white leaders in nearby Salisbury, who accepted the inevitability of racial integration, the white establishment in Cambridge, Durham argued, "reacted to the Negro demands . . . with bitter intransigence." The result was racial peace in Salisbury and "racial war" in Cambridge.[10]

In contrast, anticipating the conservative critique of the Kerner Report and right-wing views of the 1960s in general, Bozell held black leaders and white liberals responsible for Cambridge's unrest. Although he rejected the conventional southern refrain that there was no racial problem until outside agitators stirred up trouble, he blamed radical blacks and their white allies for stepping outside traditional political channels to express their views. Bozell even suggested that if black activists had not resorted to direct action they would have achieved more of their goals and avoided white backlash. "It was not a matter of good guys and bad guys. Cambridge was singled out for violence by Negro leadership; Salisbury was not." Even if their grievances were legitimate, Bozell argued, the source of the trouble was that "Negroes lost patience" and thereby "shattered" the process for gaining change, poisoning a "reasonably congenial atmosphere."[11]

While Durham and Bozell differed on the origins of racial strife in Cambridge, they agreed on the outcome. Even before George Wallace used Cambridge as a launching pad for his forays into the North, and prior to Spiro Agnew's metamorphosis from a moderate Republican into a darling of the far Right, Durham and Bozell argued that white backlash would be the long-lasting result of the strife.[12] Whatever their conclusions, Cambridge presented an interesting case study to journalists like Durham and Bozell. Reared on stories about the Montgomery bus boycott and the confrontations in Birmingham, Selma, and the Mississippi Delta, students today tend to think of the civil rights movement as a phenomenon of the Deep South. Before the urban riots of the latter half of the 1960s, many northerners likewise believed that the "race problem" existed only in the South. By dividing the United States neatly into North and South, historians of the civil rights movement have contributed to this misunderstanding of the recent past. They have missed some of the ways that the particular geography of the border states produced local movements that were neither northern nor southern but both, movements that mesh with neither the traditional chronology nor the geography of the civil rights years. By following a chronologically linear description of the movement, existing studies assume that the fight for economic and cultural equality, or the turn to black power, took place after the battle against Jim Crow. As this study of Cambridge will show, that was not always the case.

The movement in Cambridge also merits our attention because it was led by a remarkable middle-aged woman, Gloria Richardson, who mobilized working- and lower-class blacks into one of the most vibrant struggles for racial equality in the nation. Moreover, unlike many of the communities we tend to associate with the civil rights movement, Cambridge had a progressive racial reputation before the 1960s. It did not join the wave of resistance to the *Brown* decision, and it pointed with pride to the fact that blacks enjoyed the franchise and had been represented on the town council for most of the twentieth century. In spite of this record, or perhaps because of it, by 1963 the movement in Cambridge was so militant that it attracted the attention of the national media and the Kennedy administration, as we have seen. And finally, like all case studies, this one allows us, as John D'Emelio has written, to "challenge, or confirm, broad generalizations and master narratives of the past by testing them 'on the ground.'"[13]

Like the movement in general, the emergence and shape of the civil rights movement in Cambridge was no accident. Two broad structural changes that followed World War II, namely, the collapse of the town's most important industry, the Phillips Packing Company, and a rapid shift in the spatial relationship of the city to the surrounding region, created the preconditions out of which the movement arose. At the height of its power during the late 1930s and 1940s, the Phillips Packing Company employed between one thousand and four thousand men and women, about half of them in its eleven Cambridge plants. During World War II, Phillips had been the leading producer of K-rations in the country and marketed a large line of food products. The company's political influence paralleled its economic fortunes. Two of its cofounders, Augustus and Levi Phillips, were power brokers in Maryland's Republican Party. Their business partner, William Winterbottom, enjoyed nearly as much influence within the Democratic Party, especially at the local level, where the Winterbottom faction of the party won nearly every important municipal election for approximately half a century.[14]

For a variety of reasons, between 1947 and 1957 the company nearly went bankrupt, its earnings plummeting from $3.64 per share in 1947 to $.02 per share in 1956. In 1957 Consolidated Foods (today Sara Lee), a diversified food-processing corporation headquartered in Chicago, acquired control of Phillips. Coastal Foods, one of Consolidated's subsidiaries, kept some of the plants open after the merger, but by 1962 it employed only two hundred to four hundred men and women in Cambridge, about one-tenth the number who had worked for Phillips at the end of World War II. As a result, unemployment in Cambridge skyrocketed to between 7 and 11 percent for whites and 20 and 30 percent for blacks.[15]

Declining profits and a smaller work force heightened black and white frustrations and ushered in a period of political instability, a condition J. Mills Thornton, for one, describes as critical to the emergence of the civil rights movement. In 1950 Cambridge native Frederick Malkus, a graduate of the University of Maryland law school and World War II veteran, mounted a successful challenge to William Winterbottom's control of the Democratic Party, winning a seat in the state legislature that he held until his retirement in 1995. In his own words, he beat the Phillips machine by building a coalition of rural farmers, muskrat hunters, and watermen.[16]

A similar development took place in the black community. From 1906 until his retirement in 1946, with one two-year hiatus, H. Maynadier St. Clair represented the all-black Second Ward on Cambridge's town council. When he retired, the Second Ward elected Charles Cornish to replace him. Throughout his career, St. Clair had taken a moderate or accommodationist position, supporting the Phillips Packing Company in exchange for economic and political favors to the Second Ward. As the company began to decline, however, more militant blacks began to advocate a more oppositional stance. Although they did not unseat Cornish, who like St. Clair was an accommodationist, their demands presented a challenge to the status quo. Ironically, the person who ultimately became most closely associated with the rising wave of black militancy was St. Clair's granddaughter, Gloria Richardson.[17]

In short, the collapse of Phillips Packing created a political vacuum into which increasingly assertive members of both races rushed. Historically, the company had had the economic and political clout to counter challenges, whether from blacks or whites, to the racial or economic status quo. In 1937 Phillips had easily crushed a strike that temporarily united more than fifteen hundred black and white workers. But with the company only a shell of its former self, the traditional white elite lacked the power to preserve the community's equilibrium.[18]

During the same period Cambridge experienced a dramatic shift in its cultural geography, specifically in its relationship to the surrounding region. Up until then the Eastern Shore had been "one of the most geographically isolated regions" in the nation, according to John Wennersten. "It was difficult to get to and difficult to leave. Over the years it grew slowly and matured as a separate society."[19] Cambridge was hardly the only, or the most, provincial town in the region, but it was more isolated from modernizing influences than most, accessible to the outside world only by boat or by a long circuitous overland drive by car. The completion of the Chesapeake Bay Bridge in 1952 changed all that. The bridge put Cambridge within easy reach of students from many colleges and universities, reporters and photographers from the most influential newspapers and magazines in the nation, and government officials, who came to see the Eastern Shore as their backyard.

Cambridge natives tended to have very different outlooks and values from the inhabitants of eastern seaboard cities and suburbs. Many eastern shoremen saw Cambridge as a hub of activity and modernity. In the 1920s Cambridge had been "the undisputed queen city of the entire Eastern Shore." It had a fairground, a professional class D baseball park, railroad and bus depots, two newspapers, a hospital, a poolroom, three hotels, two movie houses, a bowling alley, two brothels, and an assortment of eating places. The town had produced two recent governors, Phillips Lee Goldsborough and Emerson Harrington, and was the favored retreat of the DuPonts and other distinguished Americans, all of this a matter of local pride. Outsiders, by contrast, perhaps influenced by H. L. Mencken's withering description of the Eastern Shore as a "bastion of racist hayseeds," saw Cambridge as a provincial backwater. Cambridge's population, understandably, resented outsiders' calls for changes in race relations. In the face of outside intervention during the early 1960s, they assumed a fortress mentality, insisting that Cambridge was progressive enough for their tastes and rejecting the presumptuous meddling of publicity-seeking zealots.[20]

No one could have predicted that Cambridge would soon become one of the most hotly contested arenas for civil rights in the country. As the decade began, Chet Huntley and David Brinkley, two of the nation's most prominent television newscasters, praised Cambridge as a "model city" in terms of interracial relations. An inspiring visit by Democratic presidential nominee John F. Kennedy, attended by both blacks and whites, seemed to suggest that Cambridge was going to weather the civil rights storm of the early 1960s without great difficulty, as did the victory, by a two-to-one margin, of reform candidate Calvin Mowbray for mayor. Even a timely study of local politics by George Kent, a black graduate student at the University of Maryland and Cambridge high school teacher, suggested that the black community remained complacent about the civil rights movement budding all around them.[21]

Unlike Birmingham and Selma, which civil rights forces targeted because of their history of racial oppression, Cambridge's association with racial turmoil happened almost by accident. In the summer and fall of 1961, civil rights activists organized sit-ins along Route 40, which ran north of Baltimore toward Philadelphia, after several restaurants along this highway refused to serve visiting African diplomats. An embarrassed Kennedy administration pressured the restaurants to serve the diplomats, and Governor Tawes pledged to enact statewide civil rights legislation. Rather than disband, however, the activists trained their sights on similar facilities along Route 50, which ran from Annapolis across the Chesapeake Bay Bridge and down Maryland's Eastern Shore. The sit-in protesters first "tested" Crisfield, the hometown of Governor Tawes, and Salisbury, the site of an infamous 1931 lynching. When these tests took place without significant resistance, the activists turned their attention to Cambridge.[22]

Before staging freedom rides in Cambridge, two SNCC field representatives, Reginald Robinson, a black man, and William Hansen, a white, met with representatives of the town council and local Equal Opportunity Commission (EOC). The town councilmen, pointing to Cambridge's progressive record on race, tried to get Hansen and Robinson to call off the planned rides. Edythe Jolley, the black principal of the all-black Mace Lane High School, also pleaded that the two men not "disturb the situation." Undeterred, on Saturday, 13 January 1962, approximately one hundred civil rights activists, led by Robinson and Hansen, sat in at segregated eateries and bars in Cambridge. The local white elite responded with accusations against the "outside agitators" for stirring up trouble. The *Cambridge Daily Banner* described Hansen as a "professional integrationist" who was ignorant of the town's progressive racial record and warned that the protests "jeopardized . . . four decades of biracial progress."[23]

Typically, these alarms were not repeated in the black part of town, where the freedom riders received a warm reception. On the Monday following the first rides, scores of black students from the Mace Lane High School walked out of classes to attend the riders' court hearings. In turn, high school officials suspended three of the students from school, but the suspensions did not deter fourteen more black students from joining Hansen and Robinson in sit-ins at Dizzyland and Collins Drug Store, two white student hangouts.[24]

Hansen and Robinson organized two more freedom rides during the month of January, each a little larger than the previous one. They drew heavily on a network of student activists from Baltimore allied with the Baltimore-based Civic Interest Group (CIG) and on students from other eastern seaboard communities. Cambridge was an attractive location for these students both because of its relatively proximity and because they expected less danger of arrest or police brutality there than in the Deep South.[25] But violence erupted at the Choptank Inn on 20 January, when a white mob kicked Hansen, whom Howard Zinn described as a "new abolitionist," into unconsciousness. After Hansen regained his wits, the mob shoved him through a glass door, knocking him unconscious a second time. Then police arrested Hansen for trespassing. Gifford Pinchot, grandson of the famous progressive conservationist, was also assaulted by the white mob and arrested by police.[26]

Since Cambridge lacked a large professional class or a cluster of students upon which to build, it had to rely on other resources, most importantly close family and communal ties. Compared to many northern cities, Cambridge's black population had remained fairly stable; families were interrelated by marriage and across generations. Confined to the all-black Second Ward and to all-black schools and churches, they knew each other intimately. Close personal connections made the organization of protests easier than it was in big cities. Cambridge's black elders helped tutor younger activists on the history of black struggles. Moreover, the movement in Cambridge built on the resources and leadership of Cambridge's most prominent black family, the St. Clairs, most importantly Gloria Richardson, who, because she was relatively free from economic pressures, was able to commit herself full-time to the local movement.[27]

Richardson grew up in Cambridge and graduated from Howard University, where she studied with E. Franklin Frazier, Rayford Logan, and Highland Lewis, three giants of black academia, and received a degree in sociology in 1942. These relatively radical professors helped shape her views of race relations, and she came to reject the privileges of the black bourgeoisie. Following graduation she married Harry Richardson and bore two children. When her marriage fell apart, she moved with her mother, Mabel St. Clair Booth, to Canada, where she felt "perfectly normal and human" for the first time.[28] Upon returning to Cambridge she expected to find a job as a social worker. Instead she ran smack into the color line, which kept blacks out of professional positions. She took on menial work, at which, due to her upbringing, she was not particularly adept.[29] While Richardson rejected the accommodationist tactics of her grandfather, in other ways she followed in his footsteps—notably, in his belief in black noblesse oblige.[30]

From the beginning Gloria Richardson built CNAC into one of the few civil rights organizations in the nation with strong support from poor and working-class blacks. She accomplished this, in large part, by shunning the town's conciliatory or "Uncle Tomish" black leaders, among them councilman Charles Cornish, school principal Edythe Jolley, and Helen Waters, the black representative on the countywide school board who owned a whites-only beauty parlor. Richardson made sure that lower- and working-class blacks, including a welfare recipient and a factory worker, served on CNAC's executive committee. Her critics claimed that recruiting uneducated men and women allowed her to dominate the committee, but Sandra Miller has convincingly shown that her real motive was the belief that lower-class blacks had the street smarts and intelligence to steer the group in a constructive direction. Richardson also won support from working-class blacks through the sheer strength of her personality, a trait acknowledged by both supporters and detractors.[31]

If the white elite of Cambridge had desegregated its public accommodations in 1962, as leaders in nearby Salisbury did, and if the school board had increased the pace of school desegregation, Cambridge's history might have turned out differently. But as late as January 1963 Mayor Mowbray refused to ask the town council to pass any sort of public accommodation law, even though several Eastern Shore communities had done so, and the school board would not budge on its desegregation plan, contending that the schools were open and blacks need only apply. As school superintendent James G. Busick put it, if the freedom riders would only leave, or if Richardson would just act reasonably, Cambridge would work out its racial problems peacefully.[32]

Cambridge's political history helps explain why local white elites acted as they did. The existence of the black franchise and black representation on the town council and school board made them sanguine about race relations in their community; they did not consider themselves racists or bigots. Black officials, for their part, were deeply schooled in the politics of accommodationism and assured whites that whatever problems existed could be resolved without outside interference. Both black and white leaders were unprepared for Richardson's and CNAC's aggressive approach to racial politics and civil rights. They also miscalculated the degree to which the collapse of the Phillips Packing Company left them vulnerable to challenges from both blacks and whites.

Cambridge's severe economic problems presented another obstacle to business as usual for Cambridge's elite. The black unemployment rate stood above 20 percent, over twice as high as the white rate and four times the national average. Although most of the town's factories were officially integrated, blacks were usually locked into menial jobs within them. The housing situation was even worse. Fewer than 20 percent of blacks in Cambridge had sound plumbing, compared to more than 80 percent of whites. The median value of homes owned by blacks was half that of white homes, and only slightly more than one-quarter of the town's black population owned a home at all, compared to more than 55 percent of white families.[33]

In the early spring of 1963, one day before Martin Luther King Jr. commenced Project C in Birmingham, Alabama, CNAC launched a broad-based campaign for racial equality in Cambridge. Even more than King's Southern Christian Leadership Conference (SCLC), CNAC supplemented its mass meetings and demonstrations by picketing and "testing" segregated establishments. When they were arrested, activists often chose jail over bail. "It was the goal of CNAC," Richardson explained, "to show, through the medium of direct action, the desperate need to eliminate discrimination." Local high school students, often organized by Gloria Richardson's daughter, Donna, and students from Swarthmore, Morgan State, and other regional colleges and universities, constituted the bulk of the demonstrators. Richardson's home and her family drugstore served as CNAC's headquarters, buzzing with activity all hours of the day.[34]

This stage of the demonstrations climaxed with the so-called "penny trials." On 7 May 1963 fifty-four civil rights activists, including Gloria Richardson, were tried together by Dorchester County circuit court judge W. Laird Henry Jr., one of the most distinguished whites in the community.[35] After the defendants agreed to waive their right to individual jury trials, Henry found forty-seven of them guilty on one count and the other seven guilt on two counts of disorderly conduct. Henry then dismissed all of the remaining charges and fined each defendant one penny.[36]

If Henry wished to restore peace and order through his actions, his hopes were soon dashed. CNAC resumed demonstrations and many lower- and working-class whites held their own counterdemonstrations. Fearing the outbreak of riots, Henry intervened again, this time by forming the Committee for Interracial Understanding (CIU). Consisting of several of Cambridge's most prominent white businessmen, the CIU called for a series of meetings to arrive at some sort of compromise. Partly out of respect for Henry, CNAC agreed to cooperate.

A CIU meeting with local restaurant owners, however, was less encouraging.[37] Years of class antagonism contributed to restaurateurs' response to the CIU. Most of the restaurant owners either came from or catered to working-class whites. Many of them had grown up in the same neighborhoods, and they saw Henry as one of the remaining symbols of the Phillips Company's power and an opportunity to get even with the company. Some of the restaurant owners accused the CIU of unfairly painting them as racists when the truth was that if they allowed blacks in, they would lose their white customers and go out of business.[38]

Tensions peaked after authorities arrested two young black activists, Dwight Cromwell and Dinez White, on charges of disorderly conduct. Judge E. McMaster Duer, whose family name was synonymous with racial repression on the Eastern Shore (he had presided over a 1931 trial that had resulted in a lynching), sentenced the two to an indefinite term in the state institution for juvenile delinquents. Before the sentencing, Dinez White wrote a "Letter from a Jail Cell," which, like Martin Luther King's famous "Letter from a Birmingham Jail," urged her fellow activists to persevere. "They think they have you scared because they are sending us away. . . . Please fight for freedom and let us know that we are not going away in vain."[39] On the day of the sentencing, the Maryland Commission on Interracial Problems and Relations concluded that there was virtually no middle ground upon which to build. At almost the same moment Judge Henry disbanded the CIU because, in his words, no progress was in sight.[40]

From 11 through 14 June, the same time span during which Alabama governor George Wallace confronted John F. Kennedy over the desegregation of the University of Alabama and Medgar Evers was assassinated in Mississippi, all hell broke loose in Cambridge. Guns were fired, white-owned buildings in the Second Ward were torched, and several whites were shot. One of those shot was Jerome Shenton, the thirty-seven-year-old owner of one of the businesses set on fire.[41] On 14 June, after attempting unsuccessfully to negotiate a last-minute compromise, Governor Tawes called out the National Guard and declared martial law in Cambridge. Five hundred soldiers rushed into town; up to fifteen hundred more readied themselves for action. Armed with bayonets and equipped with rifles and tear gas, they encamped themselves on Cambridge's main artery, Race Street, the dividing line between the white and black sections of town. (The aptness of the street name was coincidental; it was named after an old mill race.) Except for a very brief interval, the Guard remained in the city for over a year, the longest peacetime occupation of an American town since Reconstruction.[42]

CNAC officials welcomed the Guard because, in their words, state troopers had "proven as intolerable and prejudiced as local police"; if the Guard had not been called in, they said, local blacks would have been forced to defend themselves. Black citizens had already shown their willingness to carry guns; at the height of the protests there were shootouts in the streets. "Men in the black community," Gloria Richardson recalled, "when they got home from work, would change clothes and go and lay in the yards and in the fields, around the perimeter of the second ward, with guns." Richardson and CNAC's implicit endorsement of the right to self-defense adds to the growing body of evidence that a significant segment of the civil rights movement was not philosophically committed to nonviolence.[43]

On 9 July the National Guard departed from town. No sooner had it left, however, than CNAC initiated a new round of demonstrations, including sit-ins at Dizzyland, located at the corner of Race and Gay streets, which earned front-page coverage in the *New York Times* and other newspapers. The following day CNAC returned to Dizzyland and several other segregated establishments. After being attacked by white mobs, CNAC staged a nighttime mass march to the downtown courthouse where some of the day's protestors were being held. Violence was averted on this occasion, but tensions remained extremely high.[44]

On 12 July, a white mob once again attacked demonstrators at Dizzyland. That evening more than 250 civil rights demonstrators staged a "freedom walk" to the courthouse, where they encountered a white mob of about seven hundred there to demand the release of a white man who had been arrested during the afternoon's melee. Whites pelted the civil rights demonstrators with rocks and eggs. As darkness fell, violence erupted. A carload of whites drove through the Second Ward and exchanged shotgun fire with black residents. White businesses were once again set on fire; stones were thrown through the window of Helen Waters's home, probably by militant blacks. George Collins, a reporter for the *Afro-American*, wrote, "For what seemed like an eternity the Second Ward was a replica of the Old West as men and boys of all ages roamed the streets, stood in the shadows, and leaned out of windows with their weapons in full view." By dawn more than twelve people had been shot. It was only through an "act of God," Collins said, that no one was killed. In the midst of the violence the governor ordered the National Guard to return to Cambridge.[45]

Meanwhile, even before this new round of violence erupted, the Kennedy administration had sought to resolve the dispute. Before the fall of 1962, President Kennedy had avoided intervening in local civil rights protests lest he lose southern support for his other initiatives, both foreign and domestic. But the proximity of Cambridge and the fear of more violence there convinced the Kennedy administration that it had to take a more aggressive stance. On 22 July, after nine grueling hours of negotiations, Robert Kennedy announced that representatives of the state of Maryland, the Justice Department, and the black community of Cambridge had signed an agreement whereby CNAC promised to suspend protests in exchange for "material and tangible" reforms. This agreement represented the most direct involvement of the Kennedy administration in the racial affairs of a local community.[46]

The agreement did not end racial turmoil, however. Within a month restaurant owners, members of the Rescue and Fire Company (RFC), and other small businessmen formed the Dorchester Business and Citizens Association (DBCA), which took as its immediate task the repeal by referendum of the cornerstone of the aforementioned agreement—namely, a pledge to amend the town's charter so as to outlaw racial discrimination in public accommodations.[47] Cambridge's white elite, fearful that repeal would exacerbate racial tensions, established the Cambridge First Committee. Headed by Arnold Deane, owner of the Cambridge *Daily Banner,* William Hart, president of the local chamber of commerce, J. Edward Walter, postmaster of Cambridge, and Levi Phillips Jr., an attorney and the son of one of the founders of the Phillips Packing Company, the committee argued that passage of the referendum would threaten the "economic welfare of the city."[48] When the DBCA protested against this elitist attack on them, the Cambridge First Committee countered with appeals to patriotism. "BUDDY, YOUR BUSINESS GREW OUT OF A FOXHOLE," declared one Cambridge First broadside. Blacks and whites had cooperated during the war to preserve American freedom. "Isn't it about time we decided if the Negro is good enough to die in our foxholes, he's good enough to eat in our restaurants?" The committee conveniently ignored the fact that the military had been segregated until the Korean War.[49]

Up until two weeks before the vote on the referendum, Richardson largely steered clear of the fray. But when the National Guard denied CNAC permission to stage a march to memorialize four young girls killed in the bombing of the Sixteenth Street Baptist Church in Birmingham, Alabama, Richardson held a press conference at which she shocked white and black moderates in Cambridge and liberals nationwide by calling on blacks to boycott the referendum. "Human rights are human rights, not white rights," Richardson explained, and they should not be left up to the whim of the white majority.[50] While CNAC endorsed Richardson's position, moderate blacks accused Richardson of betraying moderate whites and enlisted the aid of the NAACP to urge blacks to vote. Regional NAACP officer Philip Savage, for one, asserted that Richardson had known that the accommodations amendment would be put up to a referendum when she had signed it.[51] At the same time liberals nationwide unleashed a barrage of attacks on Richardson for betraying the principles of the movement. *Saturday Evening Post* columnist Robert Liston argued that Richardson's action could only be explained by her own quest for "power and fame."[52]

Richardson, while acknowledging the importance of the right to vote, advanced a different view. As far as she was concerned, liberals had always overestimated the power of the franchise. Blacks in Cambridge had enjoyed the franchise for a generation, and they had elected representatives, but as a minority they remained powerless. Like the student leaders of the New Left, Richardson saw the limits of electoral democracy and advocated fundamental social and economic reforms that might actually increase racial equality. Prior to the vote, CNAC and students from Swarthmore College conducted a door-to-door survey on the concerns of Cambridge's black residents; the responses indicated that a mere 6 percent considered equal access to public accommodations the most pressing problem they faced, while 42 percent named unemployment and 26 percent housing as the top priority.[53]

Sandra Miller and other historians contend that Richardson's gender influenced her politics. Richardson denies this, and Miller's own argument suggests that Richardson's family reputation had a far greater impact. But Richardson's sex did influence the way others saw her. While most Americans could accept and even applaud the dignified activism of Rosa Parks, Richardson's aggressive approach did not sit as well. Reporters described her as "irrational," "temperamental," and "insecure"—the usual sexist language employed to dismiss "troublesome" women. President Kennedy allegedly called her a "dragonlady." Liberals tended to discount Richardson on the ground that, as a woman, she did not know better.[54]

Historians of the New Left have also done a poor job of assessing Richardson. Her absence from most works on the New Left attests to the overemphasis historians have put on white, middle-class students.[55] Richardson's distance from the mainstream civil rights movement, her distrust of electoral politics, her informal ties with Malcolm X and other independent black radicals, and her influence on many black and white student activists, all place her squarely in the company of the New Left. She had contact with Stokely Carmichael, Cleveland Sellers, H. Rap Brown, and Courtland Cox, all prominent SNCC leaders, and hundreds of students, white and black, from tens of eastern colleges, most prominently Swarthmore College, one of the incubators of the New Left. Nearly all who knew Richardson expressed great admiration for her and acknowledged her influence on their political development.[56]

During the winter of 1963–64, Richardson grew closer to a loose network of independent black radicals, several of whom journeyed to Cambridge. New York Congressman Adam Clayton Powell Jr. praised Richardson as "one of the greatest women in America today" and urged Cambridge blacks to demonstrate until they won equal rights. Fannie Lou Hamer, soon to gain fame through her leadership of the Mississippi Freedom Democratic Party, echoed Powell's sentiments. Although she was unimpressed by Louis Farrakhan, Richardson responded very favorably to Malcolm X, whom she met for the first time in November 1963. Shortly thereafter she attended a meeting in Chester, Pennsylvania, which led to the formation of Associated Community Teams, better known as ACT, the immediate predecessor of the Organization of Afro American Unity, Malcolm X's alternative to the Nation of Islam and the Big Five.[57]

At the same time that Richardson and other black leaders were urging blacks to fight on, the DBCA was waging its own battle against Cambridge's white elite. DBCA leader William Wise declared that the Human Relations Committee (the renamed Cambridge First Committee) would accomplish nothing. Rejecting moderates' calls for racial harmony and the economic revival it would allegedly promote, Wise pledged to help Cambridge become known as "America's Fortress of Freedom." Although the DBCA turned down invitations to affiliate with the Ku Klux Klan and White Citizenship Council, it spearheaded an effort to hold a national referendum on the Civil Rights Act of 1964, then pending action by Congress. Local politicians associated with the DBCA called for the passage of several measures aimed at punishing the civil rights movement.

In addition, as mentioned above, on the eve of Maryland's 1964 Democratic presidential primary, the DBCA invited George Wallace to speak in Cambridge in the hope that this would put his campaign in Maryland over the top.[58] Although Wallace knew that the situation in Cambridge was explosive, he decided to accept the DBCA's invitations, on the heels of surprisingly strong showings in Indiana and Wisconsin. He addressed an all-white crowd of between fifteen hundred and two thousand who packed the RFC's arena. "I have spoken all the way from New Hampshire to Alabama," Wallace began, "and I believe there are in this country hundreds of thousands who say stand firm and keep working." Careful to avoid blatant racist appeals, Wallace nevertheless proclaimed that the American way of life was at stake. American citizens had to protect their individual rights from the encroachment of the federal government; local communities had to defend their autonomy. Wallace had faced hecklers at most of his appearances outside the Deep South, but he met only with applause in the RFC's arena.[59]

CNAC held a counterrally during Wallace's speech. Not only did hundreds of blacks from Cambridge turn out, so too did civil rights activists and sympathizers from all over the region, including Stokely Carmichael, Cleveland Sellers, and H. Rap Brown, three of SNCC's most militant members.[60] A week later the Alabama governor nearly won Maryland's Democratic primary. In Dorchester County, which had supported John F. Kennedy in 1960, Wallace won by a four-to-one margin, even though 95 percent of the voters of the Second Ward voted against him.[61]

In the mayoral race, Charles Walls, a former Phillips Packing Company official and racial moderate, ran against Osvrey Pritchett, a one-time chief of the RFC and law-and-order candidate endorsed by the DBCA and the Harrington faction of the Democratic Party. The DBCA also endorsed a slate of candidates for the town council, all of whom emphasized that the incumbents had supported the public accommodations charter amendment. Four years earlier Mowbray had defeated Pritchett by a nearly two-to-one margin. This time Pritchett won in a landslide, capturing more than 75 percent of the total vote and an even higher percentage in the working-class Fourth and Fifth Wards.

(Pritchett received only 25 out of 710 votes cast in the all-black Second Ward.) Two of three DBCA candidates for the town council, Robert Anderson and Thomas Hoover, won as well.[62]

Ironically, in the midst of this tumult, there were signs of an end to the conflict. Days before Pritchett's victory the National Guard left town, and civil rights activists "tested" the new federal Civil Rights Act, largely without incident. Shortly after the election the town council elected Charles Cornish, the symbol of black moderation, as its president. SNCC field representative Stanley Wise wrote: "If developments in Cambridge follow their present course, perhaps we can go back [to college] soon." Over the next few months the once-vibrant civil rights movement dissipated to the extent that Steve Fraser, a SNCC volunteer, complained of the apathy he encountered upon his arrival in early 1965. Even the FBI, which in its anticommunist mania had placed CNAC under investigation, closed its investigation of the movement in Cambridge.[63]

Moderate and conservative whites welcomed the apparent revival of "a more normal and peaceful way of life." Having believed all along that the trouble had been caused by Richardson and outsiders, they attributed the peace to their departure from Cambridge. (Richardson left in December 1964 to join her new husband, Frank Dandridge, a black photographer whom she met during the protests, in New York City.) Economics lessened tension as well. Between 1957 and 1962 the unemployment rate for blacks had hovered above 20 percent; by 1965 it had fallen to less than 10 percent.

In addition, Pritchett and his colleagues steered a much more moderate course than would have been expected on the basis of their 1964 campaign rhetoric. Rather than encourage Cambridge whites to defy the Civil Rights Act, they applied for federal funds for an assortment of projects that ameliorated many of the conditions that gave rise to racial tensions in the first place. Moreover, the representatives of white backlash never totally dislodged moderates from power. Charles Cornish was elected president of Cambridge's town council because three of the five seats on the council, including his own, remained in the hands of moderates (two of the seats were not contested in 1964). So even if Pritchett and the new council members had wanted to pursue a more reactionary course, they would have found it difficult to do so.[64]

Even so, many moderates exhibited wishful thinking when they declared in the early spring of 1967 that racial harmony had returned. The process of building public housing, desegregating schools, and distributing federal dollars was painful, leaving a bad taste in the mouths of many blacks, especially young blacks, in spite of the benefits of these programs. In each instance, white leaders implemented reforms slowly and reluctantly. Never did they acknowledge their own complicity in the perpetuation of racial inequality or credit CNAC with initiating needed reforms. The RFC's refusal to desegregate its pool—it ultimately sold its facility, rather than desegregate—added to this bad taste. So too did the vote of whites in the 1966 gubernatorial election, which pitted George P. Mahoney, a seven-time loser for statewide office who ran on the slogan, "Your Home Is Your Castle—Protect It!" against Spiro T. Agnew, the moderate Republican from Baltimore County. Mahoney won overwhelmingly among Cambridge whites. Agnew won the state largely because of the support he received from minorities, including blacks in Cambridge, who supported him by an eleven-to-one margin.[65]

In the late spring and early summer of 1967, signs of racial discord began to reappear in Cambridge, for local more than national reasons. A fight between a black and a white student on the last day of school produced heated exchanges. Then several fires erupted in the Second Ward, largely at white establishments. After deeming the fires the work of arsonists, authorities arrested Dwight Cromwell for making a false alarm. Upon his arrest, Cromwell declared that Gloria Richardson "is back and she is going to tear the town down." In fact Richardson was still living in New York, but she did arrange to bring H. Rap Brown to speak at a Cambridge rally organized by the Black Action Federation, the successor of CNAC.[66]

On the evening of 24 June, Brown delivered a fiery address to a crowd of between two- and four-hundred from atop a car parked across from the Pine Street Elementary School. An even larger assembly of law enforcement authorities mustered nearby. "What happens to a dream deferred? Does it dry up like a raisin in the sun? . . . Or does it explode?" Brown began. "Detroit exploded, Newark exploded. . . . It's time for Cambridge to explode." Following this dramatic introduction, Brown rambled through a vitriolic speech that lambasted white honkies, extolled black power, admonished "Uncle Toms" (including Cambridge's black policemen, who stood on the edge of the crowd), and demanded retribution. Peppered with calls to "get some guns," the speech aroused some and bored others. At one point Brown declared, "you see that school over there—I don't know whether the honkey burned that school or not but you all should have burned that school a long time ago. . . . If this town don't come round, this town should be burned down." Later that night a fire erupted at the Pine Street school, spread to nearly twenty other buildings, and earned Cambridge front-page coverage alongside several other riot-torn cities, including Detroit, the site of one of the worst riots in American history.[67]

Whether Brown actually caused a riot or explicitly directed blacks to burn down the school remains a matter of controversy. Gloria Richardson claimed that Brown was not responsible because he had delivered the same speech elsewhere without causing riots, while police chief Brice Kinnamon told a Senate subcommittee that Brown was "the sole reason" for the riot. While the national news media, local and national politicians, historians, and most townspeople tended to take one side or the other in this debate, no one paid much attention to an unpublished report of the staff of the Kerner Commission, which concluded that no riot had even taken place. What is usually known as the Brown riot, the Kerner report concluded, was more accurately described as a "low-level civil disturbance." If the RFC, long at odds with the black community, had responded promptly to the initial fire, the incident would have attracted little attention. But the Kerner report would not go so far as to accuse the RFC of gross negligence.[68]

Ironically, the non-riot had a tremendous impact on the national scene. For one thing, it catapulted Spiro T. Agnew into the national limelight. On the morning of 25 June, Agnew rushed to Cambridge from Ocean City, Maryland, where he issued a statement expressing his "perplexity at this senseless destruction precipitated by a professional agitator whose inflammatory statements deliberately provoked the outbreak of violence." After pledging help to the community, Agnew directed authorities to "seek out H. Rap Brown and bring him to justice." While Agnew claimed to deplore slum conditions and racial discrimination, these problems did not "give any person or group a license to commit crimes." (Agnew responded similarly to the Baltimore riots that erupted after Martin Luther King was assassinated.) Agnew led the conservative attack on the Kerner Commission. Whereas the commission saw white racism as the root cause of the riots and called for massive federal programs to alleviate the problems of the ghetto, Agnew blamed liberal permissiveness, which he said had created the environment in which such violence flourished. New federal programs would only fan the flames.[69]

Contemporary observers and historians alike have downplayed Agnew's significance, portraying George Wallace as the chief agent of the conservative resurgence of the 1970s and 1980s. But it is important to understand why so many Americans, including Richard Nixon, who selected him as his running mate in 1968, found Agnew attractive. As much as any other leader of the time, Agnew enabled the Republican Party to coax away "middle Americans," especially working- and middle-class Catholic males, from the Democratic Party. Even though the press consistently belittled him for his blunders on the campaign trail—as well as his disdain for the mass media—many "middle Americans" saw him as a more legitimate torchbearer of the Right than George Wallace, in part because Agnew had not championed segregation. As county executive and then as governor, Agnew supported the basic goals of the civil rights movement and enjoyed the backing of many moderate blacks. Having served in the military during World War II and worked hard to make a successful career, he, like other white urban ethnics who made it in suburbia in the postwar era, resented those who condemned him as a symbol of white privilege. Raised in a world in which civility mattered a great deal, he was appalled by its rapid decline. And while he acknowledged the American system's flaws, Agnew defended it passionately against those who saw violence as a necessary means of achieving a more just society. Indeed, had Agnew not been indicted for a petty crime that he committed before he became governor, he might have become president and thus the symbol of the new Right nearly a decade before Ronald Reagan was elected president.[70]

While Agnew was profitably capitalizing on white backlash in Cambridge and elsewhere, H. Rap Brown and other radicals were attempting to use the riots to spark a revolution. On 26 July, upon his arrest for allegedly inciting the Cambridge "riot," Brown declared that he considered himself neither "morally nor legally bound to obey laws made by a body in which I have no representation. . . . These rebellions are but a dress rehearsal for real revolution. Neither imprisonment nor threats of death will sway me from the path that I have taken, nor will they sway others like me."[71] In the weeks that followed, Brown repeated this line, telling a large crowd in Detroit after the riots there, "you did a good job here," and predicting that if blacks united they could "make the Detroit 'rebellion' look like a picnic."[72] Most leftists saw Brown as a symbol of liberation being persecuted by racist authorities. When Congress finally enacted weak "open housing" legislation in 1968, it attached a rider, known as the Brown amendment, which made it illegal to cross state lines to incite a riot. The "Brown riot," like the real riots of the mid- to late 1960s, undermined public support for civil rights goals, increased calls for law and order, and made the new Right seem alluring to significant segments of the liberal coalition. The Democrat-controlled Congress, for its part, ignored the Kerner Commission's recommendation for federal programs aimed at eradicating poverty and racism.

To make matters worse, as the economy stalled, black economic gains, which had been gradually increasing since the beginning of World War II, diminished. The economic downturn also undercut the public's belief that the federal government could overcome poverty through large-scale welfare programs.[73]

Ironically, while it helped polarize the nation, the "Brown riot" seemed to inoculate Cambridge against further uprisings. Whereas Martin Luther King's assassination unleashed the worst wave of rioting in American history, Cambridge experienced only a very small disturbance. H. Rap Brown's reappearance in Cambridge for a court hearing, which took place two weeks after King's assassination, produced no disruptions. Evidence of a new willingness to cooperate came in the form of interracial religious services, the construction of rent-subsidized housing, and the establishment of a community center headed by several of the most militant blacks in the community. Even though the DBCA's candidates continued to win at the polls, by 1968 they were displaying a much more conciliatory attitude toward black activists. Mayor Pritchett even declared, "The time has come to think as highly of human values as we have of property values," and the city council, under the urging of Octavene Saunders, a militant black leader, passed a resolution that had been stalled for months allowing for the construction of seventy-five new public housing units.[74]

Economic growth was the chief cause of the improvement in race relations in Cambridge. By the end of the decade, median income for black families stood at $5,335, up from $2,250 in 1960. During the same period, black unemployment declined dramatically, from nearly 30 percent at its high to 6.8 percent. While Cambridge's economy stagnated during the mid-1970s and 1980s, it rebounded somewhat during the 1990s, and as the new century dawned many citizens looked hopefully toward the construction of a massive retirement and recreational community as the key to economic revival. Moreover, throughout the post–civil rights years, the types of jobs open to blacks expanded considerably. In 1960 blacks were disproportionately employed as unskilled workers. One in five black women, for instance, was employed as a domestic worker. By 1990 only 2 percent of all black women worked as domestics. Similarly, between 1960 and 1990 the number of black males and females employed as sales, professional, technical, or clerical workers increased 500 percent. These shifts support Clayborne Carson's thesis that the most important legacy of the civil rights movement was a shift in social identities. The movement not only forced whites to open doors; it prodded blacks to push them open.[75]

Housing conditions for blacks also improved throughout the 1960s, although the gap between whites and blacks did not close significantly. By 1980 only 3 percent of all homes in the Second Ward were deemed substandard, compared to almost a third twenty years earlier. But more than two-thirds of all blacks in Cambridge remained renters (by contrast, two-thirds of whites owned their own homes). This gap revealed one of the ongoing legacies of past discrimination. Residential segregation coupled with job and educational discrimination made it more difficult for blacks than whites to accumulate wealth. They had great difficulty becoming homeowners and in turn were unable to pass on their assets to future generations or weather economic downturns.[76]

In the realm of education Cambridge blacks made important strides in the wake of the civil rights protests of the 1960s. At the end of the 1970–71 school year, the Republican-run Department of Health, Education and Welfare threatened to suspend payments of federal assistance to the county unless it speeded up the desegregation process. Rather than risk the loss of badly needed funds, the school board forced longtime superintendent James Busick to resign and replaced him with an outsider who quickly consolidated black and white schools. When school resumed in the fall of 1971, the ratio of blacks and whites in the classrooms resembled that in the community. This rapid desegregation of Cambridge's schools met with little protest. Indeed, based on the results of the new plan, the U.S. Commission on Civil Rights deemed Dorchester County a model of successful school desegregation. And while desegregation was not the panacea that many liberals anticipated, black pupils did benefit significantly. In 1960, for example, less than 3 percent of the black population had any college education. By 1980 10 percent did and by 2000 the number who attended at least some college had nearly doubled again.[77]

Ironically, the primary conflict between blacks and whites in the post–civil rights era took place in the political arena, specifically over voting rights. Blacks' complaints about the lack of voting rights grew out of the persistence of residential segregation, which left blacks underrepresented on the town council. In 1969 representation by ward was replaced by at-large elections, which diluted the black vote. Hence, when Lemuel Chester, one of the most prominent civil rights activists in Cambridge, ran for town council in 1984, he won the majority of votes in the Second Ward but lost the election. It was not until 1984 that the U.S. Justice Department filed suit against the city for violating the Voting Rights Act of 1965 and the at-large election system was thrown out in federal court. Shortly thereafter, Octavene Saunders, the erstwhile leader of the Black Action Federation, became the second black representative on the council.[78]

For years, an additional source of friction was the Rescue and Fire Company, which remained an all-white institution until the mid-1980s. While few residents explicitly defended public segregation, many continued to believe that segregation in the private sphere was natural and right; and the RFC was considered a private institution. A 1986 court order finally desegregated the RFC, but even then, not surprisingly, racist attitudes persisted. Enez Grubb, one of CNAC's cofounders, and her cousin George Meekins were the first blacks admitted to the RFC, but they were ostracized and treated as unequal to the white firefighters.[79]

The racial divide is alive and well in Cambridge today, as can be seen in the differences between blacks and whites in terms of historical memory. Again unsurprisingly, most black civil rights veterans look back fondly on the 1960s and seek to keep alive the memory of the movement, while most whites prefer not to discuss those days. Maryland state senator Frederick Malkus, for one, encouraged me not to pursue my research because "nothing positive" could come of it. Edward Kinnamon, police chief Brice Kinnamon's son, concurred: "Most people here just want to forget it. It's not something we're proud of." Gloria Richardson and Enez Grubb, by contrast, welcomed inquiries into the past, shared their personal recollections and papers, and encouraged additional research.[80]

There are signs of racial goodwill in Cambridge, however. The local Episcopal church, one of the central white institutions in Cambridge since before the American Revolution, recently nominated Harriet Tubman, the famous "conductor" on the underground railroad and a native of Dorchester County, as a "saint," and the chamber of commerce and other civic groups promote the Harriet Tubman Center as a tourist attraction. Perhaps in time blacks and whites will go a step further and celebrate the civil rights movement and the role that Gloria Richardson and other local blacks played in it. But historical memory is long, and we must not hold our breath.[81]

Notes

1. Arthur M. Schlesinger Jr., *A Thousand Days: John F. Kennedy in the White House* (Boston: Houghton Mifflin, 1965), 965–73; Carl Brauer, *John F. Kennedy and the Second Reconstruction* (New York: Columbia University Press, 1977); *New York Times*, 18 July 1963, 1.

2. *Public Papers of the Presidents, John F. Kennedy, 1963* (Washington, D.C.: Government Printing Office, 1964), 572; *New York Times*, 18 July 1963, 1.

3. "Agreement," 22 July 1963, in *Civil Rights during the Kennedy Administration, 1961–63* (Bethesda, Maryland: University Publications of America, 1986), 47 reels microfilm, part 2, Papers of Burke Marshall, Assistant Attorney General for Civil Rights, reel 26 [henceforth Burke Marshall Papers].

4. William G. Jones, *The Wallace Story* (Northport, Ala.: American Southern Publishing, 1968), 281; *Cambridge Daily Banner*, 12 May 1964.

5. Cleveland Sellers, *The River of No Return* (New York: William Morrow, 1973), 68.

6. Brown's speech can be found in *Is Baltimore Burning? Maryland State Archives: Documents for the Classroom* (Annapolis: Maryland State Archives, 1993). This collection of documents is also available online at www.msa.gov.

7. Jules Witcover, *White Knight: The Rise of Spiro T. Agnew* (New York: Random House, 1972), 126–29.

8. Anthony Lewis, *Portrait of a Decade* (New York: Times Books, 1965), 100–103; *Public Papers of the Presidents*, 305–6.

9. Juan Williams, *Eyes on the Prize* (New York: Viking, 1987); Taylor Branch, *Parting the Waters* (New York: Simon and Schuster, 1998); Taylor Branch, *Pillar of Fire* (New York: Simon and Schuster, 1998); Thomas Brooks, *Walls Came Tumbling Down* (Englewood, N.J.: Prentice Hall, 1974); Stephen Lawson, *Running for Freedom* (Philadelphia: Temple University Press, 1991); Mary King, *Freedom Song* (New York: William Morrow, 1987); Manning Marable, *Race, Reform and Rebellion* (Jackson: University of Mississippi Press, 1989); Harvard Sitkoff, *The Struggle for Black Equality, 1954–1992*, rev. ed. (New York: Hill and Wang, 1993); Robert Weisbrot,

Freedom Bond (New York: Norton, 1990); Rhoda Louis Blumberg, *Civil Rights* (New York: Twayne, 1984); Robert Cook, *Sweet Land of Liberty?* (London: Longman, 1998); Charles Loery and John Marszalek, eds., *Encyclopedia of African-American Civil Rights* (Westport, Conn.: Greenwood Press, 1992).

10. Michael Durham, "Thirty Miles Divide Folly and Reason; Cambridge and Salisbury, Maryland," *Life,* 26 July 1963, 18–25. See also "Why Race Troubles Hit One City, Spare Another; A Case Study: Cambridge and Salisbury, Maryland," *U.S. News,* 5 Aug. 1963), 78–80.

11. L. Brent Bozell, "The Lessons of Cambridge and Salisbury: Was Violence Necessary?" *National Review,* 27 Aug. 1963, 145–48.

12. Studies of massive resistance and white backlash include Numan Bartley, *The Rise of Massive Resistance* (Baton Rouge: Louisiana State University Press, 1969); Dan Carter, *The Politics of Rage* (Baton Rouge: Louisiana State University Press, 1995); Thomas Byrne Edsall, with Mary D. Edsall, *Chain Reaction: The Impact of Race, Rights, and Taxes on American Politics* (New York: Norton, 1992); Jonathan Rieder, *Canarsie* (Cambridge: Harvard University Press, 1985); J. Anthony Lukas, *Common Ground: A Turbulent Decade in the Lives of Three American Families* (New York: Knopf, 1985).

13. John D'Emilio, review of Brett Beemyn, ed., *Creating a Place for Ourselves, Journal of American History* 85 (1998): 540.

14. On Phillips in general see Phillips Packing Company, "Vertical File," Enoch Pratt Free Library, Baltimore, Maryland, and Phillips Packing Company, "Annual Reports," 1939–56, *FTA News,* 5 Jan. 1947.

15. *Moody's Manual of Investment American and Foreign* (1957); Phillips Packing Co., vertical file; Phillips Packing Co., annual reports, vertical file, Enoch Pratt Free Library, Baltimore; Hobart Taylor Jr. to John E. Nolan (employment in Cambridge), 19 June 1963, Burke Marshall Papers, reel 26.

16. Frederick Malkus, interview by author, Annapolis, Md., 2 Feb. 1993; J. Mills Thornton III, "Municipal Politics and the Course of the Civil Rights Movement," in *New Directions in Civil Rights Studies,* ed. Armstead L. Robinson and Patricia Sullivan (Charlottesville: University Press of Virginia, 1991), 38–64.

17. George R. Kent, "The Negro in Politics in Dorchester County" (master's thesis, University of Maryland, 1961).

18. For an interesting description of this strike, see John Barth, *The Last Voyage of Somebody the Sailor* (Boston: Little, Brown, 1991), 36–37.

19. John R. Wennersten, *Maryland's Eastern Shore: A Journey in Time and Place* (Centreville, Md.: Tidewater Press, 1992), 3–4.

20. Mencken quoted in Wennersten, *Maryland's Eastern Shore,* 228.

21. *New York Times,* 11 Sept. 1960; *Baltimore News-American,* 2 March 1947; Huntley and Brinkley quoted in *National Review,* 23 Aug. 1963, 47; *Cambridge Daily Banner,* 10, 14, and 30 Sept. 1960; *Time,* 19 July 1963, 17–18; Kent, "The Negro in Politics."

22. George Calcott, *Maryland and America, 1940–1980* (Baltimore: Johns Hopkins University Press, 1985), 155–56; *New York Times,* 12 July 1961, 13; 4 Sept. 1961, 1; 16 Sept. 1961, 2; 21 Sept. 1961, 20; 27 Sept. 1961, 2; 5 Oct. 1961, 24; 8 Oct. 1961, 56; 28 Oct. 1961, 24; 29 Oct. 1961, 52; 2 Nov. 1961, 28; August Meier, *A White Scholar and the Black Community, 1945–1965* (Amherst, Mass.: University of Massachusetts Press, 1992), 26–27, 198 and 206–7; William Hansen, interview by author, 2 April 1992; Gloria Richardson, interview by author, 21 March 1993.

23. "Field Reports, 1962–63," Student Nonviolent Coordinating Committee (SNCC) Papers, Martin Luther King Jr. Center for Nonviolent Social Change, Atlanta, box 96; "Cambridge Report," Congress of Racial Equality (CORE) Papers, 1944–68, Martin Luther King Jr. Center for Nonviolent Social Change, Atlanta, reel 21; *Daily Banner,* 15, 22, 24, 29 Jan. and 2 Feb. 1962.

24. "Field Reports, 1962–63," SNCC Papers.

25. Meier, *A White Scholar,* 206–7; August Meier, interview by author, 29 April 1996. Meier was a professor at Morgan State University during the early 1960s and an advisor to the Civic Interest Group.

26. *Afro-American,* 27 Jan. 1962; "Cambridge Report," CORE Papers; "Field Reports, 1962–63," SNCC Papers; Howard Zinn, *The New Abolitionists* (Boston: Beacon Press, 1964). Hansen was a twenty-two-year-old white student from Xavier University in Cincinnati, Ohio.

27. Kent, "The Negro in Politics"; Richardson, interview; Annette K. Brock, "Gloria Richardson and the Cambridge Movement," in *Women in the Civil Rights Movement: Trailblazers and Torchbearers,* ed. Vicki L. Crawford et al. (Bloomington: Indiana University Press, 1993), 121–44.

28. "Gloria Richardson," *Ebony,* July 1964, 23–30.

29. Melanie B. Cook, "Gloria Richardson," *Sage* [Student Supplement] (1988); Brock, "Gloria Richardson"; Richardson, interview; Howard Schneider, "Summer of Fire," *Washington Post Magazine,* 26 July 1992, 18, 25; Sandra Y. Miller, "Recasting Civil Rights Leadership," *Journal of Black Studies* 26 (July 1996): 668–87; Edward K. Trever, "Gloria Richardson and the Cambridge Civil Rights Movement" (master's thesis, Morgan State University, 1994).

30. "Gloria Richardson," *Ebony,* July 1964, 23–30; Murray Kempton, "Gloria, Gloria," *New Republic,* 11 Nov. 1963, 15–17; Robert Liston, "Who Can We Surrender To?" *Saturday Evening Post,* 5 Oct. 1963, 78–80; Cook, "Gloria Richardson"; Cambridge Nonviolent Action Committee (CNAC), "Study," CNAC Papers, State Historical Society of Wisconsin, Madison; Kent, "The Negro in Politics"; Lemuel Chester, interview by Sandra Harney, Maryland Public Television, 2 Aug. 1997, transcript.

31. Liston, "Who Can We Surrender To?"; Kempton, "Gloria, Gloria."

32. *Afro-American,* 15 June 1962, 4, and 20 April 1963; *Daily Banner,* 15 Jan. 1962 and 4 Sept. 1962; "Editorial: WJZ-TV by Herbert Cahan," 24 July 1963, Governor J. Millard Tawes Papers, Maryland State Archives, Annapolis [hereafter Tawes Papers], S1041–1530; Richardson, interview; Schneider, "Summer of Fire," 10.

33. CNAC, "Study," CNAC Papers; Hobart Taylor Jr. to John E. Nolan Jr., 19 July 1963, and memo to attorney general (employment in Cambridge), 18 July 1963, both in Burke Marshall Papers.

34. CNAC, "Study," CNAC Papers; Downs quoted in "Cambridge Fears D-Day," *Afro-American,* 18 May 1963, 1.

35. On the Henry family, see Elias Jones, *New Revised History of Dorchester County, Maryland* (Cambridge, Md.: Tidewater Publishers, 1966), 331–37.

36. *Baltimore Sun,* 8 May 1963; *Cambridge Daily Banner,* 8 May 1963, 1; Brock, "Gloria Richardson," 128.

37. MICRPR, "Report on Racial Situation in Cambridge," 12 June 1963, Tawes Papers; "Cambridge Report," CORE Papers; *New York Times,* 5–11 June 1963; *Afro-American,* 18 May and 8 June 1963.

38. "Report on Racial Situation in Cambridge," Tawes Papers; G. Roland Harper Jr., "Letter to the Editor," *Cambridge Daily Banner,* 19 July 1963.

39. White's letter quoted in Schneider, "Summer of Fire," 8.

40. "Cambridge Report," CORE Papers; *New York Times*, 5–11 June 1963; *Afro-American*, 18 May and 8 June 1963; Burke Marshall, "memorandum," 17 June 1963, Burke Marshall Papers.

41. *New York Times*, 11–15 June 1963; *Cambridge Daily Banner*, 11–15 June 1963; *Afro-American*, 15 June 1963.

42. Governor Tawes, press release, 14 June 1963, Tawes Papers, S1041–1530.

43. Gloria Richardson to Governor Tawes, 12 June 1963, Tawes Papers, "CAM-CAN"; Gloria Richardson, interview by Sandra Harney, Maryland Public Television, 7 July 1967; Sandra Miller, "Recasting Civil Rights Leadership"; Brock, "Gloria Richardson"; Kempton, "Gloria, Gloria." On the tradition of self-defense, see Timothy Tyson, "Robert F. Williams, 'Black Power,' and the Roots of the African American Freedom Struggle," *Journal of American History* 85 (1998): 540.

44. *New York Times*, 9 July 1963; *Cambridge Daily Banner*, 7–12 July 1963; "Cambridge Report," CORE Papers.

45. *New York Times*, 13 July 1963; "Cambridge Report," CORE Papers; *Afro-American*, 13 July 1963, 1; Governor J. Millard Tawes, speech, 19 July 1963, Tawes Papers, S1041–1557.

46. *Afro-American*, 20 July 1963; "Agreement," 22 July 1963, Burke Marshall Papers. On the civil rights record of the Kennedy administration, see Branch, *Parting the Waters*, and Brauer, *John F. Kennedy and the Second Reconstruction*. Ironically, shortly before RFK announced the agreement, President Kennedy singled out Cambridge for criticism, claiming that the movement there had lost track of what it was protesting (*Public Papers of the Presidents*, 304–5).

47. *New York Times*, 24 July 1963, 1; *Cambridge Daily Banner*, 2, 4, 9, 10 Aug. 1963.

48. *Cambridge Daily Banner*, 23 Aug., 25 and 28 Sept. 1963.

49. *Cambridge Daily Banner*, 20 Sept. 1963.

50. Richardson quoted in press release, Student Nonviolent Coordinating Committee (SNCC) Papers, 1959–72, microfilm ed.; (Frederick, Md.: University Publications of America), reel 15; *Cambridge Daily Banner*, 28 Sept. 1963; *Afro-American*, 28 Sept., 5 Oct. 1963; "Field Reports," 1962–63, SNCC Papers, reel 17; CNAC, "Statement," Burke Marshall Papers; CNAC, "Study," CNAC Papers.

51. *Cambridge Daily Banner*, 28 Sept. 1963; CNAC, "Study," CNAC Papers; *Afro-American*, 5 Oct. 1963; Philip Savage, interview by John Britton, 20 Sept. 1967, Civil Rights Documentation Project, Howard University; Philip Savage folders, 1962–65, NAACP Papers, IIIC, Library of Congress, Washington, D.C.

52. Lewis, *Portrait of a Decade*, 100–103; *Saturday Evening Post*, 5 Oct. 1963, 78–80; *New Republic*, 11 Nov. 1963, 15–17; *Time*, 11 Oct. 1963, 30.

53. CNAC, "Study," CNAC Papers.

54. See "Minutes, (Notes) of (Miles) Governor Committee Meetings," Cambridge, Md., 18 June 1964, Tawes Papers, S1041–1557; Kempton, "Gloria, Gloria," *New Republic*, 11 Nov. 1963, 15–17; Liston, "Who Can We Surrender To?"; Miller, "Recasting Civil Rights Leadership"; Richardson, interview by Harney.

55. Among those who have noted the narrowness of scholarship on the New Left are Wini Breines, "Whose New Left?" *Journal of American History* 75 (Sept. 1988): 528–45, and Maurice Isserman, "The Not-So-Dark and Bloody Ground: New Works on the 1960s," *American Historical Review* 94 (Oct. 1989): 990–1010. The indexes of ten of the best-known and most prominent works on the 1960s contain not a single reference to Gloria Richardson.

56. Gloria Richardson, "Freedom—Here and Now," *Freedomways* 4 (winter 1964): 33–34; Peter Goldman, *The Death and Life of Malcolm X,* 2d ed. (Urbana: University of Illinois Press, 1979), 119; Sellers, *River of No Return.*

57. See "Human Relations Committee Notes Progress," *Cambridge Daily Banner,* 18 Dec. 1963; Major Jack Koulman to General Reckford, 4 Feb. 1964, and "Report of the Miles Committee," both in Tawes Papers, general file; Federal Bureau of Investigation, "Cambridge Nonviolent Action Committee," 100-442079, FOIA Reading Room, FBI; Goldman, *Malcolm X,* 116; *Cambridge Daily Banner,* 8 Nov., 30 Dec., 31 Dec. 1963. The Big Five consisted of the NAACP, SCLC, SNCC, CORE, and the National Urban League.

58. "Wise and the DBCA," *Cambridge Daily Banner,* 15 Nov. 1963; Louis G. Panos, "DBCA President's Views on Rights Movement Described by Newsman," *Cambridge Daily Banner,* 11 May 1964; "News Control Bill," *New York Times,* 13 Feb. 1964; "Incident Imperils Truce in Maryland," *New York Times,* 4 March 1964; "Maryland Limits Civil Rights Bill," *New York Times,* 14 April 1964, 10; Jones, *The Wallace Story,* 276–80.

59. Jones, *The Wallace Story,* 276–80; *Cambridge Daily Banner,* 12 May 1964; *New York Times,* 12 May 1964, 1.

60. Sellers, *River of No Return,* 71; *New York Times,* 13 and 15 May, 21.

61. *Cambridge Daily Banner,* 27 and 28 May, 5 June 1964; "Interracial-Cambridge, 1964," Tawes Papers.

62. *Cambridge Daily Banner,* 5 and 8 June, 13 and 14 July 1964.

63. "Last Troops Quit Cambridge, Maryland," *New York Times,* 12 July 1964, 54; "Negro Elected to Head Cambridge, Md., Council," *New York Times,* 21 July 1964, 20; *Cambridge Daily Banner,* 6, 7, 8, 23 July 1964; Steve Fraser, interview by author, 30 March 1996; FBI, 100-442079.

64. *Cambridge Daily Banner,* 11 July 1964; U.S. Dept. of Commerce, "ARA Field Report," Nov. 1964, U.S. Dept. of Commerce Papers, 378-67A-4033, box 44; Office of Economic Opportunity Papers, RG 381, National Archives, College Park, Md.; Housing and Urban Development (HUD) Papers, RG 207, National Archives, College Park, Md.; Maryland Division of Economic Development, *Community Economic Inventory: Dorchester County Maryland* (Annapolis: Division of Economic Development, 1971).

65. *Joseph W. Williams, et al. v. Rescue and Fire Company* 254 F. Supp. 556 (1966); "Reconnaissance Survey: Field Research Report," 14 Aug. 1968, Spiro T. Agnew Papers, general file, box 11, Maryland State Archives (hereafter MSA); U.S. Commission on Civil Rights, "School Desegregation in Dorchester County, Maryland," Sept. 1977; "Agnew Wins, Dorchester County Favors Demos," *Cambridge Daily Banner,* 9 Nov. 1966.

66. *Cambridge Daily Banner,* 16, 23, 26, 27, 28, 29 June 1967; "Analysis of the Cambridge Disturbance," *Civil Rights during the Johnson Administration, 1963–1968: Part 5: Records of the National Advisory Commission on Civil Disorders,* reel 6, microfilm, ed. Steven Lawson (Frederick, Md.: University Publications of America, 1984); Gloria Richardson Dandridge, interview by John Britton, 11 Oct. 1967, Civil Rights Documentation Project, Howard University.

67. Different versions of Brown's speech exist. For a collection of transcripts and newspaper clippings on the fire and riot, see *Is Baltimore Burning?;* Wayne Page, "H. Rap Brown and the Cambridge Incident: A Case Study" (master's thesis, University of Maryland, 1970).

68. Novelist John Barth, a native of Cambridge, and National Guard commander George Gelston both blamed white officials, particularly Kinnamon and the RFC, for the tragedy.

69. Spiro T. Agnew, "A Critique of the Kerner Commission Report," 23 July 1968, in Frank Burdett, ed. *Addresses and State Papers of Spiro T. Agnew.*

70. Witcover, *White Knight*. On Agnew's racial record as governor, see "Civil Rights Accomplishments of the Agnew Administration," n.d., box 11, Spiro T. Agnew Papers, MSA; "Dr. Ware Eases Agnew's Burdens," *Afro-American,* 8 April 1967; "Transcript—News Conference with Roy Wilkins," 19 July 1967, Papers of Spiro T. Agnew, box 5, subseries 3, Archives and Manuscript Department, University of Maryland, College Park, Md.

71. Clayborne Carson, *In Struggle: SNCC and the Black Awakening of the 1960s* (Cambridge: Harvard University Press, 1981), 252–57; "H. Rap 'The Lamb' Turns Erring Lion," *Afro-American,* 19 Aug. 1967; "Rap Brown—Revolutionary Violence," *The Movement,* Aug. 1967, 11; "No Formal Extradition Request Made by Maryland Yet," *Baltimore Sun,* 27 July 1967.

72. "Report of Office of Investigations," 25 March 1968, in *Civil Rights during the Johnson Administration,* reel 17; "Rap Brown Predicts More U.S. Violence," *Afro-American,* 2 Sept. 1967.

73. Robert Collins, "Growth Liberalism in the Sixties," in *The Sixties: From Memory to History,* ed. David Farber (Chapel Hill: University of North Carolina Press, 1994), 11–14.

74. *Cambridge Daily Banner,* 2, 3, 7 Oct. 1967; 22 Jan., 2 Feb., 29 Oct., 4 and 5 Nov. 1968. On housing, see HUD Papers, RG 207, entry 55, box 342, folders 42–69, National Archives, College Park, Md.; William Chaffinch to Governor Agnew, 25 Jan. 1968, Agnew Papers, MSA.

75. U.S. Department of Commerce, *1960 Census of Population: General Social and Economic Characteristics, Maryland*; U.S. Department of Commerce, *1970 Census of Population: General Social and Economic Characteristics, Maryland*; Maryland Division of Economic Development, *Community Economic Inventory: Dorchester County,* Maryland (Annapolis: Division of Economic Development, 1971); <http://www.skipjack.net/le_shore/b-envir/accra.html>.

76. U.S. Dept. of Commerce, *United States Census of Housing, 1960: Maryland*; U.S. Dept. of Commerce, *United States Census of Housing, 1990,* vol. 1 part 22; Christopher Jenks and Paul E. Peterson, eds., *The Urban Underclass* (Washington D.C.: Brookings Institute, 1991), especially the essay in that volume by Reynolds Farley, "Residential Segregation of Social and Economic Groups among Blacks, 1970–1980."

77. *School Desegregation in Dorchester County, Maryland* (U.S. Commission on Civil Rights, Sept. 1977); *1980 Census Profile: Social, Economic and Housing Profile for Maryland,* vol. 2 (Baltimore: Maryland Department of Planning, 1983).

78. *United States of America v. City of Cambridge, Maryland* 799 F. 2nd 137 (14th Cir. 1986); case file of same case, No. 86-3533, RG 84-4411, box 45, National Archives, Mid-Atlantic Region, Philadelphia; Stephen Sachs, "At-large Elections of County Commissioners: An Audit Conducted by the Office of the Attorney General," 18 July 1985 (Baltimore: Office of the Attorney General, 1985).

79. *Washington Post,* 26 No. 1987; C5; *Washington Post,* 18 Aug. 1986, B1; Enez Grubb, interview by author, March 2000.

80. Malkus, interview; "Tensions Remain in Cambridge," *Baltimore Sun,* 26 July, 1992, 1C; "Marking the 30th Anniversary of the Cambridge Pine Street Fire," vertical file, Dorchester County Public Library; Gloria Richardson, interview by author, May 2000.

81. On Tubman, see *Baltimore Sun,* 11 Jan. 1987, 20 Dec. 1986; 26 July 1992.

CHAPTER 5

Organizing from the Bottom Up: Lillian Craig, Dovie Thurman, and the Politics of ERAP

Jennifer Frost

In 1964–65 Lillian Craig, a white welfare recipient and resident of Cleveland's Near West Side, and Dovie Thurman, an African American welfare recipient and resident of Chicago's Uptown neighborhood, joined community organizing projects in their neighborhoods. Students for a Democratic Society (SDS) had recently begun community organizing under the auspices of its Economic Research and Action Project (ERAP). Inspired by the civil rights movement, especially by the Student Nonviolent Coordinating Committee (SNCC), SDS aimed to build "an interracial movement of the poor" to abolish poverty, end racial injustice, and expand democracy in America.[1] Over the next few years, SDS organizers initiated thirteen official ERAP projects in racially diverse low-income neighborhoods. Although most of these projects failed in short order, and SDS never sparked a social movement of poor Americans, Dovie Thurman and Lillian Craig shared SDS's aims and helped to make the Chicago and Cleveland projects among ERAP's largest, most successful, and longest-lived.

Scholars of the New Left in the 1960s have paid scant attention to neighborhood participants in SDS's community organizing like Lillian Craig and Dovie Thurman. New Left organizers are assumed to be ERAP's only participants, while community residents are often portrayed as passive, acted upon rather than acting. The significant exception to the rule is Sara Evans, who first documented the leadership role of community women in ERAP and their successes with welfare rights organizing.[2] When most scholars mention the projects' constituency, however, it has been to point out ERAP's failure. As Todd Gitlin put it in *The Sixties,* "The demoralized and skeptical poor were not eager to march."[3] Others accuse SDS and other New Left activists of romanticizing the poor, of seeing them as somehow above the American culture of consumption and progress, even as "antimodern." In Milton Viorst's words, "Having romanticized the urban poor, SDS organizers were disappointed to find that in reality they were suspicious, insensitive, and quite often unlikable."[4] Either way, community participants in the ERAP projects have been caricatured and dismissed rather than taken seriously. This is ironic, given ERAP's commitment to organizing from the bottom up. The involvement of neighborhood residents in ERAP programs was to be a living embodiment of the New Left principle of "participatory democracy," in which people take part in the decisions that shape their lives. New Left organizers listened to and took seriously the ideas and requests of those whom they sought to mobilize. This essay attempts to do the same for Lillian Craig and Dovie Thurman, by examining SDS's community organizing from the perspective of two low-income women, one white, one black, at the grassroots. In the tradition of the social history that began to flourish during the 1960s—in no small part due to leftist historians—this is a history of ERAP from the bottom up.[5]

For Dovie Thurman and Lillian Craig, ERAP provided both focus and resources for their community activism. Their activism, particularly on welfare issues, challenged New Left assumptions about movement strategy and goals. ERAP was a turning point for both women, and their self-confidence, political knowledge, and organizing skills expanded dramatically as a result of their participation. Their interactions with New Left organizers and other community participants revealed both the limits and the possibilities of building "an interracial movement of the poor" in the 1960s. And after the ERAP projects were disbanded in 1967 and 1968, both women continued their efforts, taking part in the welfare rights movement, community activism, and government service into the 1970s. The stories of Lillian Craig and Dovie Thurman broaden our understanding of New Left activism in the 1960s.

In arguing for the significance of the lives and activism of Lillian Craig and Dovie Thurman in the history of the New Left, the question arises, how representative were these two women of the residents in the communities where ERAP projects were initiated? Not very, if "representativeness" is defined in quantitative terms. As only two of many thousands of community residents, they are hardly a statistically significant sample. Yet their lives and their voices matter. In the words of oral historian Alessandro Portelli, the participation of people like Dovie Thurman and Lillian Craig "offers less a grid of standard experiences than a horizon of shared possibilities, real or imagined."[6]

Motivations

Sharon Jeffrey knocked on my door and asked me if I was registered to vote. I asked her in, and after a while I told her I was on welfare. That's how our friendship began.
—Lillian Craig[7]

I was organized by Rennie Davis. My aunt, Big Dovie, had gone to the welfare office to get supplementary aid for my children. Rennie was passing out leaflets for JOIN. . . . I saw this leaflet Rennie was passing out: "Are you tired of late checks, no checks, midnight raids, caseworkers' harassment? Come to a meeting." I couldn't believe they were saying this openly. My aunt said, "Oh, we need to go there. I'm tired of all this." —Dovie Thurman[8]

In 1964 Lillian Craig lived on Cleveland's Near West Side, and, by the following year, Dovie Thurman resided in Chicago's Uptown neighborhood. These neighborhoods were both in the process of being reshaped by black and white migration from the South, competition from the growing suburbs, deindustrialization, and urban blight, which meant few jobs and poor living conditions for inner-city residents.[9] Lillian Craig lived amid the narrow alleys and densely packed housing of the Near West Side, a neighborhood near downtown Cleveland west of the Cuyahoga River, which divided the city both geographically and racially. As blacks crowded into neighborhoods on the East Side, white Appalachian migrants settled mostly in the West Side's "Hillbilly Heaven."[10] Unemployment rates there ranged from 8 to 19 percent, compared to a citywide rate of 5.5 percent, and recipients of general relief and Aid to Families with Dependent Children (AFDC)—a joint federal-state public assistance program popularly known as "welfare" by the early 1960s—had increased by 35 and 96 percent, respectively, since 1956.[11]

Dovie Thurman lived on a predominantly black block—"the remnants of the servant quarters of rich homes along the Outer Drive"—in Uptown, a neighborhood encompassing 120 square blocks about five miles north of downtown Chicago.[12] A primary destination of Appalachian and southern migrants, Uptown was known as the city's "white ghetto."[13] In December 1964, when Chicago's unemployment rate was less than 3 percent, one study found that 51 percent of heads of households in Uptown were either unemployed or made less than $3,000, which put them below the poverty level.[14] Although the majority of residents were white, the number of Native Americans, Latinos, and African Americans increased during the 1960s.[15]

Both Lillian Craig and Dovie Thurman had lived their lives in poverty. Born in 1937 of Czech heritage, Craig was raised in Cleveland. Her mother died when she was twelve, and her violent, alcoholic father was unable to care for her and her two sisters. The girls were separated, and Craig was put into foster care; she remained isolated from her family for the rest of her life. In the mid-1960s she was a divorced, full-time mother of three children.[16] Dovie Thurman was nearly ten years younger than Craig. "I'm a black woman who grew up in poverty and on a welfare roll," says Thurman. "I was raised in the Pruitt-Igoe Projects in St. Louis. They blew them up, they were so bad. I moved to Chicago when I was eighteen with three kids. My husband was in Vietnam at the time."[17] Like many African Americans, Thurman remained connected to her extended family. Raised by her grandmother in St. Louis, she joined her aunt, "Big Dovie" Coleman, when she moved to Chicago.[18] In the mid-1960s, both women were still struggling with poverty, trying to support themselves and their children on the inadequate benefits provided by AFDC.

Craig and Thurman were approached by two of the most important and influential organizers in ERAP. Sharon Jeffrey and Rennie Davis had held leadership positions in SDS—Jeffrey was one of the few women to do so—and both were strong advocates of

SDS's move into community organizing in 1963. In 1964 Jeffrey was the full-time director of the Cleveland Community Project, while Davis was the director of ERAP at national SDS headquarters in Ann Arbor, Michigan, until he joined the Chicago "JOIN" project as part of the decentralization of ERAP in 1965. Both Jeffrey and Davis excelled at the interpersonal contact and trust building—often across the barriers of class, race, and gender—that community organizing involved.[19]

Unlike the vast majority of community residents contacted by New Left organizers, Dovie Thurman and Lillian Craig were quick to join ERAP. Both women were angry about their desperate economic situations. Craig's welfare benefits came to only 70 percent of Ohio's "minimum standard of need" set in 1959, and Thurman found it "impossible to live under" Illinois's welfare budget levels.[20] Thurman had long experience with the inequities and indignities of the welfare system.

> As a child growing up, I hated the welfare system. I didn't like white caseworkers. I thought they were all like the one who visited my grandmother when I lived with her. . . . She always hated welfare because she had to lick their behinds, and she couldn't tell them how she felt or else they would cut our check off. I said, "When I get grown, Mama, I'm gonna whup me some caseworkers." I didn't like what they did to my mama.[21]

Craig's mother had told her, when she was a young child, "I will never raise a doormat," and indeed she did not. As an adult Craig did not hesitate to challenge her employers. While working at Stouffer's as a young woman, for example, she attempted to organize a union and was summarily fired.[22] In the early 1960s she became involved in a welfare rights group sponsored by the Inner City Protestant Parish, an ecumenical group ministry that worked with the poor of all races. "When SDS came," she said, "I was ready for something."[23] In short, Thurman and Craig were "empowered personalities" before they ever met an organizer.

Yet there is no doubt that ERAP activism "took their empowerment to another level."[24] Despite their history of anger toward the welfare system and their attempts to challenge that system, both women experienced the stigma, shame, and powerlessness associated with being poor and on welfare in America. Craig, especially, felt ashamed of her status as a single mother on welfare; she used to tell people that her husband was in the service. When she first met Sharon Jeffrey, Craig hesitated to express her concerns about welfare and informed Jeffrey of her status as a welfare recipient only "after a while." "I am nobody, and nobody cares, and there is no escape," she remembered feeling.[25] Although Thurman, whose husband really was in the military, did not blame herself for her economic situation, she still felt powerless to change it. When she met Rennie Davis, Thurman "couldn't believe" the Chicago project's bold, open criticism of the welfare system. To involve themselves in ERAP, both women needed the strength and confidence to overcome their reluctance to identify themselves publicly as welfare recipients.

In their interest in ERAP, Dovie Thurman and Lillian Craig were more typical of women than of men in the neighborhoods. ERAP's primary method of recruitment, the door-to-door canvass, brought more women than men into the projects. Because women tended to be home during the day, when organizers came to call, they were easier to meet than men, and more receptive.[26] Their early discussions with the ERAP organizers focused primarily on community problems—problems that particularly concerned women as the caretakers of households and families. Women residents saw community improvement as a logical extension of their domestic responsibilities.[27] They also created many of the social ties that laid the foundation for neighborhood organizing—ties based as much on pooling economic resources as on friendship. "Being poor can bring you closer together," Craig noted. "I haven't got anything, you haven't got anything, but together we might have something."[28] As a consequence, women like Thurman and Craig were ERAP's first and largest constituency and provided the most consistent leadership.

The recruitment of female welfare recipients like Dovie Thurman and Lillian Craig signaled a transformation in ERAP's strategy and goals. ERAP represented SDS's attempt to formulate a strategy for social change appropriate to the political and economic conditions of the post-1945 United States. Initially ERAP sought to spark an "interracial movement of the poor" by organizing jobless men to demand full employment or a guaranteed income from the state. By late summer 1964, it was clear that this approach had failed, and SDS organizers decided that it made sense to focus on the issues and goals residents themselves defined as most important. In the end, ERAP mobilized a constituency largely of women around issues such as welfare, housing, and recreation, with the aim of changing welfare state agencies and programs.

This shift in strategy and goals was not without conflict, however. In the late summer and fall of 1964, an important debate, known as the "JOIN-GROIN" debate, arose over whether the organizing issues proposed by community residents had political content and could contribute to social change. Organizers still committed to the original ERAP strategy became known as the "Jobs or Income Now (or JOIN)" faction, while those urging the new approach were dubbed derisively the "Garbage Removal or Income Now (or GROIN)" faction.[29] As leftists historically had done, organizers on both sides of the debate considered unemployment a political issue because it revealed fundamental inequalities in American society and challenged entrenched power relations.[30] But the JOIN faction questioned whether GROIN issues posed the same radical challenge or would actually bring about social change. As Kim Moody of the Baltimore project put it, "It is difficult to see how an organization of women built on neighborhood concerns will lead to anything else."[31]

The GROIN faction countered that its approach was most consistent with ERAP's dedication to organizing from the bottom up. The largely female constituency for welfare, housing, and recreation was large, stable, and ready to organize. Moreover, they argued, these issues were connected to fundamental social, economic, and political inequalities and could spark a social movement of poor Americans. Women welfare recipients, asserted Chicago organizer Casey Hayden, "are tied to the state through the welfare system, and thus their gripes are easily politicized."[32] Prompted by the concerns of community residents like Lillian Craig and Dovie Thurman, this debate illuminated the New Left's struggle to expand the definition of "politics" to encompass new constituencies, issues, and goals.

Meanings

I stood up and made a couple of statements. "I'm sick and tired of this welfare system. I don't know what to do about it, but I want to fight, too. It's doing the same to all of us." It was my first encounter speaking to a group of people, and I got a big hand. . . . At the next meeting I was nominated to be chairperson. Just that quick. What was most exciting was somebody wanted me. I didn't even know what a chairperson was. I had a lot inside of me that I always wanted to say, but I never knew how to get it out. I didn't use to be a person that would speak out a lot. 'Cause I was angry that night, it just came out real easy. —Dovie Thurman[33]

The first sit-in was very exciting. The mothers had met and decided what we wanted to do. We wanted to do a "takeover" of the Welfare Department. We weren't even sure what that meant . . . we just knew that we were going to take over desks. And then it grew. We went during the day . . . we pushed workers out of their chairs and sat in them. Then we went into the switchboard area and started answering the phones, "This is the People's Welfare Department. Come on down and join us!" —Lillian Craig[34]

Dovie Thurman and Lillian Craig came to see the Chicago and Cleveland ERAP projects as vehicles for political expression and participation. As their self-confidence grew, both women began to shed the sense of shame and powerlessness they associated with receiving AFDC payments. Thurman, who "didn't use to be a person that would speak out a lot," always expressed surprise that she had become a public figure.[35] Craig, by contrast, proudly claimed that she had "a big mouth" and enjoyed being known as the most vocal of all of the community women involved in the Cleveland project. "At first it was important that I was in the spotlight . . . the spokesperson, with my picture in the papers and on TV," she recalled. "That came out of my past. . . . I needed to feel that I was *somebody*. I hadn't been sure I was anybody." This sense of being somebody— something Martin Luther King Jr. also talked about—conveyed her growing self-respect and self-confidence.[36] Both women had been shaped by their experience of economic hardship and insecurity, and ERAP challenged them to confront and overcome their pasts.

Thurman and Craig quickly became leaders of their respective projects and played important roles in ERAP's welfare rights activism. Craig helped ERAP organizers revive her Cleveland welfare rights group, Citizens United for Adequate Welfare (CUFAW). In 1964–65 she helped lead CUFAW's successful campaign to rescind a new fifteen-cent lunch fee for middle and high school students of welfare parents. Since family breakfasts generally consisted of oats or cornmeal, school lunches were a fundamental part of children's diet.[37] After several months of organizing and a letter-writing campaign, CUFAW held a demonstration and attended a meeting of the county commissioners. When one member of the commission asserted that if welfare recipients simply budgeted properly welfare payments would cover lunch costs, Craig replied in anger, explaining her basic expenses, her income, and how she could barely make ends meet. "I stood up and blasted the whole power structure sitting up on the platform in front of the room," she said.[38] In April CUFAW won the five-month battle, and students no longer had to pay the fifteen cents for lunch.[39]

Confronting the "power structure" was not always easy for Craig, however. One of the first ERAP welfare rights demonstrations in Cleveland took place outside the downtown Sheraton Hotel, where the governor of Ohio was to appear. Craig got into an argument with a man there who believed the popular myth that welfare mothers purposely had additional children in order to receive higher benefits.

> The man talked about sterilizing welfare mothers, and I told him that I would be willing to be sterilized if every woman on any kind of assistance—unemployment, Social Security, etc.—was also sterilized. The man said, "But those are only temporary kinds of assistance." I answered, "So is welfare." The experience shook me up so bad that after he went in I gave my sign to Charlotte [Phillips, an ERAP organizer] and just started crying.[40]

In the face of harsh personal attacks, Craig's newfound self-confidence wavered, but she gradually became more comfortable with challenging the stereotype of welfare recipients as "dumb, lazy, alcoholic, pregnant, immature."[41]

Dovie Thurman found that speaking out could make her vulnerable as well. In January 1966 she testified for the second time before the Legislative Advisory Committee on Public Aid for the state of Illinois. "I'm here because of the laws you made about rent ceilings and budget levels, which are impossible to live under," she began. "I'm here also to tell you how welfare operates to take away my rights as an American citizen."[42] Thurman repeated the testimony she had given during her first appearance before the committee about how difficult it was to manage financially on a monthly rent budget of $104.15 when her rent was $110. Then she detailed the harassment she had endured at the hands of the welfare department in the intervening time: She had been told her to find a less expensive apartment or have her benefits reduced. "I think my caseworker is using me as an example of how welfare recipients should never question the welfare department or take their problems to the legislative committee when they feel they are being treated unfairly. Welfare is trying to punish me for complaining to you that the budgets welfare recipients are forced to live on are much too low."[43]

For Dovie Thurman and Lillian Craig, participation in ERAP's welfare rights activism demanded courage and resiliency; public speaking and political organizing left them both empowered and exposed. Even so, both women emphasized the power and positive outcomes of their activism. Both described their ERAP participation as "exciting." "There was a lot of excitement and it felt good, because you'd been told by the Welfare Department you're just a piece of shit," Craig recalled. "And then getting to see something coming up, seeing your kids have a new jacket. It's one thing to demonstrate for the sake of demonstration but it's another thing [when] the mothers won something."[44] Thurman, too, recalled instances of solidarity, organization, and accomplishment.

> Back in Chicago, they wanted to put me out of the apartment because we had too many "undesirables" coming to my house, all these hippies. I was organizing these white kids, too. And the hillbillies, as they called themselves. All these folks are not supposed to get along, right? They were all walking together, saying they couldn't put us out. They raised so much Cain, marching around the building, the news media came out, until they sent an apology letter.[45]

Within a national political context of civil rights and anti-poverty efforts, Thurman and Craig discovered through their activism how individual problems could be linked to a broader set of concerns and successfully targeted.

They also expanded their organizing skills and political knowledge, for which they credited ERAP organizers. Public speaking became "easy" for Thurman, and running meetings, writing petitions, and organizing marches or pickets became familiar. Craig felt she had received "good basic training" from ERAP. "You have skills that you don't know about," she said. "I had learned that I could do things." Their testimony demonstrated the importance of people's speaking for themselves, one of the aims of building grassroots leadership in ERAP, and their activism helped introduce a broader political vocabulary, "chairperson" and "takeover" for example.[46]

ERAP's emphasis on the connection between individual grievances and the structural roots of economic inequality expanded the political consciousness of both Lillian Craig and Dovie Thurman. The aim, according to SDS leader Todd Gitlin, "was to demonstrate that problems were not personal but rather systemic and historical."[47] This kind of educational effort was time-consuming, but "listening to people's problems, their ideas, their fears, their aspirations," was necessary in order for ERAP organizers to encourage a broader perspective.[48] Craig wrote later that "SDS sharpened my already burgeoning ability to view my experiences in a political and analytic framework."[49] Thurman's involvement in the Chicago project likewise prompted her to think in new ways, with new categories of analysis. "I wasn't thinking on the race side. My thoughts were on the poor versus the rich. I began to learn about class."[50]

ERAP was a turning point for Lillian Craig and Dovie Thurman. Through political participation, they began to confront, and to demand respect from, people and institutions that condemned them as lazy, undeserving welfare recipients. Gradually they gained the confidence, skills, and knowledge to change their lives, and they helped to redefine the relationship of welfare recipients to the welfare system from one of stigma and powerlessness to one of citizenship and entitlement.[51] For these two women, involvement with ERAP meant both personal and political transformation. "Politics," according to SDS's 1962 *Port Huron Statement*, "has the function of bringing people out of isolation and into community, thus being a necessary, though not sufficient, means of finding meaning in personal life." Dovie Thurman and Lillian Craig embodied this message.

Conflict and Negotiation

I think all women tend to do and say what's expected of us—not just when we're politically involved. I think I've grown up enough now, though, that I no longer have to do things as expected. —Lillian Craig[52]

They were southern whites, who didn't like blacks at all. I was surprised when they applauded. They were surprised, too. They invited us to come back again. —Dovie Thurman[53]

Dovie Thurman and Lillian Craig helped organize their communities across racial and class barriers. The predominantly middle-class ERAP organizers who came into Cleveland, Chicago, and other cities, saw themselves as catalysts in building "an interracial movement of the poor." The real agents of social change were the black and white Americans who lived in America's poor and working-class neighborhoods. "The elimination of poverty, we think, requires the mobilization of all the power of the 75 or 100 million Americans who suffer it or suffer over it," wrote Carl Wittman and Tom Hayden in their position paper for ERAP.[54] The task was to build interracial solidarity by demonstrating to poor people, both black and white, that they held similar economic positions and therefore had common interests. "Their common consciousness of poverty and economic superfluousness will ultimately have to bring them together," asserted Hayden and Wittman.[55] With ERAP, Lillian Craig and Dovie Thurman committed themselves to cross-race organizing and to working with middle-class New Left activists.

Initially, both women were uncomfortable with idea of interracial organizing. As Dovie Thurman said of her first ERAP meeting, "I walked in and saw this smoky room. I will never forget. A group of people was sitting around, but I didn't see nobody black there. We hesitated. It was me and my aunt. 'Do you think it's all right to go in?' I wasn't used to being around all those white people."[56] Lillian Craig had the same experience when she joined the Cleveland project: "It was scary. I had never been around groups of black people. I didn't even know how to express my fear of blacks."[57]

Through ERAP, however, both women changed their views about race. ERAP organizers sought to transcend racial and ethnic divisions by creating an environment in which people of different backgrounds could meet and learn about each other. "This technique," according to one ERAP proposal, "rests on the assumption that . . . consciousness and imagination can be broadened by structured discussion with people . . . doing similar work."[58] This assumption fit with "the belief that the oppressed themselves, collectively, already have much of the knowledge needed to produce change," a position advocated by Myles Horton at Highlander Folk School and adopted by civil rights activists such as Ella Baker.[59] It also informed ERAP's two community conferences, in Cleveland in February 1965 and in Newark in August 1965, which brought together guests such as SNCC activist Fannie Lou Hamer and participants from all the ERAP projects to discuss the problems and significance of organizing across racial lines. Blacks met whites who were poor and on welfare, and were able to see that poverty was not only racial but systemic.[60] For whites, cooperating in an organization with African Americans and Latinos would, according to Chicago organizer Richard Rothstein, "change whatever racism exists, in the long run."[61] Of course, the strong interracial commitment probably kept the most hardened racists away from ERAP, but undoubtedly racial barriers were broken down on both sides, and racist views amended through exposure to each other.

Lillian Craig and Dovie Thurman were among the many community residents who committed themselves to an interracial movement. "That's one of the things I liked about the group," Thurman recalled. "I found out that poor white people ate like poor black people. They eat greens, they eat chitlins, they eat grits. We found out they were living in some worse apartments than we were."[62] The Cleveland Community Conference in February 1965 inspired Craig to declare that "poverty does not choose its colors." "By accepting participants of the Conference for themselves, we could then focus on the basic problems we all face, Poverty!"[63] Importantly, community participants like Thurman and Craig also used religious belief and language to express their commonality with all impoverished Americans. For example, Lillian Craig often spoke of the need for "an interracial and *interfaith* organization of the poor."[64]

But not all ERAP participants became enlightened on this score. Organizers reported numerous instances of white racism in the ERAP projects. In Cleveland, for example, the racism of Near West Side residents was fueled by a "backlash" attitude against the civil rights movement, and they believed "that the National Association for the Advancement of White People [was] their group, or, as they put it, 'for us whites.'"[65] Thurman herself pointed out that she and her aunt were welcomed by white members of the Chicago project because they were women. "If we had been men, they would never have accepted us," she believed.[66] Moreover, the rise of black power and militant separatism after 1965 encouraged black community residents like Thurman to identify along the lines of race and ethnicity. Community participants, one SDS member wrote, did not think of themselves as "poor," but "as a Negro who is poor or a Hillbilly who is poor."[67] As it turned out, ERAP's integrationist stance was out of step with changing ideas about race and politics in the mid-1960s.

Similarly, ERAP's understanding of middle-class activists as catalysts for social change in poor neighborhoods became increasingly controversial over the course of the decade. At first, Lillian Craig and Dovie Thurman appreciated the presence of middle-class ERAP organizers in their neighborhoods. ERAP brought resources and attention to the Near West Side and Uptown. Its commitment to organizing from the bottom up also helped, because it demonstrated a commitment to grassroots democracy.[68] As Craig recalled: "I felt so much older than those SDS kids . . . and I was only two years older than Sharon [Jeffrey]. But in many ways I *was* older. . . . They were book-wise and common sense foolish. They didn't have the 'mother wit' that I had learned from my mother. . . . They used to ask my advice and that made me feel good because I still thought, most of the time, that all I was good for was cooking supper and raising kids."[69] For Thurman, contact with ERAP organizers led to other opportunities. "I used to sit in on [veteran community organizer] Saul Alinsky's classes," she reminisced. "We began to meet other people from across the city. I began to seek more education. Me and Big Dovie were really eating up this knowledge."[70]

Even with bottom-up leadership and direction like that provided by Craig and Thurman, entire areas of practice and decision making had remained under the purview of middle-class ERAP staff. Craig often felt that she was "programmed" by project staff and that she did what was expected of her rather than direct her own actions. Organizers were far more knowledgeable than community leaders about the day-to-day running of the ERAP projects, especially fund-raising and finances.[71] To rectify this imbalance, organizers decided to involve community members more closely in the running of the projects by bringing them on as paid staff—a decision that created further complications and misunderstandings.

For one thing, ERAP organizers were often disappointed when community staff did not meet their expectations of work and responsibility. Most community staff members were women who also had households to run and children to raise, and Craig and Thurman were no exception. Both women eventually took paid staff positions with ERAP, but ERAP organizers had a hard time making room in their abstract definition of a "leader" for a working mother. The Chicago project had difficulty assigning work to community staff that was "suitable to their capabilities and to the time they can devote to community work," while in Cleveland organizers argued that few neighborhood women could make "the kind of ongoing commitment to the organization required from a leadership person."[72] In this way ERAP organizers demonstrated the limits of their understanding of the lives and practical realities of ERAP's community participants.[73]

At the same time, community staff members like Craig and Thurman were not immune to the desire for power and control.[74] When Craig felt she was doing more than her fair share of work, she lost her temper. According to Sharon Jeffrey, at one meeting Craig "began by screaming out at those who claim to belong to CUFAW but who do no work. She blasted away for about a half an hour." As a result of all the attention Craig was beginning to get, her sense of self-importance grew. Meanwhile, according to Jeffrey, "others in the organization begin to feel more and more separated from her and thus she becomes disliked."[75] In Chicago, when Thurman's aunt felt she was not getting her way, she would yell, "I quit!" ERAP organizers would then have to appease her.[76] Community staff knew that ERAP needed them, and sometimes they exploited the power this gave them.

Over time, these class differences between outside ERAP staff and community residents grew, and racial tensions were also exacerbated, with the result that ERAP projects were disbanded. By 1967 charges of "elitism" and "manipulation" began to be directed at ERAP, while solidarity among community participants was increasingly defined in terms of race. Riots in Cleveland in 1966 and in Newark in 1967 signaled the end of ERAP's efforts in African American communities. The riots, as Tom Hayden put it, "exhausted the dreams of the early sixties and climaxed the period of [ERAP's] vitality."[77] In the spring of 1967, neighborhood women like Dovie Thurman left the Chicago project to form their own welfare rights group, Welfare Recipients Demand Action (WRDA). In January 1968 community participants asked organizers to pull out of the Chicago project altogether. The last remaining ERAP project had ended.[78]

ERAP's work in the neighborhoods of Cleveland, Chicago, and other American cities was marked by both failure and success. The "interracial movement of the poor" certainly never materialized, and ERAP's self-appointed role as a catalyst for social change in poor communities led to much anger and resentment. Even so, ERAP's attempt to challenge the barriers of class and race in America was important and not without its achievements. At the very least, ERAP changed many individual lives. Lillian Craig and Dovie Thurman remained committed to both political activism and interracial cooperation for the rest of their lives, a commitment reflected in the WRDA and elsewhere. And although community participants and ERAP organizers eventually parted ways, together, for a brief historical moment, they achieved a sense of community that bridged class differences. When asked what summed up "the sixties" for her, Craig said, "Excitement. And a sense of belonging. The country music song 'May the Circle Be Unbroken' reminds me of those years."[79]

After ERAP

When they left . . . I felt disillusioned. "How *could* they—they get me all involved, and then they go." I resented their mobility. —Lillian Craig[80]

By then I had converted to my Afro and my dashiki and my wire-rimmed glasses. I was Right On, Sister, all the way there. [*Laughs.*] I am a little different now, but I had to get my black identification then. —Dovie Thurman[81]

As ERAP projects disbanded, community leaders like Craig and Thurman found their way into local social welfare agencies, city governments, and political organizations. That they persisted in their activism after ERAP's demise testifies to the strength of their commitment and what they had learned by working in the Cleveland and Chicago projects. Of course ERAP's victories were very modest in comparison with its goals. The intransigence of city officials and the erosion of funding and support for the War on Poverty undermined the projects' efforts. In fighting inner-city poverty, "we were resisting large demographic and economic forces that proved too strong to withstand," Stanley Aronowitz concluded.[82]

But Dovie Thurman and Lillian Craig continued to fight. When ERAP organizers first drifted away from Cleveland, Lillian Craig recalled, "I thought, 'Why should I stay involved? Why should I even bother?' But then something good would always happen."[83] Craig held a series of community-based social service jobs in the late 1960s and 1970s. "For me, work is very good," she said. "The ideal is to have a job you feel good about, and where payday means something."[84] She worked with youth and in a lead-poisoning and environmental education program until she was chosen to direct Cleveland's new Near West Side Multi-Service Center in 1976, where she felt she could use her skills and philosophy. "Phenomenal" was the description applied to her accomplishments at the center.[85]

Craig gradually came to identify more publicly with women, although not necessarily with feminism. She was "not one of your women's libbers," as she put it. Yet she was very concerned about finding a way to shelter battered women in Cleveland, and she proposed that local feminists "get a house—a place where [women] can go to get away from the men who are beating them and their children."[86] And when she began to collaborate on her memoirs with her friend Marge Grevatt, she wanted her story to be a gift to "the ordinary women" of the world. "The audience," she said, "should be the woman who says 'I'm just a woman,' or 'I'm just a welfare mother,' or 'I'm just a housewife.'" She believed she was an ordinary woman who had found meaning in her life through politics and community activism. "Women must see that if I could do it, any woman can."[87]

Dovie Thurman gravitated toward civil rights organizing and black identity politics. She met Martin Luther King Jr. while she was a leader of the Chicago project, and she and her aunt soon began to work as welfare rights organizers for the Southern Christian Leadership Conference. They established welfare rights groups on Chicago's South Side, and Thurman traveled to Birmingham, Alabama, where she initiated the city's first welfare rights march. "They had them dogs out, and the fire trucks. I had never been exposed to that before, and let me tell you I was scared. But I called myself bad: 'I'll die fighting; you can kill me, but you can't eat me.' Right on! [Laughs]." Later on she organized tenants in Chicago.[88]

Thurman also started to express her black cultural identity in her appearance, dress, and hairstyle, and she briefly adopted a black separatist stance after King's assassination in 1968. "This is when I went into my supermilitant thing. I'm sick of white people. . . . I just broke loose from all my white friends. I didn't want to see them, I didn't want to talk to them. . . . It took me three, four months before I could get myself reorganized," she recalled. "Then I had to begin all over again, do some soul-searching of my own. I hated not talking to my friends, 'cause we went through a lot together. I had to cool it and take a little break."[89]

By the 1980s Dovie Thurman had become a Christian evangelist. "I am not into organizing anymore. . . . I got called to the ministry." As a young woman, she had always considered herself a Baptist, but she was never really "living it." Significantly, Thurman attributed her new religiosity to frustration and a sense of failure with political activism. "I had marched and demonstrated and protested so long, taking thousands and thousands of people to Washington, D.C., and we don't get heard. They act like we ain't even there. And things is getting worse and worse. There's gotta be something else."[90] Thurman shared the political pessimism that afflicted progressives during the Reagan-Bush years; for her, the source of social change shifted from politics to religion.

Over time, both Thurman and Craig began to experience severe health problems. Their ill health revealed both the physical costs of poverty and the failure of the U.S. health care system to meet the needs of poor Americans. "I had done so much marching and demonstrating, I wore my heart valve out," asserted Thurman. "I ended up having open-heart surgery twice. Thank God, I'm okay now. I just don't get overexerted. I've slowed down completely."[91] Craig had lived her entire life in poor health. She suffered from asthma, eye difficulties, and gall bladder problems. During gall bladder surgery, physicians discovered that she had an inoperable type of cancer. "I've never been a quitter and I don't want my kids to think of me as a quitter, but in this battle you can't win."[92] In late 1979—two days after she organized a food drive and took part in a demonstration protesting patient abuse at a nursing home—Lillian Craig died.

In the end, both women articulated philosophies that supported their political activism. Craig believed that she had lived according to the maxim that "we are all responsible for other people's lives. We hold their lives in our hands." She tried to be a "friend to people." "If I hadn't lived like that, I would not have meant anything to myself."[93] Thurman's political experiences and strong Christian faith shaped her outlook. "I don't even look at race anymore. Color of skin doesn't make a person good or bad.

Dr. King saw that. I'm looking for the inner, not the outer. In the end we are all going to be together one way or the other. We will all be in heaven together or in hell. How are you going to get separated then? At the end, people won't win when they're separated here on earth or up there. Or down there."[94] Dovie Thurman and Lillian Craig's ongoing commitment to social and economic justice is part of ERAP's legacy.

Participants at the time believed, and scholars since agree, that SDS's experiment in community organizing was a short-lived, failed attempt to build a social movement of poor Americans. Yet, as a story of large defeats and small victories, ERAP fits with the larger history of twentieth-century neighborhood organizing. According to historians Neil Betten and Michael J. Austin, limited achievements have always been the rule for community organizing efforts.[95] In fact, if community organizing is understood as the slow, undramatic process of helping people develop their powers, then ERAP succeeded with at least a few community residents.[96] For Craig, Thurman, and a handful of others, participation in ERAP was a transformational experience, politically and personally. Community organizing projects of the 1960s created opportunities for such people to develop confidence, skills, and experience, and provided a spur to political activism and a means of upward mobility.

ERAP was also an important moment in the history of the New Left in the 1960s, as the stories of Lillian Craig and Dovie Thurman reveal. If ERAP represented SDS's dedication to social change and participatory democracy, Thurman and Craig, along with other community participants, helped to realize those goals, if only for a time. They spurred mostly white, middle-class organizers to expand their definitions of "the political" to incorporate new constituencies and new issues. And, as we have seen, they continued their political activism into the 1970s and 1980s, long after both ERAP and SDS were history. For Thurman and Craig, participation in the struggles of the New Left was a beginning, not the end, of the search for democracy and justice.

Notes

1. This phrase is taken from the position paper that laid out the rationale and strategy for SDS's community organizing. Carl Wittman and Tom Hayden, "An Interracial Movement of the Poor?" SDS pamphlet, [1964].

2. Sara Evans, *Personal Politics: The Roots of Women's Liberation in the Civil Rights Movement and the New Left* (New York: Knopf, 1979), 148–49, 154–55.

3. Todd Gitlin, *The Sixties: Years of Hope, Days of Rage* (New York: Bantam Books, 1987), 367.

4. Milton Viorst, *Fire in the Streets: America in the 1960s* (New York: Simon and Schuster, 1979), 394.

5. For a similar critique of scholarship on SDS, see Maurice Isserman, "The Not-So-Dark and Bloody Ground: New Works on the 1960s," *American Historical Review* 94 (1989): 990–1010.

6. Alessandro Portelli, "Philosophy and the Facts: Subjectivity and Narrative Form in Autobiography and Oral History," in Alessandro Portelli, *The Battle of Valle Giulia: Oral History and the Art of Dialogue* (Madison: University of Wisconsin Press, 1997), 88.

7. Lillian Craig, with Marge Grevatt, *Just a Woman: Memoirs of Lillian Craig* (Cleveland: Orange Blossom Press, 1981), 12, 17.

8. Dovie Thurman quoted in Studs Terkel, *Race: How Blacks and Whites Think and Feel about the American Obsession* (New York: New Press, 1992), 57.

9. John H. Mollenkopf, *The Contested City* (Princeton: Princeton University Press, 1983), 93; Jon C. Teaford, *The Rough Road to Renaissance: Urban Revitalization in America, 1940–1985* (Baltimore: Johns Hopkins University Press, 1990), 5.

10. Thomas F. Campbell, "Cleveland: The Struggle for Stability," in *Snowbelt Cities: Metropolitan Politics in the Northeast and Midwest since World War II,* ed. Richard M. Bernard (Bloomington: Indiana University Press, 1990), 111, 114, 119.

11. Sharon Jeffrey, "Prospectus for the Cleveland Community Project," [1964], 1; Students for a Democratic Society Records, 1958–1970, State Historical Society of Wisconsin, series 2B [hereafter SDS-2B], box 25, folder 4; Cleveland Fundraising Prospectus, [1965], 4; SDS-2B, box 17, folder 2.

12. Rich Rothstein quoted in "Chicago: JOIN Project," *Studies on the Left* 5 (1965), 111–12.

13. Jacqueline Jones, "Southern Diaspora: Origins of the Northern 'Underclass,'" in *The "Underclass" Debate: Views from History,* ed. Michael B. Katz (Princeton: Princeton University Press, 1993), 42; Todd Gitlin and Nanci Hollander, *Uptown: Poor Whites in Chicago* (New York: Harper and Row, 1970).

14. Anne Thureson to advisory committee, 14 Jan. 1965, SDS-2B, box 19, folder 5.

15. In 1960 Uptown's Latino and African American residents together constituted less than 2 percent of the total population. By 1970 they had risen to 13 percent and 4 percent respectively. Chicago Fact Book Consortium, *Local Community Factbook: Chicago Metropolitan Area, 1980;* Richard Rothstein to Peter Freedman, 22 Nov. 1964, SDS-2B, box 19, folder 1.

16. Craig, *Just a Woman,* 11–12.

17. Thurman quoted in Terkel, *Race,* 57.

18. See Michael B. Katz, "Reframing the 'Underclass' Debate," in *The "Underclass" Debate: Views from History,* ed. Michael B. Katz (Princeton: Princeton University Press, 1993), 172.

19. Cathy Wilkerson, "Rats, Washtubs, and Block Organizations," SDS pamphlet, [1964], 3–5, Lee D. Webb Papers, 1955–68, State Historical Society of Wisconsin, Madison, box 1, folder 6a; Evans, *Personal Politics,* 141.

20. Joan Bradbury, Sharon Jeffrey, and Oliver Fein, "The Cleveland Welfare System," [Aug. 1964], SDS-2B, box 25, folder 1; Statement of Dovie Thurman before the Legislative Advisory Committee on Public Aid, 9 Jan. 1966, SDS-2B, box 21, folder 5 [hereafter "Statement of Dovie Thurman"].

21. Thurman, quoted in Terkel, *Race,* 57.

22. Craig, *Just a Woman,* 26, 12.

23. Ibid., 31.

24. Charles M. Payne, *I've Got the Light of Freedom: The Organizing Tradition and the Mississippi Freedom Struggle* (Berkeley: University of California Press, 1995), 331.

25. Craig, *Just a Woman,* 16, 27.

26. Evans, *Personal Politics,* 141.

27. Ann Bookman and Sandra Morgen, eds., *Women and the Politics of Empowerment* (Philadelphia: Temple University Press, 1988); Guida West and Rhoda Lois Blumberg, "Reconstructing Social Protest from a Feminist Perspective," in *Women and Social Protest,* ed. Guida West and Rhoda Lois Blumberg (New York: Oxford University Press, 1990), 3–35.

28. Craig, *Just a Woman,* 27.

29. Evans, *Personal Politics,* 140.

30. Dick Flacks, "Organizing the Unemployed: The Chicago Project," 7 April 1964, 1, SDS-2B, box 21, folder 8.

31. Kim Moody, "ERAP, Ideology, and Social Change" [1964–65], 2, SDS-2B, box 22, folder 13.

32. Casey Hayden, "Notes on Organizing Poor Southern Whites," *ERAP Newsletter* (27 Aug. 1965), 8.

33. Thurman quoted in Terkel, *Race,* 58.

34. Craig, *Just a Woman,* 39.

35. Thurman quoted in Terkel, *Race,* 60.

36. Craig, *Just a Woman,* 19; "Cleveland Report," *ERAP Newsletter* (19–29 Oct. 1964).

37. "Cleveland Report," (19 Nov. 1964 and 27 Jan. 1965), SDS-2B, box 15, folder 5; Elaine Maramick to Pat [Hammond], reprinted in *ERAP Newsletter* (16–23 Nov. 1964); Dorothy Hammer to Ralph McAllister, 18 Feb. 1965, reprinted in *ERAP Newsletter* (4 March 1965).

38. Lillian Craig, "The Power of the Few," in *CUFAW Speaks for Itself* (Feb. 1965), pamphlet, Carol McEldowney Papers, 1964–68, State Historical Society of Wisconsin, Madison.

39. "Cleveland Report," *ERAP Newsletter* (1 April 1965).

40. Craig, *Just a Woman,* 18.

41. Ibid., 43.

42. Statement of Dovie Thurman; JOIN, "Press Release," 22 Dec. 1965, SDS-2B, box 21, folder 5.

43. Statement of Dovie Thurman.

44. Craig, *Just a Woman,* 42.

45. Thurman quoted in Terkel, *Race,* 60–61.

46. Craig, *Just a Woman,* 33.

47. Todd Gitlin, "On Organizing the Poor in America," *New Left Notes* (23 Dec. 1966); Tom Hayden, *Reunion: A Memoir* (New York: Random House, 1988), 131. See also Lily Venson, "Defend 'Good Work' of JOIN," news clipping (7 July 1965), SDS-2B, box 19, folder 6.

48. Cleveland project staff to applicant, 23 April 1965, SDS-2B, box 24, folder 6. Saul Alinsky pursued precisely the same aim in his community organizing. See Alan S. Miller, "Saul Alinsky: America's Radical Reactionary," *Radical America* 21 (1987), 13.

49. Craig, *Just a Woman,* 17.

50. Thurman quoted in Terkel, *Race,* 60.

51. Barbara J. Nelson, "Help-Seeking from Public Authorities: Who Arrives at the Agency Door?" *Policy Studies* 12 (1980): 175–92; Linda Gordon, "What Does Welfare Regulate?" *Social Research* 55 (1988): 609–30.

52. Craig, *Just a Woman,* 32.

53. Thurman quoted in Terkel, *Race,* 58.

54. Wittman and Hayden, "An Interracial Movement of the Poor?" 26, 21.

55. Ibid., 7–8.

56. Thurman quoted in Terkel, *Race,* 58.

57. Craig, *Just a Woman,* 17.

58. Cleveland ERAP, "Poverty and Community Movements," prospectus for People's Community Conference, Dec. 1964, SDS-2B, box 17, folder 2.

59. Payne, *I've Got the Light of Freedom,* 70–71.

60. Allen W. Batteau, *The Invention of Appalachia* (Tucson: University of Arizona Press, 1990), 7–8.

61. Richard Rothstein to Dorothy Burlage, 22 March 1965, SDS-2B, box 19, folder 4.

62. Thurman quoted in Terkel, *Race*, 59.

63. Lillian Craig, "Community People's Conference," *ERAP Newsletter* (25 Feb. 1965).

64. Ibid.

65. "Cleveland Report" [2 Aug. 1964], SDS-2B, box 15, folder 5.

66. Thurman quoted in Terkel, *Race*, 58.

67. "Parallel Organizing: An Alternative to the 'Interracial Movement of the Poor,'" SDS-3, box 46, folder 8.

68. Edward P. Morgan, *The 60s Experience: Hard Lessons about Modern America* (Philadelphia: Temple University Press, 1991), 99; James Miller, *"Democracy Is in the Streets": From Port Huron to the Siege of Chicago* (New York: Simon and Schuster, 1987), 147.

69. Craig, *Just a Woman*, 31.

70. Thurman quoted in Terkel, *Race*, 60.

71. Marya Levenson to members of MAW, reprinted in *ERAP Newsletter* (17 Jan. 1966); Carol McEldowney to Mike Miller, 9 Feb. 1965, SDS-2B, box 24, folder 8; Miller, *"Democracy Is in the Streets,"* 209.

72. "JOIN Proposal" [1965], SDS-3, box 46, folder 2; "Cleveland Report" (23 July 1964), SDS-2B, box 15, folder 5.

73. For similar conclusions, see Gary Delgado, *Organizing the Movement: The Roots and Growth of ACORN* (Philadelphia: Temple University Press, 1986), 193, 197.

74. Paul Bullock, "Morality and Tactics in Community Organizing," in *Poverty: Views from the Left,* ed. Jeremy Larner and Irving Howe (New York: William Morrow, 1968), 142.

75. Sharon Jeffrey, "CUFAW Meeting Report," 12 Oct. [1964], SDS-2B, box 25, folder 2; Sharon Jeffrey to Rennie Davis [Aug. 1964], SDS-2B, box 24, folder 5.

76. Steve Goldsmith, interview by author, 18 Feb. 1993.

77. Hayden, *Reunion*, 153, 160–61.

78. Peggy Terry, "JOIN/NCU to End Rumors," *New Left Notes* (26 Feb. 1968), 5, 8.

79. Craig, *Just a Woman*, 45.

80. Ibid., 33.

81. Thurman quoted in Terkel, *Race*, 60–61.

82. Stanley Aronowitz, "When the New Left Was New," in *The '60s without Apology*, ed. Sohnya Sayres et al. (Minneapolis: University of Minnesota Press, 1984), 22–23.

83. Craig, *Just a Woman*, 33.

84. Ibid., 57.

85. Marge Grevatt quoted in Craig, *Just a Woman*, 20–22.

86. Lillian Craig quoted in Margaret Grevatt, "Sisters to the Dispossessed," *Affilia: Journal of Women and Social Work* 2 (1987): 67.

87. Craig, *Just a Woman*, 8.

88. Thurman quoted in Terkel, *Race*, 60.

89. Ibid., 60–61.

90. Ibid., 62.

91. Ibid., 62.

92. Craig, *Just a Woman*, 22.

93. Ibid., 55.

94. Thurman quoted in Terkel, *Race*, 63.

95. Neil Betten and Michael J. Austin, "The Cincinnati Unit Experiment, 1917–1920," in *The Roots of Community Organizing,* ed. Neil Betten and Michael J. Austin (Philadelphia: Temple University Press, 1990), 35.

96. Payne, *I've Got the Light of Freedom,* 306.

CHAPTER 6

Death City Radicals: The Counterculture in Los Angeles

David McBride

In 1964 Art Kunkin, a former New York machinist and longtime member of the Congress for Racial Equality (CORE), launched the *Los Angeles Free Press* from offices located in the heart of the city's coalescing hippie bohemia, Sunset Strip. Partly because of its location, the *Free Press*—which later became the most widely circulated underground paper in the nation—devoted extensive coverage to "freak" and bohemian issues from its inception. In 1965, however, the paper's coverage of the Watts riots was better than any other local paper's, including that of the *Los Angeles Times*.[1] In retrospect, Kunkin claimed that the Watts riot had made his paper: "Watts proved that this was a serious paper, not a sheet about Happenings attended by two hundred people." Now, Kunkin thought, he had some credibility.[2] The "*Freep*" would still be a landmark countercultural paper, but it had also become an important champion of a key New Left issue.

Not long afterward, in 1966, Frank Zappa's Mothers of Invention released their first album, *Freak Out!* An outrageous, gaudy, psychedelicized hodgepodge replete with jarring dissonance, camped-up pop art, and the odd anthem to groupies, the album nonetheless revealed the hybrid nature of 1960s radicalism. Zappa himself was one of the most important figures working within the vast milieu of hip Los Angeles; the "freak-outs" he organized in 1966 drew thousands, and he was regarded by the local underground press as perhaps the most sage commentator on the state of the perpetually transforming "scene." His first album displayed elements we typically associate with the more exuberant varieties of that era's political radicalism—although it was certainly an ur-freak text as well. The album's opener, "Hungry Freaks, Daddy," lashed out (through an ironic quote of a Rolling Stones riff) at a banal, soul-crushing "Mr. America," reminding him that "the emptiness that's you inside, will not forestall the rising tide of hungry freaks, daddy!" This confrontational—if decidedly vague—attack on an allegedly inauthentic mainstream was not the only countercultural manifesto that veered into New Left terrain; "Trouble Comin' Everyday" described, over a rumbling fuzz-toned riff, Zappa's feelings as he sat glued to the television set watching the Watts riots.[3]

Memories of Radicalism and 1960s Los Angeles

The rise of the *Free Press* and the release of *Freak Out!*—both of which occurred relatively early in the trajectory of "the sixties" as an era of mass youth radicalism—showed that in Los Angeles, at least, political and aesthetic radicalism in everyday life meshed considerably. In other words, the familiar argument that the counterculture and the New Left were distinct entities (at least before New Leftists succumbed to the pleasures of pot, free love, and acid rock) cannot hold when applied to the admittedly unique Los Angeles region.[4] Of course, the questioning of this shaky divide is hardly new; many historians, including Alice Echols, Doug Rossinow, and Julie Stephens have recently challenged this rigid separation between radical culture and radical politics in the 1960s.[5]

Yet the case of Los Angeles throws the flaws of this model into starker relief than would, say, Austin or San Francisco. At the most basic level, radicals in the nerve center of mass culture felt compelled to treat cultural production as a fundamental concern. Also, the region's relative lack of a tightly knit, college-based Left meant that cultural and political radicals shared the same spaces and faced the same harassers from the mid-1960s onward. And historically, Los Angeles—unlike San Francisco, famously—did not possess much of a historical legacy of leftist radicalism, except for a few episodes; in fact, the region was famous for its right-wing tradition and apolitical anomie. Writing at the end of the 1960s, Michael Rogin and John Shover employed a close statistical, political, and psychological analysis to explain the remarkable popularity of Reagan and right-wing sentiment in southern California in the mid-1960s. Angelenos, they argued, were unable to imagine solutions for their problems outside the ideological parameters of right-wing individualism, racism, mass conformity, and law-and-order sentiment.[6]

Equally critical to Los Angeles's uniqueness was the omnipresence of the mass cultural production system, which critics held responsible for the fakery and shallowness of mainstream culture. To those trying to create a new, radicalized culture characterized by openness to experimentation, freedom from market dictates, and tolerance, the film, television, and music industries seemed omnipresent, injecting the debilitating tedium of the constant hustle into the "underground" zones of L.A. To many observers, the culture industries colored the character of the rest of the region as well, making it a strangely disorienting and inhuman place, without grounding in "real" life. And the area's seemingly endless, centerless suburban sprawl only enhanced the sense of weightlessness. In 1964 Theodore Roszak wrote in the *Free Press,* "There is perhaps no modern city where the sense of community is so dissipated as in Los Angeles. . . . It lacks even the physical integrity of a metropolis. . . . In reality, Los Angeles . . . is a case study in social disorganization . . . where the bonds of community life have grown hopelessly slack." Cribbing from Nathanael West, Phil Ochs offered an even more damning indictment in 1967: "Los Angeles is Death City. . . . It is the land of the Philistines. Los Angeles is the ultimate in the materialistic exaggeration of America. It's almost like the barbarians throwing themselves into the materialistic fires."[7]

Here, then, are some of the reasons why concerns over "culture"—the processes and contexts through which people receive and create meaning via their interactions with others and their environment—were such loaded issues in Los Angeles. Because they viewed their environs with such rancor, activists coming out of a leftist framework could not help but be animated by pleas to transform the culture. This did not mean that such people simply became hippies, however. New Leftists like Kunkin remained committed to the causes traditionally associated with the New Left—participatory democracy, racial justice, opposition to the Vietnam War, and so on. But the countervailing tendency to vilify the counterculture as misguided or dangerously quietist was simply less present in Los Angeles than in other major American cities. Students for a Democratic Society (SDS) had a presence in Los Angeles, of course; UCLA was an outpost, and both that school and San Fernando Valley State (later Cal State–Northridge) were quite tumultuous in the late 1960s.[8] Still, the brand of student radicalism we associate with Berkeley, New York, Madison, Austin, and Ann Arbor was much less visible in Los Angeles. White radicals for the most part occupied hip zones: Hollywood, Venice, and the city's canyons. Inevitably, such radicals had to intermix with the massive population of more aesthetically inclined radicals—the "freaks."

That brings us to Los Angeles hippies, or "freaks," themselves, who numbered in the scores of thousands by 1967. Some scholars have corrected the traditional view of the New Left/counterculture split by reformulating the "political" so that it encompasses the counterculture's "anti-disciplinary" politics.[9] Others, through careful social histories, have shown how the two formations converged to a point through their common enemies and common efforts to replace the "death culture" of corporate America. Rossinow's remarkable book *The Politics of Authenticity* is the most empirically extensive in this regard, although others recognized the phenomenon. Yet even Rossinow has determined that in Austin, at least, "the notion of an early united front between the new left and the counterculture was a myth. . . . The distances separating them were clear." Moreover, the usual tactic in studying this phenomenon has been to look at a couple of always-the-same locales—the San Francisco Bay area and Manhattan—and always-the-same activists—the San Francisco Diggers and the Yippies. Perhaps most tellingly, Rossinow, a student of the hinterlands who should know better, repeats the truism of New York and San Francisco's centrality, stating that in 1966 most of the underground papers in the country were located in those cities. Los Angeles, in fact, was as much a destination as the other two cities for youthful rebels and radicals.[10] It also possessed at least as many underground papers, including the *Free Press,* the *Open City,* the *Los Angeles Underground, Provo,* the *Oracle of Southern California,* and a host of others.

Doubtless, investigating the Diggers, the Yippies, Berkeley, the Haight, and the East Village tells us much about the era's radical politics. But Abbie Hoffman, Jerry Rubin,

Emmett Grogan, and the like were not the era's only important hip politicos, and rely-ing strictly on them gives us a curious portrait of America, one in which New York, San Francisco, and a couple of college towns are synecdoches for the rest of the nation, and mostly unconvincing ones at that.

In sum, focusing solely on these admittedly captivating figures and locales leaves us with a void. For if we believe that one of the most crucial stories of 1960s America was the mass culture industries' final envelopment of American popular culture, we need to account for it.[11] Moreover, the flip side of that story—the "massification" of bohemian themes, the summons to release oneself from all inhibitions manifesting itself through-out the circuitry of mass cultural production, the dissemination of (usually bowdlerized) radical themes in mass cultural texts—was most pronounced in Los Angeles. The effect was to magnify concerns among "tuned-in" residents about the authenticity of culture. The signs of co-optation were so ubiquitous in Los Angeles (and the agents of this pro-cess so shameless) that the issue captured the attention of local radicals throughout the period.[12]

My purpose is not simply to point out the need to look at other locales besides "the biggies" in order to further the cause of historical parochialism. Analyzing a gargantuan local hippie scene reaching close to one hundred thousand acolytes—some of whom were truly committed while others were, as one hip wag put it, "establishment finks in paisley"—who shared the same neighborhoods as "politicos" raises two compelling is-sues.[13] The first is the unusually high level of fraternization that occurred. The local strains of radicalism—political and cultural—both invested a great deal of energy in fo-menting an experimental "life" culture typified by shoestring book stores, underground rags, and communes. And because they lived and worked together so closely, the inter-sections where their paths crossed very often seemed muddy and indistinguishable. Typ-ically, local hippies and politicos advanced the same micro and macro political causes and defended the enclaves they mutually inhabited from encroachment by local au-thorities. In addition, because the local New Left was so concerned with cultural poli-tics, the split between it and hippies was much less evident than elsewhere.

The second issue is one of framing. If we accept at least a portion of Daniel Bell's con-tention that of all the 1960s movements, the counterculture proved the most influential, then perhaps we need to explore the demarcations within 1960s radicalism differently.[14] That is, it should be a productive exercise to frame the topic so as to highlight the de-gree to which the counterculture shaded into New Left territory rather than the reverse. Since the dominant historiographical approach is to look at the extent to which the New Left drank from the fountain of hip, refashioning the relationship by accentuating the counterculture makes the standard view problematical. As well, scrutinizing a place like Los Angeles, where cultural politics held such sway, should provide us with fruit-ful new paths in reevaluating 1960s radicalism.

Los Angeles was a radical lodestar for other reasons as well. No issue was so instru-mental in the development of 1960s radicalism as the battle for racial justice, a cause that went through a series of permutations throughout the 1950s and 1960s. While Harlem experienced a relatively small riot in 1964, the Watts riots signaled most clearly the arrival of "the fire next time." In the years following Watts, black and brown radi-calism in Los Angeles increased in intensity. By the end of the decade, Los Angeles—which was well on its way to becoming a prototypical polyglot city—had an increas-ingly racialized politics. It witnessed the emergence of both La Raza and a large local Black Panther chapter, and saw a series of violent conflagrations between the Los An-geles police department and minority activists.[15] I do not mean to suggest that Los An-geles was in any way unique with regard to racial conflict. But given the pervasive view among contemporaries that Los Angeles was not a serious place, it is hardly surprising that scholars and laypersons alike have tended to accept this cliché without delving fur-ther. And while the argument that the city as a social entity lacked *gravitas* due to its widespread anomie, its residents' refusal to acknowledge tragedy, and its privileging of images over "the real," certainly contains more than a grain of truth, it is an oversim-plification. Although the city was always peopled by non-Anglos in large numbers, the immigration act of 1965 and the subsequent waves of migrants have remade Los An-geles into one of the two most ethnically diverse megalopolises in the nation. Since the 1960s, in fact, it has been a place where identity politics, the claims of aggrieved mi-norities, and ethnic/racial pride are essential to the region's society, culture, and poli-tics.[16] The local variants of cultural and political radicalism served as important sup-ports—even as they were often scorned and ignored by local elites—in the 1960s, a period in which interest in and conflict over such issues increased dramatically.

The Rise of Countercultural Space: Hip Zones in 1960s Los Angeles

Before I return to the broader issues of race and authenticity, any discussion of the rad-icalism of the era has to locate it in its material context, particularly in urban space. Cul-tural and political radicalism were not simply free-floating clouds of signifiers—long hair, draft cards aflame, free love, Che-style machismo—detached from a physical base. Those histories that firmly embed the era's radicalism within a local social, political, and cultural context are almost invariably the most persuasive, partly because this method forces one to account for gray areas, overlap, and the more prosaic concerns of every-day participants.[17] Even if the counterculture and New Left in Los Angeles were ani-mated by national and international ideas and dilemmas, the battles they fought with authorities were almost always inflected by local concerns, and the most rancorous con-flicts were often regional in nature. Examining these clashes, especially ones over the shape and character of the city's urban space, reveals that the various forms of 1960s radicalism were not separable entities that commingled only infrequently but a loose, elastic, hip-politico agglomeration fused by local circumstance. Furthermore, the peri-odic sweeps of "underground" zones by local authorities engendered clearly "political" reactions from hippies, responses that were in the main "New Leftist" in tone.

In keeping with the metro area's sprawling nature, countercultural Los Angeles was relatively far flung, as hippies occupied a number of neighborhoods. The most important ones, however, were Hollywood and Venice, each of which drew tens of thousands of adherents over the course of the era.[18] There was a New Left presence in these enclaves as well. By 1966 Hollywood's Sunset Strip had become the center of Los Angeles's new youth bohemia, transforming it from a glittery icon of "old" Hollywood dotted by "sophisticated, expensive supper clubs" for the "mink and diamond set."[19] By the mid-1960s, "Hollywood's last sanctuary of chi-chi for the middle-aged" was no more. Instead, the region had become "a 3,000 yard thorn in the sides of those Los Angeles citizens who believe in decorum and haircuts," where one had to "buck a mob of beatniks for the pleasure of sitting down to a $50 dinner."[20] Thousands of freaks—outrageously dressed mod youths, pop artists, bikers, and bohemian holdovers from the 1950s—flooded the Strip every night to shop at the new stores that hawked hip paraphernalia, attend the numerous acid rock clubs and underground cinemas, buy drugs, or simply hang out on the streets. Adjacent areas—including the art gallery district on La Cienega Boulevard—experienced a similar influx. By mid-1966 the neighborhood was a hip zone.[21]

At the same time the zone became a haven for the local white New Left and its variants. Most significantly, in 1965, the *Free Press* located its office to the basement of the Fifth Estate, a notorious freak coffeehouse on the Strip. Owned by Al Mitchell—a forty-two-year-old divorcee, parent, World War II naval veteran, and orphan—the coffeehouse, which featured both European art films and impromptu folk guitar shows, became a central gathering point for cultural rebels. (Mitchell himself began his own short-lived paper in 1967, the *Los Angeles Underground*).[22] More than simply "the unofficial pied piper of youthful Sunset Strip habitues," as the *Los Angeles Herald Examiner* dubbed him, Mitchell espoused New Left causes.[23] Enraged by the LAPD's persistent harassment of hippies, Mitchell made a documentary film entitled *Blue Fascism*. And when organizing the widely publicized antipolice demonstrations by Strip hippies in late 1966, he stressed that "the demonstrations . . . were not just protests against the juvenile curfew law but were an attempt to focus community attention on a condition of police lawlessness, . . . brutality and gangsterism which plagues every Los Angeles minority including Negroes, Mexican-Americans, the poor, and the rebellious young."[24] In short, Mitchell moved easily between both milieus.

The Strip-based *Los Angeles Free Press* was essentially the local New Left paper, for all its countercultural bluster. As a source of information on racial injustice, SDS, local New Left schools, demonstrations, and antiwar activities, the *Freep* was authoritative. The *Open City*, a paper that lasted from May 1967 through early 1969 (when the publisher went bankrupt defending the paper from an obscenity charge), had a similar editorial style, but its estimated readership of thirty thousand paled in comparison to the one hundred thousand plus readers of the *Freep*.[25] What tends to be forgotten about these papers is just how much they were of the New Left and perceived themselves as such. While certainly eclectic enterprises, both the *Free Press* and the *Open City* paid equal attention to the concerns of hippies and "politicos," in large part because they were located at the epicenter of both populations.[26] As well as scooping the *Los Angeles Times* on two of the era's biggest stories—the Watts riots and the mid-1967 demonstration in Century City against Johnson's Vietnam policy—the *Freep* sponsored hip "happenings" and outdoor rock concerts on Venice beach.[27] It was also a boisterous advocate of underground film, rock, and drugs. The paper's work environment reflected its politics, with one visitor noticing in 1970 "kids, dogs, cats, barefoot waifs, teenyboppers in see-through blouses, assorted losers, [and] Indian chiefs wander[ing] in and out, while somewhere a radio plays endless rock music. . . . It's all ferociously informal."[28]

Venice, the poorest and most dilapidated of all Los Angeles communities abutting the ocean, had been a beat mecca in the fifties; it remained a radical and freak magnet afterward, even as it lost some of its boho luster to Hollywood. One of the Venice underground's most colorful figures, John Haag, was an enthusiastic organizer of demonstrations, a committed leftist, a vociferous advocate of experimental culture, and the owner of a landmark beat coffeehouse.[29] Like Mitchell, Haag straddled the countercultural and leftist provinces effortlessly. He led the local W.E.B. Du Bois club chapter, and was both a Wobbly enthusiast and an exponent of organic American socialism. Yet he also demonstrated on behalf of hippie protestors on Sunset Strip and organized Venice freaks against a police crackdown. And when an affluent local high school, with the LAPD's aid, clamped down on longhaired males in 1966, Haag and an assortment of "sandaled women from the Hollywood hangouts" rushed to the scene and demonstrated.[30]

Haag was both unique and curiously representative of Venice itself. While populated by bohemians and radicals of all hues, Venice also possessed a sizable black ghetto. Activists there were the most radical in Los Angeles, always viewing the city—and, more generally, "the establishment"—as a ruthless enemy. As we shall see, ongoing police harassment in combination with a city-approved attempt to redevelop Venice provoked solidarity across the community's radical spectrum.[31]

By mid-1967 certain of the city's neighborhoods had become underground zones, populated by a loose alliance of hippies and leftists (many more of the former, actually) numbering in the scores of thousands.[32] This vast expansion of the "turned-on" population had happened rather suddenly, and given the conservative political culture of the city—personified by its pugnacious, red-baiting mayor, Sam Yorty, as well as the notoriously intolerant LAPD—it was not hard to foresee trouble. Exhibitionist flair, demonstrative public behavior, and a brash experimentalism constituted the new tenor of these neighborhoods, and their facades were transformed accordingly within a two-year span. On the Strip, for example, an environment of transgressive libertarianism had replaced the "old Hollywood" edifice, which had suggested to all the power of wealth and exclusivity. Previously the area had possessed an intimidating figurative, if not literal, giganticism that complemented the mythic "great man" blockbuster films of the pre-1960s era. In effect, the old Strip's giganticist architecture "articulated" a spatial code proscribing certain types of people and behavior, and its physical and ideological constitution helped determine its constituency.[33] The new constellation of cultural and political radicalism, accompanied by the mushrooming shops and fly-by-night institutions that catered to it, invited a response.

According to Henri LeFebvre, the alteration of spatial codes constitutes a direct assault on an authority's power, which employs such codes to fix what is accepted and forbidden. The presence of two opposing cultural blocs led to what LeFebvre referred to as a "spatial duality," a situation of "contradiction and conflict" that "creates the strong impression that there exists a duality of political power."[34] The point here is that because hippies and politicos acted in concert to transform Hollywood and Venice into hospitable zones for experimentation and dissent, they appeared as a single, fixed target in the minds of authorities, who viewed the spatial metamorphoses with genuine alarm. In the resulting conflicts that occurred regularly from late 1966 onward, hippies and politicos worked together *despite* their clear differences on certain issues. To de-emphasize this pragmatic tactical alliance would be unwise, for it colored and animated everyday life. The effect of repression, in most cases, was—at least temporarily—radicalizing.

The first major clash over space, the nationally publicized Sunset Strip "riot" of late 1966, was at first simply a protest by youthful mods against the sudden police enforcement of a long-ignored curfew law.[35] Since by this point thousands of full-fledged hippies and less committed youths looking only for a good time were occupying the Strip nightly, the city felt compelled to act. Pressed by Strip establishments catering to an older, less flamboyant clientele, nightly arrests multiplied into the hundreds by mid-1966.[36] The Strip fell within two jurisdictions; part was in the city of Los Angeles while the rest was in an unincorporated section of Los Angeles County. Regardless of the partition, both city and county authorities sought to eradicate what one L.A. County supervisor called "the elements who would destroy the neighborhood by making the Sunset Strip the national headquarters for freaks, for delinquent juveniles or obscenity."[37] To be sure, crime on the Strip both minor and major skyrocketed in the mid-1960s, but the evidence suggests that a more basic revulsion against nonconformity was the impetus here.[38]

Although the riot generated both a camp B-movie (the 1967 AIP film *Riot on Sunset Strip*) and a hit rock song (Buffalo Springfield's "For What It's Worth"), it was a decidedly minor affair. As more than one thousand hip youths organized by Al Mitchell marched on behalf of hippie rights, a few scaled and vandalized two mass transit buses and hurled some rocks. That was about it, and damage was negligible.[39] Still, the hubbub initiated a wave of larger demonstrations over the next couple of months, some of them attracting a few thousand souls. The goal of the protests, at least initially, was to protect the right of free expression, which in this case meant the right of freaks to roam freely in a sophisticated, alternative consumption zone free from limits and custom.[40] Yet because the events transpired in a space populated by a range of dissenters, all of whom felt persecuted by "the fuzz," elements from all factions joined in. A *New Yorker* reporter noted that one protest included members of the W.E.B. Du Bois club, clergymen, and a motley assortment of "New Left radicals, Zen mystics, aesthetic avant-gardists, and drug proselytizers."[41] Indeed, the amalgamation was so apparent that the *New Yorker* reporter criticized the alleged dogma of the protestors, pointing to the "constellation that is long hair, bohemia, the New Left, individualism, sexual freedom, the

East, drugs, [and] the arts." In this case at least, isolating the sundry components of "the underground" was no easy task. That, I would argue, is because control over the city's physical terrain was the fundamental issue, and it naturally drew all sorts of radicals.

Protests continued into 1967, but by the end of January matters had been resolved in favor of the burgeoning counterculture. Basically, attempts to restrict access to the Strip had merely shuttled the same youths into other neighborhoods where they were tolerated even less.[42] After much negotiating between protest organizers and local officials, the county eased restrictions, and the Strip remained a bohemian haven. Al Mitchell was not content, however, with what he felt was a minor victory; to him the battle was part of a much larger cause to extend social justice to African Americans and Chicanos. For the final mid-February protest, he organized a series of simultaneous demonstrations on the Strip, in the budding gay district of Silverlake, in Venice, in Watts, and in East Los Angeles. While the turnout in Venice, East L.A., and Watts was negligible, the Strip and Silverlake protests attracted hundreds.

The event required a degree of organization for which Mitchell lacked the resources, and in any case Latinos and blacks were deeply suspicious of white hippies who spuriously ennobled poverty.[43] Still, here was a series of events that began over an issue affecting hippies—whether they could maintain their neighborhoods as freak zones—yet expanded to encompass issues animating the New Left, including racial and social justice as well as police brutality. As such, it upsets the standard tale: New Left activists demonstrating over a particular social or political injustice, only to be joined later by an enthusiastic but ill-informed, naive counterculture that diluted the movement's focus.[44]

Ironically, this episode would replay itself in the fall of 1968, when the county again tried to rid the Strip of the counterculture by enforcing loitering laws. Again demonstrators marched, only this time the scene was more farce than tragedy. Only about five hundred protestors turned out, and they concluded the march by surrounding the sheriff's station and oinking like pigs. Yet even this protest had a dual purpose—to free both the Strip and jailed Black Panther leader Huey Newton. The organizers insisted that "the tie-in between the Newton protest and the Strip protest is a natural one. . . . After all, the middle-class white kids who are being rousted by the sheriff's deputies are finally finding out just what the black people have had to take for years." Just as authorities had oppressed blacks for centuries, Peace and Freedom Party organizer Ed Pearl argued, hippies of "middle-class" origin were "being told where to sit, . . . where to stand, . . . and even when to die."[45] The comment was preposterous, yet Pearl's chutzpah indicated the degree to which hippies and politicos saw their causes as ideologically adjacent.

"Space" encompasses more than residential and commercial areas, of course; it also includes the "public" territory. And all varieties of 1960s dissenters invested "the street" with both emancipatory power and portentous meaning.[46] Radicals, as well as sufficiently enraged liberals, cherished "the street" as a central public ground. Indeed, some of the most memorable local events of the era took place in the streets, and more broadly in public space. The 1967 anti-Vietnam protest in the Century City district was one such incident, and it remains perhaps the most momentous local protest of the era.[47] And because virtually every shade of dissenter opposed the war—albeit some in more organized fashion than others—the participants in antiwar protests ran the gamut.[48]

The Century City demonstration certainly fit this model, as hippies composed roughly one-quarter of the ten to fifteen thousand demonstrators. Noting that hippies participated in antiwar protests alongside the New Left is neither novel nor interesting; after all, one would expect this essentially pacifistic lot to oppose the war. More importantly, though, this event and others like it show that regardless of ideological deviations, circumstances consistently forced the two crowds together. They inhabited the same enclaves, contested the same police, and often championed the same causes. Their ideological premises may have been distinct, but the physical ground on which they operated was usually the same; they squared off against the same opponents. Tactical alliances were the predictable by-product.

The protest itself was tumultuous. In June 1967 President Johnson arrived in Los Angeles for a fund-raiser at a hotel in Century City, a sleek, antiseptic corporate district nearly devoid of residents. On the night of the protest, the demonstrators approached a wall of police in front of the hotel, who ordered them to march past. When the protestors held their ground, the police descended, starting a bloody melee in which dozens were wounded and arrested.[49] The crowd itself was diverse, as "women of high fashion strode beside the hippie-clad." Civil rights organizations, local communists, hippies, and antiwar liberals all participated, as did Dr. Benjamin Spock, prizefighter Muhammad Ali, Student Nonviolent Coordinating Committee (SNCC) leader H. Rap Brown, and the Women's Strike for Peace. Some of those present even strained to legitimize the demonstration by pointing to the presence of older members of the respectable middle class and downplaying the role of "the costumed, bizarre element."[50] Yet, according to most observers, the counterculture was at Century City in force. One sympathetic middle-aged commentator estimated that hippies numbered four thousand, a figure with which the less friendly LAPD agreed. The *Los Angeles Herald-Examiner* reporter covering the event also concurred, noting that "several thousand of the demonstrators—mostly teenagers and young adults—danced at the protest to the music of a wildly gyrating rock and roll band" playing on a flatbed truck.[51]

To the surprise of few, the institutions representing the Los Angeles "establishment"—the interlocking alliance of dominant public and private entities that strove to shape the city's public life—exonerated the LAPD and blamed the protestors. The establishment included the relatively august *Los Angeles Times* (which at this point was lurching slowly from reaction toward liberalism), although after Art Kunkin's *Free Press* issued an extra issue that convincingly debunked the official line reported in the *Times*, that paper redid its story entirely. In any event, the exculpation had the signal effect of radicalizing those so inclined, but it also locked the local New Left and their hip compatriots more closely together at a practical level. Few hippies were being politicized for the first time, of course. Most were sustaining a relationship with politicos that had already been fostered, in part through clashes with authorities over public space.

The Hip Worldview

The more strictly *ideological* relationship between the counterculture and the New Left also merits consideration. The local counterculture's ideas and actions concerning racial inequality constitute the most important issue here, and in the Los Angeles context are especially telling. To reiterate, the *Free Press,* equally a leftist and hip paper, offered the best local coverage of the Watts riot, printing the justly famous headline, "The Negroes Have Voted!"[52] In Art Kunkin's eyes, he was now legitimate, perhaps fulfilling the role he had envisioned when he joined CORE in the late 1940s.

Hipsters' concern over racial inequality would remain high. Certainly, Al Mitchell's attempt to connect the issue of hip youths' access to the Strip with racial injustice in East L.A. and Watts was one indication of this, albeit a strained and ultimately unsuccessful one. A few months after that abortive alliance, the *Open City* envisioned the possibility of cementing the coalition. On the eve of the much ballyhooed "summer of love," as the local scene prepared for an influx of hip initiates from across the nation, an editor hoped that by the end of the summer the hip community would channel its energy into an effort to "brighten the ghettoes, turn the older generation on to the loving directness and humanism of their kids, break down racial barriers, . . . provide numerical and spiritual muscle in a fantastically heightened program of protest against the Vietnam war, inane laws about drugs, [and] general injustice and established cruelty."

The *Open City* compared the hippies to SNCC and Southern Christian Leadership Conference (SCLC) volunteers who left the North during the summer to combat racist institutions in the Deep South, and even hoped that the counterculture would "organize love-teams to canvass areas where Negroes and Mexicans and hippies are moving and help convince old residents that their new neighbors are to be welcomed, not retreated from."[53] The twenty-two-year-old Elliot Mintz, a hippie activist, gadfly, and radio host, agreed enthusiastically that "we are literally going to change the state of the nation this summer."[54]

While nothing so dramatic ever occurred, the local community did launch visible and sporadically successful efforts to attack racism in solidarity with ghetto residents. The most notable results of this half-formed alliance were the countercultural happenings and "love-ins" held in Watts and East Los Angeles. The first such event, an acid test organized by the Merry Pranksters in 1965, took place at a hall in Watts. It was almost entirely a white affair, however. Residents viewed it as a curiosity, and were—according to Tom Wolfe, at least—apparently nonplussed by the fact that organizers saw the locale as a "humorous—ironical?—site for such carryings on."[55]

The interracial love-ins of summer 1967 were far more earnest affairs. Love-ins, modeled after the "human be-in" that took place in San Francisco earlier that year, were outdoor "happenings" filled with acid rock, various amateur entertainers, free-form dancing, sex, drugs, and a healthy dollop of Eastern mysticism. Held in the city's major parks beginning in the spring, love-ins became stock events for the next few years, sometimes attracting crowds numbering over ten thousand. In mid-summer 1967 the *Open City* announced the first Watts love-in, intended as a "historic bringing together of the city's two hip communities, the white hippy [*sic*] and his black brother who has long provided the model for his way of life."[56] When the love-in took place, hip spokespersons were delighted. The hippie/anarchist paper *Provo*—whose staff, a local offshoot of the better-known Dutch collective, handed out leaflets on the Strip and provided information on transportation to the event—counted more than seven thousand attendees.[57] Strip denizen and artist Vito, a well-known "freak," brought his dance troupe, which "made an obvious impression on white people who had 'never seen white folks act that way before.'" A number of black rock and electric blues acts performed, including Taj Mahal and the Chambers Brothers. And, as at hippie love-ins, there were "spontaneous bongo drummers, flutists, and other music makers." *Open City* reporter Bob Garcia deemed the event a total success: "The hippies short-circuited the ghetto's mental hate syndrome with smiles, freaky renaissance clothes, bare feet, free food, and an open attitude which became contagious as the day wore on." The distrust palpable at the love-in's start "vanished," Garcia reported, "into common humanity" as blacks and whites danced together. For good measure, boxes of cigarette lighters with "burn, baby, burn!" stamped on them were available.[58]

Two other such love-ins followed, one in Watts and the other in East L.A. Neither was nearly as successful, but they did indicate where hip sentiment lay.[59] And these were not the only examples of attempted fellowship. The *Open City* and the *Free Press* always devoted considerable coverage to racial issues, and each had a number of Latino and black writers.[60] Perhaps most interestingly, in 1969 Kathleen Cleaver and James Baldwin held a benefit for Huey Newton at Hollywood High School, then a locus of hip youth culture. White acid bands Country Joe and the Fish and Pacific Gas and Electric played at the event.[61] Also, while two UCLA psychiatric researchers of the scene were mostly correct in stating that "the hippie is not negro," African Americans and Latinos did participate. Two of the era's most illustrious local rock bands, Love and War, featured interracial lineups. This participation was not limited to entertainers, who, as the scene's quasi-royalty, were admittedly atypical. In a 1966 photo essay of the Strip, roughly 8 percent of the hundred plus individuals photographed who looked at least vaguely hip were African American, a percentage closely proportionate to that of the greater Los Angeles black population.[62]

One should not make too much of this fraternization, though; there was plenty of discord. The point is that many hippies were hardly quietist in addressing racial inequality (indeed, given the era, they were remarkably tolerant and accepting of other races). And while it is easy to criticize the loopiness of their tactics for effecting change, one cannot question either the intention or the real interaction that did occur. Still, friction was equally noticeable. The negligible turnout by blacks and Chicanos in East L.A., Watts, and Venice for Al Mitchell's final Strip-based protest spoke volumes. It underscored the counterculture's chronic difficulty in allying with aggrieved populations, and pointed to a dilemma embedded in the counterculture's rejection of "traditional" values such as respect for elders. Likewise, their contempt for middle-class materialism was problematic. Economically and socially deprived minorities like African Americans and Chicanos might view such attitudes as both frivolous and ignorant of the role traditional forms of authority played in different cultures, especially when such institutions might protect a culture from assimilation. "Strippies" generally came from privilege, and their desire to roam freely on the alternative shopping paradise of the Strip, and to preserve its status as a countercultural stronghold, probably struck poorer Angelenos as an attempt by spoiled brats to enjoy their wealth more effectively. A few months after the events, the comments of H. Rap Brown, the incendiary leader of SNCC, lent credence to this speculation. Visiting Los Angeles in the summer of 1967 and speaking in general terms about hippies, Brown told the *Free Press,* "As long as they're unknown longhairs who get fucked over by the law, they're all for changing things. But when they get on top of the game, like some of them do in the music thing, they forget how it used to be, and pretty soon they treat money the same way all white Americans do—they get in a position to exploit and they'll do it." While he regarded hippies as benign, Brown made clear that he did not expect much from them:

> I wish all white Americans were like the hippies, because they ARE peaceful, and that's more than can be said for most honkies. . . . As far as I can see the hippies don't generate much anger among militant black people. Black people tend to see hippies—well, like white people do—as the sick element of white society. . . . They don't see them as the enemy. . . . Really, the black political people, the militants, see the hippies as more or less politically irrelevant.[63]

Even more revealing of the gulf separating hippies and minorities were the disputes that occurred during the final two interracial love-ins. The second one occurred three weeks after the first and, despite the *Free Press*'s provision of "thousands of small love gifts," was a failure, marred by open antagonism between blacks and white hippies. It was almost canceled because of the recent Detroit riot, and the *Free Press* announced beforehand that black militants "who had been kicked out . . . during the first love-in planned to make trouble if white hippies attended." According to the *Open City,* the situation did not deteriorate to such an extent, but the few whites attending the mostly black event were fearful. This was especially apparent when a young black militant climbed onstage and "began to lay down a barrage of hate about getting whitey." Other black youths there "seemed particularly hostile."[64]

The last summer love-in, a month later, intended to "break the love barrier" between races. Even more than the second Watts love-in, the third one—a "be-in" in East Los Angeles at the end of August—proved to one observer that "Hippies have quite a bit to learn about people in general, and this is especially true if they are poor and not white Anglo Saxons." Apparently, the mostly poor attendees from the surrounding area were outraged by the "stale food" from "people who accept poverty as a mask of liberation from the materialistic codes of the establishment but who have had 'it' in the past." When a black child pelted a young hippie woman with a piece of stale bread, she proceeded to chase the child. When met with cries of protest and derision, she reportedly complained that "we came out to help you people and this is the thanks we get!"[65] The East L.A. be-in fiasco was not anomalous; minority communities throughout the nation rejected what they felt was patronizing assistance from white radicals.

The manifest dissension between the counterculture and minority rights movements raises another equally important issue: For all the New Left and countercultural cross-breeding, the terms still referred to distinct entities. To overlook the obvious and fundamental dissimilarities between the hip and New Left outlooks is to create a skewed, imperfect portrait. The Strip demonstrations of 1966–67, for instance, were certainly infused with leftist undercurrents, but a pivotal motivation of the demonstrators was to ensure that the area remained a certain type of consumption zone, albeit a more colorful and raucous one than official Los Angeles would have liked. At any rate, by mid-1967 the Strip was booming, as new shops serving the consumer youthquake opened their doors *en masse*. One model for the mass consumption of hip, a shop called the Stash, even gave hippies "'hanging about privileges,' and they don't have to spend any money while they're at it. To [the owner] this is how it should be—straight people buy and hippies provide atmosphere."[66] And the Stash was but one among many equally exploitive examples of this phenomenon. Consumer-driven hedonism, of course, was a far cry from the SDS ideal of participatory democracy.[67]

There were other gaping ideological chasms as well. As Doug Rossinow has shown, the New Left emerged in large part as a consequence of postwar youth's yearning for an existential breakthrough to a more authentic life. This quest for authenticity, alleged to exist beneath layers of banal artifice, motivated all varieties of 1960s radicalism, including the counterculture. In fact, the extent to which hippies idealized "the authentic" surpassed even the New Left. For many in the counterculture, living "authentically" was an all-consuming passion, and the intensity of it separated them qualitatively from the New Left. Talk of stripping away the conventions of a bankrupt, plastic civilization permeated the local hip scene. To Frank Zappa, the "freak outs" he organized abetted the effort:

> On a personal level, Freaking Out is a process whereby an individual casts off outmoded and restricted standards of thinking, dress, and social etiquette. . . . On a collective level, when . . . freaks gather and express themselves, . . . it is . . . a FREAK OUT. The participants, already emancipated from our national social slavery, dressed in their most inspired apparel, realize as a group whatever potential they possess for free expression.

All the trappings of modern life were suspect, from time clocks to science itself. To "break on through," as L.A. rock star Jim Morrison so famously put it, necessitated transgression of both custom and morality in order to reach a realm of immediate feeling, preferably via the avenues of hedonistic pleasure—sex and drugs.[68] Most in the New Left never explored this dictum quite like the counterculture did.

Reestablishing an organic link with "nature" was another key feature of the hip worldview. Many took to the city's rugged canyons, trying to establish "more or less self-sustaining communes" where one could "take acid in a relatively paranoia free atmosphere." There, "man could know his god, nature, and his unity with life."[69] Music industry scenester Kim Fowley rhapsodized about "canyon living," where hippies could

> groove on each other and introduce to some of their spiritual contemporaries the joy of living un-hung-up outside the city thing, living in the country and nature, instinct; like a

Thoreau trip. . . . You can trap your own food here [and] . . . make your own clothes and grow your own food. . . . We want to do our own thing. And so it's hard to do your own thing when you live next door to a bank or something in Hollywood or Los Angeles . . . so if you live here you can do your own thing honestly.[70]

Often, though, the counterculture took its search for the authentic beyond this rather prosaic condemnation of modernity into more extreme territories. Hippies' willingness to extend this impulse into the nether regions of primitivist essentialism, atavism, and mysticism is what most differentiated them from the New Left, which, after all, remained wedded to a basically goal-oriented progressive agenda. Locally, hippies evinced primitivism in myriad ways, from their self-identification as a tribe to their idealization of the Indians as authentic noble savages.[71] Love-ins were integral to the process of reclaiming the primitive, as they helped to both reconnect hippies to a primordial soil and nurture vitalism. As Lawrence Lipton—beat chronicler, poet, and longtime *Free Press* columnist—suggested after the first love-in, "atavis[m] was a positive as long as it stood against the city of cement and steel."[72] Hip mysticism was of a piece. Enthusiasm for Eastern religions derived from their alleged prioritization of the circular over the linear and rejection of the individualized ego, all of which stood in contrast to the deadening belief systems of the West.[73]

Problematically, this primitivism was closely allied with an essentialist vision of human nature, one that had deeply sexist tendencies. Ideally, men and women were one with nature and free from the falsifications of modern life. Men were virile, wild he-men, a vision best encapsulated by Jim Morrison's lizard king persona.[74] On the other hand, Lipton described "girls" at the first love-in as "bacchanates celebrating the orgiastic rites of the Spring fertility rites, which they had come for, knowing it was expected of them at a love-in." At a later love-in, an observer claimed that "the girls with the jugs [of wine] were like maidens from a virginal temple, poised and innocent." Such banalities were not restricted to language; the *Oracle* continually displayed clichéd drawings of anatomically "perfect" nude women at one with a psychedelicized nature.[75] To be sure, sexism was a major problem within the New Left throughout the era. But when the local women's liberation movement began to challenge that sexism vocally—particularly the ribald sex ads in the *Free Press*—those from a New Left perspective at least responded to and addressed the complaints, partly because they saw issues of social equality and liberation as paramount. The local counterculture, which was hamstrung by an essentialist sexism, did not even consider offering a response.[76]

Hip primitivism often degenerated into outright anti-intellectualism, and here is where the cleavage was most stark. Hip figures who thought about the issue held that film and music, as full sensory experiences of the body, could supplant a debilitating reliance on intellect and linearity. In this view, connection and communication were more genuine if they involved all stimuli receptors. Hippies' glorification of children as prelapsarian innocents tended to anti-intellectualism as well. The *Oracle* trumpeted the virtues of naive art, publishing poems "by children and the childlike."[77] This irrationalist streak was also apparent in comments about political change. Instead of New Left strategizing, one local hippie commented, "we don't think in . . . terms . . . of plans and objectives." A *Provo* editorial was more effusive, stating that "the power of empathy, championed by the acid heads, is going to carry the first wave of the revolution." Finally, actor Peter Fonda, who was deeply involved in the local hippie scene, defended the Sunset Strip protests by saying they weren't political. An admirer of McCluhan, Fonda maintained that young cultural radicals "need much cooler leadership. Mario Savio is a jerk."[78] Such sentiments put hippies at a loss as to how to go about formulating social reconstruction. Their vague, half-baked notions appeared silly, particularly when they were considering the revolutionary potential of "acid-head empathy." Old Leftists may have assailed New Leftists for depending on emotion and action at the expense of analysis, but when compared to hippies, New Leftists were veritable logicians.

As has often been said, these aspects of the hip *weltanschauung* did not have much political content; directives to embrace primitivism, mysticism, and so forth were effectively about transforming one's own head. Yet despite the dead ends and plain silliness manifest in this realm of countercultural thought, hippies were still talking about authenticity and the lack of it in contemporary American mass culture. And while the New Left eschewed the counterculture's more theatrical methods of reclaiming authenticity, they did see it as a crucial personal and political issue. The pervasiveness of mass cultural production in Los Angeles meant that the "inauthentic" images produced by the system suffused the entire environment so entirely that no one could escape their reach.

As a consequence, the underground press devoted much ink to assessing the problem using leftist rhetorical devices, particularly regarding the ability of the local entertainment industries to effortlessly co-opt ostensibly oppositional culture. For example, a *Free Press* columnist complained about major label co-optation of hip music, detailing how large corporations were using seemingly independent front labels to give their acts the veneer of independence.[79] In a similar vein, Lawrence Lipton offered a wildly paranoid review in mid-1966 of a record purporting to capture and describe the nature of the LSD experience. To him, it was symptomatic of co-optation.[80] Another *Free Press* writer complained that in comparison to San Francisco, local hippie radio personalities "seem[ed] less pure, less sincere. . . . It is a mirror reality of what was once spiritual, but in their hands becomes saran wrapped and exploitative." The writer did not consider Los Angeles "real" but "a haven for star-tripping success worshipping punks, ex-Hippies turned . . . entertainment company whores."[81] Ultimately, the attention paid to the issue proved that concern over "culture" resonated beyond the confines of the hip world.

There is yet another reason to qualify the admittedly undeniable rift between the two camps. In certain pockets of the local underground by 1970, the hip-Left union extended beyond an awareness of the machinery of cultural fakery and neighborhood-based resistance to a deep correspondence between outlooks and objectives. Michael Letwin, for example, who began his career in 1971 as a local high school radical by helping to organize the Red Tide, a teenage collective, was strongly influenced by Michigander John Sinclair's White Panther Party. Their most notorious mouthpiece, the hard rock band the MC5, joined wild-eyed hedonism with left-wing politics to great effect. Letwin, who lived near UCLA on the city's west side, identified himself at the time primarily as a "freak," yet drew on this worldview to become a labor organizer years later (in fact, he said that by 1969 "hippie" had become a term of opprobrium directed at listless, apolitical heads). For him and many others, the solution at the time was the hip-New Left hybrid of the "freak." He moved in and out of both worlds with such ease that for him, and doubtless for many others, the two were indistinguishable. While perhaps atypical of the broader counterculture, Letwin's activities spoke to the porousness of the boundary between the two groups. Just as important, his hybrid positioning again attests to the intertwined trajectories of the counterculture and New Left, in spite of the clear fissures separating them.[82]

Venice and the New Left–Hip Amalgamation

Despite the notable differences between hippies and New Left politicos, then, the contours of environment, circumstance, and place often forced each into the other's territory, both ideologically and practically. As has been stressed, this tendency toward superimposition was present as early as 1965. And on many occasions, the counterculture was effectively in the New Left, reacting to contingency by adopting its framework and tactics. Nowhere was this more evident than in the Venice district of Los Angeles in the late 1960s. Venice witnessed an especially intense conflict between local authorities and real estate developers on one side and a fluctuating hip-politico coalition on the other. The relatively poor neighborhood and longtime bohemian enclave remained relatively funky and seedy in the late 1960s. An interracial district now populated by hippies, radicals, and assorted iconoclasts, it was quite different from the relatively upscale Hollywood zone—although Venice saw its share of hip commerce—yet still possessed a vibrant street culture that gravitated toward the beach.

But because Venice was potentially a prime beach community, developers eyed it jealously. Among the various Los Angeles beach communities, Venice was the poorest and least hospitable to the southern California high life. The Venice-based Oceanfront Improvement Association (OIA), a group of developers, recognized this, but they hoped to transform the area into a "new Miami Beach." They planned to lobby the city government into approving a plan to "upscale" Venice through devices such as increased property assessments, eminent domain, and sales of public property. Interested property owners and speculators would do their part, demolishing dilapidated, inexpensive housing for the poor and replacing it with beachfront high-rises. In addition, as an anti-development informant claimed to have heard at an OIA meeting, a campaign to "sweep the undesirables [off] our beach" was necessary in order to realize Venice's potential as a moneyed enclave.[83] The editors of the unabashedly pro-development *Evening Outlook* (a widely circulated west side daily that served Venice) felt likewise, favoring the completion of a canal improvement project that would raise property values and, as an added benefit, drive out the poor. As the editors put it, "The Venice canals will become part of the first-class Marina Del Rey project [an affluent subdivision]. The canals and their perimeters should be first-class as well."[84] And clearly, the assorted cultural and political radicals were not "first class."

The city obliged the developers. Beginning in early 1968 the LAPD periodically sent in its crack metro squad to patrol the area, ostensibly to aid the regular Venice division in battling an unprecedented crime wave (a true claim, although the district was not unique in this respect). Not only did the elite squad single out hippies; it was by all accounts gleefully brutal. In February 1968 the squad shuttered hip institutions, breaking windows in the process, and apprehended more than one hundred hippies, often basing arrests on appearance alone. Police had been hassling area bohemians for years, but never to this extent. According to the *Free Press,* one Venice "hippie leader asked [a squad member] why they were there. And they answered, 'We're going to clean the trash out of Venice. If you want to stay out of jail, move out of Venice.'"[85]

Two subsequent sweeps increased the tension. That autumn, the *Los Angeles Times* surmised that "hippies, property owners, . . . and police are involved in a conflict with social overtones that far transcend Venice." The police hated the hippies, "whom they regarded as wastrels infiltrated by hard-core criminals and left-wing political extremists." Hippies responded in kind, "believ[ing] that property owners—eager to make a luxurious high rise community out of Venice—had talked the police into frightening them out of the area with massive sweeps and pointless arrests."[86] Following the first metro squad raid, an *Open City* writer asserted that the officers "were not men. These were pigs. Brutal, thick-necked, pink."[87] Indeed, to sociologist Anthony Giddens, then a visiting professor at UCLA and a Venice resident, the scene in general was reminiscent of the "fall of the Roman Empire." He recalled nearly thirty years later that "the coast was lined with armed cops and . . . thousands of hippies strewn across the beach wearing all sorts of strange clothes." Given the situation, many observers thought Venice was due for a riot.[88]

As redevelopment plans proceeded, local freak and leftist activists organized to defend from a sterilizing renewal effort what a visiting UCLA professor from Germany identified as a community of "spontaneous human exchange," "participatory directness," and an exhilarating "unpredictability."[89] The city's plan to augment "renewal" by building a freeway through Venice that would separate the ghetto from the beachfront only made locals more suspicious, especially when a city planning commissioner said that "probably 90 percent of the people living in Venice won't be there when the freeway comes." The future for the existing Venice looked bleak: "The colonial office downtown formulated the master plan; the natives will formulate their plan; then the master will put his plan into effect and the natives will become natives of Watts or Big Sur [a countercultural redoubt]." In their place would be a "machine-made noncommunity with its faceless institutional architecture, bland middle-class conformity, its relentless image of clean, sterile streets and houses full of happy people with happy problems. The city will have made another cultural desert."[90]

In residents' persistent complaints about the city's intentions was the recognition that they, along with ghetto blacks, were living, breathing impediments to renewal. The community only tightened in response to the repression, however. After the first raid, activists from a coalition of leftist and liberal organizations, including the ACLU and the Peace and Freedom Party, formed the Venice Survival Committee (which the *Evening Outlook* contended was composed almost solely of hippies). During the raid itself and in the days immediately following, the committee demonstrated in front of the Venice police building, chanting, "We won't move from Venice, No!"[91] In late 1968 the committee began publishing its own newspaper, the *Free Venice Beachhead*, which served as a broadside for antidevelopment forces.[92]

Through the *Free Venice Beachhead* and more established underground papers like the *Free Press*, the Venice Survival Committee provided residents with sharp analyses of the developers' underlying motives. The *Beachhead* also delighted in exposing the city's duplicity—despite officials' protestations to the contrary—in trying to eradicate hippies and blacks through excessive property assessments and building condemnations. The Free Venice Committee, led by John Haag, was also active; it gathered more than two thousand signatures—5 percent of Venice's population—for a petition opposing redevelopment.[93] And throughout the late 1960s, demonstrations, both major and minor, were commonplace in the area.

After the city council approved a property assessment hike in the canal district—which, incidentally, would drive out the current poorer residents—activists from the Survival Committee and the Peace and Freedom Party formed a secessionist organization, "Free Venice." And though "Free Venice" was not successful, neither the city nor developers could claim victory. For even as redevelopment plowed forward, Venice never really changed that much; to this day it remains a downbeat district filled with nonconformists, aesthetes, minorities, radicals, and crime. In their spirited defense of a certain vision of Venice, local radicals undercut the potential of the alternative. New buildings simply could not attract a wealthy "mainstream" to an area so notorious for political radicalism and cultural transgression.

The role of hippies in Venice was a culmination of sorts. For while leftists certainly participated, as evidenced by John Haag's leadership, hippies comprised the bulk of activists. They were also the primary targets of redevelopers and the LAPD. Furthermore, their vision was an essentially New Leftist one—participatory democracy, social and racial egalitarianism, authenticity, and cultural experimentalism. And again, it was a contest over a discrete spatial zone that drew such sentiments to the fore. Indeed, competing visions of the built environment engendered the most passionate reactions. When Horst Schmidt-Brummer juxtaposed in his Venice photo essay the old, whimsically decorated buildings of Venice with the new, spare, linear, security-oriented buildings envisioned in the master plan, he captured well the hip/politico coalition's ability to blend concerns about authenticity, freedom, experimentation, and technocracy.[94]

Coda

Nineteen-seventy saw the release of Italian director Michelangelo Antonioni's *Zabriskie Point,* a film that revolved around the relationship between a radicalized Los Angeles college student and a young woman working for a local real estate developer. Both start out as relatively apolitical. In the film's opening scene, the student, Mark, rejects the group-oriented leftist/Black Panther radicalism espoused by his fellow classmates (including, in a cameo, Kathleen Cleaver) in favor of a less systematic tactic of individual action. And although the woman (Daria) wears hip clothes and listens to hip music, she is neither aware of nor concerned about the crisis facing political radicals, either locally or nationally. Through a sequence of happenstance events, however, both become radicalized. After witnessing a trigger-happy LAPD officer gun down a black campus radical, Mark shoots the officer and flees to Arizona. It takes Mark's own death at the hands of yet another LAPD automaton to radicalize Daria, who had fallen in love with him in the "authentic" natural setting of the Arizona desert. This radicalization occurs in the film's climax, as Daria envisions a spectacular explosion of an Arizona desert resort that the company she works for is using for a business meeting. In the throes of her violent fantasy, she goes a step further: Not only is the resort blown sky high, but all the consumerist garbage produced by such a barbaric social system explodes as well—television sets, refrigerators, even a loaf of Wonder Bread.[95]

That the film was set primarily in Los Angeles was no mistake. As Antonioni makes clear throughout, Los Angeles, although seemingly crawling with leftist white radicals and Black Panthers, is a black hole of artificiality and gross consumerism. Tacky billboards and smog range as far as the eye can see. Such an alienating environment, Antonioni seems to suggest, was fully capable of producing virulent forms of political and cultural radicalism. Moreover, as the film progresses, the barriers compartmentalizing 1960s radicalism dissolve, and the setting fosters a seamless matrix of "the underground." Mass culture, combined with authoritarian repression, forces radical subcurrents to flow into each other.

In his earlier film documenting the London counterculture, *Blow-Up* (1966), authenticity is the sole issue at stake, and rebellion is purely aesthetic.[96] There are two ways to read Antonioni's shift in emphasis. One is that he was simply following headlines, as political radicalism increased its mass appeal after 1966. In this narrative, a formerly apolitical counterculture moved toward radicalism, though with questionable conviction and rigor. The second reading is that Los Angeles was simply different, although a bellwether just the same. There the fusion had occurred years before, and the camaraderie between hippies and the New Left derived from the omnipresence of mass cultural production and living in close quarters. Priorities were different in L.A., *Zabriskie Point* suggests. The steady barrage of billboards, advertisements, and the mass media enveloped one, and local radicals had to account for the debilitating sense of unreality this produced.

Antonioni is hardly a reliable reporter, of course; his evocation of Nathanael West's themes of cultural decadence and his employment of the hoary trope of L.A.-as-grand-metaphor were stock. Moreover, audiences may have been oblivious to these messages; they may simply have liked the film for the heady cinematography. Still, the director was on to something. The way each subculture feeds off the other, mass culture's nourishment of radicalism, hippies' vaguely New Leftist operational framework, and the primacy of racial identity politics all reflected ongoing trends in the city.

Thus the emphases on the crucial importance of the politics of culture and identity were not merely the refuse of the "true" spirit of 1960s radicalism, epigones emerging after a classical New Left imploded. At least in Los Angeles, such concerns infused a broader political radicalism from the Watts riot onward. By the same token, the support offered by politicos to these causes probably made hippies receptive to political radicalism. Repression was equally important in fomenting radicalism, especially since local authorities were not very adept at discriminating between targets. Palpable dissension between politicos, hippies, and black radicals erupted at times, enough to justify categorizing to an extent. But the case of Los Angeles forces us to reconsider two analytical strategies: the notion that the New Left became countercultural rather than the reverse, and the too-easy detachment of a politically committed and publicly oriented New Left from an apolitical and "alternative" (rather than oppositional) counterculture. The cliché certainly holds in some instances, but too frequently it has been overplayed.

Notes

1. *Los Angeles Free Press,* 20 Aug. 1965, 1, 27 Aug. 1965, 1.

2. "The *L.A. Free Press* Is Rich," *Esquire,* June 1970, 56.

3. For an example of Zappa's role as reliable commentator, see *Los Angeles Free Press,* 13 Jan. 1967, 1.

4. Examples include (in varying degrees) Thomas Frank, *The Conquest of Cool: Business Culture, Counterculture, and the Rise of Hip Consumerism* (Chicago: University of Chicago Press, 1997); Todd Gitlin, *The Sixties: Years of Hope, Days of Rage* (New York: Bantam, 1987); David Caute, *The Year of the Barricades: A Journey through 1968* (New York: Harper and Row, 1988); W. J. Rorabaugh, *Berkeley at War: The 1960s* (New York: Oxford University Press 1989); Peter Levy, *The New Left and Labor in the 1960s* (Urbana: University of Illinois Press, 1994); Allen Matusow, *The Unraveling of America: A History of Liberalism in the 1960s* (New York: Harper and Row, 1984); Daniel Bell, *The Cultural Contradictions of Capitalism* (New York: Basic Books, 1976).

5. Doug Rossinow, *The Politics of Authenticity: Liberalism, Christianity, and the New Left in America* (New York: Columbia University Press, 1998); Julie Stephens, *Anti-Disciplinary Protest: Sixties Radicalism and Postmodernism* (New York: Cambridge University Press, 1998); Alice Echols, "We Gotta Get Outta this Place: Notes toward a Remapping of the Sixties," *Socialist Review* 22 (spring 1992): 26–28; Alice Echols, "Nothing Distant about It: Women's Liberation and Sixties Radicalism," in *The Sixties: From Memory to History,* ed. David Farber (Chapel Hill: University of North Carolina Press, 1994), 149–74; Gitlin, *The Sixties.* Other examples of this increasing sophistication include David Farber, *Chicago '68* (Chicago: University of Chicago Press, 1988) and Richard Candida-Smith, *Utopia and Dissent: Art, Politics, and Poetry in California* (Berkeley: University of California Press, 1995). Aniko Bodroghkozy contended recently that "these delineations [separating the New Left from the counterculture] are rather arbitrary and do not properly suggest the merging between these two tendencies. Activists embraced many of the aspects of countercultural 'lifestyle politics' such as drug use, engagement with the burgeoning music scene, and experimentation with different modes of living. Hippies, especially after becoming recipients of law and order disciplining, tended to move in more confrontational directions. So when I think it is important to distinguish these two modes of youth rebelliousness in

the 1960s, I think it is important to emphasize their common roots" (Aniko Bodraghkozy, "Groove Tube and Reel Revolution: The Youth Rebellions of the 1960s and Popular Culture" [Ph.D. diss., University of Wisconsin, 1994], 40–41).

6. The authors speculated that locals' lack of either a sense of tradition or an acceptance of limits made the city an exaggerated, grotesque version of the American Dream and a dismal realization of Tocqueville's fears of a conformist, authoritarian democracy. See Michael Rogin and John Shrover, *Political Change in California: Critical Elections and Social Movements, 1890–1966* (Westport, Conn.: Greenwood, 1970), 153–212.

7. *Los Angeles Free Press*, 27 Aug. 1964, 1; *Open City*, 9 June 1967, 3, 11, 14.

8. L.A. County sheriff Peter Pitchess delivered an alarmist report regarding local campus-based SDS and black nationalist radicalism to the Los Angeles Chamber of Commerce in early 1969. He focused in particular on San Fernando Valley State (minutes of board of directors meetings, Los Angeles Chamber of Commerce, 20 Feb. 1969, USC Regional History Archive, box 34, 16-3). Regarding UCLA, the firing of radical professor Angela Davis in 1969 as well as the murder of Black Panthers Bunchie Carter and John Huggins on campus the same year by black nationalists indicated the level of tumult. And like hundreds of other universities throughout America, UCLA experienced massive protests and police-student confrontations in the wake of the 1970 Cambodia invasion (Michael Letwin, interview by author, 27 Nov. 2000). Robert Brenner, later a well-known leftist academic, was also involved with the radical Student Worker Action Committee (SWAC) at UCLA in the early to mid-1970s. Thanks to Steven Brier for information on Letwin and Brenner. Regarding Carter's murder, see David Hilliard, *This Side of Glory: The Autobiography of David Hilliard and the Story of the Black Panther Party* (Boston: Little, Brown, 1993). The *Free Press* also devoted extensive coverage to this murder.

9. Stephens, *Anti-Disciplinary Protest*.

10. Rossinow, *The Politics of Authenticity*, 260; Stephens, *Anti-Disciplinary Protest*; Farber, *Chicago '68*; Matusow, *The Unraveling of America*; Gitlin, *The Sixties*. One exception is Simon Frith, who has recognized L.A.'s centrality to the counterculture. See Simon Frith, "Rock and the Politics of Memory," in *The Sixties without Apology*, ed. Sohnya Sayres (Minneapolis: University of Minnesota Press, 1982), 59–69, esp. 54.

11. To be fair, this process gathered momentum earlier, with the rise of television (and even earlier still through radio). The rise of television and its impact on culture is documented in Lynn Spigel, *Make Room for TV: Television and the Family Ideal in Postwar America* (Chicago: University of Chicago Press, 1992) and James Baughman, *The Republic of Mass Culture: Journalism, Filmmaking, and Broadcasting in America since 1941* (Baltimore: Johns Hopkins University Press, 1992).

12. Michael Letwin, a radical from Los Angeles who began his career as a radical "freak" in a local high school in 1969–70, said that growing up in Los Angeles, one always felt the presence of the industry. He personally grew up being interested in it and said that co-optation was noticed by all. He later helped organize a leftist-freak polyglot high school student collective named the Red Tide.

13. *Open City*, 21 July 1967, 12.

14. Bell, *The Cultural Contradictions of Capitalism*.

15. In late 1969 there was a major shootout between Black Panthers and the LAPD (*Los Angeles Times*, 2 Dec. 1969, 1, 3; 10 Dec. 1969, 6).

16. For a more extensive discussion of minority radicalism in late 1960s Los Angeles, see Laura Pulido, "Race and Revolutionary Politics: Black Chicano/a, and Asian American Leftists

in Southern California," *Antipode* 34 (2002). For the cultural dimensions of black radicalism in the period, see Daniel Widener, "'Way Out West': Expressive Art, Music, and Culture in Black LA," *Emergences* 9 (1999): 271–89.

17. Rossinow's *The Politics of Authenticity* and Farber's *Chicago '68* are the best examples of this.

18. "The Mad New Scene on Sunset Strip," *Life,* 26 Aug. 1966, 75–83; "Sunset Boulevard's New Bohemia," *Los Angeles Magazine,* Dec. 1965, 34–42; "The Hippie Invasion," *Los Angeles Magazine,* May 1967, 30; *Los Angeles Times,* 4 June 1967, W1, W4; "The Sunset Strip," *New York Review of Books* (hereafter NYRB), 9 March 1967, 8–13; *Los Angeles Times,* 10 March 1966, pt. 2, 1, 8; "Could Your Daughter Kill?" *Los Angeles Magazine,* Feb. 1970, 30; Los Angeles County Ordinance No. 8874, 29 June 1965; Gordon Nesvig, clerk of the County Board of Supervisors, to Sybil Brand of the County Public Welfare Commission (with attachments), 31 May 1965, Los Angeles County Board of Supervisors Archives, file 330; Paul Hyman and Robert Wallach, "The Hippies and the New Values," (paper given at the UCLA Neuropsychiatric Institute, 1969), 4, 9, 21.

19. *Los Angeles Times,* 10 March 1966, pt. 2, 1, 8; "Sunset Strip—A City in Self-Defense?" *Los Angeles Newsletter,* 29 Oct. 1966, 3–5; "Sunset for the Strip," *Newsweek,* 4 July 1966, 22–23; *Los Angeles Times,* 28 Feb. 1966, 3; *Life,* 26 Aug. 1966, 75–83; *Los Angeles Magazine,* Dec. 1965, 34–40.

20. *Life,* 26 Aug. 1966, 77; *Newsweek,* 4 July 1966, 22; *Los Angeles Times,* 10 March 1966, pt. 2, 8; 20 March 1966, W4.

21. Ralph Gibson and Roger Kennedy, *The Strip: A Graphic Portrait of Sunset Boulevard, Fall 1966* (Los Angeles: Roger Kennedy Graphics, 1966), 1; *NYRB,* 9 March 1967, 10; *Los Angeles Free Press,* 14 Jan. 1966, 6–7; *Newsweek,* 4 July 1966, 22–23.

22. *Los Angeles Magazine,* May 1967, 30–37, 70–71. The Fifth Estate opened in 1961. See also *Los Angeles Free Press,* 17 Sept. 1964, 1; 22 Oct. 1965, 6; 13 Jan. 1967, 18.

23. *Los Angeles Free Press,* 13 Jan. 1967, 8–9; *Los Angeles Herald-Examiner,* 24 Nov. 1966, 2.

24. Al Mitchell, interview, *Los Angeles Free Press,* 13 Jan. 1967, 8–9.

25. *Esquire,* June 1970, 55–64; *Los Angeles Free Press,* 27 June 1969, 10, 16, 23; 19 July 1968, 3, 6; 1 Nov. 1968, 34–35; *Open City,* 9 June 1967, 11; "LA's *Open City* Closed Down," *Rolling Stone,* 19 April 1969, 14.

26. When the *Free Press* moved to the nearby Jewish neighborhood of Fairfax in 1967, the ambiance was the same—a hodgepodge of political radicals and hippies living in a relatively cheap neighborhood. See *Los Angeles Times, West Magazine* section, 14 May 1967, 8–9; *Los Angeles Times,* 5 June 1966, W1, W5. See also *Los Angeles Underground,* 1 April 1967, 7. Issues of the *Los Angeles Underground* are located in the UCLA Special Collections Archive.

27. *Los Angeles Free Press,* 20 Aug. 1965, 1; 26 June 1967 (extra ed.), entire issue; 24 June 1966, 12; 4 Aug. 1967, 9; 23 Aug. 1968, 33; 25 April 1969, 14–15.

28. *Esquire,* June 1970, 58.

29. The coffeehouse Venice West Café Expresso was a notorious gathering place for beats in the fifties, but it closed in early 1965. See John Maynard, *Venice West* (New Brunswick, N.J.: Rutgers University Press, 1991), 161–68; *Los Angeles Free Press,* 21 Sept. 1964, 1–2; 1 Jan. 1965, 4; 15 Jan. 1965, 2; 25 June 1965, 3; 2 July 1965, 2; *Los Angeles Times,* 27 Jan. 1966, W1–2.

30. *Los Angeles Times,* 8 March 1966, pt. 2, 1; 10 March 1966, 3; 13 March 1966, C1, C11; *Los Angeles Free Press,* 25 June 1965, 3; 18 March 1966, 3, 5; 20 Sept. 1968, 8.

31. *Los Angeles Free Press*, 16 Feb. 1968, 1, 15; *Open City*, 16 Feb. 1968, 4; *Los Angeles Times*, 25 March 1968, 1, 10–11; *Evening Outlook*, 8 Feb. 1968, 1–2; "Damn It, We'd Rather Do It Ourselves," *Los Angeles Magazine*, April 1969, 32–35.

32. *Los Angeles Times*, 4 June 1967, W1, W4; Hyman and Wallach, "Hippies and the New Values," 3; *Los Angeles Magazine*, Feb. 1970, 30.

33. *Los Angeles Times*, 1 April 1966, pt. 2, 1, 8; *Los Angeles Herald-Examiner*, 19 Nov. 1966, C6; 28 Nov. 1966, B2; *NYRB*, 9 March 1967, 8–13. Henri LeFebvre, *The Production of Space* (Cambridge: Blackwell, 1991), 142.

34. LeFebvre, *The Production of Space*, 374. This was a much discussed topic in the local press, both mainstream and underground. See Gibson and Kennedy, *The Strip*, 1; *Los Angeles Free Press*, 30 June 1967, 18; *Open City*, 20 Dec. 1968, 2; *Los Angeles Magazine*, April 1969, 35; Horst Schmidt-Brummer, *Venice, California: An Urban Fantasy* (New York: Grossman, 1973).

35. *Los Angeles Herald-Examiner*, 13 Nov. 1966, 1, 6; *Los Angeles Free Press*, 18 Nov. 1966, 3; *Los Angeles Times*, 14 Nov. 1966, 3; *New York Times*, 14 Nov. 1966, 36.

36. On 11 November, the night before the riot, 85 were arrested, while on 9 July 1966, 276 youths were rounded up by police. *Los Angeles Herald-Examiner*, 12 Nov. 1966, 1; *Los Angeles Free Press*, 15 July 1966, 5. Before the summer of 1966, the curfew, which had been enacted decades earlier, was rarely enforced.

37. *Los Angeles Times*, 8 Jan. 1967, W5.

38. *Los Angeles Times*, 22 Nov. 1966, pt. 2, 1; 16 Jan. 1966, W1, W8; 20 Feb. 1966, W1, W8.

39. *Los Angeles Times*, 14 Nov. 1966, 3. One set of reporters even called the incident a "pseudo-event." They cited evidence that the "riot" was staged by television crewmen who egged the youths on, saying, "You're not just going to stand there, are you? Do something!" (*NYRB*, 9 March 1967, 8–13).

40. *Los Angeles Times*, 27 Nov. 1966, 1, B4, 28 Nov. 1966, 3, 15 Dec. 1966, W14; *Los Angeles Free Press*, 16 Dec. 1966, 1, 21.

41. "Fly Trans-Love Airways," *New Yorker*, 25 Feb. 1967, 121.

42. *Los Angeles Times*, 5 Jan. 1967, pt.2, 1, 2; *Evening Outlook*, 2 Dec. 1966, 10. One observer stated in early 1967, "youngsters have been talking about spreading out and moving into the nearby San Fernando Valley, where the whole cycle will probably begin again with fresh protagonists" (*NYRB*, 9 March 1967); *Los Angeles Herald-Examiner*, 21 Dec. 1966, 3. The conservative *Evening Outlook* editorialized that the arrest of a few Santa Monica High School students on narcotics charges "will serve to awaken many young people and their parents to the ugly realization that the Sunset Strip kind of sickness is a fact of life in every community" (*Evening Outlook*, 1 Dec. 1966, 1).

43. One Chicano writing to the *Free Press* in 1968 explained that Mexicans forced to live in places like Tijuana could not understand hippies who chose to live in squalor (*Los Angeles Free Press*, 19 April 1968, 4).

44. Works that, in varying degrees, take this approach include Rossinow, *The Politics of Authenticity*, Gitlin, *The Sixties*, Rorabaugh, *Berkeley at War*, and Caute, *The Year of the Barricades*.

45. *Open City*, 20 Sept. 1968, 2. In a strange mix of nostalgia and absurdism, protesters planned to "re-enact [their] great victories" immediately afterward. After removing themselves to the exclusive Pacific Palisades neighborhood, they would surround and block a police car to memorialize the Berkeley Free Speech Movement; hold a free store "loot-in"; symbolically reconstruct the old Strip hip nightclub Pandora's Box; conduct a ritual "unmasking" of the police in

memory of the 1967 Century City antiwar demonstration; and, finally, throw a party celebrating the electoral victory of new president of the Peace and Freedom Party Eldridge Cleaver (*Los Angeles Free Press,* 20 Sept. 1968, 8).

46. Perhaps the baldest example of this was the slogan of John Sinclair's White Panther Party (of which the great Detroit rock band MC-5 were the most famous members), "Dope, Guns, and Fucking in the Streets!" For a less ecstatic discussion of the issue, see George Lipsitz, "Who'll Stop the Rain? Youth Culture, Rock 'n' Roll, and Social Crises," in Farber, *The Sixties,* 206–34, esp. 213–14.

47. In a feature article marking the thirtieth anniversary of the march, the *Los Angeles Times* argued that the "bloody, panicked clash left an indelible mark on politics, protests and police relations. It marked a turning point for Los Angeles, a city not known for drawing demonstrators to marches in sizable numbers. . . . The Century Plaza confrontation foreshadowed the explosive growth [nationally] of the antiwar movement and its inevitable confrontations with police. It shaped the movement's rising militancy, particularly among the sizable number of middle-class protesters." A police officer stated that the impact of the demonstration "cannot be underestimated, in terms of its relevance to the LAPD, to the magnitude and effectiveness of the antiwar movement and to what kind of public appearances President Johnson would make in the future" (*Los Angeles Times,* 23 June 1997, A1, A15).

48. Norman Mailer noticed that among the thousands of demonstrators at the October 1967 march on the Pentagon, many were hippies (Norman Mailer, *Armies of the Night: History as a Novel, the Novel as History* [New York: New American Library, 1968], 108–11).

49. *Los Angeles Free Press,* 26 June 1967 (extra edition), entire issue; *Los Angeles Times,* 24 June 1967, 1, 2 July 1967, 1, 20–21; *Los Angeles Herald-Examiner,* 24 June 1967, 1, 3–4, 25 June 1967, 1, 3. One of the main organizers of the protest itself was Donn Healey, who had been married to local communist leader Dorothea Healey. I am indebted to an anonymous reviewer for this information.

50. *Los Angeles Times,* 2 July 1967, 1, 20–21.

51. *Los Angeles Herald-Examiner,* 24 June 1967, 1, 4, 25 June 1967, 3.

52. *Los Angeles Free Press,* 20 Aug. 1965, 1.

53. *Open City,* 26 May 1967, 4.

54. *Los Angeles Magazine,* May 1967, 72.

55. The best description of the Watts "acid test" and the other "tests" held in Los Angeles is in Tom Wolfe, *The Electric Kool-Aid Acid Test* (New York: Farrar, Straus & Giroux, 1968), 267–86.

56. *Open City,* 7 July 1967, 10.

57. *Provo,* 1 Aug. 1967, 13.

58. *Open City,* 14 July 1967, 8, 9, 16; *Los Angeles Free Press,* 14 July 1967, 7, 12.

59. *Open City,* 4 Aug. 1967, 9; *Los Angeles Free Press,* 4 Aug. 1967, 17; *Open City,* 2 Sept. 1967, 7. Indeed, local hip music acts participated in a number of benefits for Native American rights in the late sixties. *Oracle of Southern California,* Aug. 1967, 15; "Festivals," *Rolling Stone,* 9 Aug. 1969, 16; "Random Notes," *Rolling Stone,* 9 Dec. 1971, 4.

60. Earl Ofari and Jerry Harrison, both black reporters, wrote respectively for the *Free Press* and *Open City.* They tended to cover political and social issues in the ghetto but also wrote frequently about the ghetto arts scene. Robert Igriega and Bob Garcia, both Latinos, wrote for the *Open City.*

61. *Open City,* 7 Feb. 1969, 2.

62. Hyman and Wallach, "Hippies and the New Values," 10; Gibson and Kennedy, *The Strip*, 2–3, 6, 10, 13, 20–21, 32–33.

63. *Los Angeles Free Press*, 18 Aug. 1967, 3, 5.

64. *Open City*, 4 Aug. 1967, 9; *Los Angeles Free Press*, 4 Aug. 1967, 17.

65. *Open City*, 2 Sept. 1967, 7. The article was entitled "Love-In That Made Mostly Enemies." Interestingly, Watts-based black director Ed Gentry filmed a mostly white love-in, *A Groovy Griffith Park Love-In*, in early 1968. In it, he "seem[ed] to be insisting that the flower experiment has failed, that if you are white and hip you are still white and middle-class, and though you have turned your back on white bourgeoise [*sic*] conventions, you still bear the guilt of whiteness. . . . Gentry superimposes art nouveau versions of the slogans of the 'beautiful people,' implying, one supposes, that the hip world has become an establishment to itself: snobbish, superior, and ambitious in its own special way." *Open City*, 8 March 1968, 12.

66. *Los Angeles Times, West Magazine* section, 28 Jan. 1967, 17.

67. The most glaring example of the commodification of the countercultural ethos occurred annually at the city's notorious teen fair. Located in Hollywood, businesses used the fair to discern what the next trends in youth culture would be. At the 1967 fair entrepreneurs emphasized psychedelic themes to determine what would be cool: "Even Sears Roebuck made its appearance in the form of a 'Psychedelic Bug-Out' complete with hallucinatory movies consisting of teens frolicking in Sears bathing suits, viewed in reverse motion and through tinted lenses." The 1969 teen fair saw the resolutely bohemian Flying Burrito Brothers and Jimi Hendrix play alongside displays of youth-oriented bric-a-brac (*Los Angeles Underground*, 23 April 1967, 5; *Los Angeles Free Press*, 8 April 1966, 1, 4 April 1, 11; *Evening Outlook*, 1 April 1969, 1A–2A).

68. Liner notes to The Mothers of Invention, *Freak Out!* (Rykodisk: RCD 10501), 1966.

69. *Oracle of Southern California*, Aug. 1967, 3–5, 18–21; Lewis Yablonsky, *The Hippie Trip* (New York: Pegasus, 1968), 47; *Open City*, 19 May 1967, 3; *Los Angeles Times*, 1 June 1967, W1, 25 May 1967, W4.

70. Kim Fowley, interview by Bob Ferris, KNX Radio, 1968. Recording included on *Highs in the Mid-Sixties*, vol. 3, *L.A. '67—Mondo Hollywood A Go Go* (Archive International Productions: AIP 10005).

71. *Los Angeles Times*, west section, 28 Jan. 1968, 17–21; "Neil Young," *Rolling Stone*, 30 April 1970, 40–43; *Oracle of Southern California*, Aug. 1967, 28, Nov. 1967, 3–9; *Los Angeles Free Press*, 7 March 1969, 6; *Open City*, 16 June 1967, 2, 29 March 1968, 8.

72. Lawrence Lipton, with Carlos Hagen, "Memories of a Love-In" (1974), sound recording with accompanying transcript, New York Public Library Recorded Sound Archive, 1–8.

73. *Oracle of Southern California*, April 1967, 4, May 1967, 3–7, June 1967, 9, July 1967, 4, 26; Lipton, "Memories of a Love-In," 2.

74. A *Free Press* writer even declared that long hair on men "function[ed] as the lion's mane, standing for pride, strength, and sexuality." Short hair, on the other hand, "symboliz[ed] the young man's willingness to submit to authority." *Los Angeles Free Press*, 30 May 1969, 40.

75. Lipton, "Memories of a Love-In," 8; *Los Angeles Free Press*, 11 April 1969, 1, 22; *Oracle of Southern California*, Oct. 1967, 1, 14, Dec. 1967, 1.

76. *Los Angeles Free Press*, 4 July 1969, 6, 1 Aug. 1969, 5, 3 April 1970, 8.

77. Gene Youngblood of the *Free Press*, aping Marshall McLuhan, argued that "Our perspectives are no longer unilateral but kaleidoscopic. Our environment is more complex, more 'total'" (*Los Angeles Free Press*, 21 June 1968, 33); see also *Los Angeles Magazine*, May 1967, 30; *Oracle of Southern California*, Dec. 1967, 4, 5, 14.

78. Hyman and Wallach, "Hippies and the New Values," 14; *Provo,* 1 May 1967, 4; *Los Angeles Times,* 26 Nov. 1966, 19.

79. *Provo,* 26 May 1967, 9; *Los Angeles Free Press,* 24 May 1968, 26–27. *Free Press* critic Harlan Ellison (a famous science fiction writer himself) skewered ABC television's appropriation of hip, *The Mod Squad* (*Los Angeles Free Press,* 11 Oct. 1968, 5, 10 Jan. 1969, 5).

80. *Los Angeles Free Press,* 26 Aug. 1966, 2.

81. Ibid., 1 Nov. 1968, 34–35, 41. For more unfavorable comparisons of Los Angeles to other scenes, see *Open City,* 17 Nov. 1967, 4, 8 Dec. 1967, 4, 14 June 1968, 8; "Pinnacle and Kaleidoscope in Los Angeles," *Rolling Stone,* 11 May 1968, 18. Barney Hoskyns concluded similarly, remarking, "As early as 1965, San Francisco hippies were routinely dismissing LA as a plastic dystopia, the polar opposite of everything San Francisco stood for. Frisco was the city of Beats, Pranksters, and Diggers, of subversive street theater: Los Angeles was a mammon of hype and freeways" (Barney Hoskyns, *Waiting for the Sun: Weird Scenes and the Sound of Los Angeles* [New York: St. Martin's, 1996], 140–42). See also "Los Angeles Scene," *Rolling Stone,* 22 June 1968, 11–15.

82. Letwin, interview.

83. *Open City,* 5 April 1968, 13, 9 June 1968, 8; *Los Angeles Magazine,* April 1969, 32–35, 56–62; *Free Venice Beachhead,* Jan. 1969, 1; *Los Angeles Free Press,* 29 Aug. 1969, 12.

84. *Evening Outlook,* 23 April 1969, 4.

85. *Los Angeles Free Press,* 16 Feb. 1968, 1, 15; *Open City,* 16 Feb. 1968, 4; *Los Angeles Times,* 25 March 1968, 1, 10, 11.

86. *Los Angeles Times,* 25 March 1968, 1, 10–11.

87. *Open City,* 16 Feb. 1968, 4. One Venice patrolman received a poster in the mail saying, "Abolish Trigger Happy Pigs" (*Los Angeles Times,* 27 Oct. 1968, W4).

88. "The Two Tonys," *New Yorker,* 6 Oct. 1997, 66–74; *Los Angeles Times,* 25 March 1968, 11, 27 Oct. 1968, W1; *Open City,* 27 Sept. 1968, 3.

89. Schmidt-Brummer, *Venice, California,* 7, 21, 24–25.

90. *Open City,* 20 Dec. 1968, 2; *Los Angeles Magazine,* April 1969, 35; *Los Angeles Times,* 28 July 1968, W1, W6; *Los Angeles Free Press,* 11 Oct. 1968, 2; *Evening Outlook,* 26 April 1969, 1–2.

91. *Open City,* 16 Feb. 1968, 3; *Los Angeles Free Press,* 16 Feb. 1968, 15, 11 Oct. 1968, 2; *Evening Outlook,* 9 Feb. 1968, 1–2, 10 Feb. 1968, 1–2, 12 Feb. 1968, 1, 8.

92. *Los Angeles Free Press,* 25 April 1969, 3.

93. *Los Angeles Magazine,* April 1969, 34–38, 56–62; *Free Venice Beachhead,* Jan. 1969, 1; *Los Angeles Free Press,* 25 April 1969, 3.

94. Schmidt-Brummer, *Venice, California,* 7, 21, 24–25.

95. *Zabriskie Point* (MGM, 1970).

96. *Blow-Up* (Premier/MGM, 1966). Given the film's opacity, it was remarkably successful in the Los Angeles area, breaking the box office record at a local theater (*Variety,* 13 March 1967, 3).

Part II

Reconsiderations

CHAPTER 7

How New Was the New Left?

Andrew Hunt

> One suspects that, when the history of the 1960s radicalization becomes more
> fully analyzed, a process that will only come about through the probing of a
> large number of individual experiences of a cross-section of activists, the na-
> ture of the phenomenon might seem very different than the popular images de-
> picted today. In fact, what are currently regarded as the conventional—one
> might even say "canonical"—features of the 1960s radicalization and its ac-
> tivists, may prove to be atypical and peripheral.
>
> —Alan Wald

In 1983 Americans flocked to see *The Big Chill,* directed by Lawrence Kasdan. Many
critics and audiences praised the film as sophisticated and witty. Pauline Kael called it
an "amiable, slick comedy with some very well-directed repartee and skillful perform-
ances," but also noted that "it isn't really political."[1] In the film, set in South Carolina
during the early 1980s, a group of seven old friends from the University of Michigan
gather at the funeral of their friend Alex, who has slashed his wrists out of disillusionment. Erstwhile campus radicals, the seven friends have become paunchy and prosperous. They drink wine, smoke dope, listen to lots of 1960s music, have sex, and, to a person, dismiss the radical activism of the 1960s as a meaningless juvenile infatuation.
After the funeral they go their separate ways, committed to making money instead of
change. It is no wonder that many 1960s radicals left the cinema feeling dispirited or
disgusted. Many of them bristled at the idea that 1960s radicals had "sold out" or
"grown up," a widely held assumption among the general public by the time the film
was made.

The Big Chill caused many former student activists to pause to reevaluate their accomplishments. The popular film reinforced a myth that proved difficult for many radicals and historians to counter. Some even began to accept it. One Marxist intellectual

noted that the 1980s "was the decade when those radicalized in the 1960s and 1970s began to enter middle age. Usually they did so with all the hope of socialist revolution gone—indeed, often having ceased to believe in the desirability of such a revolution."[2] Perhaps unintentionally, the pioneers of 1960s history contributed to the *Big Chill* myth. By portraying the New Left as unique to the era, these early scholars of 1960s history lent credence to the notion that most activists had followed the same path as the characters in Kasdan's film. None probed the similarities between the Old and the New Left. Instead, they celebrated the exceptional nature of the New Left, or the ways in which the New Left continued to have an impact on American politics after the 1970s. Allen Matusow, among others, expressed this view:

> The old left consisted of various sects exhausted by pointless intramural feuding and subsisting on an archaic faith in the revolutionary potential of the working class. . . . Impatient with Marxism as a social theory and contemptuous of the parties that treated its texts as sacred, the new left intended to let its ideology emerge from action and chose men of action, not mere thinkers, as its early heroes—Robert Moses walking alone into Mississippi, Fidel Castro in the Sierra Maestra Mountains with his tiny rebel band, and [C. Wright] Mills, the lonely rebel fighting complacency in academe.[3]

Matusow's assessment is echoed in countless books about the 1960s in general and the New Left in particular, both those who wrote before Matusow and those who came after. Irwin Unger's *The Movement: A History of the American New Left* (1974), set the tone for the steady stream of books on the subject that appeared in the 1980s.[4] According to Unger, the young radicals of the period, prone to experimentation and highly critical of theory, were "anti-imperialist," and "concerned with personal liberation and life-style issues." Ultimately, their affluence, contempt for "bourgeois values and institutions," and rejection of the "bureaucratic Old Left" made this generation of leftists distinct from their forebears.[5] In 1988 the British historian David Caute argued that the Left, before the explosion of radicalism of the 1960s, consisted of a mixture of social democratic and communist elements. This tradition emphasized class conflict, worked within trade unions, embraced technological and material progress, seldom challenged the paternalism of universities or the right of administrators to enact antidemocratic regulations, and lived largely conventional lives that rendered them virtually indistinguishable in appearance or material possessions from their neighbors.[6] "The Old Left," he wrote, "was not without passion (and anger), but held the mind must govern the heart. . . . The New Left's relaxed, permissive attitude to sex and drugs often offended the Old Left, who in turn seemed 'square,' 'hung up,' and therefore repressive to the young."[7] By contrast, the New Left, taking its cues from Camus, Sartre, Mills, and Marcuse, embraced a more libertarian kind of radicalism, inspired by the civil rights movement and the Cuban revolution, and directed its opposition against the arms race, corporate liberalism, the Cold War, and racial and economic inequality.[8] The tendency to stress New Left exceptionalism still persists. Paul Boyer observed in 1995, "In contrast to 1930s radicals, 1960s activists sought to change consciousness and attitudes as well as the political system. . . . Depression-era radicals had identified with workers, as in

Clifford Odets's 1935 play, *Waiting for Lefty*. New Left radicals . . . allied themselves more often with social outcasts, even those stigmatized as insane."[9]

One of the few books to explore the relationship between the old and New Left in any depth is Maurice Isserman's *"If I Had a Hammer . . .": The Death of the Old Left and the Birth of the New Left* (1987). Isserman traces the complex relationship between those embers of Old Left radicalism still glowing in the early 1960s—tiny enclaves of CPers, Schactmanites, radical pacifists, *Dissent* contributors, and so on—and the young drafters of the SDS's influential 1962 manifesto, the *Port Huron Statement*. Isserman concludes that youthful New Left pioneers focused primarily on the shortcomings of their precursors, while failing to learn a number of important lessons, particularly the importance of their elders' "sense of historical irony that would allow its adherents to keep both victories and defeats in perspective."[10]

Isserman's book was a welcome antidote to the standard interpretation of New Left exceptionalism. But it was primarily an exploration of the decline of American radicalism in the aftermath of McCarthyism and the Cold War, and the ways in which its declension gave rise to the New Left. He traced the roots of the New Left without placing it in a larger tradition of American radicalism.

The task of developing a deeper understanding of the New Left and its place in American cultural history has been impeded by the lack of consensus on exactly how to define the New Left. Some observers emphasize the organic nature of the New Left. David Caute identified three "phases" through which the New Left passed, before disintegrating in the early 1970s.[11] Kenneth Kenniston, a professor of psychology who had witnessed the student movement of the 1960s, distinguished between "the old New Left" and "the new New Left."[12] In 1981 Staughton Lynd identified a "first New Left," which "was made up of radicals in the years 1930–45 who broke not only from Stalinism but also from Leninism, and not only from Leninism, but also from Trotskyism, and not only from Trotskyism, but in part from Marxism itself."[13] A narrower definition of the New Left has come from a cluster of intellectuals, among them Todd Gitlin and James Miller, who have effectively reduced the New Left to a small clique based in the national office of Students for a Democratic Society. When SDS grew, the New Left grew; when SDS collapsed, the New Left died. Others have traced the intellectual origins of the New Left to Madison, Wisconsin, a cauldron of progressive thought and experimentation for decades before the 1960s. In *History and the New Left* (1990), for example, Paul Buhle collected a fascinating series of essays by prominent writers, historians, and public figures who did their graduate work at the University of Wisconsin's history department in the 1950s and 1960s, and whose contributions to the early New Left were vital.[14]

There is even more confusion about what constitutes the Old Left. Most narratives treat the Left before around 1959 as an amorphous amalgamation of every form of social, cultural, intellectual, and political radicalism that existed on both sides of the Atlantic. Among the few historians to attempt to sort out the various pre-1960s strains of radicalism, John Patrick Diggins identifies two categories: the "Lyrical Left," or early-twentieth-century band of socialists, anarchists, free lovers, birth control advocates, guests of Mabel Dodge's Greenwich Village salon, radical clergy, and Wobblies (members of the Industrial Workers of the World), and particularly around the cluster of intellectuals gathered around the radical periodical the *Masses;* and the "Old Left," the Great Depression Left, which consisted primarily of the Communist Party, but also the Socialist Party under Norman Thomas, the Trotskyist Socialist Workers Party, and various postwar, anti-Stalinist intellectuals.

Each generation of radicals creates its own new Left, with new agendas and ideological axes to grind. Once upon a time, Debs's Socialist Party and the Industrial Workers of the World represented a new Left. So, too, did the Communist Party. In many respects, the Communist Party underwent a more dramatic break with earlier American radical movements than did the New Left of the 1960s. Diggins found that what he called the Lyrical Left drew several of its major figures from "small towns in the Midwest or rural Northeast," while his "Old Left" attracted "many of Russian Jewish or east European ancestry."[15] The Lyrical Left looked to American cultural radicalism for inspiration—particularly to the writings of Thoreau and Whitman—but the Old Left intellectuals "were more inclined to turn away from American intellectual traditions to look elsewhere for an inspiring radical ideology."[16] A telling example of this divide, writes Diggins, is the sharp contrast between the *Masses* of the World War I years, with its poetic innocence, and the *New Masses* of the 1930s, typically full of dry, jargon-filled essays. He also draws parallels between the Lyrical Left and the New Left of the 1960s: "In spirit, the New Left was originally closer to the 1913 rebels than to the Marxists of the thirties. . . . In its élan and anarchist bravado the New Left . . . resembled the Lyrical rebels."[17] Reading Diggins, one cannot escape the conclusion that in the history of twentieth-century American radicalism, the Communist Party was a greater anomaly than the 1960s New Left. With its unwavering allegiance to Moscow, authoritarian democratic centralism, clandestine tactics, fixed hierarchy, and rigid emphasis on Marxism-Leninism, the party departed sharply from the more decentralized and libertarian radical movements of the twentieth century.[18] Still, unlike the 1960s New Left, the CP never made any attempt to disown its radical heritage. On the contrary, during the Great Depression, party members and so-called fellow travelers elevated radical luminaries such as Eugene Debs, Sacco and Vanzetti, Big Bill Haywood, and the Wobblies to mythic status.[19]

Though a clear definition of these various incarnations of "the Left" remains elusive, a central tenet of the New-Left-as-exception view is that the New Left of the 1960s was separate and distinct from all that came before it. "It is important to understand," wrote Barbara Ehrenreich in 1992, "how much the New Left represented not just an upsurge of 'the Left,' but a radical break from the socialist and communist traditions that for so long defined leftism."[20] This assumption has been the foundation of historical writing on the 1960s for the past twenty years, but a closer examination suggests a great deal more fluidity between the two lefts. Perhaps the most telling indicator of their overlap is that New Left idol Herbert Marcuse's most famous disciple, Angela Davis, was a member of the Communist Party—tarred as an Old Left organization by Tom Hayden and co.—and she assumed a prominent place in the party's leadership. "I needed comrades," Davis recalled in her autobiography, "with whom I could share a common ideology. I was tired of ephemeral ad-hoc groups that fell apart when faced with the slightest difficulty; tired of men who measured their sexual height by women's intellectual genuflection."[21]

Davis was by no means unique. Several of the most respected antiwar leaders of the 1960s were schooled by groups and individuals who most scholars have dismissed as "Old Left" and therefore insignificant. One of these, Dorothy Healey, found herself lionized by young activists in southern California, and her call-in radio show on Los Angeles's KPFK became legendary in radical circles.[22] Younger militants like Davis discovered Healey and other veteran radicals and found that they had much to learn from them. "I began to pay visits to Dorothy Healey, who was the District Organizer of Southern California. We had long, involved discussions—sometimes arguments—about the party, its role within the movement. . . . I immensely enjoyed these discussions with Dorothy and felt that I was learning a great deal from them, regardless of whether I ultimately decided to become a Communist myself," Davis wrote.[23]

Davis's experience reflected a broader trend. Movement luminaries who were either members of "Old Left" organizations or who cut their political teeth among earlier generations of activists include Healey, Dave Dellinger, Fred Halstead, Michael Harrington, A. J. Muste, Barbara Deming, I. F. Stone, Pete Seeger, Anne and Carl Braden, Bettina Aptheker, David McReynolds, Peter Camejo, Doug Dowd, Hal Draper, and many others. The infusion of "red diaper" babies into the movement was in part responsible for bridging the gap between the new generation of radicals and their forebears.[24] Because of their unique upbringing—many had witnessed firsthand the demoralizing effects of McCarthyism on their families and friends—the red diaper babies usually had a better grasp of historical ironies, and contributed a more levelheaded approach to organizing. As Judy Kaplan and Linn Shapiro have observed, "During the sixties, many Red Diaper babies who joined the New Left offered a competing point of view to the belief that revolution was around the corner and that college students would make it happen. Radical change, we had been taught, results from painstaking organizing, often requiring a lifetime commitment, among the working masses."[25]

Scholars have never properly credited the Trotskyist Socialist Workers Party (SWP) for its diligent and often effective organizing efforts.[26] "In the course of the 1960s," writes Alan Wald (who proves the exception to the rule), "the SWP's vitality was revealed through a surprising initial responsiveness to feminism, gay rights, and even some aspects of the counter-culture."[27] And in fact the SWP contributed significantly to the student movement, notably in leading antiwar efforts through its Student Mobilization Committee to End the War in Vietnam (SMC). In 1965 it appeared that SDS was poised to assume a prominent role in coordinating antiwar actions. The organization had sponsored the highly effective 17 April antiwar demonstration in Washington, D.C., which by conservative estimates drew twenty thousand protesters. Despite this early success, SDS officially abdicated its leadership position in the antiwar movement at its national convention at Camp Kewadin, Michigan, in June 1965.[28] This was a divisive move for SDS, and many local chapters questioned its wisdom and continued antiwar organizing on their own. In the 4 December 1967 issue of the SDS periodical *New*

Left Notes, Carl Davidson and Gregg Calvert editorialized: "To continue our previous position of separating ourselves from other antiwar forces, without advocating an independent program of our own, would be an indulgence in sectarianism which neither we nor the movement could afford."[29] The decision left the door wide open for the SMC, a coalition firmly under the control of the SWP, to maneuver into the void left by SDS's departure. At this point, writes Fred Halstead, "the Communist Party and the Socialist Workers Party—and the youth groups allied with them—were beginning to play a more central role in the movement."[30] Thereafter SMC, not SDS, would emerge as the main student organization in the national antiwar coalition.[31]

The so-called "Old Left" played a more vital role in the movement than scholars have supposed, and its impact on young radicals was constantly in evidence. Nevertheless, some of the most influential accounts of the 1960s insist that movement youths rejected both the practical experience and the socialist ideology of their elders. Particularly controversial is the question of whether early SDSers endorsed Marxism, and to what extent. The debaters range from Todd Gitlin, who insisted in 1995 that "the movement . . . felt no attachment to the promise of the 'socialist' camp," to former *Ramparts* editor David Horowitz, then a Marxist and now a conservative activist, who claims, "we were Marxist revolutionaries when we began the New Left."[32] Whatever the original intentions of the founders of SDS and other pioneers of the New Left, by the late 1960s the carefully reasoned language of the *Port Huron Statement* had been supplanted by more militant, confrontational rhetoric. Sources once dismissed as "Old Left"—namely, Marx, Lenin, and Rosa Luxemburg—enjoyed a revival among the newly militant engaged in street fights at home and protests against the horrific war in Vietnam.

Some of the most prominent historians of the era have romanticized the early 1960s while following Diggins's reading of the later years: "Although the New Left started out as an open, democratic, and nonideological movement, by the end of the sixties much of the New Left had reverted to the clichés of economic Marxism; it had succumbed to the fury of sectarianism and even to the 'cult of personality.'"[33] Allen Matusow was even more unequivocal in his denunciation of late-1960s radicals: "By the time of the SDS national convention at East Lansing, Michigan, June 1968, the new left was rapidly coming to resemble the old. Pictures of Mao and Lenin hung on the walls, and copies of Mao's little red book were everywhere. Not long ago Marx had been regarded as an old fogy from the Victorian past."[34]

Almost all of the SDS-centered accounts treat even the nominal presence of what they derisively call "ideology" (read Marxism) as threatening, paving the way for a takeover by tiny ultra-leftist sects. What these scholars ignore in their glorification of the early New Left is that SDS was confined largely to pockets of campus intellectuals in the San Francisco Bay Area, Madison, Wisconsin, and Ann Arbor, Michigan. The more militant New Left that dominated the later part of the decade, by contrast, radicalized movement participants in ways that the SDS, with its limited scope and pragmatic idealism, never could.[35] Contrary to Gitlin, Miller, et al., the New Left did not end with the demise of SDS. Had the movement been so vulnerable as to fall prey to the Weather Underground and the Progressive Labor Party (PLP)—two tiny sects no more significant than the Symbionese Liberation Army—then it would hardly be worth all the trees that have been destroyed in chronicling its existence.[36] But the New Left was made of tougher stuff and enjoyed a much broader base of support than that, as Terry Anderson and other historians have documented.[37] For every person who gravitated into the orbit of the Weathermen or PLP, there were countless others who rejected such foolishness in favor of meaningful, nonviolent, socialist activism. The conventional "death-of-the-sixties" myth espoused by writers like Gitlin has eliminated the contradictions and complexities of the period. Even if we ignore developments after 1968—feminism, environmentalism, neighborhood organizing, G.I. and Vietnam veterans' struggles, Chicano and American Indian activism, gay and lesbian liberation, communes, huge antiwar demonstrations, and an explosion of cultural radicalism and experimentation—the trite SDS "death-of-the-sixties" account sheds little light on some of the most tumultuous years in American history.

An even less supportable claim is that the early New Left invented the concept of participatory democracy, which reverberates through much of the literature of the period. Milton Viorst, for example, attributes the origins of participatory democracy to C. Wright Mills.[38] The *Port Huron Statement* may have secured a prominent place for the term "participatory democracy," but it was hardly a new idea. The concept, by other names, had deep roots in American—and indeed in European—history and culture. The historical record fairly brims with attempts since colonial times to fashion sovereign, decentralized communities, built from the "bottom up," populated by enlightened and engaged citizens. When radical activists began to "rediscover" American history in the late 1960s, they found that previous generations of Transcendentalists, populists, socialists, communists, Wobblies, anarchists, and others had struggled against tremendous odds to empower ordinary Americans with a sense of self-worth. The Owenite and Fourierist socialist communes in antebellum America represented some of the earliest forms of participatory democracy in this country.[39] General strikes in 1876 and 1919, the unemployment councils and renters strikes of the early 1930s, the Flint sit-down strike of 1937, the radical pacifist communes of World War II, are only a few of the many experiments in egalitarian, humanistic "group-centered" decision making of the sort advocated by student radicals in the 1960s.

If the history of attempts to realize participatory democracy has been overlooked, so too have their intellectual origins. Whether or not the drafters of the *Port Huron Statement* knew it, their ideal of participatory democracy was indebted to the writings of utopian socialists such as St. Simon and Fourier, early-twentieth-century British socialists Sidney and Beatrice Webb,[40] French syndicalist Georges Sorel, anarchist Emma Goldman, and more contemporary political thinkers such as Saul Alinsky, Dave Dellinger, and Dwight McDonald.

A pervasive and typically unchallenged assumption in the literature on protest movements of the 1960s is that young radicals were anti-intellectual and largely ignorant of history. Many chroniclers have argued that the New Left's rejection of all things theoretical and abstract represented a discontinuity between the New Left and the Old Left. But historical amnesia was not as prevalent among sixties radicals as the secondary accounts suggest. Younger radicals were by no means ignorant of history. In fact, during the early seventies numerous so-called "movement people" went from the streets to the graduate schools, and the field of American history proved a direct beneficiary of this shift. Journals like *Radical America, Studies on the Left,* and, later, *Radical History Review,* reflected the developing historical consciousness of the New Left. Radicals went from graduate school to tenure-track jobs in record numbers, a trend that prompted University of Alabama professor Forrest McDonald to lament that "left-wingers" controlled the "history departments of the most prestigious schools as well as the two major associations of professional historians."[41] By the mid-1970s, new books had appeared on resistance and social movements in American history, as scholars attempted to develop a deeper understanding of the failures and triumphs of previous generations of the American Left. The popularization of Dee Brown's American Indian history *Bury My Heart at Wounded Knee* (1970) and Howard Zinn's *A People's History of the United States* (1970) heralded the radicalization of American history. Outside the classroom, campus revival houses began showing Herbert Biberman's 1954 film *Salt of the Earth,* an uncompromising look at a bitter miners' strike in New Mexico produced by blacklisted Hollywood filmmakers. *Salt of the Earth* acquired a cult following in the 1960s because of its nuanced and sensitive treatment of women, Latinos, and union organizing. Film historian Danny Peary wrote:

> Indeed, *Salt of the Earth,* though intended for working-class people of all eras, was the one nondocumentary with which student activists of the protest era could identify. . . . They saw triumphant militant protest against a seemingly invincible authoritarian foe; characters like themselves whose political consciousness is raised . . . as they engage in political activity; and a film that speaks out for *solidarity* and against the power elite, encompassing racial brotherhood and sexual equality.[42]

The revival of *Salt of the Earth* on college campuses, the growing enrollment of young radicals in humanities and the social sciences, and the appearance of left-leaning history texts signaled a shift in academia that, given the times, made a great deal of sense. Gone were the days when a C. Wright Mills or a William Appleman Williams stood out as a heretic.

Despite the march of movement radicals into academia, most scholars continued to accept the Old Left–New Left dichotomy without question in the 1980s and 1990s, particularly the patently false claim that the 1960s represented the first outburst of student activism in the United States.[43] C. Wright Mills popularized this idea in his influential "Letter to the New Left," which appeared in the *New Left Review* in 1960. Mills attacked the Marxist theory of the working class as the vanguard of revolution, an antiquated notion that belonged in the dustbin, in Mills's view. Students and intellectuals, not workers, were the "possible, immediate, radical agency of change," he wrote.[44] Of course, this was not a new idea either, though it was widely considered novel at the time. Campus unrest, in fact, dates back to 1766, when students at Harvard College revolted over rancid butter being served in the commons. Between 1800 and 1830 students at Princeton staged at least six violent demonstrations, including one riot in which students seized control of several buildings and defied authorities to halt the takeover. At Brown, a series of "deliberate, organized, and protracted" campus uprisings forced the president to resign. In the wake of such riots, John Wheelock, president of Dartmouth, noted, "Melancholy must be the prospect . . . of our country, when students . . . undertake to insult humanity and justice, to prostrate laws and overturn the social order."[45]

From the abolitionist student groups of the 1830s to student settlement house volunteers seventy years later, student activism persisted throughout the nineteenth century. Pacifist organizations emerged on campuses across the country during World War I, most notably the Intercollegiate Socialist Society (ISS), founded in 1905 by Jack London, Upton Sinclair, and Clarence Darrow.[46] After the war, the ISS evolved into the League for Industrial Democracy, which boasted two thousand members by 1927 and some seventy-five college chapters. In the meantime, two groups, the Intercollegiate Liberal League and the more activist National Student Forum (NSF) emerged in the 1920s as important vehicles for nationwide student protest. The NSF's biweekly *New Student* reported routinely on resistance and upheavals at institutions of higher education across the United States. When the first issue of the *New Student* appeared in 1922, students at the University of Wisconsin protested the president's decision to ban such prominent intellectuals as radical University of Pennsylvania sociologist Scott Nearing, author Upton Sinclair, and socialist writer Kate Richards O'Hare from speaking on campus. After much agitation, and the rental of an off-campus hall for Sinclair, the students won their demands, an important victory for academic freedom.[47] From 1922 until 1929 the *New Student* reported on academic freedom battles, student strikes, campus communist clubs, student civil disobedience, anti-ROTC demonstrations, and other acts of nonconformity.

If the 1920s gave rise to the small but steadily growing student movement in the United States, the Great Depression witnessed its flowering. This renaissance of student activism is the subject of Robert Cohen's recent book, *When the Old Left Was Young: Student Radicals and America's First Mass Student Movement* (1993). Relying on student newspapers, oral histories, university administrative files, previously classified FBI files, U.S. Office of Education documents, and many other sources, Cohen reconstructs a period of American history in which student activism rivaled, if it did not surpass, the unrest of the 1960s. Such groups as the American Student Union, the Young People's Socialist League (the youth wing of the Socialist Party), the Young Communist League, the National Student League, and countless individual students launched free speech fights, academic freedom battles, student strikes, antiwar rallies, and demonstrations against racial discrimination. Cohen reminds us that UC Berkeley's first free speech fight erupted not in 1964 but in 1934. University of California chancellor Clark Kerr's crackdown on free speech activists paled in comparison to the methods used in the Depression, when Berkeley dean Louis O'Brien worked with "undergraduate vigilantes" from fraternity row and the football team to violently disrupt the free speech strike.[48] Cohen quotes playwright Arthur Miller's reminiscence of his days as a student at the University of Michigan in the 1930s, which could have applied to UC Berkeley thirty years later:

It was a time when frats, like the football team, were losing their glamor. . . . Instead my generation thirsted for another kind of action, and we took great pleasure from the sit-down strikes that burst loose in Flint and Detroit. . . . We saw a new world coming every third morning. . . . When I think of the library I think of the sound of a stump speaker on the lawn outside because so many times I looked up from what I was reading to try to hear what issue they were debating now. The place was full of speeches, meetings, and leaflets. It was jumping with issues.[49]

Not only was the Depression a watershed for campus activism; student radicals keenly understood university power relations. During the Berkeley Free Speech Movement of 1964, Mario Savio's influential essay "The End of History" criticized the culture of conformity at the postwar "multiversity." Savio's critique of the university as an assembly line made to "serve the need of American industry" mirrored earlier student complaints.[50] Forty years earlier, for example, William Ross of Brookwood Labor College acknowledged that for years students had been "aware of the domination of institutions of higher learning by business interests" and sought ways to undo the relationship.[51] Another 1920s student activist, Douglas Haskell, declared, "With all respect to the older generation, . . . spiritually this is an age of ruin, of nausea. Mechanization must go."[52]

Much has been made of the so-called generation gap of the 1960s. "Never trust anyone over thirty," a statement often attributed to Berkeley Free Speech Movement activist Jack Weinberg, became one of the most ubiquitous slogans of the era. But even this sentiment can be traced back to the youthful radicals of World War I, free spirits such as John Reed and Floyd Dell, who feared that age thirty marked a turning point after which youthful idealism would begin to wane. "Adolescence is the true day of revolt," wrote Walter Weyl of the youthful World War I–era militants, "the day when obscure forces, as mysterious as growth, push us, trembling, out of our narrow lives into the wide throbbing life beyond self."[53]

Students in the interwar years showed an ingenuity that would make 1960s militants proud. In December 1922 a three-day student conference sponsored in Hartsdale, New York, by the National Student Forum (NSF) listed grievances similar to those voiced by campus radicals more than forty years later. Approximately sixty students from schools across the country discussed ways of transforming their roles "from that of audience to that of actor."[54] The NSF issued a broad critique of higher education in particular and war and capitalism in general. The report concluded that "academic freedom is frequently suppressed"; "the existing marking system had a stultifying effect on whatever . . . intellectual intentions a student might have"; "a great deal of college is just so much deadly boredom" lacking "insight into human problems"; and the "college president . . . [and] the board of trustees . . . have effective control over the affairs of college, both as to what shall be taught, and how, and who shall teach it."[55] A conference participant proposed that students resist these disturbing trends in higher education by engaging in "unselfish service" as the first "step toward the freedom of that social order which we seek to bring about."[56]

Nor was the New Left of the 1960s unique in suggesting that students and intellectuals should be natural agents of social change. Student activists had made this argument for decades before the *Port Huron Statement.* In 1933 a radical journalist commented on the meteoric growth of leftist politics on American university campuses: "Radical parties have grasped this opportunity to entrench themselves within the [student] movement. Organizations such as the National Student League have done much in making the student socially conscious. Various radical social science clubs have sprung up in colleges. These should lead, be the vanguard, and hasten the natural growth of the movement."[57]

Five years later, in a foreshadowing of things to come, anarchist Stephen Craig explored this idea further in the pages of *Vanguard:*

> The students, armed with better facilities of education, and soon to become (for the most part) an integral part of the proletariat, should be the vanguard in this struggle which is basically that of socialism. By opposing this course, they place themselves and the workers in the mire of patriotism and become supporters of capitalism. The libertarian youth will fight this treacherous tendency among the students and will exert all their efforts in directing it along the lines of anti-statism and anti-capitalism through solid links with the working class.[58]

The Depression had its own Mario Savios, now largely forgotten. The University of Virginia, for example, was a relatively conservative campus before 1932, its student government controlled by fraternities. In the fall of 1932, as the climate of the country began to sour, a student named Chance Stoner established a Marxist study class on campus that quickly gained a large following. Stoner eventually "organized the rest of the student body," became its president, and rewrote the college's constitution. In 1935 he led Virginia's first pacifist student strike, which "shut down all university classes."[59]

Of course, World War II and the end of the Depression took the wind out of the sails of student protest movements, and student radicalism remained dormant in the 1940s and 1950s, except for pockets of resistance and revolt. The 1960s marked a renaissance for young radicals, but historians of the 1960s have overemphasized the discontinuity between the new wave of radicalism and its predecessors. Writers examining the decade from the vantage point of the Reagan era would have us believe that the New Left began with the founding of SDS and the drafting of the *Port Huron Statement* and ended with either a) the Democratic National Convention of 1968 in Chicago; b) the Weathermen's Days of Rage in 1969; c) the Altamont rock concert at the end of 1969; or d) the Kent State shootings of 4 May 1970. This version of the 1960s, with an easily identifiable beginning and end, eliminates all fluidity between the New Left and its forebears and descendants. In fact, elements of the New Left were constantly present on the political scene before SDS and Port Huron, and they lived on, in different forms, after SDS's collapse.

By the close of the 1980s, several historians had begun to challenge the traditional SDS-centered narratives and to shift the spotlight to previously neglected constituencies. Among these were David Farber's *Chicago '68* (1988), about the 1968 Democratic National Convention, Alice Echols's *Daring to Be Bad* (1989), about the rise of radical feminism in the early 1970s, and Kenneth J. Heineman's *Campus Wars* (1992), about protest at various state universities.[60] Echols's work in particular extended the era of the 1960s into the 1970s and also emphasized a segment of activists whose origins and development differed sharply from the SDS-centered model. Other historians began to explore the radical movements that emerged in the early 1970s: gay rights, Chicano power, the American Indian movement, G.I. and veterans' resistance, communes, and environmentalism. During the 1990s several works documented New Left activism in the 1970s. Terry Anderson's *The Movement and the Sixties* (1994) was among the first and most ambitious books to challenge the standard SDS model. By illuminating grassroots resistance movements of the early 1970s, Anderson's book represented a fresh alternative to the works of the 1980s.[61] "When my students talk about the Sixties," says a professor quoted by Anderson, "they really mean the early 1970s."[62]

Four years after *The Movement and the Sixties* appeared, the publication of Doug Rossinow's *The Politics of Authenticity* generated excitement in the field.[63] Rossinow's book, about the New Left in Austin, Texas, shattered many assumptions about the roots and demise of 1960s radicalism. Rossinow discovered a different set of seeds that led to the flowering of radicalism in Austin—namely, the harassment of progressives at the University of Texas in the 1940s, the influence of humanistic Christian intellectuals and progressive religious leaders, and the Christian activism of the UT campus YMCA and YWCA. Rossinow also documents the presence of a vibrant New Left in Austin in the 1970s; but he rejects both the New-Left-as-historical-exception argument and the excessive optimism of those who insist that the New Left never really died. Rossinow presents a more balanced, qualified view: "In the twenty-five years since the New Left unraveled, the United States has not seen a cohesive, organized left group. . . . Many Americans continue to hold leftist views, and there has been plenty of leftist activism between the mid-1970s and the late 1990s, but leftists generally have carried on their politics as individuals, mainly in issue-specific organizations in which they have collaborated with liberals."[64] My book on Vietnam Veterans against the War (VVAW) similarly contends that the gritty working-class activists of VVAW, with their counseling services for poor veterans and unique methods of protest, fashioned a branch of the New Left completely independent of the SDS variety. The memorable line from the famous *Port Huron Statement*—"We are the people of this generation, bred at least in modest comfort, housed now in universities, looking uncomfortably to the world we inherit"—did not apply to VVAW.[65]

All of this begs the questions: How new was the New Left? If the New Left *is* synonymous with SDS, why use the term "New Left" at all? Or does the New Left encompass other actors, such as Vietnam veterans, feminists of the early 1970s, gay rights activists, American Indian militants, environmentalists, and many other groups that occupy various points on the progressive political and cultural spectrum? Todd Gitlin's argument that identity politics have robbed the Left of a grand vision of social change can be challenged by insisting that identity politics was necessary to forge a more inclusive movement.[66] Moreover, SDS's own ideology in the mid-1960s was itself often nebulous, problematic, and in many cases not terribly different from early variants of libertarian radicalism.

It is time to reconsider how we conceptualize the 1960s. The view of New Left exceptionalism relies on historical amnesia. We can reject that narrow view while still acknowledging that the best minds of the 1960s successfully challenged old paradigms, untested models, and accepted modes of behavior. By the 1970s, ideas and theories that had once been accepted as gospel, such as Frederick Jackson Turner's frontier thesis, had been tested and refuted by a new generation of insurgent intellectuals yearning for fresh insights. Why, in this charged atmosphere of intellectual inquiry, has the notion that the New Left was exceptional gone largely unchallenged?

Rossinow suggests that the last quarter of the twentieth century witnessed a prolonged lull in radical activism. Still, the effects of the upheavals and transformations, as antiwar activist Rennie Davis noted, "have by now permeated every nook and cranny of our culture."[67] We cannot hope to understand the period between 1975 and 2000 unless we can meaningfully assess the profound, complex, and lasting legacies of the 1960s. To do that, we must stop thinking in terms of beginnings, middles, and ends, and adopt a more cyclical, less progressive view of history that acknowledges the many neglected constituencies of social protest movements in the 1960s.

Still, as problematic as the Old Left/New Left paradigm is, it should not be jettisoned altogether. It must be preserved if for no other reason than that some very influential figures of the 1960s characterized themselves as part of the "new" Left, as distinct from the "old" Left. And in any case it would be foolish to suggest that the New Left offered *nothing* new. At their best, the 1960s insurgents furnished a moral appeal to action that still resonates today. They were the first generation of radicals to criticize the poverty of abundance, rather than the abundance of poverty (to borrow a term from John Patrick Diggins). The brightest among them provided humanistic visions to counter the pervasive ideology of the state and the corporate elite. At a time of unprecedented growth and prosperity, the youthful radicals of the 1960s played a key role in forging a renaissance of grassroots resistance to entrenched power. Their search for authenticity in a world beset by war, overpopulation, environmental degradation, and corporate control of mainstream politics and media remains of interest and value. It is one thing to acknowledge these contributions to American cultural history. It is another to accept the old/new paradigm without argument, to treat the writings of C. Wright Mills and the *Port Huron Statement* as unprecedented, and, ultimately, to regard the "old" and "new" Lefts as static, easily identifiable entities. The American Left was never so simple. In the end, the old/new paradigm insults everybody. Pre-1960s radicals are reduced to one-dimensional, card-carrying ideologues who left no real legacy, while 1960s militants become hedonistic, irrational, and ultimately anti-intellectual, just the kind of portrait we get in movies such as *The Big Chill*.

Notes

Epigraph: Alan Wald, *The Responsibility of Intellectuals: Selected Essays on Marxist Traditions in Cultural Commitment* (Atlantic Highlands, N.J.: Humanities Press, 1992), 74.

1. Pauline Kael, *5001 Nights at the Movies* (New York: Henry Holt, 1991), 69.

2. Alex Callinicos, *Against Postmodernism: A Marxist Critique* (Cambridge: Polity Press, 1989), 168. Despite this bleak assessment, there were other books written around the same time that emphasized the lifelong commitment of 1960s radicals to progressive causes, including Doug

McAdam's *Freedom Summer* (New York: Oxford University Press, 1988), and Jack Whalen and Richard Flacks, *Beyond the Barricades: The Sixties Generation Grows Up* (Philadelphia: Temple University Press, 1989).

3. Allen Matusow, *The Unraveling of America: A History of Liberalism in the 1960s* (New York: Basic Books, 1984), 310–11.

4. Another early influential work was Kirkpatrick Sale's *SDS* (New York: Random House, 1973).

5. Irwin Unger, *The Movement: A History of the American New Left, 1959–1972* (New York: Dodd, Mead, 1974), 150.

6. David Caute, *The Year of the Barricades: A Journey through 1968* (New York: Harper and Row, 1988), 34–37.

7. Ibid., 36.

8. Ibid., 37–38.

9. Paul Boyer, *Promises to Keep: The United States since World War II* (Lexington, Mass.: D.C. Heath, 1995), 294.

10. Maurice Isserman, *"If I Had a Hammer . . .": The Death of the Old Left and the Birth of the New Left* (New York: Basic Books, 1987), 219.

11. Caute, *The Year of the Barricades,* 37–39.

12. Kenneth Keniston, *Young Radicals: Notes on Committed Youth* (New York: Harcourt Brace Jovanovich, 1968), 15.

13. Staughton Lynd, *Living Inside Our Hope* (Ithaca: Cornell University Press, 1997), 67.

14. Paul Buhle, ed., *History and the New Left: Madison Wisconsin, 1950–1970* (Philadelphia: Temple University Press, 1990).

15. John Patrick Diggins, *The Rise and Fall of the American Left* (New York: Norton, 1992), 155.

16. Ibid.

17. Ibid., 233–34.

18. Despite these negative qualities, I prefer to insert a disclaimer distinguishing the CP leadership from the party's rank and file. Historian Albert Fried noted insightfully: "No institution, however hieratic its structure of organization, however centralized its bureaucracy, is as tightly controlled as the Party was alleged to be. At the lower levels, in the units and branches, the faithful exercised a greater degree of individual initiative and tended to be more principled, ingeniously so, than the leaders" (Albert Fried, *Communism in America: A History in Documents* [New York: Columbia University Press, 1997], 6–7).

19. Ibid., 20, 165.

20. Barbara Ehrenreich, "Legacies of the 1960s: New Rights and New Lefts," in *Sights on the Sixties,* ed. Barbara L. Tischler (New Brunswick: Rutgers University Press, 1992), 233.

21. Fried, *Communism in America,* 386.

22. See Dorothy Healey's memoir, *California Red: A Life in the American Communist Party,* with Maurice Isserman (Urbana: University of Illinois Press, 1993).

23. Ibid., 387.

24. James Miller should be commended for noting the presence of red diaper babies in SDS. Prominent SDSers Steve Max, Bob Ross, Richard Flacks, and Mickey Flacks all fell into this category. See James Miller, *"Democracy Is in the Streets": From Port Huron to the Siege of Chicago* (New York: Simon and Schuster, 1987), 136–37.

25. Judy Kaplan and Linn Shapiro, eds., *Red Diapers: Growing Up in the Communist Left* (Urbana: University of Illinois Press, 1998), 9.

26. The reasons for this are not terribly complicated. In the 1960s and early 1970s, numerous movement organizers who were not in the SWP disliked and distrusted the organization. Only SWP leader Fred Halstead's sprawling *Out Now! A Participant's Account of the American Movement against the Vietnam War* (New York: Monad Press, 1978) has offered a sympathetic account of the SWP during this period. Much of the literature ignores the SWP altogether. The one exception is Tom Wells's masterful *The War Within: America's Battle over Vietnam* (Berkeley: University of California Press, 1994), which spotlights some SWP luminaries (including Halstead). Wells is decidedly unsympathetic toward the SWP, and spends much time on the internecine battles between the Trotskyites and the CP, as well as the hostility toward the SWP among other movement activists.

27. Wald, *The Responsibility of Intellectuals,* 77.

28. Wells, *The War Within,* 45.

29. *New Left Notes,* 4 Dec. 1967, quoted in Halstead, *Out Now!,* 368.

30. Halstead, *Out Now!,* 75.

31. Nancy Zaroulis and Gerald Sullivan, *Who Spoke Up? American Protest against the War in Vietnam* (New York: Doubleday, 1984), 98.

32. Todd Gitlin, *The Twilight of Common Dreams: Why America is Wracked by Culture Wars* (New York: Metropolitan Books, 1995), 96; David Horowitz, *Radical Son: A Generational Odyssey* (New York: Free Press, 1997), 104. Horowitz's motives are readily apparent. Having leapt from the far Left to the far Right, he has spent years depicting the New Left as dangerous fifth columnists serving their Red masters in Moscow in a manner reminiscent of Herbert Philbrick.

33. Diggins, *The Rise and Fall of the American Left,* 238.

34. Matusow, *The Unraveling of America,* 335.

35. To make matters worse, many of the SDS-centered histories focus on about a dozen or so important SDS members. With the exception of some detailed discussions of SDS's Economic Research and Action Project (ERAP) and the organization's short-lived foray into the antiwar movement, these histories largely neglect the influence of these radical activists and intellectuals outside the major college towns that served as their headquarters.

36. Former Weatherman Bill Ayers placed the Weather Underground's contribution in perspective: "If you read the FBI documents from 1973, say, there were tens of thousands of political bombings in the country. Every draft board, every ROTC building, every recruiting station had problems in those years. It was really a phenomenon that was quite widespread. So the fact that the Weather Underground took credit for twenty bombings was in that context." Quoted in Joan and Robert K. Morrison, *From Camelot to Kent State: The Sixties Experience in the Words of Those Who Lived It* (New York: Times Books, 1987), 321.

37. Terry H. Anderson, *The Movement and the Sixties: Protest in America from Greensboro to Wounded Knee* (New York: Oxford University Press, 1995).

38. Viorst, *Fire in the Streets,* 190.

39. Carl Guarneri, *Utopian Alternative: Fourierism in Nineteenth-Century America* (New York: Cornell University Press, 1991), and Donald E. Pitzer, ed., *America's Communal Utopias* (Chapel Hill: University of North Carolina Press, 1997).

40. Particularly the ideas outlined in the Webbs' *A Constitution of the Socialist Commonwealth of Great Britain* (London: Longmans, Green, 1920).

41. Bruce J. Schulman, "Out of the Streets and into the Classroom? The New Left and the Counterculture in United States History Textbooks," *Journal of American History* 85 (1999): 1527.

42. Danny Peary, *Cult Movies 2* (New York: Dell, 1983), 135.

43. David Caute wrote, "Socialists of the Old Left rarely challenged the paternalism of the schools and universities they attended, the moral right of administrators or faculty to lay down the law on curriculum, examinations, and rules for personal conduct. Nor did they question competition at the service of political ambition. . . . The most far-reaching innovation of the New Left was to challenge these time-honored hierarchies. For the Old Left, the existence of elites—whether based on power or skills—was a fact of life" (Caute, *The Year of the Barricades,* 35). Similarly, Mossimo Teodori, editor of an influential anthology titled *The New Left: A Documentary History* (Indianapolis: Bobbs-Merrill, 1969), wrote: "The Student Peace Union, [formed in Chicago in 1959], was the first nationwide political association of a student character" (Teodori, *The New Left,* 125).

44. C. Wright Mills, "Letter to the New Left," in *"Takin' It to the Streets": A Sixties Reader,* ed. Alexander Bloom and Wini Breines (New York: Oxford University Press, 1995), 79.

45. Ralph S. Brax, *The First Student Movement: Student Activism in the United States during the 1930s* (Port Washington, N.Y.: Kennikat Press, 1981), 3–4.

46. Ibid., 20.

47. *The New Student,* 7 June 1922, 1–2.

48. Robert Cohen, *When the Old Left Was Young: Student Radicals and America's First Mass Student Movement* (New York: Oxford University Press, 1993), 122. Unlike the Berkeley FSM of the mid-1960s, which failed to immediately inspire similar actions, the U.C. Berkeley Free Speech Movement of 1934 was but one of a wave of similar free speech fights on university campuses across the country. See Cohen, *When the Old Left Was Young,* 98–133.

49. Ibid., xiii.

50. Mario Savio, "The End of History," in Bloom and Breines, *"Takin' It to the Streets,"* 114–15. In several issues of the *New Student,* critics of higher education in the 1920s frequently cited two influential works on the corporate control of American universities, Upton Sinclair's *The Goose-Step: A Study of American Education* (1923) and Thorstein Veblen's *The Higher Education in America: A Memorandum on the Conduct of Universities by Businessmen* (1918).

51. *New Student,* 2 Feb. 1924, 7.

52. Brax, *The First Student Movement,* 5.

53. Diggins, *The Rise and Fall of the American Left,* 234.

54. No author, "The Student Conference at Hartsdale, New York," supplement to the *New Student,* 13 Jan. 1923, 1–5.

55. Ibid., 6.

56. Ibid., 12.

57. *Vanguard, an Anarchist-Communist Journal,* Jan. 1933, 5–6.

58. Stephen Craig, "The Student in Politics," ibid., April 1938, 12.

59. Brax, *The First Student Movement,* 108.

60. David Farber, *Chicago '68* (Chicago: University of Chicago Press, 1988); Alice Echols, *Daring to Be Bad: Radical Feminism in America, 1967–1975* (Minneapolis: University of Minnesota Press, 1989); Kenneth J. Heineman, *Campus Wars: The Peace Movement at American State Universities in the Vietnam Era* (New York: New York University Press, 1993).

61. Terry H. Anderson, *The Movement and the Sixties: Protest in America from Greensboro to Wounded Knee* (New York: Oxford University Press, 1995).

62. Anderson, *The Movement and the Sixties,* 357–58.

63. Doug Rossinow, *The Politics of Authenticity: Liberalism, Christianity, and the New Left in America* (New York: Columbia University Press, 1998).

64. Ibid., 338.

65. See Andrew E. Hunt, *The Turning: A History of Vietnam Veterans against the War* (New York: New York University Press, 1999), 192.

66. Todd Gitlin, *The Twilight of Common Dreams*.

67. Douglas T. Miller, *On Our Own: Americans in the Sixties* (Lexington, Mass.: D.C. Heath, 1995), vi.

CHAPTER 8

Strategy and Democracy in the New Left

Francesca Polletta

In 1965 twenty-eight-year-old Norm Fruchter, an editor at *Studies on the Left*, returned from a trip to Mississippi to herald profound changes in the civil rights movement. Black Mississippians and the Student Nonviolent Coordinating Committee (SNCC) activists they worked with had "abandoned the goal of eventual integration into existing Mississippi society as both unrealistic and undesirable," he wrote. Rejecting the "totemic demands" of the Left—for federal housing and employment programs, national health insurance, and the like—they were working instead to create counter-institutions and relationships "based on assumptions about identity, personality, work, meaning, and aspirations not accepted in the majority society." Probably even more "disconcerting" to "orthodox left-wingers," Fruchter speculated, they were challenging what counted as radical organization. SNCC was "primarily a movement . . . only incidentally an organization," and its bureaucratic inefficiency should not be condemned, since one of its chief purposes was "to raise the question of just how well all the organizations operating on bureaucratic assumptions within the majority society have served human freedom."[1]

Fruchter's piece provoked an indignant response from Old Left stalwart Victor Rabinowitz. "For many of the young of our nation, including, of course, many in the Movement, freedom may mean the right to smoke pot, to drive a car while drunk and to goof off when the sprit so moves," Rabinowitz observed. "To a Negro farmer in Mississippi, it means the opportunity to organize to achieve the right to vote, the right to be treated like a human being, the right to be integrated into the human brotherhood. These rights come along with the right to eat a square meal and to live in a house with flush toilets." To gain those rights required a political program and a "disciplined, efficient organization," precisely what SNCC was attempting to become—with a coordinating committee, executive committee and secretariat, a policy statement, and formal rules for personnel decisions. Such a "bureaucracy" would be anathema to Fruchter and his friends, but to suggest that program, organization, and "totemic" political demands were of no interest to Mississippi blacks was at best romantic, at worst "both condescending and insulting."[2]

This debate is interesting for several reasons. It captures the tenor of the battle between Old and New Leftists for the helm of American radicalism, a battle that was often fought on the terrain of the black freedom struggle. As it had before and would again, the New Left staked its claim to political authority on its capacity to celebrate and, not least, to interpret the purposes of its civil rights heroes. Challenges to the Old Left's misplaced faith in bureaucracy, its myopic focus on securing federal programs that were no more realistic than grassroots revolution, its obsequious allegiance to the Democratic Party, its stodginess, would all be made in the name of the alternatives being advanced by activists in the Deep South. The debate is interesting, second, for articulating two conceptions of movement organization that competed—and still compete—for leftists' allegiance. One is bureaucratic, conventional, strategic—organization aimed at effecting institutional change, at gaining power. The other is collectivist, participatory-democratic, "prefigurative," its purpose to enact within the movement itself the desired society, to effect a cultural revolution rather than mere political reform. The New Left's genius, according to most observers, was to join the two commitments. Inspired by SNCC's version of the "beloved community," in which a "band of brothers" transcended not only race but the impersonalism and alienation of modern American life, New Leftists undertook a variety of social experiments under the banner of "participatory democracy." Yet the "dilemma inherited from SNCC," chroniclers agree, was that building the better society was different from living it, and demanded different skills. The movement foundered, by most accounts, because it was unwilling to create the kind of reformist, bureaucratic organization that might have endured but was antithetical to its antihierarchical values. Norm Fruchter was thus the voice of prefigurative politics, the "ultra-democratic mystique" that Students for a Democratic Society (SDS) inherited from SNCC, Rabinowitz that of political convention.[3]

The Fruchter/Rabinowitz debate is interesting, finally, for what it missed. SNCC staffer Mike Miller wrote but did not publish another response to Fruchter's piece. Both Fruchter's and Rabinowitz's renderings bore "so little resemblance to the day to day realities" of SNCC "as to be almost frightening," Miller wrote. SNCC's goal was not to develop new assumptions "about identity, personality, work, meaning, and aspirations not accepted in the majority society," as Fruchter claimed, but to gain "power to break into the society and get a share of its resources." "Believe it or not," Miller went on, SNCC had an administration. "It has offices in Atlanta. Checks are made out there by an honest to goodness book-keeper, there are files, forms, duplicate copies, secretaries, machines and all the rest of the paraphernalia of bureaucracy." But Rabinowitz was equally off the mark in reducing SNCC to its policy statements and organizational charts. SNCC workers were experimenting with "decentralized forms of administration," but their purpose was practical: They sought organization "designed to effectively service the staff and field without controlling all activity at the local level." SNCC's day-to-day operations were driven above all, and this apparently eluded both commentators, by its staffers' commitment to "being 'an organizer' and being in the field." To Fruchter's and Rabinowitz's characterizations—SNCC as utopian community or SNCC as a "disciplined army"—Miller countered, "many of us in SNCC prefer a different formulation. We are a band of organizers seeking to open the tremendous potential of human resources that has been locked up in the racism of the South. That potential cannot be opened by anyone but the Negro people who live in Southern bondage." SNCC organizers eschewed neither political power nor the "totemic demands" of Old Leftists. "It is the additions to the old demands, not their dismissal, that is important. It is the new demands of participation, local control in decision making, leadership from below rather than from above that distinguish SNCC from the old left."[4]

Like Miller's, the SNCC that I describe in this chapter is different from the one that figures in popular narratives of participatory democracy's rise and fall. "I really don't remember ever being at a meeting where somebody would say, 'Well, now, the job at hand is to create the beloved community,'" Mississippi SNCC organizer Martha Prescod Norman recalls. The "band of brothers" was not the beloved community. It was self-consciously black; its members were dispatched to locations and delegated tasks on the orders of state, district, and project directors; and they believed that freedom would be gained more effectively through political power than through moral suasion. SNCC workers did operate on the basis of practices we would call participatory-democratic—but more for practical reasons than for "prefigurative" ones. Decentralized, participatory decision making helped to sustain the commitment of overworked and underpaid organizers, provided them the flexibility they needed to respond to local conditions, and created mechanisms for keeping future political leaders responsible to their constituents. That SNCC workers experienced themselves as a "band of brothers," a tightly knit group of friends operating in deadly conditions, also made for relations of mutual trust and deference that discouraged the challenges to informal leadership that prove so time-consuming in participatory-democratic organizations. Betty Garman Robinson, who was a member of SDS before she became a SNCC staffer, recalls that "participatory democracy was more of a concept in SDS. It was a goal, an ideal. In SNCC it was very practical." Her comment suggests that the supposedly fundamental tension between democracy and efficacy may not be so fundamental after all.[5]

But Garman Robinson's point raises a tricky question. If decentralized and participatory organizational forms were so effective, then why did SNCC abandon them in 1965, centralizing resources and fund-raising, vesting more power in the executive secretary, and ridding the organization of "freedom high" proponents of loose structure? At the very time that SDS was decentralizing further under the banner of participatory democracy, eliminating national offices and programs, SNCC was moving in the other direction. In fact, the two developments were not unconnected. Collectivist modes of organization, initially appealing for their practical uses, came to be viewed in SNCC as inefficient and self-indulgent, in part because they were failing to generate the programmatic agenda that was desperately needed. But participatory democracy was also damned by its association with white New Leftists. As racial tensions within the movement sharpened, black SNCC activists found increasing fault with a mode of decision making that had come to be seen as the prerogative of the northern New Left.

What I present here is neither a history of participatory democracy nor a full account of SNCC's and SDS's mutation over the course of the 1960s. And although I emphasize the practical purposes of decentralized and participatory decision making, it is clear that some people came to SNCC because they saw its chief purpose as modeling an alternative society, and were never swayed in that perception. In stressing the practical functions of participatory democracy, my aim is rather to challenge the supposedly intrinsic and unavoidable opposition between democracy and efficacy that has informed narratives of the New Left. A second purpose is to identify different tensions at the heart of participatory-democratic projects, namely, the difficulties of basing democratic decision making on friendship and of using it to negotiate divergent political aspirations. Finally, historians have emphasized the New Left's indebtedness to SNCC, but they have tended to reproduce SDS leaders' professions of admiration for SNCC without exploring their more ambivalent aspects. By focusing on the interaction between SNCC and SDS, and their mutual influence on the issue of internal democracy, I hope to contribute to understanding the relationship between the white New Left and the civil rights movement.

From the "Beloved Community" to the "Band of Brothers"

On 1 February 1960, four black students from Greensboro A&T sat down at a segregated lunch counter in a downtown Woolworth's and refused to get up until the store closed. The next day students from surrounding colleges took up the sit-in, and in the following days demonstrations spread to other establishments in Greensboro, then to other cities. By the end of the month, sit-ins had begun in thirty cities in seven states, and by the end of March in fifty-four cities in nine states. In early April, Southern Christian Leadership Conference (SLC) official Ella Baker invited student sit-in leaders to a coordinating conference in Raleigh, North Carolina. Students insisted that the organization they formed there, SNCC, remain independent of the "adult" civil rights organizations—the National Association for the Advancement of Colored People, the Congress of Racial Equality (CORE), and SLC. They agreed that SNCC would serve only as an information-sharing body. The student movement's decentralization was its strength, they believed.[6]

SNCC's early leadership was dominated by Nashville student John Lewis and sit-in participants Diane Nash and Marion Barry. They had studied Gandhian techniques of nonviolent direct action before launching sit-ins that other students viewed as especially well organized. From their advisor, Fellowship of Reconciliation worker James Lawson, they absorbed a vision of racial reconciliation through morally persuasive action. That vision—of a "beloved community"—was an animating ideal for the Nashville students, describing both a future of racial harmony and the bonds of trust and love enacted within the movement itself. Decisions were made by consensus among Nashville students—James Lawson saw it as "the true Gandhian way"—and they brought that style with them to SNCC. Within a year of its founding, however, SNCC was moving from lunch counter sit-ins to community organizing in the most repressive areas of the Mississippi Delta, and from a campus coordinating body to a cadre of full-time organizers. The Nashville students' leadership had been eclipsed by a new group of personally religious but much more politically oriented students. For these activists, "power" was appealing rather than suspect. While SNCC retained a formal governing structure of campus representatives, decisions were increasingly made by SNCC's Atlanta staff and by project directors and field secretaries in Mississippi and Southwest Georgia.[7]

Faced with daily harassment and terrified local residents, SNCC organizers survived by combining movement ideals with a heavy dose of pragmatism. Charles Sherrod, an organizer in Albany, Georgia, urged his colleagues not to "let the project go to the dogs because you feel you must be democratic to the letter." At the same time, lacking resources and political connections, SNCC organizers believed that their only hope of gaining a foothold in black communities was to secure the support of community leaders. The challenge was to push leaders into more activist stances. Decisions—whether to hold a march in response to an arrest, how to persuade a minister to allow a mass meeting in his church—had to be made with the community rather than for it. Field reports show organizers struggling to resolve local conflicts over turf, leadership, and strategy without imposing their own agendas. After ministers in Albany charged that SNCC was trying to run the show there, organizers discussed the situation. "Miss Baker pointed out that it might have been better all around to have shifted the car pool to local handling as soon as possible. That part of our strategy in each local community should be to shift as much of the responsibility as soon as possible to local handling." Staffers agreed, while noting "the difficulty of doing this at the time when the pressures are upon you."[8]

Although their first contacts were usually with black ministers and civic leaders, SNCC workers discovered that those most willing to bear the costs of retaliation for joining the movement—"strong" people, they called them—were often farmers, sharecroppers, and domestic workers. Poorly schooled, sometimes illiterate, these were people deemed "unqualified" for political participation. Involving them in making decisions was a way to allay their acute sensitivity about their lack of political sophistication, and to train them to do politics. "People learned how to stand up and speak," Mississippi project head Robert Moses says now. "The meeting itself, or the meetings, became the tools. . . . Folks were feeling themselves out, learning how to use words to articulate what they wanted and needed. In these meetings, they were taking the first step toward gaining control over their lives, by making demands on themselves. . . . They were not credentialed people; they did not have high school diplomas for the most part. They were not members of labor unions or national church associations. Yet, through the process, they became leaders."

Organizers also began to see collective decision making within local movements as essential to developing the mechanisms that would keep future black leaders directly responsible to their constituents. A movement politics that developed leaders—many leaders—was the way to prevent the co-optation to which all movements were vulnerable. By actively remaking conventions and criteria of leadership, participatory deliberative practices would ensure that a future black politics remained truly collective, responsive to its most disenfranchised participants.[9]

Among SNCC field secretaries, too, group decision making was the norm. "The dangers that we all faced were too great to risk the possibility of someone not implementing a decision made by the group because he personally disagreed with it," executive secretary James Forman later explained. "We had to talk things out until we all agreed on all decisions." "People were making a decision about how they were going to use their lives," adds staffer Muriel Tillinghast. "And that's not something that you could vote on. That was something that everybody was going to have to grope for. So these meetings would go on, you could not believe how long these meetings went on." In addition, many project staff were young and inexperienced, and SNCC workers knew they were training staff as much as they were community activists. Hollis Watkins was a Mississippian just out of high school when he joined SNCC. "To me, understanding was the most important part. Through the participatory process, all of the things that we were dealing with would be brought out, explained, and talked about."[10]

SNCC workers' respect for "being 'an organizer' and being in the field," as Mike Miller put it, meant that organizers' individual initiative was rewarded and their autonomy protected. Direction from SNCC's Atlanta headquarters was minimal and, staffers agreed, "a basic principle in decision making is that people who do the work make the decisions." To be sure, former staffers refer to the disproportionate authority of Forman and Moses. Yet, by all accounts, both men were careful to give away their power. When both Moses and Forman were jailed in Greenwood, Mississippi, in April 1963, and the project there was left without a leader, the two men nixed the person elected as acting director and urged instead that the project form a decision-making committee. Former SNCC staffers remember that Forman was the one who cleaned the bathrooms, and that he often sent less experienced staffers to high-level meetings for a crash course in political negotiation.[11]

What I have briefly described might be characterized as a "tutelary" rationale for democratic procedure. Involving novices in decision making, establishing a norm of participation, rotating leadership tasks—all these helped to develop movement leaders. From veteran activists like Ella Baker, Myles Horton, Bernice Robinson, and Septima Clark, SNCC workers learned an organizing strategy that emphasized the development of local leadership. Firm in their dislike of utopian communities, Baker and Horton treated group decision making as fertile ground for radical education. Continuing in that tradition, SNCC workers saw decentralized and participatory practices not as contrary to effective political action but as essential preparation for it. Of course, a practice can be embraced for a variety of reasons. Whereas former seminarian and SNCC's first administrative secretary Jane Stembridge always viewed SNCC's commitment to being a community rather than an organization as its strength, James Forman, a veteran of political battles and firm believer in clear chains of command, was more enthusiastic about the solidarity-building functions of participation, and was much more willing to sacrifice democracy for organizational efficiency. All SNCC workers were proud of the supportive and intellectually exciting community they had created. But this was the product of friendships forged in the midst of grueling and dangerous activism, more than a deliberate attempt to model an alternative mode of governance.[12]

SDS and Participatory Democracy

If SNCC's deliberative style was based more on friendship and the practical demands of organizing in that time and place than on principle, what about SDS? Was SDS's version of participatory democracy really prefigurative in intent? Or was SNCC's influence on SDS actually less important than commentators have supposed? Casey Hayden, SNCC staffer and SDS member, emphasizes the differences between the two groups. The drive to create accountable leaders that animated SNCC's participatory decision making was "a different existential situation than the alienation and relationship to elite government which spawned participatory democracy as a call to arms for the white new left," she says. For SDS members, participatory democracy "spoke to people's sense of what happened in community to us. . . . It had a lot to do with being a non-alienated person. So that we experienced that non-alienated community in our work with each other." The picture is more complicated, though. For the *Port Huron Statement*'s framers, "participatory democracy" referred not to a method of making decisions but to a macro-political vision in which institutions were governed by their constituents. "Participatory democracy did not mean abandoning organizational structures of the usual sort, like elected officers and parliamentary procedure," SDS leader Richard Flacks insists. "We were thinking of participatory democracy at that time as a concept of social change, not as a set of principles for guiding the internal organizational life of SDS." Bob Ross writes that although "the phrase was interpreted, by some mass media and even friendly observers, to imply 'consensus in group decision-making' . . . to this author's knowledge, that meaning was not used at all at the Port Huron meeting in 1962, and rarely until 1965–66." For several years after its founding, SDS relied on deliberative structures similar to those of the college student councils and national student organizations with which its members were familiar: formal offices of president, vice president, and national secretary; a full-time paid staff; and decisions between conventions made by a national council (made up of national executive committee members and chapter representatives).[13]

Yet the confusion of "participatory democracy" with consensus-based decision making is understandable. The students at Port Huron experienced a powerful sense of community both as personally satisfying and as offering new political possibilities. They saw the trust, respect, and affection that informed their deliberations as a radical break with the position-staking wrangling and egotism that characterized the Left, and as embodying the values of personal commitment and caring that they wanted to see on a grand scale. Moreover, within a year of Port Huron, SDS leaders were discouraging each other from holding the same office twice; by 1964, in SDS's urban organizing projects, group process had become "more important than any other issue," as one organizer put it. So, even if it did not mean decision making by consensus at the outset, "participatory democracy" had by 1965 become that.[14]

What was SNCC's role in this evolution? SDS's fortunes were intertwined with SNCC's from its inception. Robert Alan Haber, a graduate student at the University of Michigan, took over the moribund campus chapter of the Student League for Industrial Democracy and began to recruit members just as northern students were launching demonstrations and pickets in support of the southern sit-ins. A fortuitously timed conference on civil rights, planned before the sit-ins erupted, became a high-profile encounter between northern white students and sit-in representatives. SDS leaders attended SNCC's inaugural conference and pledged their assistance with fund-raising and political lobbying. Campus SDS chapters began to spring up around the country after Tom Hayden was dispatched to cover the southern movement as SDS's first field secretary. His accounts of SNCC organizing in southwest Georgia and Mississippi were riveting. "Revolution permeates discussion like never before," Hayden wrote about SNCC workers in the fall of 1961. "In our future dealings we should be aware that they have changed down there, and we should speak their revolutionary language without mocking it. . . . The Southern movement has turned itself into that revolution we hoped for, and we didn't have much to do with its turning at all. . . . We had better be there."[15]

Hayden's reproach was directed to fellow SDS members who had criticized the southern student movement for being "moralistic" and "non-political" (as Hayden himself had done). Yet Hayden's ambivalence persisted. Several months later, as he began taking notes for what would become the *Port Huron Statement*, he again cautioned that the southern movement's "moral clarity has not always been accompanied by precise political vision, and sometimes not even by a real political consciousness." SDS would supply the larger ideological picture, he promised, would show how, in a phrase popular among the group, the issues were related. In statements like these, James Miller argues, "Hayden was complaining that the civil rights movement lacked an adequate understanding of participatory democracy." Indeed, Miller goes on, "Hayden's almost patronizing call for a 'precise political vision' to guide the civil rights movement should help lay to rest the misconception that the idea of participatory democracy was a product of this movement." The term itself came from Hayden's philosophy professor, Arnold Kaufman. Following Kaufman, Hayden in his draft notes conceptualized participatory institutions as distinct from but complementary to representative ones, providing citizens the education to participate wisely. But, drawing on C. Wright Mills, Hayden went on to define the key political task as piercing robotic, "acquiescent dread" that made Americans' participation rote and meaningless.[16]

The origins of participatory democracy were, as Miller suggests, bookish. But Hayden, by his own account, was mining the literature for a theoretical framework in which to place his experiences as a student and as an activist in the South. In SNCC projects in McComb and Albany, Hayden later recounted, he had experienced the core components of what would become participatory democracy. A Camus-flavored willingness to lay one's body on the line for justice, to *act*—this was the existential commitment that, as Miller points out, was joined somewhat uneasily with a Rousseauean vision of civic republicanism. But Hayden was also influenced by the experience of watching black southerners sacrifice jobs, homes, and personal safety for the civil rights that whites took for granted. Participatory democracy lay in the gap between the grassroots activism that he observed in Mississippi and the sterility of northern electoral politics. It held out the hope that mainstream political institutions could be made deserving of citizens' allegiance.[17]

The southern movement influenced not only the substance of New Leftists' commitment but its style—a style that would early on be confused with participatory democracy in its original sense. "Much care was expended to encourage reticent members to express their views," Barbara Haber wrote later of the discussions at Port Huron. "Ideas and questions were responded to without condescension or acrimony. Good-naturedness, tolerance, and curiosity characterized our discussions. In plenaries, though there were hot and heavy debates (mostly participated in by men), trust, affection, and the desire to make it work seemed to predominate." "We were in love with each other," Richard Flacks says simply. In a political wilderness of flag-waving conformity and student apathy, SDSers were "drawn into the circle and kept there by powerful personal bonds—bonds that were more important than political analyses or positions," according to Todd Gitlin. But early SDS members also felt they were reproducing an ethos they had encountered in the southern civil rights movement, whether directly or secondhand. Richard Flacks remembers that in SDS meetings Casey Hayden, who had authority as a civil rights leader, would halt discussions that were becoming competitive or pedantic. For those who had worked in the South, Barbara Haber wrote later, "the black struggle, and the vibrant communities that sprang up within it, was a harsh mirror in which we saw reflected the banalities and complacency of white, middle-class life."[18]

If SDS leaders, like later chroniclers, tended to see the SNCC community as more deliberate and self-conscious than it was, more of a political project in itself, it is striking that in both organizations, a participatory style of decision making coexisted so easily with conventional organization. Formal offices and elections, chains of command and *Robert's Rules of Order*—SNCC and SDS had these. Participatory democracy in the procedural sense was an ethos, a set of informal understandings more than formal procedures. It worked because it responded to organizers' needs for independence and flexibility, in the case of SNCC, and, in both organizations, because it was based on bonds of friendship. Friends are familiar with each other's preferences and idiosyncrasies. Their mutual affection gives each a stake in issues the other thinks important. Their mutual respect and trust makes it easier to defer to each other's expertise. When a friend makes a decision unilaterally, we tend to assume that it is because the issue is either very complex or trivial. In the early days of both SDS and SNCC, friendship among the group minimized the need for background information, challenge, and negotiation in collective decision making.

As models for democratic decision making, however, neither friendship nor political organizing is without problems. "Letting the people decide" works as long as the organizer can harness her aspirations to those of the people with whom she works, and as long as "the people" are agreed on their aspirations. This is not always the case. When next steps are ambiguous or contested, "letting the people decide" requires much more than a simple openness to residents' direction. The danger of confusing democracy with friendship, meanwhile, is that friendship's exclusiveness makes it difficult to expand the group beyond the original circle, and friendship's determined informality makes it difficult to implement more formal mechanisms for ensuring equality and accountability. SNCC and SDS confronted both these problems, which I treat only briefly here.

SNCC after Atlantic City

In the fall of 1964 SNCC was a very different organization than it had been six months earlier. From a tight-knit cadre organizing quietly in the rural South, it had become a geographically dispersed and nationally known organization whose spokespeople attracted the kind of media attention reserved for film stars and Martin Luther King Jr. SNCC's sponsorship of the Mississippi Summer Project was in large part responsible for the group's suddenly high profile. Eight hundred, mainly white, volunteers were recruited to register voters and run freedom schools and community centers, bringing national attention to the violence and harassment that civil rights workers had endured for years. In August the Mississippi Freedom Democratic Party (MFDP), which SNCC had organized, challenged the seating of the segregationist Mississippi regulars at the Democratic National Convention in Atlantic City. Though the challenge was unsuccessful—the MFDP refused a compromise of two non-voting seats—it demonstrated SNCC's ability to mobilize national support. SNCC's future as one of the "Big Five" civil rights organizations seemed secure.[19]

Instead of capitalizing on its new stature, however, the group was plunged into a series of rancorous debates about organizational structure and decision making. Meetings convened to map out new programs dissolved into battles in which proponents of individual autonomy and participatory democracy were pitted against defenders of centralized structure and top-down decision making. The latter, who dubbed themselves "hardliners," charged those they called "freedom highs" with over-intellectualizing instead of organizing, abandoning hard-won political bases to float around the country on a whim, and squandering resources as they pursued their own liberation. SNCC's antielitism and individualism had once been sources of political creativity, James Forman wrote later, but the new opposition to all authority was debilitating. By the time the hardliners won the battle, in the spring of 1965, and began replacing SNCC's decentralized and consensus-based decision-making structure with a more centralized administration and majority voting, the divisiveness had taken its toll. By the fall of 1965,

SNCC's Mississippi staff had shrunk by two-thirds, and SNCC had lost its place on the cutting edge of the state's black politics.[20]

Historians have tended to see the battles over structure as reflecting the opposition between prefigurative and strategic orientations, or between principle and pragmatism, that had been there from the start. Participatory democracy was simply too unwieldy for a group that had grown so fast and was pressed to respond quickly to new national opportunities. SNCC workers who resisted the trend to tighter structure were closer to the group's earlier utopian aspirations, but they were simply out of touch with the demands of organizational effectiveness. What this explanation misses is that initially both sides argued in terms of strategy. The advocates of loose structure, many SNCC veterans among them, worried that further centralization would undermine SNCC's Mississippi projects and that more bureaucracy would only multiply the roadblocks that kept resources from reaching the field. A closer examination of discussion in SNCC during this period suggests that the battle over decision making reflected less a conflict between democratic absolutists and political pragmatists than it did programmatic confusion and racial tensions within the group.[21]

Although the convention challenge earned SNCC kudos for its political novelty, its defeat was profoundly dispiriting—and confusing. "We were kind of at loose ends," communications director Julian Bond remembers. "There was no plan, no operational plan, absent any kind of theory or anything, there was just no plan to go beyond that. It was sort of, what do we do now? What comes next?" Should black southerners continue to seek access to the Democratic Party or abandon it altogether? Should SNCC concentrate on voter registration or move into economic programs? SNCC workers were determined to return to the grassroots local organizing that had been their forte before the convention. They would not impose their agendas on the people they organized; they would not reproduce the manipulation they had witnessed in Atlantic City. They would "let the people decide." But, in many counties, they soon discovered that this approach was not generating the radical programs it was supposed to. "So far I've been using the SNCC technique of prying and prodding with questions until the idea comes out," said one organizer, "but it is slow . . . people really have no ideas for programs." The author of a field report from Monroe County, Mississippi, noted, "there has been a stopping of all projects, [and] an attempt to let the local people say what they want," but she confessed that "the programs have been very slow. In fact I can't think of one program that is progressing." A staffer in Meridian wrote, "What we've had so far is discussion and workshops, but no programs." "You talk about we gotta have a program," one worker said, satirizing SNCC workers' attitude. "Baby, just talking to people is a program."[22]

In some communities the publicity from the convention challenge mobilized previously quiescent black leaders, who now competed for leadership of the movement. SNCC organizers confronted competing leaders, agendas, and constituencies within black communities. When they were able to get programs off the ground, they faced criticism from other SNCC staff that community centers, freedom schools, and welfare initiatives were not sufficiently radical. "Too damn many nursery schools, and milk programs," one organizer wrote. "Maybe I don't see the connection between the type of center program we have and the long range community organization clearly enough, but I do feel too much of our time and people are taken up in this," said another. "Many of us do not see the relationship between community centers, sewing classes and political and economic freedom." Complaints like these revealed, but did not resolve, the conflict between SNCC workers' commitments to "letting the people decide" and making radical change.[23]

Project workers found little guidance in SNCC's regional and national meetings. Efforts to thrash out agendas dissolved into debates about decision making and chains of command. A position paper prepared for a staff retreat in November 1964 argued, "It is admirable to talk of democracy and giving the staff full participation but at the moment this is not what needs full attention. . . . We as an organization have never sat down and decided what needed to be done as a long term drive, why it needed to be done, whether or not we were going to do it and if we were, how were we going to do it." But the paper was ignored as staffers battled over structure. Indeed, minutes of meetings during this period show that when issues of agenda were introduced, the discussion often shifted, sometimes rather abruptly, to issues of organizational structure. "For most of the time I was with SNCC, I felt we knew, as SNCC staff, what we were doing, and how each person's work fit into that," Casey Hayden explains. When that was no longer true, after the summer of 1964, "the structure discussion reflected that confusion. Structure was a secondary problem." The voter registration campaign that anchored SNCC's early organizing efforts had invested moderate goals with radical potential, uniting young activists who saw themselves on the cutting edge of protest with older local residents and established civil rights organizations. Now that the convention experience had thrown into question the wisdom of an alliance with the Democratic Party, and the prospect of national voting rights legislation undermined the radicalism of voter registration, there were no obvious strategies to unite such disparate groups. One problem with participatory decision making as a means of radical education and leadership training is that it depends on a commonality of aspirations between an organizer and those being organized. In fact, SNCC workers had defined their radicalism in terms of their willingness to defer to local people's objectives. But that role had always coexisted with another: SNCC was the cutting edge and conscience of the national movement. For much of its career, that had meant forcing the federal government to intervene in the Deep South. SNCC workers saw themselves as a "vanguard, pushing ahead," said a volunteer in 1965. "Other people follow . . . sort of keeping things intact." So far, SNCC had succeeded in joining roles of local movement catalyst and radical vanguard. But could nineteen- and twenty-year-old radicals be expected to commit to an agenda of local incremental change for the long-term?[24]

Staffer Ed Brown describes one response to the crisis within SNCC: "We were beginning to really force our various points of view on the community. . . . 'Let the people decide' became a very popular argument . . . [but only] when local people were deciding in accordance with what the staff thought; and when local people deviated, then they were to be ostracized. They were sellouts; this SNCC group didn't want to deal with them any more." Few SNCC workers were so judgmental or, given the general confusion about available options, so assured. The more common response was to turn to reforming the decision-making process. SNCC workers attacked each other for "manipulating" the people and for giving insufficient autonomy to organizers. Debates over styles, structures, and criteria of decision making substituted for and, just as important, deferred debates over goals. But in that context, proposals for tightening up the organization began to gain support. Departing from SNCC's old freewheeling, decentralized, and participatory structure was becoming appealing as a way out of the group's programmatic impasse.[25]

As some staffers noted, however, there was no guarantee that a more hierarchical structure would supply the programs that were so badly needed. Stokely Carmichael complained that "people here are incapable of dealing with the real problem, which is lack of programs." But drawing attention to the group's avoidance of the topic did not seem to do much good. Minutes of meetings during this period show that when issues of agenda were introduced, the discussion often shifted to organizational structure. Why? "Sometimes it's more comfortable to talk about structure, because it's so concrete," staffer Judy Richardson explains now. "And goals were so much more difficult to talk about." In other words, SNCC workers battled over how decisions were made and how resources were allocated because the real problem—generating the sense of radical purpose that would reenergize organizers and appeal to residents—was difficult to get a handle on. For all contenders, then, the preoccupation with structure both substituted for and thwarted a discussion of goals.[26]

In a curious way, the growing support within SNCC for a more bureaucratic structure also reflected a desire to recapture the group's early identity as a "band of brothers." It is curious because bureaucratic structure would seem precisely the opposite of a small community of friends. But by the spring of 1965 "tight structure" had come to be seen as a bulwark against the dominance of whites. In the early days SNCC had been a predominantly black organization. Many staffers had opposed the influx of volunteers in the summer of 1964 not only on the grounds that well-educated whites would unintentionally reproduce patterns of racial deference but that the movement itself would be irreversibly changed. When almost a hundred volunteers were added to the staff in September, they were angry that a decision had been made with so little consultation. By fall the tight-knit cadre began to feel undermined. "It used to be a band of brothers, a circle of trust, but that's not true anymore," said one SNCC veteran. "The movement talks a lot of the 'good old days,'" white staffer Elaine DeLott Baker wrote in her diary in December 1964. "The kids worked together, went to jail together, suffered together, at times starved together. They were, for the most part, black. . . . When I see the old staff stick together, when I feel the resistance on their part to accept the new people who have been around now for five and six months, I feel sad now, not angry. The anger I feel is rather directed at these people." Newcomers were easy to resent. On local projects they came into conflict with black project directors they perceived as uncommunicative and sometimes downright hostile. They were asking for guidance as much as for democracy. But they used an idiom that was intellectual, individualistic, and increasingly associated with the white New Leftists trooping south to experience—and interpret to the world—SNCC's brand of participatory democracy. "We should all have some say . . . COFO [Council of Federated Organizations, the Mississippi civil rights umbrella group] has degenerated into a clique of people who have been here," one new project worker declared. "Authority lies in some vague place, decisions come from some mysterious oligarch. Maybe we should define big brother." "I was told by a person of some authority that the role of the project director is left totally vague to keep new people in check," another complained. "This sounds pretty undemocratic."[27]

What accounted for the increasingly hostile character of SNCC deliberations in the fall of 1964 was not only the size of the organization but the rifts emerging among its oldest members. The repeated betrayals by white liberal allies, the media's fascination with the white volunteers, and the volunteers' often inadvertent breaches of the complex etiquette of race relations within the movement inevitably produced racial tensions within the group. In addition, black staffers were becoming interested in issues of racial identity and consciousness and some wondered whether these issues could be addressed openly in integrated gatherings. Still, it was difficult to renounce the determined interracialism of the original group of friends, according to former staffers. Racial antagonisms surfaced instead in disputes over the decision-making process. After a long debate at one meeting about the nature of legitimate authority—just the kind of discussion that drove hardliners mad—one participant, an older minister, remarked, "the thing that bothers me is that there really is a black-white problem here which you don't say but which is at the bottom of a lot of what you're saying. Why don't you deal with your black-white problem?" But the "black-white" problem was tough for an interracial group to confront, let alone resolve. Instead, debates over organizational structure were increasingly viewed in terms of their racial associations. The loose-structure argument came to be seen as ideological rather than instrumental, and as white.[28]

In fact, many of the proponents of loose structure were black, and some of the hardliners were white. In retrospect, black SNCC staffers describe the debate in terms of class and regional differences, as pitting Atlanta staff against Mississippi field organizers and northern student sophisticates (black and white) against native Mississippians. But in early 1965 the loose-structure advocates, or "freedom highs," were seen as white. "The 'freedom highs' are essentially white intellectuals, hung up in various ways," one staffer wrote. Today another former staffer recalls that the insistence on consensus in meetings was seen as "a northern white import from SDS. . . . A lot of people felt that the black people who were arguing for [consensus decision making] had been influenced by these ideas through white participation." Forman likewise attributed the organization's antiauthoritarian "neurosis" to "the middle class-element and especially . . . those who had been strongly influenced by ideas about participatory democracy coming out of Students for a Democratic Society." A number of white SNCC staff did have close ties to SDS and were comfortable with that group's more abstract intellectual style. Some did see loose structure as an ideological commitment with radical implications. But others continued to argue for decentralized and participatory decision making on practical grounds. Such arguments now held little water, however. Whites and "their" antiorganizational animus were coming to be seen as responsible for the organization's paralysis. A white staffer described a rumor of a "conspiracy" circulating among hard-liners: "It sounds something like this: 'All the people . . . who don't want structure are white, intellectuals, and not doing any specific job, they claim to speak for the people who don't talk-up; but do they?"[29]

Those promoting more centralized, hierarchical structure were not an organizational faction bent on ridding the organization of whites by adopting a new structure. The appeal of bureaucracy lay rather in its relationship to inchoate preferences and problems. Tightening up organizationally was a bid to recuperate the sense of purpose and solidarity that had characterized the earlier group. The irony was that the argument for more radical democracy within SDS had credence because of its association with SNCC, while the same argument in SNCC was tainted by its association with the white New Left.

Old Guard and Prairie People

SDS was obviously a very different organization from SNCC. Although it began SNCC-style community organizing in 1963, SDS had always seen itself as operating on multiple fronts: campus activism, electoral campaigns, and direct action. Its deliberative style was never guided solely by the imperatives of community organizing. And although SDS was founded and led by a small group of committed friends, its chapter organization made for very different relations between leaders and members. But SDS still experienced some of the same problems in trying to sustain decentralized participatory decision making. And just as an allegedly ineluctable tension between prefigurative and strategic aims cannot fully account for the crisis over decision making that rent SNCC, it cannot explain similar debates within SDS.

Participatory democracy—in its procedural version—"became an article of faith" in SDS as the organization shifted to urban organizing efforts directly modeled on SNCC's. In the spring of 1964, as part of its Economic Research and Action Project (ERAP), SDS began sending student activists to Chicago, Cleveland, Newark, Trenton, and other cities. Their object was to build "an interracial movement of the poor." Activists in many local projects experimented with rigorously democratic procedures. In the Cleveland project, making decisions by consensus and refusing all hierarchies among the staff was a self-conscious effort to model new relationships. In Cleveland and elsewhere, however, staffers also sought to involve local people in decision making as a practical way to build their leadership capacities.[30]

For all ERAP's populist fervor, however, the drive to fully democratize SDS's national structure came not from ERAP but from members new to the organization. After an SDS-sponsored antiwar march in April 1965 drew twenty thousand participants, SDS was thrust into the media spotlight. Chapters mushroomed as newcomers flocked to the organization. New members differed from the SDS "old guard," as they were now called. They were predominantly from the West, less intellectual, and not from political families. They had little interest in the careful intellectual analyses that had been the old SDS style, and were unconcerned with maintaining the sympathies of liberal allies. They wanted action now. The term "prairie people" captured their western origins and outlaw image.[31]

Veterans interpreted the newcomers' challenge to SDS's national structure in terms of their determined antiauthoritarianism. Of course, veterans too were hostile to centralized, top-down organizations. But at SDS's national convention in Kewadin in June 1965, the old-timers seemed powerless in the face of an antiorganization impulse that was immune to considerations of organizational survival. Workshops were unchaired. Chairs for the plenary sessions, often with more than 250 participants, were selected at random and votes were not counted. There were frequent references to elitism and alienation (bad) and "getting with the people" and "non projects" (good). Radical democrats called for eliminating the offices of president and vice president and were stopped only by the promise of a member referendum on the issue. "Structural democracy is an obvious fraud; out with it! Representative government doesn't really represent anyone; out with it!" was how veteran Steve Max characterized the discussion. In the fall, the new guard threw the national office into chaos when it began a collectivist experiment in the office, just when SDS was being flooded with requests for membership and for its position on the war. The trend toward democracy at any cost seemed unstoppable, however, and SDS eagerly surrendered any claim to be the chief coordinator of the antiwar movement. Within a year the old guard was voted out office, and SDS embraced decentralized, regional organization.[32]

The opposition between old and new guards in SDS reflected more than newcomers' extreme antiauthoritarianism, however. In fact, newcomers' ideological commitments were diverse, including everything "from counterculture utopianism to a budding Marxism," says early SDSer Bob Ross. In the Austin SDS, wrote Jeff (Shero) Nightbyrd in 1964, "we have Leninists, Humanists, social democrats, liberal democrats, and a couple of beatniks." The latter observation is interesting since it was Shero who led the effort to eliminate the offices of president and vice president. He and the Austin SDS chapter were widely seen as quintessential prairie people: confrontational, unafraid of taking on the old guard, and uninterested in the demands of organizational survival. However, Shero's personal correspondence at the time reveals something different: a combination of admiration for SDS's founders and frustration with what he perceived as his exclusion from the club. "I'm writing to you because we folk in the boondock[s] seem to get forgotten by the vast N[ational] O[ffice]," he wrote to assistant national secretary Helen Garvy. He was "burbling over with ideas and thoughts and other various insanities," and he was eager to reconnect with the SDS heavies he had met earlier. But he was sensitive to their indifference.[33]

Shero was not alone. Letters by new chapter members to the national office during this period refer repeatedly and enviously to the founding generation of SDS as a group of "friends." "The main problem seems to be to reach new people," Helen Garvy wrote to a chapter member who complained of being shut out of "the mysterious inner workings of SDS." "You weren't alone in feeling lost at the convention." To SDS's leadership, she wondered, "How do we permeate an informal leadership that grew from the days when SDS was a small group of friends?" The problem was not entirely new: SDS leaders had worried as early as 1962 about how to maintain the intimacy of the early group. It had been easier to integrate newcomers when veterans knew them, though. Friends brought friends into the group. They were likely to tap people who were like themselves—an obstacle to diversity but a way to sustain the integrity of existing friendships. Now there were hundreds of new people. "The friendship group just reached the saturation point," Tom Hayden recalls.[34]

The problems confronting SDS are understandable. Friendships among the early group supplied the trust, mutual affection, and respect that made for easy decision making. But they also made it difficult to expand the deliberative group beyond the original circle. Newcomers to a group of friends lack not only information about how the group works but also affective bonds with veterans. Newcomers threaten existing friendships and for that reason alone they may find it difficult to secure the trust and respect of the inner circle. Even if veterans actively try to integrate newcomers, they are likely to be suspected of exclusiveness, no matter what they do.

New SDS members got, they said, a clear message that they were unwanted. Old-timers did not solicit their advice, seek their company, or credit their opinions. This was not deliberate. SDS leaders were highly conscious of the need to give newcomers a sense of belonging, and generous in their desire to turn over the reins of power. But they also enjoyed an easy camaraderie with each other and could speak in shorthand about complex issues. Veterans sat in informally on the National Council meetings, where they probably spoke more than newcomers did. They naturally called their friends for advice and gravitated to each other at meetings. "We weren't saints," Bob Ross says. "Maybe at a conference we'd be having a conversation and wouldn't be as welcoming to a new person as we should have been. But we were really very conscious of trying to integrate them." Nevertheless, even something as relatively trivial as not being warmly welcomed at a meeting could confirm newcomers' anxieties. Indeed, Austin activist Robert Pardun remembers wondering at the Kewadin convention "why the old guard seemed so standoffish." Instead of "personal conversations and friendships that would have helped to break down the boundaries between 'us' and 'them,'" newcomers heard speeches by male old guard leaders, who "intimidated less articulate or less experienced members and made them feel excluded or irrelevant."[35]

New members responded by accusing the old guard of hypocrisy. What kind of participatory democracy could be practiced by an elitist clique? When Pardun and others called for dismantling the group's national structure, he explains now, they were expressing their frustration with officers' lack of accountability. But Pardun also admits that the challengers had not worked out much of an alternative. Moreover, with the discussion of organizational structure cast as a battle between new and old guards, and between centralized structure and no structure, little attention was paid to other, less dramatic proposals for organizational reform. The same thing happened at SDS's "Rethinking Conference" in December. In advance of the conference, many participants had submitted proposals for linking chapters to the national office and for better integrating newcomers into the organization. Some of the proposals were unrealistic, but many were sensible and creative. The memos and position papers were ignored, however, and the meeting dissolved into speechmaking and factionalism. After that, old guard members began to drift away from the organization.[36]

The eclipse of SDS's old guard was not, in itself, the cause of SDS's collapse in 1968 and 1969. But the manner of the succession that took place in 1965 set a precedent for complete turnovers in office almost every year, with little contact between old and new officers. As the organization exploded in size, calls to make the national office more representative were met with pledges to restrict the power of national officers. Less attention was paid to how membership would have input into the positions and policies of the national office. The result was a national office that was remote from the chapters. What suffered was not its ability to offer direction—few chapters would have accepted its direction, anyway—but its ability to provide information, advice, and a sense of programmatic coherence.[37]

As in the case of SNCC, the conflict between old and new within SDS can be viewed narrowly as a showdown between ideological absolutists and democratic pragmatists. But that view would miss the fact that the new guard initially lacked a coherent ideology—antiauthoritarian or otherwise—and that the old guard was itself committed to decentralized, participatory organization. Newcomers' interest in radical democracy crystallized in and through their experience of exclusion. Old guard leaders, for their part, wanted newcomers to be full participants in the group. But their tendency to turn to each other for advice and companionship in some instances excluded people, and in others it was easily perceived that way. The stakes of the conflict were less ideological than a place in the group of friends.

This brief look at participatory democracy in SNCC and SDS lends itself to some rather sweeping conclusions. It suggests, first, that more democracy does not necessarily mean less efficacy. Involving novices in strategic and tactical decisions can be effective in training them to confront and change oppressive institutions. Collectivist decision making can build solidarity and spur tactical innovation. If done right, it can help to discover common interests and forge common goals. It is less effective, however, in negotiating differences of aspiration between organizer and community—especially when those differences are not acknowledged. Ritual injunctions to "let the people decide" can end up deferring questions about longer-term goals rather than taking them on.[38]

SNCC and SDS were not the first movement groups to experiment with radical democracy. Quakers, anarchists, and pacifists had all attempted to abolish internal hierarchies, relying variously on rotating offices, consensus-based decision making, and decentralized decisions. There were models for participatory democracy, but they were less available to student activists in the 1960s than we tend to imagine. Nevertheless, student activists did not entirely lack guidance on how to frame issues, lodge complaints, defuse tensions, and resolve disputes—the complex interactional norms that make any deliberative system possible. SNCC workers built participatory decision making into an older strand of community organizing in which the relationship between organizer and resident was a tutelary one. And in their staff decision making, SNCC, like SDS, relied on the bonds of trust, respect, and affection that joined a group of friends.[39]

Collective decision making among friends is in some ways "naturally" participatory, egalitarian, and efficient. But its intimacy and exclusivity make it difficult to expand beyond a core group of founders. And its determined informality discourages the use of formal mechanisms for guaranteeing participation and accountability when the group does expand. In both SNCC and SDS, the same thing that made participatory democracy easy in the first place made it difficult to sustain.

Notes

1. Norm Fruchter, "Mississippi: Notes on SNCC," *Studies on the Left* 5 (1965): 76–78.

2. Victor Rabinowitz, "An Exchange on SNCC," ibid., 87–88.

3. In *Community and Organization in the New Left: The Great Refusal* (New Brunswick: Rutgers University Press, 1989), Wini Breines describes SNCC and the New Left as inspired by a "prefigurative" commitment, and notes the "dilemma inherited from SNCC." Barbara Epstein, in *Political Protest and Cultural Revolution: Nonviolent Direct Action in the 1970s and 1980s* (Berkeley: University of California Press, 1991), describes such movements as aimed at "cultural reform." On the New Left's prefigurative/strategic or expressive/instrumental tension, see Peter Clecak, "The Movement and Its Legacy," *Social Research* 48 (1981): 521–56; Emily Stoper, *The Student Nonviolent Coordinating Committee* (Brooklyn: Carlson, 1989); Richard King, *Civil Rights and the Idea of Freedom* (New York: Oxford University Press, 1992); Edward Morgan, *The 60's Experience: Hard Lessons about Modern America* (Philadelphia: Temple University Press, 1991); Paul Starr, "The Phantom Community," in *Co-Ops, Communes, and Collectives: Experiments in Social Change in the 1960s and 1970s,* ed. John Case and Rosemary C. R. Taylor (New York: Pantheon, 1979), 245–73. For a critique of analyses centered on these alleged tensions, see Maurice Isserman, "The Not-So-Dark and Bloody Ground: New Works on the 1960s," *American Historical Review* 94 (1989): 990–1010. Richard Rothstein refers to SNCC's "ultra-democratic mystique" in his "Representative Democracy in SDS," *Liberation* 16 (Feb. 1972): 15.

4. Mike Miller, "To the Editors of *Studies on the Left,*" 20 Aug. 1965 (typescript), Mike Miller Papers, private collection.

5. Martha Prescod Norman, interview by Bret Eynon, 26 Oct. 1984, Columbia University Oral History Collection; Betty Garman Robinson, interview by author, 29 June 1996.

6. Baker was supportive. Long frustrated by SCLC's charismatic leadership style and its failure to nurture grassroots organization, she saw in the student movement the potential for mass mobilization anchored in local movements. On SNCC's founding, see Clayborne Carson, *In Struggle: SNCC and the Black Awakening of the 1960s* (Cambridge: Harvard University Press, 1981), and for Baker's role in it, see Charles M. Payne, *I've Got the Light of Freedom: The Organizing Tradition and the Mississippi Freedom Struggle* (Berkeley: University of California Press, 1995); David Garrow, *Bearing the Cross* (New York: William Morrow, 1986); and Joanne Grant, *Ella Baker: Freedom Bound* (New York: John Wiley, 1998).

7. See David Halberstam, *The Children* (New York: Random House, 1998), 141; and Aldon Morris, *The Origins of the Civil Rights Movement: Black Communities Organizing for Change* (New York: Free Press, 1984). See also transcripts of Martha Prescod Norman and John O'Neal

oral histories, Columbia University Oral History Collection. Bob Moses and Mike Thelwell described the "beloved community" as an animating ideal for SNCC's early, Nashville-based leadership (interviews with Bob Moses, 9 Dec. 1992, and Mike Thelwell, 28 June 1995, by author).

8. Sherrod quoted in Fred Powledge, *Free at Last? The Civil Rights Movement and the People Who Made It* (Boston: Little, Brown, 1991), 343; SNCC staff meeting, 6 March 1962, Student Nonviolent Coordinating Committee Papers, microfilm, 1959–1972 (Sanford, N.C.: Microfilming Corporation of America, 1982) (hereafter SNCC Papers), reel 3, 798–800.

9. Robert P. Moses and Charles E. Cobb Jr., *Radical Equations: Math Literacy and Civil Rights* (Boston: Beacon Press, 2001), 81, 87.

10. James Forman, *The Making of Black Revolutionaries* (Seattle: Open Hand, 1985), 419; Muriel Tillinghast, interview by author, 5 June 1996; Hollis Watkins, interview by author, 22 Nov. 1996.

11. Staff meeting minutes, 9–11 June 1964, SNCC Papers, reel 3 975–92. On Moses and Forman's authority, see author's interviews with Judy Richardson (10 Sept. 1992) and Julian Bond (23 March 1992).

12. Participatory democracy as tutelage for citizenship has long been an important theme in political argument. The project I describe here differs in its application to oppositional movements. The point is not merely to train people to be better citizens but to be activists—citizens who confront and challenge institutional politics as they exist. I develop this idea at greater length in *Freedom Is an Endless Meeting: Democracy in American Social Movements* (Chicago: University of Chicago Press, 2002).

13. Casey Hayden, interview by author, 22 May 1995; Richard Flacks quoted in James Miller, *"Democracy Is in the Streets": From Port Huron to the Siege of Chicago* (New York: Simon and Schuster, 1987), 43; Robert Ross, "Primary Groups in Social Movements: A Memoir and Interpretation," *Journal of Voluntary Action Research* (July–Oct. 1977): 143.

14. Quoted in Miller, *"Democracy Is in the Streets,"* 206.

15. On SDS's early support for SNCC, see Haber to Charles Jones, Charles McDew et al., 14 Oct. 1961, SNCC Papers, reel 4, 1150; "Southern Report #2 To Campus Contacts By Al Haber gleaned from Tom Hayden . . . UPI dispatches, Tom Gaither and Connie Curry," 7 Oct. 1961, SNCC Papers, reel 44, 890; "To: Haber, From: Hayden," SNCC Papers, reel 4, 1138–40.

16. Robert A. Haber, "From Protest to Radicalism: An Appraisal of the Student Movement," *Venture* (fall 1960), reprinted in *The New Student Left*, ed. Mitchell Cohen and Dennis Hale (Boston: Beacon Press, 1966), 40; Miller, *"Democracy Is in the Streets,"* 102–3.

17. Tom Hayden, *Reunion: A Memoir* (New York: Random House, 1988).

18. Barbara Haber, "A Manifesto of Hope," *Socialist Review* 93/94 (1987): 162; Richard Flacks, interview by author, 11 Aug. 1999; Todd Gitlin, *The Sixties: Years of Hope, Days of Rage* (New York: Bantam Books, 1987), 106; Haber, "A Manifesto of Hope," 162.

19. Forman, *The Making of Black Revolutionaries;* see also Carson, *In Struggle;* Dittmer, *Local People;* Doug McAdam, *Freedom Summer* (New York: Oxford, 1988); Gitlin, *The Sixties.*

20. Forman, *The Making of Black Revolutionaries.* On Mississippi, see Carson, *In Struggle.*

21. Carson, *In Struggle;* Stoper, *The Student Nonviolent Coordinating Committee;* King, *Civil Rights and the Idea of Freedom.*

22. Julian Bond, interview by author, 23 March 1992; on programmatic confusion, see Nancy and Gene Turvitz to Dear Friends, 10–14 July 1965, SNCC Papers, reel 61, 1071–72; "Report for Monroe County" 3 March 1965, SNCC Papers, reel 20, 976; Mary Brumder report, [fall 1964], SNCC Papers, reel 66, 1265; Liz Fusco, "To Blur the Focus of What You Came Here to Know," [1966], SNCC Papers, reel 20, 46–54.

23. On the new cleavages in Mississippi communities, see John Dittmer, *Local People;* Carson, *In Struggle;* "Hattiesburg Report from Barbara Schwartzbaum," [Nov. 1964], SNCC Papers, reel 66, 1270; "November 28, 1964—Dick Kelley" [field report], Samuel Walker Papers, State Historical Society of Wisconsin, Madison (hereafter SHSW).

24. "Introduction: Semi-Introspective," anonymous, [Nov. 1964], SNCC Papers, reel 3, 440–43; Casey Hayden, personal communication, 29 Aug. 2001; transcribed interview [with summer volunteer] no. 408, 1965, Stanford University Project, South Oral History Collection.

25. Transcript of Ed Brown interview, Moorland-Spingarn Research Center, Howard University.

26. Stokely Carmichael in Executive Committee meeting minutes, 12–14 April 1965, SNCC Papers, reel 3, 410–26; Richardson, interview. Alabama project worker Silas Norman broke into another discussion at the same meeting to say, "It seems to me that the last six months I have been coming to meetings, everyone always leaves before we get around to discussing programs." The meeting ended almost immediately after; programs were apparently not discussed. In a meeting a few months before, Courtland Cox charged that "a lot of people got up and began to discuss their [programmatic] needs . . . and we cut them off to talk of structure." In spite of Cox's intervention, the discussion remained fixed on structure (meeting notes [Feb. 1965], Mary E. King papers, SHSW).

27. Minutes of staff meeting in Hattiesburg, 22 Dec. 1964, Elaine DeLott Baker Papers, private collection; Elayne DeLott Baker, "Reflection, probably written in December 1964," Baker Papers; minutes of Fourth District staff meeting, Harmony, Mississippi, 15–17 Jan. 1965, JoAnn Robinson papers, SHSW. On SNCC staffers' experience of racial tensions, see also Bond and Garman Robinson, interviews, and interviews in Francesca Polletta, *Freedom Is an Endless Meeting,* chap. 4.

28. Minister quoted in minutes, Fifth District meeting, 25 Nov. 1964, Mary E. King Papers, SHSW. On black SNCC staffers' interest in issues of identity, see Cleveland Sellers and Robert Terrell, *The River of No Return: The Autobiography of a Black Militant and the Life and Death of SNCC* (Jackson: University of Mississippi Press, 1990).

29. Charlie Cobb, "On SNICK/Revolution/and Freedom," [April 1965], SNCC Papers, reel 33, 269–72; SNCC staffer, interview by author, 29 June 1995; Forman, *The Making of Black Revolutionaries,* 419; staffer quoted in Mary King, *Freedom Song: A Personal Story of the 1960s Civil Rights Movement* (New York: William Morrow, 1985), 485.

30. "Can the methods of SNCC be applied to the North?" Hayden asked fellow SDSers in the March/April 1963 SDS bulletin, quoted in Sale, *SDS,* 97. On ERAP, see Breines, *Community and Organization;* Miller, *"Democracy Is in the Streets";* and Jennifer Frost, *An Interracial Movement of the Poor: Community Organizing and the New Left in the 1960s* (New York: New York University Press, 2001).

31. See Todd Gitlin, *The Whole World Is Watching: Mass Media in the Making and Unmaking of the New Left* (Berkeley: University of California Press, 1980) 25 ff., on the effects of the March on Washington on SDS's membership. On the "prairie people," see Sale, *SDS;* also Paul Buhle, *Marxism in the United States: Remapping the History of the American Left* (London: Verso, 1987); Gitlin, *The Sixties;* Robert J. Ross, "Generational Change and Primary Groups in a Social Movement," in *Social Movements of the Sixties and Seventies,* ed. Jo Freeman (New York: Longman, 1983).

32. Steve Max, "The 1965 Convention: From Port Huron to Maplehurst," summer 1965, Students for a Democratic Society Papers, microfilm, 1958–70 (Glen Rock, N.J.: Microfilming Corporation of America, 1977) (hereafter SDS Papers), series 3, no. 3; on Kewadin, see also Sale, *SDS;* and Gitlin, *The Sixties.*

33. Ross, "Generational Change," 185; Jeffrey Shero, "SDS, Organization and the South," 1964, SDS Papers, series 2a, no. 130; Jeffrey [Shero] to Helen [Garvy], 28 Nov. 1964, SDS Papers, series 2a, no. 92.

34. On SDS as group of friends, see for example, Paul Cowan, "An Open Letter to Tom Hayden," n.d. [May–June 1965], SDS Papers, series 2a, no. 16, and other letters in that series. H[elen Garvy] to Barry Goldstein, 20 Oct. 1964, SDS Papers, series 2a, no. 79; To Worklist and friends from Helen Garvy, National Office, National Council Meeting, 18–20 April 1965, SDS Papers, series 2a, no. 13; on earlier concerns about newcomers, see Sale, SDS, 81; Tom Hayden, interview by author, 21 Sept. 2000.

35. Ross, interview; Robert Pardun, *Prairie Radical: A Journey through the Sixties* (Los Gatos, Calif.: Shire Press, 2001), 115–116. Like SNCC, SDS did plan programs designed to integrate newcomers and, in SDS's case, to ease out veterans. However, in the press of other business, none of these got off the ground.

36. See, e.g., Potter to Worklist, n.d. [1965], SDS Papers, series 2a, no. 29, and other memos and letters in that collection.

37. On the "Rethinking Conference" and its aftermath, see Gitlin, *The Sixties*, and Sale, *SDS*.

38. Readers of Jane Mansbridge's *Beyond Adversary Democracy* (Chicago: University of Chicago Press, 1983) will find this argument familiar. However, her argument that unitary democratic procedures require unified interests gives inadequate attention to the role of the decision-making process itself in reconfiguring people's "interests."

39. Some SDSers had had exposure to Quaker decision making through their contacts with the American Friends Service Committee, CORE, and Women Strike for Peace. SDS's Swarthmore contingent brought a respect for Quaker methods. Richard Flacks was an eager reader of A. J. Muste's *Liberation* and has since described his admiration for Muste's belief in decentralized and participatory organizations. On SDS's organizational models, see also Richard Rothstein, "Representative Democracy in SDS"; Richard Flacks, "A. J. Muste," *Social Policy* 30 (1999): 7–12; and Miller, *"Democracy Is in the Streets."*

CHAPTER 9

The "Point of Ultimate Indignity" or a "Beloved Community"? The Draft Resistance Movement and New Left Gender Dynamics

Michael S. Foley

Of all the movements huddled under the New Left umbrella, draft resistance has long been perceived as the most exclusively male and one of the most sexist. And so, when I first began research for a history of the draft resistance movement in Boston during the Vietnam War, I was not surprised to find that in the course of compiling a database of 575 activists' names, only 72 belonged to women. In a movement that emphasized open defiance of Selective Service laws—laws that applied only to men—the small number of women's names in movement documents reflected the masculine public face that draft resistance organizations presented in their newsletters and publications.

Still, preliminary oral history interviews indicated that a significant number of women actively participated in Boston's draft resistance movement and, at times, seemed to hold positions of responsibility within the Boston Draft Resistance Group and the New England Resistance, the two most prominent movement organizations in the city. In addition, a questionnaire administered to 310 draft resistance activists (including 45 women) revealed varying degrees of agreement or disagreement with several generalizations about the role of women in the movement. The overwhelming majority of respondents (92 percent), both men and women, agreed that women "played an important role in the draft resistance movement," and a smaller but significant proportion agreed that while women did not "often" assume leadership positions (77 percent), they did "sometimes" (78 percent), and they "often participated in determining important policy and procedure issues" (57 percent). Moreover, most respondents disagreed with the common perception that "women were marginalized in the movement and mostly limited to clerical work" (56 percent).[1]

When the answers of the twenty-four women who responded to the questionnaire were isolated, however, the results were more contradictory. Consistent with the rest of the respondents, 95 percent of the women agreed that women played an important role in the draft resistance movement. Likewise, while 87 percent disagreed with the statement that women "often" attained positions of leadership, 74 percent of women said that women "sometimes" held leadership positions. Most telling, however, is that 71 percent of the women (compared to 44 percent of the total population) said that they believed the movement limited them primarily to clerical work; only 45 percent recall women determining policy or procedural issues. These results seem inconsistent, but they also suggest that these women believe that the draft resistance work they did do, if largely behind the scenes, was critical to the functioning of their respective antidraft organizations.[2] Perhaps it did not mean that women *led* these organizations, but to the extent that they participated, equally or not, the evidence suggests that these women found their draft resistance work both important and fulfilling.

The results of this initial investigation into draft resistance gender dynamics contradicted my expectation that women who worked in the draft resistance movement would report persistent marginalization and sexism. After all, the masculine bravado that was part of the culture of the New Left, and its attendant sexism, have been well documented; New Left men and women wrote about it as early as 1968, and it is a central theme in the historiography of both the New Left and the women's liberation movement. Indeed, Sara Evans's thesis that women's liberation arose out of the civil rights movement and the New Left, first spelled out in her influential *Personal Politics* (1979), is one of those rare scholarly arguments that has persisted virtually unchallenged for more than two decades. Evans argued that women who had gained valuable organizing experience and insight into the meaning of equality within the civil rights movement and the New Left faced constant unequal treatment within those movements, thus necessitating their own movement for gender equality.[3]

To date, however, comparatively little has been written about women and draft resistance. Two essays by sociologist Barrie Thorne (herself a participant in Boston) in 1975 and 1977 informed Sara Evans's brief treatment of the topic in *Personal Politics*. Thorne (and then Evans) argued that although draft resistance ideology stressed equality and freedom, "the draft resistance movement was, in a sense, the point of ultimate indignity in the experience of New Left women." Unlike the civil rights and other student movements, draft resistance targeted an institution—the Selective Service System—that directly affected only men. Consequently, many of the tactics and strategies employed by the Resistance emphasized male action. Women could not refuse induction, nor could they turn in or burn their draft cards. Women who wanted to work in the movement often did so only in clearly defined subsidiary roles; and this ultimately led to the rise of sexually coded stereotypes, the most memorable of which was declared in the infamous slogan, "Girls Say 'Yes' to Guys Who Say 'No.'" Participation in draft resistance organizations, then, ranked among the worst New Left experiences for women, and in some cities it sparked the call for women's liberation.[4]

There is much merit in Thorne's and Evans's analyses of women in draft resistance, but the enduring image of draft resistance as the "point of ultimate indignity" for New

Left women, an image sustained by the few memoirs that reflect on the subject, has become too totalizing: It portrays women mostly as victims, largely denies female agency, and generally obscures a much more complicated dynamic that existed between men and women.[5] Although the sexist treatment of women in draft resistance organizations in Boston created a kind of flashpoint that ultimately led women to recognize their shared oppression (and to then form the first women's consciousness raising groups in that city), the usual generalizations about New Left women are difficult to make here.

This essay argues for a fuller, richer picture of gender dynamics in the draft resistance movement and the New Left, one that situates inspiration and empowerment alongside repression and sexism. In the Boston draft resistance movement, depending on backgrounds, expectations and aspirations, and the organization in which they worked, women's sense of marginalization—and their response to it—differed significantly. Despite obvious inequities, draft resistance provided a nurturing environment in which some women could do the kind of antiwar work they wanted to do, and with room to grow; for others, it offered only limitations, frustration, and conflict, and thus served as a catalyst for women's liberation.

Draft resisters adopted and promoted a self-conscious image of manliness as a defining trait of the movement, primarily because of early criticism leveled against them and their methods of dissent. Dating to some of the earliest draft protests, detractors questioned the patriotism and masculinity of draft resisters. On 26 March 1966, the Boston Committee for Non-Violent Action (CNVA) participated in the Second International Days of Protest against the Vietnam War by sitting in the path of buses carrying draftees into the Boston army base. As police arrested eleven CNVA members, hundreds of burly longshoremen and other onlookers yelled obscenities and called them "cowards." In anticipation of their 31 March court date, four of the arrested men issued press releases announcing that they planned to burn their draft cards on the South Boston district courthouse steps before they went in to face the judge. By the time they arrived that morning, a mob of more than 250 people had assembled in the street outside the courthouse. When the eleven defendants ascended the building's steps, the crowd immediately began calling them "yellow" and "cowards." As the first pacifist lit a portable gas burner and held his card to the flame, some in the crowd shouted, "shoot them!" and "kill them!" Before any of the four draft card burners could make a statement, a group of about seventy-five high school boys broke from the rest of the crowd, rushed up the steps, and attacked them. Three government agents who had infiltrated the crowd to witness the card-burning crime pushed and dragged the resisters from the mob and may have saved their lives, though not before the mob broke the nose of one of the resisters.[6]

The events surrounding these early challenges to the draft system made it clear that those who chose to resist the draft would constantly see their masculinity, and their manhood, questioned. For some segment of the public, refusal to serve one's country—or support for those who refused—could be explained only as cowardice or weakness. As protesters marched through South Boston a week later to protest the beatings, onlookers again yelled "cowards," "sissies," and "faggots." One heckler walked up to the group with a live chicken and broke its neck in an unsubtle warning; he then followed the group with the dead animal dangling from the end of a stick. Compared to the image of the manly warriors who accepted conscription and combat, draft resisters had to confront a popular image of themselves as cowards, or chickens, who could be beaten and intimidated.[7]

The draft resisters' struggle to overcome this image did much to shape the culture of the draft resistance movement, particularly its gender dynamics. In Boston, as draft resistance came to dominate antiwar efforts in the city, organizers not only emphasized the risk attached to open defiance of draft laws but also fostered a kind of machismo that did much to frame the experience of both men and women in the movement. This at first seems consistent with Doug Rossinow's findings elsewhere in the New Left that "sexuality and danger mingled closely in the existential search for a fuller life and a just society." Certainly the draft resistance movement could trace some of its ideological origins to existential and Judeo-Christian traditions—but in the more apocalyptic ethos of late 1967 to late 1969, stopping the war took precedence over the search for a fuller life.[8]

Although the draft resistance movement generally supported any challenge to the Selective Service System, including avoidance, draft resisters themselves went to great lengths to distinguish themselves from draft dodgers. Instead of evading service by leaving the country or pretending to be psychologically unfit—which often meant pretending to be gay—at the pre-induction physical, draft resisters openly courted confrontation with the government. Beginning in October 1967, the New England Resistance (NER), in coordination with Resistance groups nationwide, held a series of mass draft card turn-ins. In Boston most turn-ins took place in solemn ceremonies in some of the city's historic churches. The cards were then delivered to the Justice Department in Washington, in part as demonstrations of moral witness, but also in the hope that the Justice Department would begin an endless series of prosecutions that would swamp the tiny federal court system and undermine the Selective Service System. By confronting the war machine instead of dodging it, draft resisters asserted their masculinity and cut for themselves an image of daring risk takers.

When FBI agents came calling soon after a draft card turn-in, resisters knew they had attracted the government's attention. Initially, FBI interviews could be intimidating for resisters and their families. But the Resistance tried to turn these visits to advantage by brazenly confronting the FBI agents on the issues of the war and the draft. The most famous example of this occurred when Alex Jack, a Boston University divinity student and New England Resistance founder, anticipated his meeting with the FBI by waiting for the agents in the offices of the *BU News*. There Jack invited the agents to sit down because, he said, he wanted to ask *them* a few questions. He gave them a questionnaire that asked questions about the war and the draft, and included a waiver of their Fifth Amendment rights. The last page doubled as a pledge sheet that FBI agents could fill out to join the Resistance. When the agents realized they were being mocked, they left immediately, only to be followed by a group of Resistance "agents" who "looked them up and down, scribbled noisily in pads, and said 'Ah yes,' and 'very interesting'" until they drove away. Similar events occurred at the University of Massachusetts campus in Boston, where a group of students burst in on an FBI interview, snapped about a dozen photographs of the agents, and published them in the student paper and in antiwar leaflets. One resister went so far as to challenge J. Edgar Hoover's masculinity by wearing a button during his FBI interview that said, "J. Edgar Hoover sleeps with a night light."[9]

If draft resisters did not always acknowledge the central role that their manly posturing played in their activism at the time, they see it clearly in retrospect. Bill Hunt, then a Ph.D. candidate in the Harvard history department and another founder of New England Resistance, acknowledges an underlying question that nagged at many resisters: "Are we doing this because really we're scared to fight?" Through it all, Hunt says, "we could never be certain. We were clear enough about our arguments against the war, but what this . . . did not do was to answer the question: would we have the guts to fight in a war that we did believe was just. We *said* we would, but that's easy to say because this wasn't 1941. So there was always that question about masculinity." The best way to answer the question was to continue to press the confrontation with the government. Confrontation could be scary, however, and some resisters attribute the "tough, macho style" adopted by the men in the movement as a way to help everyone feel "less frightened."[10]

The male swagger sustained the courage of some draft resisters, but it alienated others, particularly gay men. Peter Schenck, a Boston University sophomore from Springfield, Massachusetts, turned in his draft card at the first Arlington Street Church turn-in largely because, as a parishioner of the church, he found the Reverend Jack Mendelsohn's calls for resistance so persuasive. But the idea of a community of draft resisters emerging from this act of defiance also appealed to him. "I certainly felt like I was giving up a lot of elements of community," he later said. "This was a decision that was going to make my life a lot more difficult with a lot of other people in my life. And I hoped that something was going to replace that." For a gay man, however, the resistance's promise of community was never fulfilled. After the FBI called to interview him, Schenck went to the Resistance office to seek advice and was alarmed to encounter a group of draft resisters "just kind of hanging out" there "telling fag jokes." Those present casually tossed about words like "faggot" and "cocksucker" as Schenck stood there wondering what to make of this new "community." He left the office and never returned.[11] It is difficult to know just how common this experience might have been, but it is clear that no openly gay men (or women) actively participated in Boston's draft resistance movement; those gay men and women who did take part, including Ray Mungo, the editor of the *BU News,* kept their sexual orientation hidden.[12]

Even so, the flair of the draft resistance movement, the commitment to confrontation, and the absolute rigidity of the resisters' moral stand, attracted many people, including women. In late 1967 and early 1968, draft resistance was the driving force of the antiwar movement in Boston, and it engaged a wide range of individuals outraged about the war. Women who chose to target the draft as their primary focus in protesting the war generally had three or four options available to them. Some worked with the local

Resistance organization, which emphasized moral witness and complete noncompliance with the draft. Others chose to work with draft counseling groups, which, unlike the Resistance, focused on community outreach and on *over-cooperating* with the Selective Service by advising men to seek every possible alternative available to them. In addition, women could join small groups of the so-called "Ultra-Resistance" in raiding draft boards to either steal or destroy draft files, or they could participate in suburban organizing.

In Boston, where all of these opportunities were open to women, the New England Resistance established itself as the highest-profile draft resistance organization. The NER's elaborate draft card turn-in ceremonies attracted considerable media attention. The first turn-in, held at the Arlington Street Church on 16 October 1967, yielded 214 cards, with another sixty-seven burned in the flame of a church candle. Although it went unnoticed by the mass of reporters in attendance, Nan Stone, a young Methodist minister then enrolled in Boston University's School of Theology and the only woman who participated in the ceremony, burned one of those cards. In fact, Stone had argued strenuously with the event's other organizers for the right to do so. In anticipation of mass arrests at the church, the planners decided that several people, including Nan Stone, would not participate, thus guaranteeing that someone would be available to arrange bail and find legal assistance for the others. But Stone, perhaps more than the others, felt a powerful need to put herself at the same level of risk as the men, not only to demonstrate her passionate stand against the war but also to prove herself their equal. As she later recalled, "most of the guys sort of dismissed that . . . they looked at me as not having the risk that they had, 'cause I didn't have a draft card, wouldn't be drafted." Steve Pailet, one of the few sympathetic men, pushed for her participation and gave her his own card to burn. Over the next few days, however, the debate over Stone's position continued, and some argued against her inclusion in the "Master File" of draft resisters then being compiled. Only when the FBI came looking for her and more of the men realized the risk that she had taken in burning Pailet's card, did they assent to labeling Stone a resister, too.[13]

This episode was typical of the kind of treatment women could expect in those resistance organizations that made noncompliance their primary tactic. Even so, some women like Stone were able to attain positions of influence in the New England Resistance, though it was, as she said, a "continual struggle." In some ways, their experience was not unlike that of women who later broke into the construction trades in the 1970s and 1980s, or entered other occupations traditionally closed to women.[14]

Women in the draft resistance movement had to overcome routine objectification, sexual harassment, and expectations of subservience. First, they had to put up with frequent sexist allusions to women that appeared in Resistance literature. One leaflet, for instance, noted that organizers were planning a "huge, incredibly noisy, chick-laden" party for the night following the 3 April 1968 draft card turn-in. Another leaflet promoting a meeting to be held the night before the turn-in stated that "lovelies will sigh 'Yes' to guys who say 'No,'" an implicit promise of women as sexual prizes for men who joined the Resistance. Indeed, several popular posters, usually featuring attractive women in short skirts (including one of Joan Baez and her sisters), promoted the idea that "Girls Say 'Yes' to Guys Who Say 'No'" and could be found in Resistance offices all over the country.[15] When the Resistance turned its attention to organizing GIs in 1968, it invited them to gatherings that would provide "beer and chicks and things." As late as January 1969, when the New England Resistance had moved away from draft resistance altogether to do GI outreach, they put out a call for "more girls" to attend Wednesday night parties for "lonely GIs."[16] In reality, of course, few women associated with the organization offered sex or even companionship as some kind of reward to new resisters, but the objectification of women in this way also served to bolster the manly, virile image of draft resisters.

At the same time, there was a kind of romantic mystique attached to the resisters, and it made them and their cause appealing. Historian and Boston draft resistance activist Ellen DuBois recalls a particular "giddiness" as late as 1968 among her female peers at Wellesley College in anticipation of a campus rally at which Michael Ferber, a nationally known draft resister and codefendant of Dr. Benjamin Spock, and several other resisters spoke.[17] For DuBois, coming from a women's college, the "presence of lots of men was a thorough attraction, not a discouragement." And their mystique was naturally rooted in rebellion. "I kind of imagined motorcycles," DuBois remembers, "that they all had motorcycles." In fact, compared to the Resistance men in California, many of whom did have motorcycles, the men in Boston seemed tame. But the act of resistance, of defiance, nevertheless fueled this romantic image.

In several instances romanticism led to romance, and some of the women who worked in the NER office became involved in relationships with men in the leadership. This sometimes resulted in feelings of distrust and competition among some of the women, particularly between those involved with men in the organization and those who were not. For example, the men would often forget to tell Nan Stone about a meeting that some of their girlfriends (who also worked in the office) were attending. Stone resented one woman in particular, she said, "because she had this boyfriend that gave her . . . an in, somebody who would listen to her. She was paid attention to because of who she was fucking." Sue Katz, another prominent woman in the New England Resistance, however, saw such relationships as useful in attaining positions of responsibility in the organization. Until she started sleeping with one of the Resistance leaders, she says today, "I know I was sort of like nobody, just a 'chick.'" Her relationship made her "somebody" and provided entree into "those . . . all-night meetings, solving the problems of the world."[18]

Regardless of intimate relationships between the men and women of the Resistance, there was a fairly pronounced sexual division of labor. Dana Densmore, who worked in both the New England Resistance and the city's leading draft counseling organization, the Boston Draft Resistance Group, has described the weekly dinner meetings of the Resistance as "exercises in self-laceration" for the women members. "It went without saying that we cooked and cleaned up while the men bonded, strategized, and postured." Indeed, as Sara Evans and others have found elsewhere in the civil rights movement and the New Left, women were expected to take on the traditionally female tasks of cooking, cleaning, and secretarial work: bookkeeping, typing, filing, stuffing envelopes. While women such as Nan Stone, Connie Field, and Rosemary Poole tended to the books, kept track of hundreds of resisters, bought office supplies, and made up leaflets on the mimeograph machine, the men held strategy sessions, met with reporters, and gave informal "raps" at colleges and churches in greater Boston.[19]

In the Boston Draft Resistance Group (BDRG), circumstances for women differed somewhat from those in the New England Resistance. Although women did most of the clerical work in the Cambridge office, participation in BDRG was not as starkly gender coded as it was in the New England Resistance.[20] Women made up at least half of the draft counselors and also took part in "Early Morning Shows," in which members of BDRG arrived at local draft boards to talk to potential draftees on the mornings that they were being bussed into the city for their physical exams. Unlike draft card turn-ins and induction refusals, such activities were open to both men and women. Ellen DuBois, who worked for BDRG while an undergraduate at Wellesley, recalls that although draft counseling was not at all sexualized, the Early Morning Shows, which were usually carried out with more men than women, did take advantage of women participants' femininity. "We wouldn't call it flirting, but we would earnestly try to convince [the inductees] to resist the draft," she recalled. "I'm not sure how conscious we were that we were playing on the fact that we were women and they were men, but somebody must have been conscious of it."[21]

BDRG women, however, disagreed then (as they do today) about the extent to which they participated in leading the organization. Generally, those who held one of the few paid staff positions claim to have experienced very little male chauvinism. Both Sasha Harmon and Bliss Matteson, successive office managers for BDRG, agree that they never "felt any particular discrimination or any particular shutdown" in weekly steering committee meetings or in the office itself. They acknowledge, however, that if they had not assumed clearly defined roles as part of the office staff, they might have felt "at more of a disadvantage."[22]

Other women in BDRG recall the situation differently. DuBois believes that although women like Harmon and Matteson were influential, a fundamental inequality kept them and other women from "advancing beyond a certain point." Women in BDRG had greater responsibility than women in the Resistance, "but there was something wrong at the top." A glass ceiling existed, and as DuBois remembers it, those women would eventually "sort of mysteriously disappear." Dana Densmore, Abby Rockefeller, and Roxanne Dunbar pushed this view further, charging that an "astonishing male hierarchy," most apparent in steering committee meetings, dominated BDRG. According to Densmore, just as at New England Resistance meetings, "if a woman spoke up" in a BDRG steering committee meeting, "there would be a dead silence for a few seconds, and then they would pointedly pick up exactly where they were before her comment." Eventually such experiences in both the New England Resistance and BDRG led Densmore, Rockefeller, and Dunbar to leave the draft resistance movement in 1968 and form Cell 16, one of the first radical feminist groups in the country.[23]

Steering committee meetings at BDRG, like those at the New England Resistance, were notoriously long, as decisions were reached by consensus rather than by majority vote. As a result, those who excelled in debate and carried themselves with confidence (the "highly aggressively verbal easterners . . . New Yorkers," according to one woman) often dominated these sessions. Although there were some exceptions, far fewer women than men felt comfortable with this kind of confrontational dynamic. One male BDRG founder remarked that he had always been proud of the organization's emphasis on this informal style of decision making until years later, when he recognized that it resulted in a kind of "tyranny of informality" that yielded to a "charisma-based" form of leadership. Since few women in those days were socialized to master the "mass-haranguing style" needed to make a point in meetings, men dominated decision making. Sue Katz later raised the issue of masculinity when she described the debates that occurred in similar meetings in the Resistance as a "dick sport for wimpy radicals." Instead of an athletic competition, the men in the Resistance jousted with one another by seeing, she said, "who could conceptualize a longer sentence that would obfuscate more ideas than the next person." Ideological discussion provided a forum to assert "who was the big cock on the block. . . . [It] was as much a competitive sport as anything else. It was just *their* competitive sport," Katz recalled. "Women were not picked for the teams until last."[24]

Ultimately, then, the evidence seems to suggest a clear-cut case of male insecurity (resulting from draft resisters' collective refusal to go to war) leading to the development of a group culture in which sexism and male chauvinism were accepted expressions of manhood. This culture, consistent with the Evans thesis, marginalized many of the women in the movement and eventually led them to create their own movement. Indeed, women from the New England Resistance and the Boston Draft Resistance Group felt sufficiently alienated to come together in the city's first consciousness-raising groups (later part of the larger socialist-feminist organization Bread and Roses) and to form Cell 16, the radical feminist group that began teaching women Tae Kwon Do to defend themselves against their male oppressors.

All of this makes for a neat and fairly predictable story. But the gender dynamics in the draft resistance movement were more complicated. Men did not simply dominate the movement, and women did not simply wait to begin fighting sexism until after they left it. To imply as much suggests that women experienced the draft resistance movement primarily as victims. In fact, however, many women found draft resistance work fulfilling in spite of male dominance, and many also challenged that dominance within the organizations long before and even after discovering women's liberation. Women certainly experienced sexism and frustration, but the extent to which they were limited varied by individual and often could be tied to individual expectations and aspirations.

Like some of the women at BDRG, female Resistance activists today disagree on the degree to which men kept them in subordinate roles. In particular, with the exception of Sue Katz, the women who were involved in relationships with Resistance men are unlikely to recall male chauvinism as a defining characteristic of their experience. Even though their very presence in the inner circle derived from their attachment to male leaders, and could be seen, consequently, as more pointedly sexist, the consensus among these women seems to be, as one put it, that "you weren't treated any differently than you were anywhere else in the movement." The male chauvinism present in the draft resistance movement, they suggest, was simply an extension of the male chauvinism that permeated American society. Another female Resistance activist is certain that women participated actively in the leadership of the organization. Women "certainly spoke out at meetings whenever they wanted; there was no attempt to silence women," she reports. "And I certainly didn't feel that I wasn't a part of the organization nor that I couldn't speak up if I wanted to speak up." Indeed, she says, "power is in the hands of those who seize the power."[25]

By the time the New England Resistance had run its course in late 1969, the two women who recall most acutely the oppression of the men in the organization, Sue Katz and Nan Stone, had largely succeeded in their personal struggles to overcome male dominance, in "seizing power." Both Katz and Stone eventually took on public speaking assignments, directed their own programs, and wrote articles for the organization. Moreover, according to Katz, the men in the group made her their head of security. All of these responsibilities had formerly been reserved solely for men.[26]

The contrasting accounts of women's experience in the draft resistance movement can be explained in part by a combination of prior activist experience, motives for joining the antiwar movement, and the expectations for each person's role. For example, the slightly older women who came to draft resistance as graduate students, or at least in their mid-twenties, arrived with years of experience in the civil rights movement or elsewhere in the New Left, where they felt they had been marginalized to a far greater degree than in their draft resistance work.

Some of these women had a comparative perspective that others did not. Unlike Nan Stone and Sue Katz, for whom draft resistance work constituted their first sustained activism of any kind, Rosemary Poole came to the Resistance after working with the Congress of Racial Equality (CORE) in California in the early 1960s, and Students for a Democratic Society (SDS) at Harvard in the mid-1960s. Poole had faced sexism in both places, and she regarded sexism at the New England Resistance as tame by comparison. Even though Poole acted as Resistance bookkeeper and did the kind of clerical work often expected of women, she asserts that "there was freedom" in the Resistance. "There was openness. There was the same old shit, but it was malleable. . . . It was really a place where things could grow. And of course we did grow and there were lots of arguments and fights and feelings . . . but it was a great situation, in my opinion, for women to move out of that kind of position." When draft resistance faded by 1970, Poole got more involved with women's liberation, but not as a direct reaction to her draft resistance experience. For her, the New England Resistance surpassed expectations. "It was *family* . . . it was just like 'God, these people really do stuff together, and have fun together, and they care about the things I care about, and they go off and do them together.' It was wonderful. It was absolutely wonderful." Penney Kurland of the Resistance agreed: "I did whatever needed to be done; I was just so happy to be doing something [to end the war]."[27]

Similarly, Janine Fay, who was instrumental in beginning BDRG's coffeehouse for GIs, Sgt. Brown's Memorial Necktie (named for the army sergeant in charge of inductions at the Boston army base, who had lost his tie in a scuffle with protesters), never felt thwarted in BDRG. She came to the organization after working on civil rights in Chester, Pennsylvania, for several years while an undergraduate at Swarthmore College.

Fay later recalled that she joined BDRG because she "just couldn't bear the news about what was going on in Vietnam and I wanted to do something." Her aspirations and expectations were not as high as they might have been later, however, as she simply sought a place in the antiwar movement that would also be enjoyable. "I tried to find a place where I could do something that I kind of liked," she later said. "Given the context [that] I wanted to participate, and give part of my life over to ending the war, to doing what I could, I made it also so I could kind of enjoy myself as much as possible." Even so, as Heather Booth, Evi Goldfield, and Sue Munaker wrote in 1968, coffeehouse work was one way that women could do antiwar work without being in an "auxiliary" position. Fay enjoyed considerable autonomy in her work for BDRG and the coffeehouse. "There wasn't something that I was yearning for that someone was stopping me from doing," she said. Years later she could see how other women with aspirations to *lead* BDRG might have felt stifled and then left the organization, but she was not one of them.[28]

Likewise, DuBois of BDRG notes that although she saw the glass ceiling that kept women from advancing beyond a certain point in the organization, she regarded BDRG as also providing the kind of "beloved community" environment associated with the early civil rights movement: It was "a place where men and women came together in loving union with hopes of transcendent goals."[29] In part, DuBois experienced this as she saw her "leadership capacities," already developing at Wellesley, "at least overlooked" at BDRG, and although she did not assert herself as strongly at BDRG as she did at Wellesley, she recalls, "I never felt that I wasn't allowed to do or say anything." DuBois and other women "didn't quite get it" that draft resistance was "supposed to be a men's movement." They tried to extend it "to be a fully integrated movement" from the start and the men in the organization did not actively restrain them. "The amazing thing is that I *didn't* hit any walls," DuBois recalled. "I sort of noticed . . . that there was something odd about the women [in BDRG], but only because they *were* in the leadership."[30]

In addition, the "beloved community" overtones at BDRG contrasted sharply with the sexually predatory nature of SDS, the Weathermen, and the macho "strutting" of the New England Resistance. As a twenty-one-year-old woman, DuBois notes that her work in BDRG coincided with her "sexually coming of age," and that BDRG was a safe place in which to "get introduced to a full-fledged heterosexual culture in the context of the movement," which, she said, "was pretty nice." Pursuit of relationships may not have been a primary motivation for most women's participation in the draft resistance movement, but the generally respectful and safe quality of those relationships contributed to a gender dynamic often overlooked in describing the subjugation of women in the New Left, which tends to emphasize the more exploitive experience of women in SDS and the Weathermen.[31]

To the extent that men did limit the roles of women in the Resistance and BDRG, some women have suggested that this occurred only as much as women allowed it; as soon as they challenged the arbitrary limits set by the men, they were given room to grow. "I dearly loved some of [the men], and none of them restricted me in a way that

I felt I didn't participate in," recalls Rosemary Poole. "[If] I was willing to put up with it, then I got it; if I wasn't willing to put up with it, then I didn't get it, 'it' being abuse." When Poole was clear about her limits, "they were respected" by Resistance men. "God knows there was a lot of sexism that went on right and left, but I didn't feel like I couldn't do something about it," she says. Women "could make an emotional space that was really good for the people involved in [the Resistance]."[32]

Perhaps the most frequently cited example of men marginalizing women in draft resistance and throughout the New Left focuses on the dominance of men in meetings. Like Dana Densmore, Roxanne Dunbar recalled women being routinely ignored in Resistance and BDRG meetings. Dunbar, a graduate student in history at UCLA who came to Boston to begin dissertation research, later remembered, "I'd be rattling off all this stuff, historical stuff and everything, and see these eyes glaze over—these men—in meetings where I'd make a suggestion . . . and I realized that it wasn't just me." Women did not speak as often as men did, "and when they did, sometimes they'd be politely listened to and then they'd go on as if that woman hadn't even spoken . . . and that really burned me, because I was used to people listening to me." Such experiences were not limited to younger women; they also occurred in meetings of Resist, the organization founded by several older "advisors" in the academic and religious community to support draft resistance organizations. Hilde Hein, then a philosophy professor at Tufts University and the only woman to serve as a regional representative for Resist, where she solicited and evaluated funding applications from various antiwar organizations in the Boston area, recalls that "tiers were evident" among steering committee members. Resist employed a woman to run the office but did not encourage women to speak in public or invite many women to serve on the steering committee. According to Hein, more prominent women, such as Grace Paley and Florence Howe, did not appear to be intimidated at steering committee meetings, but Hein was: "I certainly know that if we went around the room expressing opinions, and I said something, nobody paid attention. And if somebody two seats down repeated exactly what I said, and was male, it would be heard. I discovered that. I didn't need to be told that."[33] The male "stars" of Resist—Noam Chomsky, Paul Lauter, Paul Goodman, and others—dictated the course of discussions.

The sense of exclusion experienced by some women did not extend to all. Rosemary Poole, for one, asserts that she was willing to tolerate the dominance of Resistance meetings by just a few men in a way that Sue Katz, Nan Stone, and Roxanne Dunbar were not. She admits that she grew accustomed to listening at meetings and could generally count on someone finally saying what she thought anyway. Likewise, Penney Kurland recalls that she did not like to see the men dominating, but that she also did not necessarily want a leadership role for herself. Kurland remembers only that the women in the New England Resistance struggled with men who "were really nice people, good intentioned, but [who] couldn't help dominating whatever situation they were in." Poole agrees that "those guys just talked their heads off—they took up too much space," but that women were not totally passive. When the women established limits, they were respected. Eventually, Poole recalls, "[we would] get up our spunk and come in and blast them all. . . . We taught teach other how to shut up a little bit so that those of us who had a harder time speaking in a group like that could speak." Bliss Matteson saw an analogous situation in BDRG. "If you're used to functioning in groups, if you're used to being listened to," she reflected, "then you just didn't let them *not* listen to you." In addition, a statistical analysis of BDRG steering committee meeting minutes done by Charles Fisher, a Brandeis University sociologist and BDRG activist, circa 1970, indicated that the ratio of women to men speaking was three to four, although, as Fisher noted, the women were "less likely to contribute to strategic or political discussions."[34]

Restricted participation in meetings also did not extend to women such as Bernardine Dorhn of SDS, who used her physical appearance and revealing attire to advance her own leadership aspirations. Both men and women in Boston's draft resistance movement remember Dorhn as much for her provocative sexuality as for her political savvy. Rosemary Poole recalls that when Dorhn once attended a Resistance meeting in Boston in 1968, wearing one of her trademark miniskirts, and sat with her legs spread apart, "all of the guys were just flipping out." According to Tim Wright, a BDRG founder, however, Dorhn was one of a few women who could be "respected intellectually and politically" even if they "dressed like sex objects." When Dorhn came to town, Wright recalled later, "not only was she bewitchingly attractive—so we all wanted to fuck her —but . . . part of her charisma was her mind, which was razor sharp: she was a lawyer [and] she was really smart."[35] Dohrn was the exception, however; most women did not participate equally with men in draft resistance meetings, either because they were less inclined to do so or because they were largely ignored when they did.

Two outgrowths of the draft resistance movement that are often overlooked and have been almost completely ignored in evaluating women's experience are suburban anti-draft organizing and the so-called Ultra-Resistance. Few records exist for either type of activity, but in Boston it is clear that a number of suburban groups grew out of BDRG's draft counseling and community-outreach approach to challenging the draft, and that at least two draft board raids associated with the Ultra-Resistance of Catholic leftist and pacifist groups heightened the intensity of Boston's draft resistance work.[36]

In the summer of 1968 BDRG made suburban antiwar and antidraft organizing a priority, and perhaps the most successful of these efforts took place in Concord, Massachusetts, where a group of students formed the Concord Area Resistance Summer (CARS) and enlisted the aid of numerous women in the community. Concord, of course, can trace its reputation for defiance and nonconformity to the American Revolution in the late eighteenth century and to Henry David Thoreau in the mid-nineteenth. Although CARS members were conscious of that history, they took most of their inspiration from the civil rights movement and more directly from Boston's draft resistance movement. CARS made education about the war and the draft its primary focus and spent much of its time providing draft counseling to young men in the area, holding teach-ins and a film series on the Vietnam War, distributing leaflets at area shopping centers, and conducting the usual "endless meetings." The group did not organize demonstrations because, as one activist later put it, "you don't demonstrate in the suburbs; people don't like it." In many ways, the work built on models of community outreach used by BDRG in working-class neighborhoods of Cambridge and Boston, which in turn had built on the SDS Economic Research and Action Projects (ERAP) of the mid-1960s. The only difference in Concord was the focus on the suburban middle class, not the urban working class.[37]

At its peak, as many as fifty people were active in CARS, with a leadership that was largely female. Many of the people involved came from the Concord Friends Meeting, the Quakers. A few of the younger members had ties to BDRG, but approximately twelve to fifteen leaders made most of the decisions. According to Susan Starr, a nineteen-year-old who grew up in Concord, CARS attracted women because women were more politically active than men in the suburbs. "Most of those women did not have full-time jobs, [and] some were young women," she recalls, "and the men were all at work. . . . There were very few of them, when they came home, who were interested in this kind of work."[38]

In practice, then, women in CARS did the secretarial work that their counterparts in BDRG and NER did, but they also experienced a leveling of hierarchy in the organization that allowed them to participate more equally with men. "We were certainly no less sexist than the society at large at that point," recalls Starr, "but we did have a little higher level of consciousness." Although women did most of the "grunt work," Starr also edited the CARS newsletter, which, unlike those of BDRG and the Resistance, contained numerous articles written by Starr and other women in the group. Sexism was not altogether absent, of course. Starr remembers that male opinion was often "taken more seriously" than female opinion but, she says, "it was not a central issue for us." By their numbers alone, women had to be at the center of the organization; and Starr claims that CARS never suffered from internal divisions or debates "about male/female dynamics or male dominance."[39] That said, unlike Women Strike for Peace, an antiwar organization founded and led by older, middle-class mothers, CARS did not seem to rely on the older women in the community for leadership; the only female names to appear in the few documents left behind by the organization are names of younger women.[40]

In contrast, men clearly dominated the pacifist and Catholic Left groups that made headlines by raiding draft boards and destroying draft files with their own blood or with paint or by burning them in homemade napalm. Suzanne Williams, who had spent at least sixty-eight days in jail on various charges resulting from her peace activism with the Committee for Non-Violent Action (CNVA) before the 1968 draft board raids, recalls that CNVA meetings operated much like those of the Resistance and BDRG.[41] "The woman would talk and those assembled would largely act as if there had been an interruption that had nothing to do with anything, as if a coal train had passed by," she said. "Two minutes later, a man might express the very same idea and where it had been treated like a coal train when the woman had said it . . . people would [now] actively discuss it and say 'Oh, what a good idea.'" Similarly, CNVA women understood that they were expected to "make coffee, and stuff envelopes, and cook dinner, and do the dishes and so forth," while the men plotted strategy.[42]

In other ways, however, women in the Ultra-Resistance also participated much more equally by taking part in the "heroic" action typically reserved only for men. On 4 June 1968, for example, Williams entered the Boston Customs House with fellow CNVA member Frank Femia, took the elevator to the floor housing Local Board 30, and poured black paint over several drawers full of draft files. When it transpired that the FBI had no idea who had perpetrated the crime, Williams and Femia claimed responsibility for it. They were quickly apprehended, brought to trial, and sentenced to four years in prison. (After a prison escape that added six months to her sentence, Williams spent eighteen months at the Federal Reformatory for Women in Alderson, West Virginia.) A few weeks after the initial sentencing, on 7 November 1968, two more women joined six men in raiding four draft boards in Boston, where they destroyed hundreds of draft files. Draft board raids provided one type of protest where women could plan an action, carry it out, and face the consequences as the equals of men. In the larger scheme of the draft resistance movement, however, they were few in number.[43]

For the most part, despite the varied experiences of women in draft resistance, the image of alienated women limited to subservient roles has long dominated all others. By the summer of 1968, both male and female writers described the second-class status of women in articles in national New Left and draft-resistance periodicals. The earliest piece, by Francine Silbar, appeared in SDS's *New Left Notes* in March 1967 (before either the BDRG or the New England Resistance had been founded). Silbar challenged the secondary role of women in the incipient antidraft movement and suggested that women organize themselves around the draft issue, and not merely as men's secretaries. In December 1967, following the second national draft card turn-in, Rodney Gage, a California resister, argued that the time had come to "bring women into essential areas of the Resistance." He urged resisters to "speak to and act against a growing feeling of impotence and stagnation among our sisters in the movement." He concluded that clerical work did not "suffice as meaningful work" for women any more than it would for men. By March 1968 another male writer described women in draft resistance as "the sleeping giant of the movement" and compared their position in the Resistance to that of "Blacks in the early '60s who felt the intimidation of White co-workers."[44]

Although these male writers were sympathetic to the plight of their female colleagues, their interpretation of the issues demonstrated that even after Resistance women had met to discuss their grievances at the national conference in Lake Geneva, Wisconsin, some men still did not fully appreciate women's fundamental feelings of alienation. One writer in *The Resistance,* the national newspaper published in Boston, noted that "many aggressive 'women liberation' types feel angered and hurt because they cannot participate" in draft card turn-ins. He then seemed to blame these particular women for their own plight in arguing that "their militant actions only intensify the strong male-chauvinistic tendencies of some Resistance organizers." Apart from office work, cooking, and taking part in demonstrations, he suggested, women could also "serve as particularly effective draft counselors and leafleters of GIs and reservists"; in other words, the effectiveness of women in the movement stemmed mostly from their sex appeal.[45] Such insensitivity only fueled the notion that the draft resistance movement was, as Barrie Thorne and Sara Evans later described it, the point of "ultimate indignity" for women in the New Left.

In the years since the end of the Vietnam War, some male draft resistance activists have expressed regret for their treatment of women. In a tenth-anniversary address at the Arlington Street Church, Michael Ferber noted that "the band of brothers born at this altar ten years ago was a band of brothers only, and the tough, macho style some of us put on to help us feel less frightened was unfair and hurtful to the women and the gay people among us." Similarly, Harold Hector of BDRG says that he would like to apologize "for being such a sexist pig." Hector recalls that the BDRG men "completely ignored" the women's contribution to the organization. Instead, they would "always slough off clerical stuff to them," and expect them "to be our girlfriends."[46]

Such apologies may be welcomed by women who were active in the draft resistance movement, but they also have the effect of perpetuating the image that, as Charles Payne has suggested with regard to the sexual division of labor in Mississippi's civil rights movement, "men led, but women organized" the Boston draft resistance movement.[47] In many ways, of course, that is true. But the evidence presented here suggests that different women experienced their work in draft resistance differently. For some, draft resistance work clearly constituted the "point of ultimate indignity," but others found inspiration and fulfillment, indignities notwithstanding. And some small number of women clearly did participate as leaders.

Some of this conflicting data can be attributed, no doubt, to the passage of thirty years and the use of oral histories. Unfortunately, unlike the military women who used the GI antiwar press as a forum, women who took part in the Boston draft resistance movement did not write extensively about their plight in underground newspapers of the time.[48] The oral histories, coupled with the survey results and the limited documentary evidence, at least suggest that further study is warranted.

Ultimately, then, although almost all of these women later became feminists, they report different experiences in the draft resistance movement. Evidence of the complex gender dynamics presented in this essay does not overturn Barrie Thorne's and Sara Evans's generalizations about the experiences of women in draft resistance and the New Left in general, because for many women draft resistance was indeed their most immediate pre-feminist experience—and it pushed them to begin their own movements for women's liberation and radical feminism. But at the same time that this macho, sexist culture served as a catalyst for a new movement, women (and men) in the movement were also in the process of first *defining* it as sexism and, consequently, as a rationale for a new gendered resistance. That process of definition, and of calling for a new movement to challenge it, however, has overshadowed other, equally valid and varied experiences. For even among participants in Boston's earliest consciousness-raising groups, some women found themselves liberated—if not as women, then as activists—through their work in draft resistance.

Notes

1. Michael S. Foley, 1997 Boston Draft Resistance Survey, author's files (raw data to be deposited in my papers and oral history tapes at Swarthmore College Peace Collection upon publication of my *Confronting the War Machine: Draft Resistance during the Vietnam War* [Chapel Hill: University of North Carolina Press, forthcoming]). The survey was administered to 310 draft resistance activists, including 45 women; 185 responded, including 25 women. Responses

to statements regarding the role of women in the movement: 1) Women "played an important role" in the movement, 150 (92%) agreed, 13 (8%) disagreed; 2) women "often attained positions of leadership in draft resistance organizations," 30 (23%) agreed, 103 (77%) disagreed; 3) women "sometimes attained positions of leadership in draft resistance organizations," 111 (78%) agreed, 32 (22%) disagreed; 4) women "often participated in determining important policy and procedure issues," 77 (57%) agreed, 59 (43%) disagreed; 5) women were "marginalized in the draft resistance movement and mostly limited to clerical work," 62 (44%) agreed, 80 (56%) disagreed. Note: A significant number of the 185 respondents either did not answer these questions or checked "don't know." This can be attributed to older supporters of the movement or rank-and-file resisters who would not have been in a position to observe the day-to-day operations of draft resistance organizations; even so, the high number of "don't know" responses can also be seen as evidence that women did not hold prominent positions in these organizations.

2. 1997 Boston Draft Resistance Survey. Responses to statements regarding the role of women in the movement: 1) Women "played an important role" in the movement, 22 (95%) agreed, 1 (5%) disagreed; 2) women "often attained positions of leadership in draft resistance organizations," 3 (13%) agreed, 20 (87%) disagreed; 3) women "sometimes attained positions of leadership in draft resistance organizations," 17 (74%) agreed, 6 (26%) disagreed; 4) women "often participated in determining important policy and procedure issues," 10 (45%) agreed, 12 (55%) disagreed; 5) women were "marginalized in the draft resistance movement and mostly limited to clerical work," 17 (71%) agreed, 7 (29%) disagreed.

3. Sara Evans, *Personal Politics: The Roots of Women's Liberation in the Civil Rights Movement and the New Left* (New York: Vintage, 1980). As evidence of the lasting impact of the Evans thesis, see Rachel Blau DuPlessis and Ann Snitow, introduction, *The Feminist Memoir Project: Voices from Women's Liberation* (New York: Three Rivers, 1998), 6–7; and Rosalyn Baxandall and Linda Gordon, introduction to *Dear Sisters: Dispatches from the Women's Liberation Movement* (New York: Basic, 2000), 7–8. Baxandall and Gordon write, "in the crucible of activism for civil rights, for peace, for the environment, for free speech, for social welfare, women have been valued participants who gained skills and self-confidence. At the same time they have been thwarted, treated as subordinates, gophers, even servants, by the men in charge—including men who considered themselves partisans of democracy and equality. Within these movements women learned to think critically about social structures and ideologies, to talk the language of freedom and tyranny, democracy and domination, power and oppression. Then they applied these concepts to question their own secondary status. It is precisely this combination of raised aspirations and frustration that gives rise to rebellion." This is a point likewise accepted by Doug Rossinow in his important revision of New Left history, though he argues that women not only rebelled but attempted to "form a new, feminist left." See Doug Rossinow, *The Politics of Authenticity: Liberalism, Christianity, and the New Left in America* (New York: Columbia University Press, 1998), 297–333.

4. Barrie Thorne, "Women in the Draft Resistance Movement: A Case Study of Sex Roles and Social Movements," *Sex Roles* 1 (1975): 179–95; Barrie Thorne, "Gender Imagery and Issues of War and Peace: The Case of the Draft Resistance Movement of the 1960s," in *The Role of Women in Conflict and Peace,* ed. Dorothy McGuigan (Ann Arbor: University of Michigan Center for the Continuing Education of Women, 1977); Sara Evans, *Personal Politics,* 179–85. This argument has been picked up by Alice Echols, in *Daring to Be Bad: Radical Feminism in America, 1967–1975* (Minneapolis: University of Minnesota Press, 1989), 37–38; and "'Women Power' and Women's Liberation: Exploring the Relationship between the Antiwar Movement and

the Women's Liberation Movement," in *Give Peace a Chance: Exploring the Vietnam Antiwar Movement*, ed. Melvin Small and William D. Hoover (Syracuse: Syracuse University Press, 1992), 173. In their popular 1971 book on the draft resistance movement, Michael Ferber and Staughton Lynd produced a 293-page national overview that included exactly one paragraph on the contribution of women to the cause (Michael Ferber and Staughton Lynd, *The Resistance* [Boston: Beacon Press, 1971] 159–60). Two years later, sociologist Michael Useem, using Boston as a case study, published his analysis of draft resistance and completely ignored gender issues (Michael Useem, *Conscription, Protest, and Social Conflict: The Life and Death of a Draft Resistance Movement* [New York: John Wiley & Sons, 1973]).

5. Memoirs that mention women in draft resistance in Boston include Dana Densmore, "A Year of Living Dangerously: 1968," and Roxanne Dunbar, "Outlaw Woman: Chapters from a Feminist Memoir-in-Progress," both in DuPlessis and Snitow, *The Feminist Memoir Project*.

6. "7 War Protesters Beaten in Boston," *New York Times*, 1 April 1966, 5; "Pacifist Group, Card Burners, Struck, Kicked," *Manchester Union-Leader*, 1 April 1966, 1; "Boston Draft Card Burnings, Beatings Jar Mayor, Police," *Boston Globe*, 8 April 1966, 1; "Draft Protester Thanks FBI Agent," *Boston Globe*, 1 June 1966, 1; "The Wrong Place," *Time*, 8 April 1966, 28; John Phillips, telephone interview by author, 29 Aug. 1997; Xenia (née Suzanne) Williams, interview by author, 28 Aug. 1997; transcript of *United States v. O'Brien*, Cr-66-91-S, 1966, National Archives, Waltham, Mass.

7. "Marchers Pelted in Boston Protest," *New York Times*, 7 April 1966, 5; "Boston Pacifist Parade Pelted," *Manchester Union-Leader*, 7 April 1966, 1; "Boston Draft Card Burnings, Beatings Jar Mayor, Police," *Boston Globe*, 8 April 1966, 8; speech by Jerome Grossman (Massachusetts ACLU annual meeting, 2 Oct. 1993). For an interesting examination of this image of manliness from another angle, see Joshua Freeman, "Hardhats: Construction Workers, Manliness, and the 1970 Pro-War Demonstrations," *Journal of Social History* 26 (summer 1993): 725–44. See also Van Gosse, *Where the Boys Are: Cuba, Cold War America, and the Making of a New Left* (London: Verso, 1993).

8. Rossinow, *The Politics of Authenticity*, 297–333. Rossinow describes the quest for an authentic masculinity as one of the pillars of the New Left; while the machismo of draft resistance neatly fits that characterization and had many of the effects on women's participation that Rossinow describes, one cannot persuasively make the case that the quest for authentic masculinity was a goal of draft resistance so much as a by-product of the movement's tactics, which emphasized male risk-taking. For more on the intellectual origins of the draft resistance movement, see Foley, *Confronting the War Machine*, chap. 3.

9. Ferber and Lynd, *The Resistance*, 153–54; Alex Jack, interview by author, 21 March 1997; New England Resistance (hereafter NER) Newsletter, n.d. [c. early Nov. 1967]; Papers of Alex Jack, privately held collection.

10. Bill Hunt, interview by author, 31 Oct. 1997; Michael Ferber, "The Politics of Memory" (sermon delivered at Arlington Street Church, Boston, 16 Oct. 1977), Arlington Street Church archives, Boston, Mass.; Larry Etscovitz, interview by author, 12 Aug. 1997.

11. Peter Schenck, interview by author, 2 Dec. 2000. A few months later, when his draft board called him for his pre-induction physical (a practice ordered by the director of Selective Service, Lewis Hershey, to punish those who returned their draft cards), Schenck, alone now in his resistance, brought a psychologist's note vouching for his homosexuality to his physical; the doctor gave him a 4-F deferment.

12. Ray Mungo, interview by author, 13 June 1997; Sue Katz, telephone interview by author, 2 March 1999. On homophobia in the New Left, see Ian Lekus, "'Nothing But a Bunch of Fag-

gots': Greg Calvert and the Politics of Homophobia in the New Left" (paper delivered at the Annual Meeting of the Organization of American Historians, Toronto, Ontario, 23 April 1999).

13. Nan Stone, interview by author, 28 March 1997; Jack, interview; Neil Robertson, interview by author, 24 Aug. 1997.

14. On women in the construction trades, see Susan Eisenberg, *We'll Call You If We Need You: Experiences of Women Working Construction* (Ithaca: Cornell University Press, 1998); Molly Martin, ed., *Hard-Hatted Women: Stories of Struggle and Success in the Trades* (Seattle: Seal Press, 1988); and Jean R. Schroedel, *Alone in a Crowd: Women in the Trades Tell Their Stories* (Philadelphia: Temple University Press, 1985).

15. NER letter, 20 March 1968, William Clusin Papers, privately held collection; "A Time to Resist," leaflet, Michael Zigmond Papers, privately held collection. One version of the "Girls Say 'Yes' to Guys Who Say 'No'" poster can be found in the Papers of Benjamin Spock, series 2, box 11, folder: miscellaneous 1968, II, Syracuse University, Bird Library.

16. Thorne, "Women in the Draft Resistance Movement," 184, 190; *Revolution Newsletter*, 9 Jan. 1969, Robert Shapiro Papers, privately held collection.

17. Ellen DuBois, interview by author, 11 June 1997.

18. Nan Stone, telephone interview by author, 8 Oct. 1997; Sue Katz, interview by author, 2 March 1999.

19. Densmore, "A Year of Living Dangerously," 73; Rosemary Poole, interview by author, 4 Dec. 2000; Connie Field, interview; Stone, interview, 28 Mar 1997.

20. One BDRG newsletter noted: "Sasha Harmon is our office manager; if you have an afternoon free and would like to lend a hand collating, stapling, folding, phoning, etc.-ing, call and ask her what's up." This instruction seems to have been aimed at all readers of the newsletter, male and female alike, but it also makes clear that Harmon, a woman, was in charge of these responsibilities. BDRG Newsletter, March 1968, Papers of Barrie Thorne, Michigan State University (hereafter BTP).

21. Ellen DuBois, telephone interview by author, 30 Nov. 2000; Tim Wright, interview by author, 25 Aug. 1997.

22. Sasha Harmon, telephone interview by author, 14 Sept. 1997; Bliss Matteson, interview by author, 29 Aug. 1997.

23. DuBois, interview, 11 June 1997; DuBois, interview, 30 Nov. 2000; Tekla Louise Haasl, "'I Want to Knock Down the World': A Study of Radical Feminism and Cell 16," (master's thesis, University of New Hampshire, 1988), 24–29; Densmore, "A Year of Living Dangerously," 73; Roxanne Dunbar-Ortiz, telephone interview by author, 17 Sept. 1997.

24. Harmon, interview; Wright, interview; Katz, interview. For more on male dominance of New Left meetings, particularly regarding the earlier New Left, see Evans, *Personal Politics*, 115.

25. Field, interview; Olene Tilton, interview by author, 16 June 1997.

26. Katz, interview; Stone, interview, 8 Oct. 1997. An example of women as public representatives of the NER is Nan Stone, "GI Support Speech," n.d., Nan Stone Papers, privately held collection.

27. Poole, interview; Penney Kurland Lagos, interview by author, 21 Feb. 1999.

28. Fay, interview, 1 Dec. 2000; see also Heather Booth, Evi Goldfield, Sue Munaker, *Toward a Radical Movement* (Boston: New England Free Press, 1968), reprinted in Barbara A. Crow, ed., *Radical Feminism: A Documentary Reader* (New York: New York University Press, 2000), 58–63.

29. DuBois, interview, 30 Nov. 2000. To the extent that anyone has made the "beloved community" analogy to draft resistance, it has been described as a "distinctly male beloved community" (Rossinow, *The Politics of Authenticity*, 230).

30. DuBois, interview, 30 Nov. 2000.

31. Ibid. On sexual exploitation in SDS and Weatherman, see for example Evans, *Personal Politics*, 152–54, 177–79; Allen Matusow, *The Unraveling of America: A History of Liberalism in the 1960s* (New York: Harper and Row, 1984), 340–41; Todd Gitlin, *The Sixties: Years of Hope, Days of Rage* (New York: Bantam Books, 1987), 371–72, 395; Rossinow, *The Politics of Authenticity*, 265–67.

32. Poole, interview.

33. Dunbar-Ortiz, interview; Hilde Hein, interview by author, 18 Sept. 1998.

34. Poole, interview; Kurland Lagos, interview, 21 Feb. 1999; Matteson, interview, 29 Aug. 1997; Charles Fisher, "Midwives to History: The Boston Draft Resistance Group" (unpublished manuscript, II–16; copy in author's files).

35. Todd Gitlin describes Dorhn as combining "lawyerly articulateness with a sexual charisma —even more than her chorus line looks—that left men dazzled" (Gitlin, *The Sixties*, 385–86); Poole, interview; Wright, interview.

36. Some might argue that to include a discussion of gender relations in these organizations and activities takes us outside the New Left, but it is clear that if both were not dominated by college students, they were still of the New Left. In the summer of 1968, BDRG, unquestionably a New Left organization, made suburban organizing a priority. Likewise, the draft board raids for which the Berrigan brothers were well known were carried out by individuals with both pacifist and leftist credentials. More importantly, draft board raids, if not endorsed by the Resistance, were seen as part of the same *movement* by people both within and outside it. As for the sparse records, sometimes BDRG members did the organizing in particular towns on their own, and in other cases they were successful in mobilizing some of the residents to lead antidraft organizing in their own communities. Few records seem to exist for any particular towns with the exception of Concord, Massachusetts; there, the Concord Area Resistance Summer put out a newsletter and kept good records, copies of which are included in Barrie Thorne's papers at Michigan State University. On the other hand, Boston's two draft board raids (in June and November 1968), did not grow out of the work of either BDRG or the Resistance, but were initiated by members of the Catholic Left and others with ties to the Committee for Non-Violent Action (CNVA) and the War Resisters League (WRL). Papers for both organizations are deposited at the Swarthmore College Peace Collection, though I rely here primarily on oral history and documents provided by Xenia Williams (nee Suzanne Williams) and a few found in the Thorne papers at MSU.

37. Susan Starr, interview by author, 4 Aug. 1997.

38. Ibid.

39. See various issues of the CARS newsletter, "CARS Mechanics," BTP; Starr, interview.

40. On Women Strike for Peace, see Amy Swerdlow, *Women Strike for Peace: Traditional Motherhood and Radical Politics in the 1960s* (Chicago: University of Chicago Press, 1993). For a related article on Women Strike for Peace fighting the draft, specifically, see Amy Swerdlow, "'Not My Son, Not Your Son, Not Their Sons': Mothers against the Vietnam Draft," in Small and Hoover, *Give Peace a Chance*, 159–70.

41. Martin Cohen, "Suzi, What's a Nice Girl Like You Doing in Jail?" *Fact*, Jan.–Feb. 1967, 31–41.

42. Williams, interview. Note that the coal train reference derives from Williams's stay in federal prison for destroying draft files. As she tells it, while a prisoner at the Alderson, West Virginia, Federal Reformatory for Women, "I was in the bend of the Greenbriar River, and also in the bend of the C&O railroad tracks, and the coal trains from Appalachia to the D.C. area were going through all the time. And when the coal train went by, it was not possible to carry on a conversation. You just stopped and waited till the noise ended."

43. Williams, interview; Caroline Surrey, "Suzi Williams, the Pacifist Who Smeared Draft Files," *Boston Sunday Globe,* 13 Oct. 1968, A3; "Frank and Suzi Sentenced," *The Peacemaker,* 19 Oct. 1968, 1; "Statement: the Boston Eight," press release, BTP.

44. Francine Silbar, "Women and the Draft Movement," *New Left Notes,* 27 March 1967, 11; Rodney Gage, "The Resistance: Oct 16–Dec 4–April 2," *Resist* (a magazine put out by the Palo Alto resistance), Dec. 1967, Papers of Michael Ferber, Swarthmore College Peace Collection; Robert Pearlman, "Two Worlds of Draft Resistance," *Paper Tiger,* 1 March 1968, BTP.

45. "Geneva Conference Plans Summer Organizing," *The Resistance,* 1 June 1968, 6, Papers of Robert Chalfen, privately held collection.

46. Ferber, "The Politics of Memory"; Hector, interview, 9 April 1997.

47. Charles M. Payne, "Men Led, but Women Organized: Movement Participation of Women in the Mississippi Delta," in *Women in the Civil Rights Movement: Trailblazers and Torchbearers, 1941–1965,* ed. Vicki L. Crawford, et al. (Bloomington: Indiana University Press, 1990) 1–11; see also Charles M. Payne, *I've Got the Light of Freedom: The Organizing Tradition and the Mississippi Freedom Struggle* (Berkeley: University of California Press, 1995).

48. See Barbara Tischler, "Voices of Protest: Women and the GI Antiwar Press," in *Sights on the Sixties,* ed. Barbara Tischler (New Brunswick: Rutgers University Press, 1992). When New Left women moved on to women's liberation, they produced countless broadsides, periodicals, and newsletters, but I've been unable to find much direct criticism of draft resistance in those writings. See, for example, recent anthologies such as Baxandall and Gordon, *Dear Sisters* and Crow, *Radical Feminism.*

CHAPTER 10

Losing Our Kids: Queer Perspectives on the Chicago Seven Conspiracy Trial

Ian Lekus

The scene: Chicago, Illinois, December 1969. The stage: Judge Julius Hoffman's courtroom in the new downtown federal building on Dearborn Street, between Adams and Morgan. The so-called Chicago Seven—pacifist David Dellinger, New Left organizers Tom Hayden and Rennie Davis, Yippies Abbie Hoffman and Jerry Rubin, and activist academics John Froines and Lee Weiner—faced charges of conspiracy to incite a riot at the 1968 Democratic National Convention, held in the Windy City. The judge had already severed the case of Bobby Seale, cofounder of the Black Panther Party, from that of the remaining seven white defendants. The courtroom drama played out for five months, premiering in September 1969 and running until the jury convicted the defendants in February 1970. The trial itself proved a remarkably queer event, an open confrontation between the state on the one hand and those who protested the racial, sexual, and generational hierarchies dominant in society on the other, between those who enforced the American order of things and those who rebelled against the norms.

Journalists, participants, and historians have written about the political spectacle of the conspiracy trial at great length. As Andrew Kopkind observed in *Hard Times,* "Dellinger's militant pacifism, Abbie Hoffman's theatrical anarchism, Hayden's visionary pan-radicalism, and Bobby Seale's black Leninism defied neat packaging." Furthermore, the government "assured confusion at the defense table by bundling widely disagreeing fellows in one bed."[1] Within the context of the state's prosecution of these strange bedfellows, perhaps the queerest two days of this judicial drama came late in 1969 when U.S. Attorney Thomas Foran cross-examined Allen Ginsberg, legendary Beat poet and witness for the defense. As prosecutor, Foran served as lead storyteller for the state, defining for the jury and the broader courtroom of public opinion how the government viewed the defendants and their allies. Ginsberg took the stand as one of the cultural icons (along with Arlo Guthrie, Pete Seeger, Phil Ochs, Judy Collins, Country Joe Mc-Donald, Timothy Leary, and others) chosen by the Chicago Seven to represent and articulate the vision of the generation of young white men and women protesting the crimes of the American Empire. On 11 and 12 December the already combative courtroom climate took a turn toward the surreal, as Ginsberg offered poetry and chanted *Om* in partial answer to Foran's questions. The judge appeared to be as hostile to the defense witness as the prosecutor was, his scorn transparently evident as Ginsberg chanted in Sanskrit. Allen Ginsberg—Buddhist and Jew, poet and unrepentant homosexual, opponent of the Vietnam War—embodied much that was anathema to the courtroom's defenders of state and national power. Foran, a loyal cog in Mayor Richard Daley's Democratic Party machine, gay-baited Ginsberg, his poetry, and his friends throughout the cross-examination. The poet's testimony climaxed explosively, bringing the defendants to tears as he recited fragments of "Howl"—while Foran could only sneer "damn fag" as Ginsberg left the stand.[2]

A week after the Chicago Seven trial ended, Thomas Foran lashed out at the threat he saw seducing the future leaders of the nation. Before a meeting of the Loyola Academy Booster Club, he fumed, "we've lost our kids to the freaking fag revolution." In *Stonewall,* Martin Duberman cites Foran's declaration as evidence of official hostility toward the gay movement, while Terence Kissack's article on the Gay Liberation Front in New York refers to Foran's outburst as one example of how Vietnam War hawks considered the "long-hairs" of the antiwar movement insufficiently manly.[3] Young men in the antiwar movement and the counterculture routinely experienced harassment that framed their political resistance in terms of gender and sexual deviance. Abbie Hoffman recalled one passerby in Times Square hissing at him, "You fuckin' coward, won't defend our country, won't go and fight, you cocksucker."[4] The insights offered by Duberman and Kissack illuminate the contexts within which gay liberation activists organized in the late 1960s and early 1970s.

Foran's temper tantrum and the conspiracy trial as a whole also provide a critical vantage point from which to reexamine the relationship between the antiwar movement and the state more broadly, using the insights of queer scholarship. Historian Donna Penn explains that "'queer' is an analytical tool that allows us to re-read personal experiences and cultural prescriptions and proscriptions through a lens focused on how the *normal* gets constructed and maintained."[5] Michael Warner, Monique Wittig, and other queer theorists critique the heteronormativity of social thought and organization. Warner describes heteronormativity as "the culture's assurance (read: insistence) that humanity and heterosexuality are synonymous," while Wittig explains that "to live in society is to live in heterosexuality. . . . Heterosexuality is always already there within all mental categories. It has sneaked into dialectical thought (or thought of differences) as its main category."[6] For establishment Democrats like Thomas Foran, whatever other legitimate ills of society demanded redress, this conflation of *normal* and *heterosexual* remained the cornerstone of society, a fact not to be questioned lest the entire foundation begin to crumble.

At the dawn of the 1960s, most activists shared the heteronormative notions endemic to the Cold War American society in which they grew up. A few spaces existed in the antiwar movement (notably in the socialist-pacifist War Resisters League) where men and women did not have to hide their attraction to the same sex, and could thus function as activists nearly as openly and honestly as did their heterosexual comrades. In many parts of the movement, however, if news spread of an activist's homosexuality, he or she encountered tense silences or awkward responses at best, and harassment, derision, and total exclusion at worst. But during the daily work of organizing, in the conversations on long road trips and at all-night meetings and conferences, in the friendships developed and in the trust won through experience over time, many heterosexual activists reexamined and rejected their assumptions. This transformation of consciousness evolved slowly, unevenly, and far from unanimously. Organizations that demanded adherence to a "correct" party line hindered the development of democratic social movement cultures within which lesbians and gay men could confide honestly in their comrades. Likewise, political spaces where men bragged about their sexual prowess with women, proclaiming their normal heterosexuality and thereby deflecting mainstream gay-baiting of longhaired activists and hippies, proved inhospitable to gay men and to many women of all sexual orientations who joined the gay liberation and feminist movements.

State-sponsored interference further hindered the development of democratic relations between activists, as infiltrators and anonymous fliers and rumors spread by FBI agents, undercover police officers, and other government representatives sowed the seeds of distrust and enmity throughout the movement. Tactical gay-baiting was one of many tools deployed by the state to undermine antiwar and civil rights organizing. This open willingness of the ruling elites to use homophobia as a weapon for dividing and conquering spurred many organizers to recognize that they and their gay and lesbian allies often stood on the same side of the state-drawn line between "normal" and "queer." Applying the tools of queer analysis to the Chicago conspiracy trial throws light on the concrete ways in which the Cold War consensus of heteronormativity began to crack open during the years of gay liberation, and suggests that Thomas Aquinas Foran might stand alongside Allen Ginsberg as one of the most unorthodox patron saints of the queer past.[7]

The conspiracy trial came more than a year after riots wracked Grant and Lincoln Parks along the lakeshore and filled the streets of downtown Chicago. The August 1968 violence erupted in a city still reeling from the April riots that followed the assassination of Dr. Martin Luther King Jr. While 168 American cities and towns faced riots, looting, and arson immediately following King's murder in Memphis, Richard Daley issued "shoot-to-kill" orders to the Chicago police force, the only such directive in the country. When Daley could not acknowledge his failure to restore peace, Thomas Foran requested that U.S. Attorney General Ramsey Clark send federal troops to Chicago, according to J. Anthony Lukas, the *New York Times* reporter assigned to cover the conspiracy trial.[8] Enraged by the riots and embarrassed by his own poor handling of the uprising, Daley was determined to prevent the counterculture Yippies and the National

Mobilization to End the War from disrupting the convention he had brought to the city. Foran himself served as one of Daley's liaisons to Rennie Davis of the Mobilization, conveying the mayor's unwillingness to issue a permit for the Mobe's planned peaceful and nondisruptive protests. For years Daley had repeatedly undermined civil rights and economic justice organizing in his city. Now local police surveillance units coordinated directly with the FBI to monitor the demonstrations planned for August.[9]

While Yippie organizers hoped to draw hundreds of thousands of demonstrators to the Democratic National Convention, the great fear of violence kept turnout down to the low thousands. Even rock bands scheduled to perform in Lincoln Park at the Yippie-sponsored Festival of Life backed out, though the Detroit-based rockers, the MC5, joined Abbie Hoffman, Allen Ginsberg, and other speakers at the event. The festival disintegrated into a battle between those in attendance and the police, with some in the crowd screaming, "Pigs eat shit!" and "Prague! Prague!"—a reference to the Soviet troops who had just invaded Czechoslovakia. As some policemen used their clubs to push the crowd back, others yelled, "Get the fuck out of town . . . go back where you came from, fags."[10] Barbara Smith, later a pioneer of black feminist writing and organizing, reported on her encounters with the Chicago police for the Mount Holyoke College newspaper. An inspiring day spent listening to Bobby Seale in Lincoln Park and to Jean Genet, William Burroughs, and Dick Gregory at the Chicago Coliseum passed peacefully, but the next day, while she was listening to SDS leader Carl Oglesby in Grant Park, the police descended on the crowd. Canisters of tear gas flew while officers beat the young people in the park. The seriousness of what was happening sank in when a boy who had been hit in the head bled onto Smith's raincoat and shirt. She reported to her classmates in South Hadley that

> it should be clearly understood by those people who were not there that violence was not planned by the demonstrators, in the sense that offensive tactics were never discussed. It was recognized however that the police officers would undoubtedly have orders directly from Mayor Daley to use the weapons at their disposal and many demonstrators were prepared for these assaults with helmets and wet cloths to breathe through. . . . It was *never* the policy of the demonstration's leaders, however, for people to reciprocate with violence.[11]

As the convention proceeded, policeman attacked hippies, pacifists, clergy, journalists, bystanders, and even delegates. Ray Warner, then a salesman in men's wear at the downtown Sears and a future member of Ann Arbor Gay Liberation Front, witnessed a handful of undercover policemen, usually assigned to his store's shoplifting squad, hurling insults and heavier objects at their uniformed counterparts in front of the Chicago Hilton. Warner's report of watching these infiltrators "provoke" the officers while most demonstrators behaved peacefully corresponds with many accounts of the "police riots" at the convention.[12]

From Daley, Hoffman, Foran, and other elected politicians and their appointees in Chicago and across the United States, to the policemen on the beat, many officials saw themselves as bulwarks against the collapse of American society. Drawing the line against what they saw as a fifth column of young Americans marching across the land, these male authorities enforced hierarchies of age, race and ethnicity, and sexuality and gender with the ends of their nightsticks and the barrels of their guns. One rookie policeman in Los Angeles reported his shock at hearing his fellow white officers claim that "the Negroes and their left-wing allies are the agitators and underminers of the American system."[13] After a Los Angeles police riot in the wake of a large antiwar demonstration protesting President Lyndon Johnson's appearance at a fund-raising dinner in June 1967, participants quoted policeman ordering, "Get that damn Jew," and describing the crowd as "a bunch of dirty, Goddamned communists."[14] Following riots in Berkeley, one patrolman there told outside observers that "if the parents of these cocksuckers had beat 'em when they were young, we wouldn't have to do it now."[15]

In Chicago during the Democratic National Convention, faced with a seventeen-year-old girl insisting on her right to stay on a sidewalk, one of Mayor Daley's finest screamed, "You hippies are all alike. All you want is free love." He then knocked her to the ground, pinned here there with his club, and threatened, "Free love, I can give you some free love."[16] A New York police officer, after breaking up the spring 1968 Yip-In at Grand Central Station, expressed his rage against the white youths he viewed as a threat to the norms of nation, gender, and sexuality: "Here's a bunch of animals who call themselves the next leaders of the country. . . . I almost had to vomit. . . . It's like dealing with any queer pervert, mother raper, or any of those other bedbugs we've got crawling around the Village. As a normal human being, you feel like knocking every one of their teeth out. It's a normal reaction."[17] To this policeman, to Foran, Daley, and Judge Hoffman, and to countless other members of what Richard Nixon claimed was the "silent majority" of Americans, activists and hippies visible in the streets, parks, and other public spaces of the nation's cities represented a queer and present danger to the "normal" relations between state and citizen and between men and women.[18]

The last two policemen quoted above, in venting their disgust at the hippies' quest for "free love," equated the countercultural rejection of one historically specific configuration of heterosexual love and family with the rejection of heterosexuality altogether.[19] Thomas Foran railed against the same threat aimed at the nuclear family in the atomic age when he warned, "we've lost our kids to the freaking fag revolution" before the two hundred people attending a meeting of the parents' booster club at the Catholic high school attended by one of his sons. His tirade came before an audience in suburban Wilmette that may well have shared his conception of children as something they controlled and thus could lose. Foran, a Daley appointee who made his fortune in Chicago's urban renewal projects, proposed that "perhaps our own prejudiced ways are responsible for losing a child, as he turns against our beliefs." He did not assail Ginsberg by name in Wilmette, at least not according to the AP or UPI wire reports or any of the books published soon after the trial. That is to say, while Thomas Foran gay-baited and insulted the poet on the stand, he did not draw a clear distinction between Ginsberg, whose poems screamed with joy in celebration of sex between men, and any of the heterosexually identified white defendants.[20]

Instead, Foran declared that Bobby Seale, the national chairman of the Black Panther Party and an original member of what started out as the Chicago Eight, "had more guts and more charisma than any of them and he was the only one I don't think was a fag."[21] Seale, who had never met any of the other defendants before the trial except Jerry Rubin, and whose involvement in the demonstrations outside the convention consisted of two brief speeches, attempted to represent himself in court, to the extreme displeasure of Judge Julius Hoffman.[22] Nor did his repeated charges of racism against Hoffman endear him to the judge. Hoffman eventually ordered Seale restrained and muffled before the court and soon severed his case altogether from the rest of the Chicago Seven.[23] The politically pornographic spectacle of the Black Panther bound and gagged in the white courtroom—resisting legal and physical assaults that included one court marshal punching the chair-bound Seale in the groin—made headlines around the world.[24] Foran called this "the most horrible sight I've ever seen in a courtroom" and blamed Seale's codefendants and counsel for manipulating him. "They used that kid as though they were masters of the plantation," he alleged.[25] Conjuring up deeply entrenched white myths that ascribed great physical and sexual prowess to African American men while denying them moral or intellectual parity with whites, the Democratic prosecutor credited the Black Panther with a strong constitution but a weak mind. In Thomas Foran's tale, Bobby Seale was simultaneously too charismatic and too courageous to be homosexual *and* a "kid" as defenseless as a slave when it came to resisting the manipulations of his "fag" codefendants.[26]

In positing this racialized queer menace to "our kids," Foran recalled the invisible, irresistible threat evoked by red-baiting politicians and journalists who warned of homosexual subversion during the peak years of McCarthyism. His speech consistently framed the generation gap in sexual and racial terms. He declared that "our kids"—our white kids, Foran implied before his fellow parents in Chicago's northern suburbs— "don't understand that we don't mean anything when we use the word 'nigger' . . . they just look at us like we were a bunch of dinosaurs."[27] According to the attorney, "the defendants are attempting to draw children into their revolution by using valid political issues such as war and racism with totally false idealism."[28] The "freaking fag revolution" that inspired Foran's tirade at Loyola Academy was winning the hearts and minds of white youth away from the American racial and sexual hierarchies he had dedicated his career to preserving. The black power movement, in the person of Bobby Seale—"the only one" of the Chicago Eight he "didn't think was a fag"—shored up the destabilized order of gender and sexuality for Foran's white kids in exchange for rhetorical concessions to racial justice. Given his admiration of "that kid" Seale and his awkward stand against prejudice, this seemed an acceptable trade to Foran, at least as long as he did not have to question his own position of power.

Thomas Foran was hardly the only white man who ambivalently eroticized the black power movement. Some counterculture and New Left leaders themselves, usually men, framed their revolt as a struggle against "castration" by the system parallel to the Panthers' battles against racism and for their own full manhood. In *Do It,* published during the conspiracy trial, Jerry Rubin argued that "Long hair is our black skin. Long hair turns white middle-class youth into niggers."[29] Jerry Farber, an instructor in English at Los Angeles State College, cited "the master-slave approach to education" in his essay

"The Student as Nigger," and compared the emasculation and lynching of black men in the South to the "kind of castration that goes on in the schools."[30] John Sinclair, manager of the MC5, found in the work of Huey Newton and Eldridge Cleaver the inspiration to launch the White Panther Party. He enumerated the White Panthers' agenda, beginning with "1. Full endorsement and support of the Black Panther Party's 10-point program and platform. 2. Total assault on the culture by any means necessary, including rock and roll, dope, and fucking in the streets."[31] To many white, generally heterosexually identified men, state representatives and protestors alike, the black power movement assumed the position laid forth by literary theorist Anne McClintock in her analysis of sexuality and European imperialism. McClintock described a "porno-tropics for the European imagination—a fantastic magic lantern of the mind onto which Europe projected its forbidden sexual desires and fears." Stateside, the internal African American colony performed a comparable role as the funhouse mirror against which sexual norms and deviance were reflected for white Americans.[32]

Black Panthers encouraged this queer adulation at times, as in Eldridge Cleaver's manifesto, *Soul on Ice,* which cast American racism in terms of the emasculation of black men. White male radicals could point to Cleaver's vicious attacks on James Baldwin and other black men "acquiescing in this racial death-wish . . . bending over and touching their toes for the white man" as the revolutionary justification grounding their own antigay prejudice.[33] The FBI exploited this tendency, deploying African American infiltrators on the Venceremos Brigades to Cuba to harass gay white male activists and force white heterosexual brigadistas to make an otherwise false choice between supporting either black power or gay liberation.[34] The FBI also used homophobia, in the form of anonymous and forged letters casting aspersions on the sexual orientation of Panther leaders, to sow dissent within the Black Panther Party.[35] The agency gay-baited white activists in SDS, the National Mobilization Committee, and other wings of the antiwar movement as well. Dave Dellinger was targeted on multiple occasions, as the FBI printed his photo on an anonymous "Gigantic 'Pick the Fag' Contest" pamphlet and distributed a flier mocking Dellinger ("looking more fairy-like than ever") and his "usual high pitched voice."[36] Sometimes, however, the government waged a direct frontal assault on the antiwar and black power movements, as in the slaying of Fred Hampton, the Illinois Black Panther Party chairman, by the Chicago police on 4 December 1969, in the middle of the conspiracy trial, a month after Seale's case was severed from the white defendants' and a week before Allen Ginsberg took the stand.

From the vantage point of a government attorney prosecuting the conspiracy trial, the escalating conflicts with the antiwar, black power, and other protest movements during the fifteen months between the Democratic Convention and Thomas Foran's meeting with Allen Ginsberg on Judge Hoffman's stage offered sufficient evidence of an ongoing conspiracy against the state—and against the nation's white youth. (Based on how the government used the charge of "conspiracy" in the Chicago trial, some members of the New Left determined that the working definition of the term was "breathing together.")[37] Shootouts raged on between Black Panthers and local police across the nation, with mounting casualties on both sides. Protests flared up on hundreds of campuses from coast to coast, perhaps most notably the armed takeover of the Cornell student union by rifle-toting African American students. The struggle over who controlled spaces inhabited by white youth extended to Berkeley's People's Park, where the National Guard occupied a predominantly white city and killed one white bystander in May 1969. Even through the fall, as SDS splintered into sectarian cadres, as the Weathermen vowed to "bring the war home" and dynamited the statue of a policeman in Chicago's Haymarket Square, and as the so-called years of hope gave way to days of rage, the antiwar movement grew larger than ever. The 15 October 1969 Moratorium organized a million Americans against the war, while the Mobilization on 15 November drew almost as many to Washington, D.C., in protest. The feminist movement attracted women dedicated to the political goals of the civil rights movement and the New Left but alienated by the misogyny they encountered in those movement cultures, while the now burgeoning Gay Liberation Front organized comparably disaffected gay men and lesbians.[38]

This context might explain Foran's impatience on the morning of 12 December, pacing in front of Barbara's Book Store in the Old Town neighborhood, waiting for the store to open. According to J. Anthony Lukas, when the owner arrived, Foran asked her if the store carried any of Allen Ginsberg's books. As she searched for the poet's works, the prosecutor badgered her, "Could you hurry up? The future of the country may depend on this."[39] Foran soon returned to the federal building, books in hand, for another day of battling those "intellectuals" and "liars" manipulating America's youth.[40] Cross-examining Ginsberg, Foran tackled the poet's role in the Lincoln Park rally, reviewing Ginsberg's religious chanting and delving into the nature of the witness's relationships with Jerry Rubin and Abbie Hoffman. After inquiring about their discussions of logistics for the Yippie Convention, Foran asked Ginsberg to confirm that he had kissed Abbie Hoffman. Ginsberg did so. Foran pressed the baiting one step further, asking whether Ginsberg considered the two Yippie leaders to be "intimate friend[s]."

The prosecution persisted in using gay-baiting in hopes of destroying the poet's credibility as a witness for the defense. Richard Schultz, the assistant government attorney, selected several poems for their shock value, poems containing references to a "dirty asshole" sandwich, sex with a newly married couple, and copious bodily parts and fluids, and the court instructed the defendant to read the poems aloud. Foran's disgust was palpable by all reports, his ears closed to the poet's odyssey exploring religious and democratic possibilities. He sneered "damn fag" even as he stood before the defendants as "Howl"'s "Moloch! Nightmare of Moloch! Moloch the loveless, Moloch the heavy judger of men! . . . Moloch whose buildings are judgment! Moloch the vast stone of war! Moloch the stunned government!" The best minds of a generation of men stood trial, literally and symbolically, before a stacked court, and all agreed that the fate of the nation rested in the verdict.[41]

As much as Foran appeared to despise Ginsberg, legally speaking the poet was not on trial. In attempting to discredit the homosexual Buddhist-Jewish poet in front of the conservative-seeming jurors, and for the broader judgment of Christian, heterosexual Americans, the prosecutor deployed another tactic familiar to the McCarthy years, the imputation of guilt by association. That is, Ginsberg's intimate friendships with Abbie Hoffman and Jerry Rubin—and by implicit extension the remaining defendants and the movement at large—implicated the Chicago Seven in a conspiracy to subvert the moral and political fiber of the nation's white youth. Foran argued later in the trial that

> there are millions of kids who, naturally, resent authority, are impatient for change . . . [after the assassinations of the Kennedys and King], the kids do feel that the lights have gone out in Camelot, the banners are furled, and the parade is over. . . . And there is another thing about a kid, if we all remember, that you have an attraction to evil. Evil is exciting and evil is interesting, and plenty of kids have a fascination for it. It is knowledge of kids that these sophisticated educated psychology majors know about. These guys take advantage of it personally, intentionally, evilly, and to corrupt those kids, and they use them.[42]

Nearly twenty years after the espionage and sex panics of the early 1950s, the U.S. Attorney prosecuting the Chicago Seven conspiracy trial used tactics and rhetoric premised upon a good-and-evil Cold War model of political and sexual predators to defend the liberal state from those who sought social and structural transformations beyond those forms of change acceptably absorbed by the system.[43]

There was one noteworthy difference between Foran's evocation of the queer menace and the McCarthy-era witch-hunts. Whereas Cold Warriors imagined a body-snatching invasion by undetectable resident aliens, long hair and androgynous clothing made 1960s-style subversives and perverts easily identifiable. After the jury delivered its guilty verdict, the *Chicago Tribune* cheerfully reported on its front page, "6 in Riot Trial Shorn by Jail Barber." Prison warden Winston Moore noted that "without their long hair, Rubin and Hoffman look like nice, clean-cut kids." Dave Dellinger, "balding and eldest of the group, conforms to jail standards" and thus was spared the blade. Running this story below its flag-waving masthead ("the American paper for Americans"), the newspaper evoked the rite of passage for young men entering the armed forces, the shaving of new recruits to eliminate any distinctiveness which might undermine the cohesion of military units. By shearing the hair of the New Left and Yippie leaders, the state chopped off their most visible marker of rebellion and individuality, hoping to redeem them as citizens in the process.[44]

Trial accounts emphatically reported the marked contrast between the defendants' youth and Foran's adult masculinity.[45] J. Anthony Lukas credited the Catholic father of six in his mid-40s with having "the stocky good looks of an Irish cop or a bantamweight prizefighter, with a hard, compact body that looked as though it had been poured into his sharply creased gabardine suits. His steel-gray hair was always combed and his cherubic cheeks closely shaved, as if he had just spent a long time in a barber's chair."[46] Alternatively, Yippie Stew Albert cast Foran as "the ideal AMERIKAN MAN. Square jawed, tight assed and short, he moved like a PATTON TANK into the courtroom."[47] At the Booster Club meeting, the onetime World War II torpedo bomber pilot and Golden Gloves boxer told his audience that to keep his sanity while prosecuting the conspiracy trial, he had attended wrestling matches on Sundays.[48] (Whether or not Foran also mentioned attending Sunday services before watching men grappling on the mat was not reported). Even the first sentence of the obituary that ran in the *New York Times* in August 2000 declared Foran "best known as the pugnacious prosecutor of the Chicago Seven conspiracy case."[49]

Unlike Judge Julius Hoffman—who "represents perfectly the decaying aristocracy of dinosaurs we see everywhere, directing universities, corporations, and draft boards," wrote Tom Hayden in 1970—Thomas Foran vigorously embodied state power. He advocated reform, having begun his career as land acquisitions counsel in the Daley Democratic machine in the office of the Chicago Corporation Counsel (he later represented property owners in the city).[50] He even condemned the Vietnam War: Years after the trial, he reflected that "the worst thing about the convention was that it gave us Richard Nixon. And because of that, it continued the war another four or five years."[51] The prosecutor emphasized his liberal credentials, frequently invoking the New Frontier and even claiming he was a "better friend" to "Bob" Kennedy than was Tom Hayden, who had stood guard at the slain presidential candidate's funeral bier.[52] Like the Kennedy brothers, cut down in their prime—themselves also virile and practicing Catholics, athletes, and war heroes—Foran cultivated the persona of liberal masculinity. This image shielded the prosecutor and professional men of his generation from the early Cold War–era suspicions of sexual deviance that might follow an educated man pursuing a career in law and politics. Now, two decades later, in the shadow of Camelot, these male reformers living the strenuous life of Cold Warriors worked to remedy the ills of society, but through political channels that left the norms of gender and sexuality unquestioned.[53] African American men—Martin Luther King, perhaps even one day that "kid" Seale—could now participate as full citizens and members of the club. Yet as the ideological lines dividing normal from deviant shifted to allow this degree of acceptance of heterosexual black leaders, they decisively cordoned off the freaking fag revolutionaries seducing the next generation of leaders.

Tom Hayden begins his 1970 account of the conspiracy trial with Foran's enraged declarations that "we've lost our kids to the freaking fag revolution" and "our kids don't understand that we don't mean anything when we use the word 'nigger.'" The former SDS leader also pointed to the Foran-Ginsberg episode on the stand as evidence of the vast cultural and generational chasm between the state and the activists. Hayden pointed directly to the prosecutor's statement about the "freaking fag revolution" as confirmation of what the defendants realized during the trial: "Foran represented imperialist, aggressive man, while we, for all our male chauvinist tendencies, represented a gentler, less aggressive type of human being."[54] Mid-trial, Stew Albert wrote a long column for the *Berkeley Tribe* savaging Foran as a self-loathing closeted homosexual and urging all his readers to remember that the struggle of gay liberation was theirs as well.[55] Hayden, once accused of gay-baiting Carl Wittman out of the SDS ERAP project in Newark, now drew the line against Foran and those like him who would dismiss Ginsberg's poetic vision or the emotive friendships between Ginsberg, Hoffman, and Rubin.[56] Albert's awkward call for solidarity with the "new and absolutely crucial liberation front" that was born when "hundreds of homosexuals poured out of a gay bar ... and fought the harassing pigs to a standstill"—one of the first such declarations from a heterosexual male author—proves especially remarkable for framing the Stonewall riots in the language of the New Left. Albert furthermore used Foran's viciousness as an emphatic example of how homophobia was an intrinsic component of American imperialism and of the repression of sexual freedom for all. At the same time, Albert came under fire from readers who interpreted his column as claiming "that it was a bad thing to have homosexual desires—and that Foran was bad because he had them." As he recalled thirty years later, the hostile response "forced me to think about the new gay movement in a deeper and more challenging way. And to see how much street Brooklyn bigotry I still possessed."[57]

These two halting but horrified responses to Foran's exaggerated masculinity and his gay-baiting of Ginsberg, the Chicago Seven, and the larger movement offer snapshots of the shifts underway in the consciousness of heterosexual movement participants. Tom Hayden argued that "Our crime was that we were beginning to live a new and contagious lifestyle without official authorization. We were tried for being out of control," for aligning themselves with Black Panthers, Ché Guevara, and the people of Vietnam.[58] For many 1960s activists, the process of aligning oneself against the bureaucrats and war makers included exaggerating one's masculinity and heterosexuality—at least for the heterosexually identified men for whom this was feasible—against charges of effeminacy and queerness. But the state's explicit use of homophobia to disrupt the personal and political relationships within social movement cultures, personified in the furious disgust of Thomas Foran at the conspiracy trial, made explicit the sexual limits to this unauthorized, contagious new lifestyle. Even as activists proclaimed personal and political liberation for all, very few extended their queer rebellion against the norms far beyond the binary of heterosexual relationships. Through the first two decades of the Cold War, homophiles and gay liberationists put sexual orientation in the public sphere as a category of political reform. Agents of the state inadvertently accelerated this transformation, as in the case of Thomas Foran, whose own days of rage laid bare the heteronormative liberal masculinity devoted at all costs to holding up the pillars of empire. In so doing, this state coercion forced members of the New Left and the counterculture to recognize, however unevenly, their direct complicity in upholding the very norms of sexuality and gender formulated by those agents of power they were aligned against.

Notes

Acknowledgments: A shorter version of this chapter was originally presented at "The Future of the Queer Past" conference at the University of Chicago in September 2000. Special thanks are due Vincent Brown, William Chafe, Derek Chang, Jay Driskell, Lisa Hazirjian, Leisa Meyer, Kevin Murphy, and Paul Ortiz for their helpful suggestions during the writing and revisions of this essay.

1. Andrew Kopkind, "The Trial," *Hard Times,* 23 Feb.–2 March 1970, reprinted in Kopkind, *The Thirty Years' War: Dispatches and Diversions of a Radical Journalist, 1965–1994* (New York: Verso, 1995), 199.

2. Allen Ginsberg, *Chicago Trial Testimony* (San Francisco: City Lights, 1975), esp. 11, 73–74; Tom Hayden, *Trial* (New York: Holt, Rinehart, and Winston, 1970), 36–39; J. Anthony Lukas, *The Barnyard Epithet and Other Obscenities: Notes on the Chicago Conspiracy Trial* (New York: Harper and Row, 1970), 30–32; Michael Schumacher, *Dharma Lion: A Critical Biography of Allen Ginsberg* (New York: St. Martin's Press, 1992), 535–37.

3. Martin Duberman, *Stonewall* (New York: Dutton, 1993), 215; Terence Kissack, "Freaking Fag Revolutionaries: New York's Gay Liberation Front, 1969–1971," *Radical History Review* 62 (spring 1995): 111.

4. Abbie Hoffman, "Revolution for the Hell of It," in *The Best of Abbie Hoffman* (New York: Four Walls Eight Windows, 1989), 22.

5. Donna Penn, "Queer: Theorizing Politics and History," *Radical History Review* 62 (spring 1995), 36.

6. Monique Wittig, *The Straight Mind* (Boston: Beacon Press, 1992), 40, 43, quoted in Michael Warner's introduction to *Fear of a Queer Planet: Queer Politics and Social Theory,* ed. Michael Warner (Minneapolis: University of Minnesota Press, 1993), xxi, xxiii.

7. For an expansion of this framework and further examples, see Ian Lekus, "Queer and Present Dangers: Homosexuality and American Antiwar Activism, 1964–1973" (Ph.D. diss., Duke University, forthcoming).

8. Adam Cohen and Elizabeth Taylor, *American Pharaoh: Mayor Richard J. Daley: His Battle for Chicago and the Nation* (Boston: Little, Brown, 2000), 452–58; Lukas, *The Barnyard Epithet,* 84–85.

9. On Mayor Daley's reign in Chicago and preparations for the Democratic National Convention, see Cohen and Taylor, *American Pharaoh,* and David Farber, *Chicago '68* (Chicago: University of Chicago Press, 1988). For more on Foran's role in these preparations, see Farber, *Chicago '68,* 105.

10. Farber, *Chicago '68,* 177–83, quote on 178.

11. Barbara Smith, "Chicago Firsthand: A Distortion of Reality," reprinted in Smith, *The Truth That Never Hurts: Writings on Race, Gender, and Freedom* (New Brunswick: Rutgers University Press, 1998), 159–60.

12. Raymond Warner, interview by author, 25 Aug. 1999, Detroit. On police infiltrators, see Farber, *Chicago '68.*

13. Quoted in Rodney Stark, *Police Riots: Collective Violence and Law Enforcement* (Belmont, Calif.: Focus Books, 1972), 102.

14. Ibid., 32.

15. Ibid., 61.

16. Farber, *Chicago '68,* 186.

17. *New York Post,* 12 Nov. 1968, 53, quoted in Stark, *Police Riots,* 110.

18. On Los Angeles, see David McBride, "On the Fault Line of Mass Culture and Counterculture: A Social History of the Hippie Counterculture in 1960s Los Angeles" (Ph.D. diss., UCLA, 1998). On Ann Arbor, see Bret Neal Eynon, "Community, Democracy, and the Reconstruction of Political Life: The Civil Rights Influence on New Left Political Culture in Ann Arbor, 1958–1966" (Ph.D. diss., New York University, 1993). On Austin, see Doug Rossinow, *The Politics of Authenticity: Liberalism, Christianity, and the New Left in America* (New York: Columbia University Press, 1998). On Lawrence, Kansas, see Beth Bailey, *Sex in the Heartland* (Cambridge: Harvard University Press, 1999).

19. On the historically specific nuclear family of the Cold War era, see Stephanie Coontz, *The Way We Never Were: American Families and the Nostalgia Trap* (New York: Basic Books, 1992).

20. "Foran Assails Conspiracy 7 Plea to Youth," *Chicago Tribune*, 27 Feb. 1970, 2; "Federal Prosecutor Criticizes the Chicago 7 Defendants and Their Lawyers," *New York Times*, 28 Feb. 1970, 9; Jason Epstein, *The Great Conspiracy Trial: An Essay on Law, Liberty, and the Constitution* (New York: Random House, 1970), 431–32; Hayden, *Trial*, 42, 53; Tom Hayden, *Reunion: A Memoir* (New York: Random House, 1988), 399–400; Lukas, *The Barnyard Epithet*, 32; Wolfgang Saxon, "Thomas Foran, 76, U.S. Attorney Who Prosecuted Chicago Seven," obituary, *New York Times*, 11 Aug. 2000, B9; John Schultz, *Motion Will Be Denied: A New Report on the Chicago Conspiracy Trial* (New York: William Morrow, 1972).

21. "Federal Prosecutor Criticizes the Chicago 7."

22. David Dellinger, *From Yale to Jail: The Life Story of a Moral Dissenter* (New York: Pantheon, 1993), 341.

23. Charles Garry, a white California lawyer who frequently represented Black Panthers on trial, originally agreed to defend Bobby Seale in Chicago. However, when he developed a gall bladder condition and required hospitalization, the defense sought a delay in the trial to allow for Garry's convalescence. Judge Hoffman turned down the usually *pro forma* request, declaring that William Kunstler, lawyer for the white defendants, adequately fulfilled Seale's constitutional right to counsel. Nonetheless, Seale attempted to represent himself, hurling a vast array of insults ("fascist dog," "racist," "pig," "rotten, low-life son of a bitch") and arguments of constitutional rights at the judge, who was infuriated, declaring that "if there's any judge on the bench who looks after underprivileged members of other races, it's me" and that he was "the best friend" Negroes had on the Chicago bench. Finally, Judge Hoffman ordered Seale bound and gagged on 29 October, severed his case from the other defendants' on 5 November, convicted him on sixteen counts of contempt, and sentenced him to four years in prison. See Marty Jezer, *Abbie Hoffman: American Rebel* (New Brunswick: Rutgers University Press, 1992), 200–203; Lukas, *The Barnyard Epithet*, 36–37, 48–49. Direct quote from Lukas, 49.

24. Schultz, *Motion Will Be Denied*, 69.

25. "Federal Prosecutor Criticizes the Chicago 7."

26. On this mythology, see Donald Bogle, *Toms, Coons, Mulattoes, Mammies, and Bucks: An Interpretive History of Blacks in American Films* (New York: Viking Press, 1973), and Michele Wallace, *Black Macho and the Myth of the Superwoman*, rev. ed. (New York: Verso, 1990). Bogle's discussion on the trope of the buck, the sexually predatory black male in American cinema, is particularly relevant to Thomas Foran's framing of Bobby Seale, as is Wallace's commentary on Bogle's analysis. Bogle notes the presence of the buck at the dawn of filmmaking (most infamously in D. W. Griffith's "The Birth of a Nation") and his subsequent disappearance, being too threatening to white audiences for American studios to allow onscreen—until the 1960s and early 1970s, when the virile, powerful buck resurfaced in the guise of characters depicting black militants.

27. Hayden, *Trial*, 29.

28. "Foran Assails Chicago 7 Plea to Youth," *Chicago Tribune*, 27 Feb. 1970, 2.

29. Jerry Rubin, *Do It: Scenarios of the Revolution* (New York: Simon and Schuster, 1970), 94; on castration, see 28, for example. Eldridge Cleaver wrote the introduction for *Do It* and sought to nominate Jerry Rubin as his choice for vice president after being nominated for president in 1968 by the Peace and Freedom Party (a choice not ratified by the party).

30. Jerry Farber, "The Student as Nigger," in Farber, *The Student as Nigger: Essays and Stories* (North Hollywood, Calif.: Contact Books, 1969), 123.

31. John Sinclair, *Guitar Army: Street Writings/Prison Writings* (New York: Douglas Book Corp., 1972), 105; also see John Sinclair, interview by Bret Eynon, 1977, Contemporary History

Project (The New Left in Ann Arbor, Mich.) transcripts of oral interviews, Bentley Historical Library, University of Michigan (see, in the same place, related interviews with White Panther Party members, their allies, and their adversaries).

32. Anne McClintock, *Imperial Leather: Race, Gender, and Sexuality in the Colonial Conquest* (New York: Routledge, 1995), 22. In addition to McClintock's writings on sexuality and imperialism in the European context, my analysis of the sexual politics of how liberal and radical white masculinities were forged and manifested during the Cold War draws on David Roediger's work on the development of ideologies of white republican freedom in the nineteenth century. Roediger argues that given the existence of slavery in republican America, blacks "could be stigmatized as the *antithesis* of republican citizens. In the changed circumstance in the nineteenth century, they would further be seen as the opposites of 'free white labor'" (David Roediger, *The Wages of Whiteness: Race and the Making of the American Working Class* [New York: Verso, 1991], 36).

33. Eldridge Cleaver, *Soul on Ice* (New York: Dell, 1968), 102.

34. "The Reminiscences of Teresa Meade," 13 April 1984, interview by Ronald J. Grele, Collection of the Columbia University Oral History Research Office, New York, 76–82.

35. FBI memorandum, COINTELPRO operation, from Newark Office to the FBI Director, 16 Oct. 1970, reproduced in Ward Churchill and Jim Vander Wall, *The COINTELPRO Papers: Documents from the FBI's Secret Wars against Domestic Dissent* (Boston: South End Press, 1990), 213; *Final Report of the Select Committee to Study Governmental Operations with Respect to Intelligence Activities, Supplementary Detailed Staff Reports on Intelligence Activities and the Rights of Americans, book 3*, 94th Cong., 2d sess., 23 April 1976, 199.

36. *Final Report of the Select Committee*, 38–39. Ché Guevara, Mark Rudd, and Herbert Marcuse were the other "contestants" in the "Pick the Fag" contest.

37. Todd Gitlin, *The Sixties: Years of Hope, Days of Rage* (New York: Bantam Books, 1987), 342. Gitlin does not specify who used this definition beyond "movement etymologists."

38. Epstein, *The Great Conspiracy Trial*, 1–24; Gitlin, *The Sixties*, 342–43, 379, 391–95; Ron Jacobs, *The Way the Wind Blew: A History of the Weather Underground* (New York: Verso, 1997), 54, 121; W. J. Rorabaugh, *Berkeley at War: The 1960s* (New York: Oxford University Press, 1969), 159–64. In his survey of the year between the police riots and the trial, Gitlin acknowledges the Stonewall rebellion, noting "In July [*sic*], homosexuals responded to the bust of a gay bar in Greenwich Village by fighting back against the police" (342). Neither the name of the Stonewall Inn nor the prior homophile or subsequent gay liberation organizing receives any mention.

39. Lukas, *The Barnyard Epithet*, 30.

40. Quoted in Hayden, *Reunion*, 398–99.

41. Ginsberg, *Chicago Trial Testimony*, esp. 65–74; Hayden, *Trial*, 38–39.

42. Quoted in Hayden, *Reunion*, 398–99.

43. On the sex panics of the early 1950s and early Cold War homophobia, see George Chauncey Jr., "The Postwar Sex Crime Panic," in *True Stories from the American Past*, ed. William Graebner (New York: McGraw-Hill, 1993), 160–78; John D'Emilio, "The Homosexual Menace: The Politics of Sexuality in Cold War America," in *Passion and Power: Sexuality in History*, ed. Kathy Peiss and Christina Simmons (Philadelphia: Temple University Press, 1989), 226–40; Estelle B. Freedman, "'Uncontrolled Desires': The Response to the Sexual Psychopath, 1920–1960," *Journal of American History* 74 (1987), 83–106; and Donna Penn, "The Meaning of Lesbianism in Postwar America," *Gender and History* 3 (summer 1991), 190–203.

44. Bernard Judge, "6 in Riot Trial Shorn by Jail Barber," *Chicago Tribune,* 1 Feb. 1970, 1. The warden officially cited "sanitary" reasons for shearing the defendants. Additionally, in considering these points, it is important to keep in mind the state's urgent desire to restore the credibility of American citizenship as exemplified through military service, given how poorly the war effort was proceeding at the time.

45. Foran, in his mid-forties, was roughly a dozen years older than most of the Chicago Seven, though barely two years older than Allen Ginsberg and ten years *younger* than David Dellinger.

46. Lukas, *The Barnyard Epithet,* 85.

47. Stew Albert, "Revolution in the Revolution," *Berkeley Tribe,* 9 Jan. 1970, 6.

48. Hayden, *Trial,* 53.

49. Foran obituary, *New York Times,* 11 Aug. 2000.

50. Cohen and Taylor, *American Pharaoh,* 499; Hayden, *Trial,* 53.

51. Thomas A. Foran, obituary, *Washington Post,* 11 Aug. 2000, B7.

52. Lukas, *The Barnyard Epithet,* 84.

53. My analysis of the Kennedys, Thomas Foran, and other Democrats cultivating this muscular liberal masculinity draws on scholarship examining Theodore Roosevelt, male Progressive Era reformers, and American foreign policy at the dawn of the twentieth century. Key works consulted include Gail Bederman, *Manliness and Civilization: A Cultural History of Gender and Race in the United States, 1880–1917* (Chicago: University of Chicago Press, 1995); Kristin L. Hoganson, *Fighting for American Manhood: How Gender Politics Provoked the Spanish-American and Philippine-American Wars* (New Haven: Yale University Press, 1998); and Kevin P. Murphy, "The Manly World of Urban Reform: Patronage, Homosocial Desire, and the Politics of Desire in New York City, 1886–1917" (Ph.D. diss., New York University, 2001).

54. Hayden, *Trial,* 29, 36–39, 42. Contrast Hayden's views on Foran to Jerry Rubin on David Dellinger: "He's in his early 50's, but he's a kid at heart, a born troublemaker. If there were a million Dave Dellingers, there'd be no generation gap." Both the agents of state power and the protestors drew a direct link between age and the proper behavior befitting an American citizen, if from diametrically opposed viewpoints.

55. Albert, "Revolution in the Revolution," 6.

56. Carl Wittman, "Us and the New Left," *Fag Rag,* fall 1978, 22–23.

57. Albert, "Revolution in the Revolution"; E-mail, Stew Albert to <sixties-l@lists.village.virginia.edu>, 28 Aug. 2000; E-mail, Stew Albert to author, 1 Sept. 2000.

58. Hayden, *Trial,* 33.

CHAPTER 11

Between Revolution 9 and Thesis 11: Or, Will We Learn (Again) to Start Worrying and Change the World?

Jeremy Varon

I

The passion, promise, dynamism, naiveté, idealism, audacity, vanity, nihilism, tragedy, and mythology of the 1960s all combine in a word that served as the animating spirit of much of the decade in the United States and large parts of the world: *revolution*. To Kirkpatrick Sale, charting in the early 1970s the seemingly inexorable transformation of the American New Left from a strategy of "protest to resistance" and beyond, revolution was the "pattern woven by all the threads of the sixties."[1] This sense of the evolution of the era's protest movements is hardly the retrospective imposition of a narrative on reality, the conceit of the historian seeking to order the past by giving it a direction. Over the course of the 1960s, activists themselves in countries of the advanced industrial world came to see revolution as the telos of their efforts, the ultimate expression of their aspirations.

Jean-Paul Sartre described the global "liberation of the imagination," inspired chiefly by the Vietnamese's implausible success against the U.S. military, as the great achievement of the 1960s.[2] Revolution was the most potent vision the imagination conceived. Its currency was evident in New Left ideology, especially as many activists turned in the late 1960s to Marxism as a language for understanding the deep structure of their societies and the means for radically changing them. The desire for revolution was evident also in the slogans of the protest culture. "Be realistic, demand the impossible" —

a phrase of the French militants of May '68 that circulated worldwide—suggested that the only path to true victory was nothing less than the total remaking of society. "Create two, three, many Columbias," a slogan adapted by American radicals from Che Guevara's global call to "Create two, three, many Vietnams," advocated the capture of institutions as a crucial means to overthrowing one's society as a whole. With steely defiance, the Black Panthers sang to rouse their armed rank and file, "Time to pick up the gu-un/Revolution has begu-un." The language of revolution pulsed as well through American rock 'n' roll of the late 1960s, which served as the lingua franca of radical movements in the Western world. In the wake of the Democratic National Convention in Chicago in 1968, Crosby, Stills, Nash and Young pronounced with millenarian optimism, "We can change the world, rearrange the world." The Jefferson Airplane, as if both to capture and to shape the Zeitgeist of 1969, declared more boldly, "Look what's happening out on the street, got a revolution, got a revolution!"

Revolution defined also activists' sense of themselves. Black Panther leader Fred Hampton, assessing what made him and the Panthers so challenging to the white power structure, explained, "I am a revolutionary."[3] One chronicler of the American student movement remarked, "In 1964 or 1965 someone in SDS [Students for a Democratic Society] declared himself a revolutionary; by 1969 it was impossible for any SDS member to admit that he was *not a* revolutionary."[4] Such self-descriptions were hardly confined to black radicals or to a narrow circle of student militants at select campuses. A 1970 poll estimated that over 1 million young Americans considered themselves "revolutionaries."[5] In 1971 fully 25 percent of students polled at the University of California at Santa Barbara (UCSB)—a school hardly thought of as a bastion of radicalism—believed that change would take place in the United States by means of "revolution." One UCSB student, describing the calling she and her radical cohort felt, declared, "For us there was no future. Revolution was the future."[6]

The hope for revolution was also the driving force behind American activists' increasing fascination in the late 1960s with violence. By the end of the decade guns and bombs had entered the imagery of the more radical sectors of the movement, and "revolutionary armed struggle" was common in discussions of political strategy, especially in the independent, widely distributed newspapers of the underground press. Though only a minority of radicals actually engaged in violence, they operated on a strikingly large scale.[7] The idea of revolution, finally, suffuses the remembrances of the children of the 1960s as they wax nostalgic about their years of living exuberantly and dangerously. Christopher Hitchens, counting his many blessings for having been alive and aware in 1968 (teaching at Berkeley, no less), expressed his deepest gratitude for the "pure, crystalline pleasure of the gift that keeps on giving—the memory of revolution."[8]

Yet the idea of revolution receded as dramatically as it had arrived. Reality proved far harder to reshape than the New Left had imagined. The resiliency of the established order was nowhere more evident than in France in 1968, where the near certain collapse of the state at the hands of students and workers was followed by the near instantaneous restoration of de Gaulle and the return to an only mildly altered status quo. In the United States, the zenith of left-wing radicalism turned out to be the moment of its decline; the more militant the student, antiwar, and black power movements became, the less they were able to maintain unity in their ranks and command the allegiance of the masses they claimed as their base. Never, hindsight suggests, did they have the numbers or resources to threaten corporate or military power with any literal collapse. In this light, 1960s talk of revolution may now seem either an indulgent delusion or a noble but impossible dream.

To be sure, the 1960s produced movements that have been the source of lasting and meaningful change. One may speak of the civil rights revolution, the feminist revolution, the queer revolution, the green revolution, and, of course, the technological revolution, which was informed by the ethos of the counterculture. All have rendered the world far different from and, in countless ways, vastly better than it was before. But the 1960s never produced the "the big one," the seismic shift in consciousness and society that would make the world decisively more humane, harmonious, and just. As easily as one can document how things have changed, one can record how they have remained the same. The collapse of the ideal of revolution was evident already in the choices made by veteran radicals in the mid-1970s. Many pursued community-based activism, worked to build alternative institutions, and sought to combine personal and political growth. Those who continued to promote a revolutionary message—especially one advocating violence—garnered little support. Efforts at social change continued, but they were informed less and less by the desire for revolution.

The language of revolution, moreover, now seems largely devoid of all oppositional content. Already in the 1960s it was invoked by advertisers and corporate leaders to celebrate expanded consumer choice, technological change, and even capitalism's ability to constantly remake and improve the world. In years since it has become more fully a part of the self-congratulatory rhetoric of corporate America. In one among dozens of possible examples, a 1999 ad for Chrysler-Plymouth announced, with no apparent irony, "By inventing the minivan, we built much more than just an alternative to the station wagon. We started a revolution."[9] The whole concept of revolution, when rendered so banal, is thrown into deep crisis.

The disenchantment with revolution has been further reinforced by recent assessments of the protest movements of the 1960s. Historians have argued that methodological biases and unchecked instincts have contributed to the overestimation of the revolutionary nature of 1960s activism. These include the narrow study of movement "elites" in major cities, focus on the leaders of organized factions, who were often more radical than rank-and-file activists, and susceptibility to the seductive power of violence to dominate attention.[10] As a result, historians have called for greater study of the movement's grass roots, where one presumably finds the more sober and, so the prevailing view goes, more inspiring reality of sustained commitment to peaceful protest and to institutional reform.[11]

But these largely fruitful correctives may yield their own distortion—one that conceals the extent to which a large, diverse, and overtly revolutionary culture (at least in aspiration and self-perception) took shape in the United States in the 1960s. By extension, they may deflect attention from what remains perhaps *the* big question of the

American 1960s: How is it that just a few decades ago a sizable number of people in a prosperous, formally democratic society thought that revolution was desirable, possible, and necessary? A cluster of questions follows: What did 1960s radicals mean by revolution? In what ways did the goal of revolution both help to energize but also to mislead the movement? What was the place of violence in the politics and culture of the movement? How and why did the revolutionary imagination of the 1960s disintegrate so quickly, and where might one see today the traces of its dissolution? What are the prospects for resurrecting something of the utopian, even revolutionary spirit, of the era? Is such a project worthwhile, if it is even possible? Addressing these questions entails reworking elements of a familiar narrative of the rise, decline, and fall of 1960s radicalism. More broadly, it requires exploring the defining tensions of the decade: those between the power and the limits of the imagination, the possible and impossible, and between desires, dreams, and delusions.

II

What makes the emergence of revolutionary politics in the United States in the 1960s so remarkable is that affluent postwar societies seemed to preclude in their very structures the possibility of revolution. Herbert Marcuse, the quintessential philosopher of the New Left, gave the most penetrating diagnosis of this condition. From his analysis, the contours of the New Left's revolutionary imaginary start to come into focus.

In his 1964 *One-Dimensional Man,* Marcuse observed that gross exploitation no longer defined the political economy of advanced industrial societies. They therefore lacked the foundational "contradiction" between capital and wage labor, capitalist and proletariat, that had served in the industrial era as the "objective" basis for revolutionary socialist politics and for the critical theory of the Frankfurt School. To the contrary, societies like the United States afforded the majority of their populations, workers included, access to a version of "the good life" (however modest in most cases). The relatively low levels of antagonism America experienced in the 1950s and early 1960s reflected in large part its "objective" achievements, chiefly its "increased standard of living" and its "overwhelming efficiency" from a technological and organizational standpoint.[12] In the face of these achievements, Marcuse lamented, "the very idea of qualitative change recedes," threatening "the paralysis of criticism."[13] With few exceptions, citizens extended their loyalty to "the whole," to the entire system they credited for their prosperity, security, and comfort.

And yet, Marcuse insisted, "this society is irrational as a whole," insofar as "its productivity is destructive of the free development of human needs and faculties"; it was in dire need of both criticism and fundamental change.[14] Given the affluence of postwar society, however, any widespread revolt in a country like the United States would have to be largely a moral and aesthetic response to the various conditions that served the interests of "domination." Chief among these were the perpetuation of unnecessary forms of alienated labor; the colonization of leisure by the "culture industry"; the persistence of poverty amid immense societal wealth; racial inequality; the maintenance of peace with the Soviets through the constant preparation for war; the degradation of the environment; and the restriction of autonomy by administration and "one-dimensional" forms of thought and culture.

Marcuse was not optimistic in the early 1960s about the prospects for a mass revolt. He vacillated between the belief that "advanced industrial society is capable of containing qualitative change for the foreseeable future" and the fainter sense that forces "exist which may break this containment and explode this society."[15] To the extent that he had hope, he vested it in the possibility that some would engage in "the Great Refusal" by rejecting the established order in its totality. Such a refusal, as the source of hope for those "without hope," was most likely to come from the "outcasts and outsiders, the exploited and persecuted of other races and colors" who were largely excluded from the benefits of advanced industrial society.[16] There was, Marcuse conceded, no guarantee of a better future, as insight into the need for change "has never sufficed for seizing the possible alternatives."[17] Yet the character of advanced industrial society remained the product of a contingent choice and could be changed through the assertion of critical reason, liberating consciousness, and political will.

Marcuse was tremendously prescient, in essence describing the 1960s before they had quite happened. His dialectical method, which fused analysis of structural tendencies with a deeply ethical commitment to judge a society by assessing its "unused or abused capabilities for improving the human condition," deserves great credit for his insights. He identified which forces and groups would provide the impetus for large-scale revolt in the 1960s in the United States. Indeed, the civil rights movement inspired and served as an example for the student and antiwar movements. The anticolonial struggles in Asia, Africa, and Latin America—the revolt of the world's "exploited and persecuted" —were a second great beacon. And although Marcuse did not foresee the emergence in a few years of a large, radical movement of white, middle-class students and youth in the United States and other Western countries, he did anticipate and help to shape its values. Young radicals not only echoed Marcuse's particular criticisms of advanced industrial society in their struggles against racism, poverty, militarism, alienation, and environmental ruin. Claiming a part in "the Great Refusal," they shared his focus on *the whole* and the attending conviction that society must be rejected *in its entirety*. They shared, that is, the goal of revolution.

III

If the gravitation of young leftists to revolution can be traced to a single observation about society, a key insight into the nature of power and resistance, it is that each injustice is linked to every other injustice, so that fighting any of them demands fighting all of them. The New Left was overwhelmingly a movement of activists, not of ideologues, and their sense that "it's all connected" did not spring from a narrowly philosophical commitment to systemic or "totalizing" critique. It was rooted in their practical efforts to change society.

In April 1965 SDS president Paul Potter addressed the first national demonstration against the Vietnam War in Washington, D.C., sponsored by SDS. His speech, commonly regarded as a threshold moment in SDS's development, has added significance as an early articulation of the ingredients that some radicals would soon weave into a revolutionary worldview. After intimating the existence of a system of oppression, Potter proclaimed:

> We must name that system. We must name it, describe it, analyze it, understand it and change it. For it is only when that system is changed . . . that there can be any hope for stopping the forces that create a war in Vietnam today or a murder in the South tomorrow or all the incalculable, innumerable more subtle atrocities that are worked on people all over—all the time. . . . In a strange way the people in Vietnam and the people in this demonstration are united in much more than a common concern that the war be ended. In both countries there are people struggling to build a movement that has the power to change their condition. The system that frustrates these movements is the same. All our lives, our destinies, our very hopes to live, depend on our ability to overcome that system.[18]

Potter posited a unified structure of domination responsible for discrete forms of oppression; its elimination required changing the whole. Consistent with this premise, leftists in the late 1960s used the term "the system" as a label for the complex entity they protested. To the system they counterposed "the movement"—an equally capacious term comprising everyone from student and antiwar activists to black militants to politically engaged hippies. It captured in a word the radicals' sense of "us," of being an extended community distinct from a common adversary. They thus cast political conflict as a battle of two fundamentally incompatible forces that could be resolved in their favor only through some radical, even revolutionary, transformation.

Though Potter himself did not name the system, capitalism was clearly the object of his polemic. New Leftists first used the language of "corporate liberalism" to describe the system but soon graduated to a more strongly Marxist vocabulary. Since Potter also asserted a direct connection between U.S. activists and the Vietnamese fighting U.S. aggression, the struggle, conceived most expansively, was an international one against a *global* system of power. Finally, Potter spoke with a sense of gravity and romantic desperation. He declared, in essence, a condition of moral emergency whose ultimate stakes were life and death and which demanded that leftists actively fight the system. Echoing Potter's spirit, one activist described how the frustration of making modest demands against an uncompromising power structure fed the more ambitious rebellion of the late 1960s: "There were very few wins in the sense that you got anything you wanted. . . . We might have fixed some smaller issues, but we didn't want to fix smaller issues. We wanted to fix issues that would change the world. It was clear to many people that something much more radical was needed."[19]

But what? How did one go about fighting the system once one had asserted its existence and begun to "name" and "analyze" it? For 1960s activists, the answer was to attack the bigger issues by attacking the smaller ones—to address the whole by first confronting its parts. This is what the students did at Columbia University in 1968 and what made their rebellion so significant. In opposing Columbia's building of a gym in Harlem, they protested racism and economic inequality more broadly; attacking Columbia's relationship with the Institute for Defense Analysis (IDA, a center that facilitated military research), they protested U.S. militarism and the university's complicity in it. Mark Rudd's infamous comment that the students used the gym and IDA as mere pretexts for instigating a major confrontation may have been obnoxious, counterproductive, and only partially true. But it nevertheless spoke to how the rebellion far transcended the particular issues under protest.[20] This became evident as the protest escalated into the momentary capture of the university by the students—many of whom saw their act as one of revolution and the occupied campus as a "liberated zone"—and the forcible recapture of Columbia by police.

This dynamic of the protest of a "local" issue escalating into a major confrontation was repeated in countless settings (though most often beyond the glare of instant celebrity that shone on Columbia's comparatively privileged radicals in America's leading city). At San Francisco State College the movement for black and ethnic studies programs was part of a larger struggle against racism. The combination of the university's intransigence and the students' militancy led to what one official described as "violence unmatched in the history of American higher education" and the continuous occupation, in the fall and winter of 1968–69, of the campus by police.[21] At the City University of New York, the 1969 battle over open admissions erupted into a major class and racial conflict. At Cornell University in the same year, students used the demand for a black studies program as a vehicle for advocating black power more generally; the photograph of black students occupying a campus building while brandishing rifles is an enduring symbol of the profound racial and social divisions of the era. In each case, radicals confronted a local injustice as an instance of a much broader system of oppression, which served as the ultimate target of their protest. Authorities fed this sense of the struggle by responding as if the very legitimacy of their power were being threatened.

IV

The confrontations at Columbia, San Francisco State, and Cornell, the storied battles at the Pentagon in 1967 and "People's Park" in Berkeley in 1969, and the countless skirmishes on campuses and at demonstrations throughout the country in the late 1960s all convey the importance of militancy to the "revolutionary" culture of the movement. Much more than a tactical orientation or style of protest, militancy was a defining ethos for young radicals that had political, ethical, and existential dimensions. Not only was militancy a way of seizing some measure of power; it provided radicals with a means of backing their words with action and of living the substance of their values. In this capacity, militancy was an experiential antidote to the complacency, dispassion, and superficial self-satisfaction that defined for young leftists the mainstream of their society.

Activist Bill Ayers, describing the priorities of New Leftists, explained:

> You had a responsibility to link your conduct to your consciousness. . . . If you believed
> something, the proof of that belief was to act on it. It wasn't to espouse it with the right trea-
> tises or manifestos. We were militants. That's what we were. We were militants before we
> were thinkers, we were militants before we were theoreticians. . . . Militancy is a stance in
> the world, a way of being in the world that says that I'm going to put my body somehow in
> the way of the normal functioning of things, and I'm going take the consequence of having
> done that. . . . The statement is my body standing in the way, and once that statement is
> made, you open up a public space where lots of people have to think and act differently. . . .
> Militancy was the standard by which we measured our aliveness.[22]

Ayers first experienced the power of militancy directly while participating in a sit-in at
the Ann Arbor draft board office in 1965. Even those among the crowd of onlookers
who "wanted to kill us," he recalls, were forced to ask themselves what political principle would drive students such as himself to risk their educations and futures. Ayers's
reflections function well as a general description of an ethic of resistance that began in
the defiant acts of the civil rights movement and ran through various forms of direct action practiced by the movement, from university sit-ins to the burning of draft cards to
the trashing of property at demonstrations. The mobilization of millions of people into
the civil rights, antiwar, and student movements testified, in part, to the catalyzing
power of action.

Militant action could also have a profoundly educational effect, insofar as it provided
an intuition or a glimpse of the "whole." Todd Gitlin recalled,

> Confrontations were moments of truth . . . bisecting life into Time Before and Time After.
> We collected these ritual punctuations as moments when the shroud that normally covers
> everyday life was torn away and we stood face to face with the true significance of things.
> Each round was an approximation of the apocalypse, in the original meaning: the revelation
> of things the way they actually stand.[23]

Put another way, confrontation could induce a near-religious sense of the disclosure of
social truth—moments of potentially terrifying clarity in which the essential nature of
"the system" and the ultimate stakes of political conflict were laid open to be experienced and understood.

Participants in the Columbia University takeovers report having just such a revela-
tion. A flier asserted that those who were arrested and beaten

> know personally the brutality and inhumanity of a System which kills its young men with-
> out remorse, and allows the poor to starve without remorse, and wages a dirty war without
> remorse. We who were there and busted discovered in that experience a solidarity with each
> other. . . . We will free Columbia of the Company men and profiteers and cake-eaters who
> control its future and direct its participation in the death industries. Our weapon is our sol-
> idarity.[24]

According to this alternately heartfelt and grandiose testimony, the Columbia rebels had
the immediate, physical experience of oppressive power in its complex dimensions—of

the militarism, inequality, and destructiveness of the system working on the body si-multaneously. Conversely, the experience enhanced their sense of the importance of sol-idarity in a movement that aspired not just to resist, but to win.

For Jeff Jones, who later helped form the Weather Underground, the protests at Co-lumbia showed that

> if you could create a confrontation with the University administration, you could expose . . . the interlocking network of imperialism as it was played out on the campuses. You could prove that the University was working hand-in-hand with the CIA, that ultimately the cam-puses would resort to the police to resolve their problems, . . . when you really pushed them they . . . would call upon all the repressive apparatuses to defend their position from their own students.[25]

Jones had the experience, in approximate form, of Louis Althusser's view of the rela-tionship between capitalism, the state, and institutions. According to Althusser, capi-talism reproduces itself through the combined functioning of "Ideological State Appa-ratuses," such as schools and the family, and "Repressive State Apparatuses," such as the police and the military.[26] The primary role of presumably benign institutions like universities is actually to maintain established patterns of ideological hegemony and po-litical authority. But when they fail in their mandate or when their true function is ex-posed and radically challenged, the state intervenes with the apparatus of repression. Vi-olence thus serves as the underlying basis of institutional authority. Confrontation at Columbia—which ended with the police raiding the campus—made that "truth" ap-parent to Jones and was one of the things that led him to conclude that the only chance for success was to fight the system's violence with violence of one's own.

Violence was the choice of only a minority of self-described revolutionaries, who were themselves only a part of the New Left. But the turn to violence was the extreme expression of beliefs present throughout the movement—above all, that the struggle was ultimately one of all or nothing against a system that would relinquish its power only when forced, by whatever varied means, to do so.[27]

Militancy, though responsible for much of the movement's dynamism, was also a source of danger. By exalting action and equating commitment with risk, advocates of militant protest threatened to shut down analysis, prompt fatally exaggerated assess-ments of the movement's strength, and alienate potential allies. Black Panther leader Huey Newton suggested that the most noble thing one could do was to commit acts so confrontational and daring that they amounted to "revolutionary suicide." The danger the Panthers courted and the losses they took were, in part, the consequences of this at-titude. (The Panthers were also, of course, the victims of merciless attacks by police and other state agents.) White radicals, in addition to praising action, sought to prove the credibility of their commitment relative to that of black radicals and other people of color, who suffered far greater state repression and who were generally more militant. At its best, this impulse motivated middle-class whites to commit acts of great sacrifice in solidarity with those whose oppression was immediate and obvious.

This linkage of risk, personal dedication, and identity could be taken, however, in a less constructive direction, notably in the practice of "gut check." Performed by a host of movement groups and collectives, gut check was a ritualized way of pressuring members who opposed or hesitated to participate in an action, whether violent in intent or not, that held the prospect of arrest or injury. Robin Palmer, who was arrested nearly twenty times in the 1960s and 1970s, recounted the substance and tone of a gut check:

> If you don't do it, you're a coward. If you don't do it, you're not thinking of the Vietnamese. . . . You're a racist because the blacks have to live like this in the ghetto all the time. You're a racist because the Vietnamese are getting bombed like crazy all the time. Children mangled, women raped. . . . And you're worried about getting arrested?! And you're worried about getting hit by a cop over the head with a billy club?![28]

In Palmer's account, gut check used the themes of race and privilege to shame and intimidate those experiencing doubt about taking some risk; any alternative amounted to cowardice, hypocrisy, or even complicity in oppression. One early leader of the Weathermen took this race-based imperative for whites to be militant to confounding extremes. In 1969 he commented that blacks, because of their oppression, should be free to pursue a variety of political approaches and strategies. "But for white people," he insisted, "there's only one form—only one form—and that's to pick up the gun."[29] Whites, because of their privilege, must not merely match but exceed the sacrifice of blacks! Militancy, within the culture of the movement, ideally served as a means of self-realization and of honoring one's deepest commitments. But for those who succumbed to the pressure of gut check and took risks for which they were not prepared, militancy was a cause of self-estrangement.

At an extreme, militancy devolved into a kind of militarism that saw violence as the only truly revolutionary act and that divided the movement by positing a hierarchy of virtue based on one's willingness to "pick up the gun." Former Weatherman David Gilbert concedes that in their most dogmatic phase the Weathermen addressed the movement by saying in effect: "We're ready to fight and die. We're ready to do anything, and you're either on our side or you're on the side of the pigs."[30] Militancy, in this unforgiving dichotomy, failed to inspire and enlighten, to produce unity, or to draw others into revolutionary politics. It functioned instead as the basis for a crude dualism that separated the saved from the damned.

V

However confidently some young leftists may have identified themselves as revolutionaries, they remained a small minority scarcely capable of waging revolution. Principally, they had failed to convince millions of Americans to break with a capitalist system that, despite growing political and economic tensions, continued to deliver very real rewards. For many on the Left, defeating capitalism remained the *sine qua non* of a true revolution. Unable to win the active allegiance of the masses, the New Left appeared to reach the structural limit of its revolt.

Marcuse, for all his analytical powers, offered little constructive perspective on this predicament. Addressing a meeting of American radicals in 1969 he managed only equivocal commentary and a vague statement of hope:

> Radical change without a mass base seems to be unimaginable. But the obtaining of a mass base—at least in this country—and in the foreseeable future—seems equally unimaginable. What are we going to do with this contradiction? The answer seems to be very easy. . . . We have to try to get this mass base. But here we meet the limits of democratic persuasion. . . . Why these limits? Because a large, perhaps a decisive part of the majority, namely the working class, is to a great extent integrated into the system; and on a rather solid material basis, and not only superficially. It is certainly not integrated forever. Nothing is forever in history.[31]

These remarks reveal the profound crisis in the revolutionary imagination of the Western Left, even as the idea of revolution enjoyed renewed vitality. At root, the master narrative of revolution that had dominated the Left for nearly a century appeared inoperative, insofar as there was no longer a "material" basis for revolutionary consciousness among workers. Constructing another narrative, however, was no easy task.

In the face of this apparent impasse, activists serious about revolution turned with great urgency in the late 1960s to the questions of what constituted revolutionary agency, what class or group might be the "revolutionary subject," and how it could be best supported or mobilized. These questions proved extremely divisive. SDS devolved into dogmatic, jargon-laden debate and then dissolved in 1969 into several warring parts, each of which claimed knowledge of the true path to revolution. The split, which left many members dispirited with the national organization and unwilling to identify with any of the organized factions, has commonly been recorded as the moment of the New Left's self-destruction—the final estrangement from its founding commitments to democracy and equality.[32] Yet the split reflects also the severity of the dilemma faced by the Left at the decade's end, at which point its ambitions vastly exceeded its capabilities. One former SDSer, reflecting on the intensity of factional debate, explains, "We went from being young kids with a moral vision, to realizing we were up against the heaviest power structure in the world. . . . And so people looked for almost what I considered magical solutions, because it was scary."[33]

One "solution" proffered by groups like Progressive Labor was to insist that the working class remained *the* agent of revolutionary change. On the basis of this belief, some New Leftists worked to forge "student-worker" alliances on campuses and entered factories to become workers themselves, in hopes of pushing unions in a more "revolutionary"—or at the very least progressive—direction.[34] However dogmatically, adherents of this "workerist" orientation served to remind the movement that its values and goals had to penetrate much more deeply and broadly into American society should the kinds of transformation it sought be at all possible.

Yet calls to class revolution by New Leftists failed, by and large, to mobilize actual workers, revealing the inability of a worker-centered narrative (certainly one in which middle-class students appointed themselves leaders) to provide any longer a viable protocol for revolutionary change. More promising and resonant with the times was "revolutionary anti-imperialism," which had adherents throughout the black power, student, and antiwar movements. Its main premise was that the prosperity of advanced industrial societies depended on the economic exploitation of developing countries. The intensity with which the United States battled left-wing movements in the Third World seemed to demonstrate its stake in maintaining its dominance; conversely, the success of Third World insurgents appeared as signs of a broad "crisis of global capitalism." The example of the Vietnamese was especially inspiring. To activist Naomi Jaffe, it showed "that the power of [the United States] wasn't infinite" and served as "an incredible ray of hope that lit up brilliantly the sixties and seventies for many of us."[35]

Some U.S. radicals derived from Third World rebellions a specific mandate for revolution in their own country by reasoning that the greatest contribution they could make to Third World struggles was to bring the war for socialism home to their own society. Anti-imperialism also provided a way to account for and work around the absence of conditions considered within a traditional Marxist view to be prerequisites for revolutionary change. Within an anti-imperialist framework, the U.S. working class could be seen as an international "labor aristocracy" that benefited from the exploitation of foreign labor and resources. The initial or even primary impetus for radical change would therefore have to come from a new set of groups and forces working in solidarity with one another: students, who were not fully integrated into the benefits of the capitalist economy or absorbed by its ideology; blacks, some of whom saw themselves as part of an internal U.S. colony and their struggle as one of "national liberation"; and insurgents in the Third World, who threatened the U.S. empire from without. However counterintuitive, anti-imperialism allowed for an indigenous, revolutionary, socialist critique of affluent societies that had satisfied many of the traditional, material demands of socialism.

Revolutionary anti-imperialism was especially important for groups like the Weathermen, who drew on Third World examples to shape their vision of "armed struggle." The Cuban experience showed that the organization of the working class into a communist party was not a necessary precondition for a successful revolution.[36] Instead, a small band of guerrillas committing "exemplary" acts of violence could incite the masses to revolt and thereby circumvent the arduous task of organizing a revolutionary movement. From these foreign models, advocates of violence in the United States inferred that the assertion of revolutionary will could create a revolutionary situation where its "objective" determinants were lacking.

The visions of revolution emerging from the New Left and black power movement ultimately suffered the same fate. The Black Panthers, despite their bravado and fierce reputation, had only a few thousand members. They proved no match for a government determined to wipe them out. Student radicals intent on reviving class politics neither joined workers' struggles en masse nor were joined in alliance by workers. Adherents of anti-imperialism misread both the global and national context. International capitalism was not nearly so vulnerable as they imagined, and the existence of a worldwide struggle did not mean that strategies that worked in Cuba and Vietnam could be applied successfully to the situation in the United States. Though the violence of New Leftists may have been rooted in moral outrage, and may have had, in cases, a limited utility as a response to gross injustice, it clearly failed to instigate the mass revolt for which many of its practitioners had hoped. More modest approaches to revolution proved equally unsuccessful. Former SDS president Greg Calvert, in response to the alleged elitism of militants preaching confrontation and posing as leaders, argued in 1969 for the "revolution that does not need vanguards because it is so deeply grounded in the lives of the majority of the people that the governing classes will have lost before they know what happened to their power."[37] However warmly populist, this "velvet revolution" never materialized in the United States. No approach to revolution was able to push through the barrier that, with all the stresses of the 1960s, would bend but not break: that in an affluent society like the United States enough people are well enough off, precluding the possibility of a movement broad enough and strong enough to create radical, lasting change.

VI

One of the dangers faced by a movement of aspiring revolutionaries is that it will fail to attract a critical mass of participants, supporters, and resources to make its goal remotely possible. Under such circumstances, being a "revolutionary" is less a form of political agency than a moral and existential stance—a way of announcing one's opposition to the established order and desire for something radically better. A second danger is that the movement does not constitute a genuine alternative to the existing society. In this scenario, no success is possible, for even if the revolutionaries seize power and seemingly "win," no transformation in values and practices—indeed no revolution—will have taken place. The challenge of making a revolution, then, lies not only in accumulating "power," but also in representing at least the promise of a society more just and humane than the one it seeks to replace. The New Left suffered from the first condition, evident in its overestimation of its size and strength and its failure to win the active support of the masses. It struggled also with the second danger, insofar as it constantly risked reproducing some of the negative features of U.S. society that it ostensibly opposed.

For the New Left, revolution was not simply the goal or endpoint of political struggle; it was also a *process* that entailed prefiguring, in one's activism and protest culture, the liberated society to come. Marcuse succinctly described this ethos, which ran through New Leftists' commitment to participatory democracy, efforts to create non-hierarchical forms of organization, experiments with cooperative forms of living, and attention to the political dimensions of personal life. Before a New Left audience in 1969 he declared, "Our goals, our values, and our own and new morality, our OWN morality, must already be visible in our actions. The new humans who we want to help to create—we must already strive to be these human beings right here and now."[38] Elsewhere Marcuse identified the creation of a "New Sensibility" resistant to "cruelty, ugliness and brutality" as both the means and the content of liberation in the developed world.[39]

The New Left's epiphanies were just those moments when it transcended what it felt were the corrupt values of "the system" and began to enact its vision of the future. Such triumphs include SDS's early efforts to replicate the sense of "beloved community" enjoyed by Student Nonviolent Coordinating Committee activists organizing in the South; the reign of participatory democracy in sit-ins and at takeovers such as Columbia; the spontaneous efforts of Berkeley residents to turn a drab plot of university-owned land into a community garden and meeting place ("People's Park"); and the countless anonymous moments when compassion, mutual respect, and commitment to a collective purpose dominated young rebels' treatment of each other.

By contrast, the movement's inability to separate itself from the perceived failings of mainstream society constituted its low points and threatened the integrity of its resistance. New Leftists were at times alert to this danger. Yippie leader Jerry Rubin denounced the New Left's debilitating factionalism and internal competitiveness by asking, "Are we creating a New Man, or are we a reflection ourselves of the bullshit we hate so much."[40] Pacifist Dave Dellinger complained that Yippie culture was, in its egotism, "distressingly like the mirror-image" of the dominant culture.[41] One underground newspaper drew comparisons between the mainstream and "alternative" culture in commenting on Altamont, the disastrous 1969 rock concert that shared nothing of Woodstock's magic and ended in shattering violence. The paper lamented that at Altamont "we were the Mother Culture" and that the event revealed that "the horror show is in all of us."[42] Weatherwoman Susan Stern described Weatherman's infamous praise for Charles Manson at a 1969 SDS meeting as an expression of "the last putrid drop of American poison still flowing in the blood of the Weathermen."[43] Robin Morgan, a leading feminist voice, charged that the militancy of the male-dominated New Left reproduced the aggressiveness and will to dominate of the reigning chauvinist culture.[44]

Concerns that the New Left would reproduce the problems of American society became especially acute as some in the movement gravitated toward violence and tried to cultivate the stern, even callous subjectivity that "armed struggle" seemed to require. While himself a fugitive, radical pacifist Daniel Berrigan wrote an open letter to the Weather Underground, in which he cautioned: "The mark of inhuman treatment of humans is a mark that also hovers over us. It is the mark of the beast, whether its insignia is the military or the movement. A revolution is interesting only insofar as it avoids like the plague the plague it hopes to heal . . . and will be no better than those who it brought into being."[45] Psychologist Kenneth Keniston described what he felt was the genuine agony and chief failing of the New Left as its "complicity with the very violence against which [it] struggled." The New Left's aggression, he asserted, was "no less a symptom of the pathological violence of American life" than were police repression and the bombing of Vietnam.[46]

Even a voice as authoritative and beloved within the counterculture as that of the Beatles expressed grave doubt about the ability of self-described revolutionaries to show a truly better way. The song "Revolution," despite its title and driving energy, was not at all an anthem to radical change. Rather, it warned of the false promise offered by "people with minds that hate," while informing listeners that their world was going to neither unravel nor experience a glorious rebirth. (And that, the Beatles sang reassuringly, was "alright.") The entirely dissonant "Revolution 9" was more cynical still about the idea of revolution. It provided no sonic intimation of the shimmering utopia to come. Instead, it presented a seeming infinity of chaos and cacophony to accompany what the song suggests is the dull seriality of a world that keeps turning, without ever quite changing. The words "number nine, number nine" are muttered over the onslaught of noise, as if to convey that no turn or numbered "revolution" has any special significance. True revolution, within the Beatles' abstract commentary, appeared impossible.[47]

Kenniston sought also to counsel, and not just criticize, the New Left. Chiefly, he urged that young radicals acknowledge "inner evil" and accept that they shared in the deficiencies of their society. With this awareness, Kenniston insisted, an activist "becomes more effective in his deeds, for he is less prone to an unconscious complicity with the forces he consciously seeks to overcome."[48] In their weaker moments activists used the apparent acceptance of this complicity to further vilify their enemy; their own failings, within a self-serving logic, became more evidence of how their society had misshaped them and why it needed to be destroyed. (One radical group, retaining a language of accusation even while confessing its fallibility, spoke of the need to "kill the inner pig.")[49] Assuming responsibility for their conduct receded as a priority.

Yet in their stronger moments, New Leftists used the recognition of "inner evil" to temper their militancy with humility and impose ethical and political limits on their conduct. The Weather Underground, commonly portrayed as the purest embodiment of the New Left's excesses, vividly illustrates this restraint. Despite its ominous rhetoric and early plans for lethal attacks, the group never practiced the brutal and indiscriminate violence its critics had feared; its modus operandi, like that of most other "armed struggle" groups, was to bomb property in response to the violence of the state after issuing warnings intended to reduce the possibility of injury.[50] The movement's aggression, Kenniston's comparison notwithstanding, ultimately shared nothing in scale and very little in kind with the violence of the system young radicals protested. The only revolution worth fighting for, most seemed to grasp, was one that offered the prospect of an improved humanity.

VII

It is impossible to know if revolution in the United States was possible—as radicals confidently asserted—or if it was utterly impossible—as most Americans seemed to believe. The more pertinent question is one of perception: How could revolution appear from a certain vantage point likely or even inevitable and, from another vantage point, little more than a mirage?

Sociologists Richard Flacks and Jack Whalen, in their study of the 1970 burning of the Isla Vista branch of the Bank of America by students at UCSB, describe this capacity of revolution to oscillate between a looming possibility and a delusion as based on one's location and angle of vision. In the wake of the bank burning, revolution became "something very tangible and real" to those immersed in the radical culture of Isla Vista, the youth "ghetto" near campus that the students had "liberated." Indeed, to UCSB activists Isla Vista and other "revolutionary battlefields" like Berkeley and Madison constituted "the only 'real' reality"; the surrounding communities of Santa Barbara and Goleta were, by contrast, "outposts of a dying culture."[51] Yet to most spectators outside the New Left the burning of the bank took no special courage and had no world-historical significance. They saw the conservative and ultimately stable worlds of Goleta and Santa Barbara as the real ones and Isla Vista as a playground where self-absorbed "radicals" acted out indulgent and at times reckless fantasies.

In trying to account for their faith in revolution, former 1960s activists often explain how their participation in radical subcultures affected their views. One UCSB activist, who had wrongly assumed that revolutionary politics dominated America, remarked, "It was easy to get isolated from the rest of the world, being surrounded by people who basically felt the same way as you did."[52] Breaking out of that isolation could mean losing the hope of revolution. Another Isla Vista activist recalls, "I finally realized there wasn't a social revolution going on, and that there wasn't going to be one, when I looked at a Gallup poll in the newspaper and realized that I was part of what was only a 10 percent that could easily be ignored or eliminated."[53]

For other radicals, revolution was more quixotic or illusory still. Some never truly believed in the viability of revolution, despite their immense sacrifice on its behalf. This contradiction was particularly striking in those who risked everything for revolution by taking up arms. Robin Palmer was a New York City Yippie who joined a local bombing collective in 1969 and, one year later, the Weather Underground. In December 1970, on the anniversary of the assassination by Chicago police of Black Panther leader Fred Hampton, he was arrested for trying to bomb a bank, tried, and sent to Attica prison.[54] During the 1971 Attica uprising, Palmer's close friend Sam Melville, himself convicted for guerrilla activity, was shot and died in Palmer's arms. Reflecting years later on his motivations, Palmer confessed, "Even though in my essence I was a Weatherman, in my quintessence I said, 'It's all bullshit, we're never going to take state power.'" He speculated that it was the Yippie in him, with its taste for the absurd and for cosmic irony, that permitted him to commit highly dangerous bombings (in which he deeply believed from a moral standpoint) while doubting that revolution was remotely possible.[55]

For those less prone to such doubt, hindsight has done little to clarify whether revolution was or wasn't a realistic goal. Another member of the "armed struggle," describing recently what he learned about U.S. power from his many years underground, echoed Marcuse's tortured reflections in 1969 on the prospects of radical change. The United States, it turns out, was

> systematically much more resilient than I would have ever thought. . . . We really thought there was a potential for revolutionary change in that period. And we were not alone, you're talking millions of people around the world. . . . We mis-estimated [the chances for revolution], but it could have gone the other way. There could have been enough international contradictions, but we were wrong about how close that was.[56]

Revolution, in this rendering, was at once desperately close and infinitely far away.

More than just the ambiguity of signs and the inscrutability of the future accounts for this equivocation. For radicals, "revolution" was a conspicuously open-ended or even vague construct. Their optimism about revolution was based in part on their reading of events, which seemed to portend dramatic change: the assassinations of 1968, urban riots, the rise of black power, U.S. losses in Vietnam, growing division over the war domestically, anticapitalist rebellion worldwide, campus protest, increasing political violence, and state repression. They vigorously debated revolutionary ideology and strategy, and their activism suggested in a general way the nature of the liberated society to come. But they never defined how turmoil would produce radical change, how they would actually seize power, or how they would reorganize politics, culture, and the economy after a revolution. To a great degree, their revolutionary ambitions were driven by an apocalyptic impulse that rested on several assumptions: that the existing order was thoroughly corrupt and had to be destroyed; that its destruction would give birth to something radically new and better; and that the transcendent nature of this leap rendered the future a largely blank or unpredictable utopia.

References to this process of chaos and rebirth and praise for the creative power of destruction abounded in movement discourse. The Black Panthers spoke enthusiastically of a final, violent showdown with white America that would clear the way for a massive shift in power. Immediately following the assassination of Martin Luther King Jr., for example, Panther leader Eldridge Cleaver declared a "requiem for non-violence" and insisted, "Now there is the gun and the bomb, dynamite and the knife, and they will be used liberally in America."[57] A radical newspaper wrote of reports of Weatherman bombings: "Our humble task is to organize the apocalypse!"[58] A communiqué accompanying a bombing by the "Volunteers of America" declared, "Out of the Bankruptcy of AmeriKKKa will come a new country and a new people."[59] And, as if to welcome a cataclysmic confrontation that would hasten the arrival of a new society, a Berkeley newspaper printed in huge letters on its cover the message from California governor Ronald Reagan in 1970 to student demonstrators: "If it takes a bloodbath, let's get it over with."[60]

Revolution, within an apocalyptic frame of reference, was less a vision of social change based on a political analysis than a structure of expectation born of outrage, and an unelaborated faith that chaos bred crisis and that from crisis a new society would emerge. In this way young radicals translated their belief that revolution was morally and politically necessary into the mistaken sense that revolution was therefore likely or even inevitable.

VIII

Whether a real possibility or only a pipe dream, revolution had in the 1960s a presence on the historical stage that it has not enjoyed since. The decline of the era's radicalism was followed by the more or less total dissolution of the revolutionary imaginary in the advanced capitalist world—the abandonment of revolution as a political ideal and a utopian structure of desire or even of faith. As Russell Jacoby lamented in 1993, "a utopian spirit—a sense that the future could transcend the present—has all but vanished."[61]

The demise of revolution coincided with the entrenchment of the postmodern condition, virtually defined by the exhaustion of utopian energies. Not only does revolution appear impossible in prosperous, stable societies in which the technology-driven principle of performance dominates; postmodern thinkers have sought to discredit the idea of revolution outright. Principally, they have accused utopian ideologies of being counterproductive or even dangerous insofar as such ideologies naively assume the possibility of a moment of emancipation or perfect justice, and promote coercive means in service of these impossible ends. Jean François Lyotard, in a seminal postmodern text, described the totalizing impulse behind utopian quests for "final solutions" as a "dangerous fantasy to seize reality."[62] Slavoj Zizek, a leading postmodern intellectual, has characterized the desire for a New Man and a New World, beyond antagonism or contradiction, as a fundamentally fascist longing, responsible for the terror of the twentieth century.[63] One of the postmodern imperatives is to purge politics of apocalyptic impulses.

Along with the abandonment of revolutionary goals, there has been in the Western world a massive reduction in the scale of political ambition. Against the broadly Marcusean premise of a unified system of domination, postmodern thinkers have developed an understanding of power as local, mobile, and dispersed. The Marcusean perspective urges the "Great Refusal" of the whole, ideally culminating in revolution; the postmodern view counsels acts of resistance, generated indefinitely as power re-forms and shifts its locus. With this turn to "resistance" comes pervasive skepticism about the possibility of any *systematic* alternative to the status quo. Moreover, commitment to resistance has largely been stripped of the militancy and sense of mission that gave 1960s activism much of its energy and political force. World developments, especially the collapse of communism and the unprecedented supremacy of democratic capitalism as a global model, affirm the sense of the absence of alternatives. This perspective, Jacoby asserts, is "the wisdom of our times, an age of political exhaustion and retreat."[64]

And yet there is a way in which resistance, rebellion, and revolution are threatened less by being marginalized or made obsolete than by being too proliferate and popular. Tom Frank's *The Conquest of Cool: Business Culture, Counterculture, and the Rise of Hip Consumerism,* though focused on the advertising and clothing industries in the 1960s, makes this point with special force. Frank does *not* argue, as one could carelessly misread him as doing, that "the Establishment" co-opted the values of the counterculture, thus limiting whatever political threat it posed. His great ambition is to smash the distinction between "authentic" and "phony" counterculture and a view of co-optation as the calculated victory of the latter over the former.[65] Frank contends that in the late 1950s and early 1960s there was a budding consensus in America that conformity was bad—for the soul and for business both. This was true on Madison Avenue, where a new generation of advertisers set out to transform their industry. They found in the counterculture "a symbolic ally in their own struggles against the mountains of deadweight procedure" and "creative dullness" of the advertising world, and drew on the language of the counterculture—mainly on its notions of authenticity, individuality, and difference—to express their own sense of rebellion.[66] According to Frank, the near instantaneous incorporation of countercultural motifs into the mainstream reflected not so much the cunning of capitalism, bent on absorbing and profiting from dissent, as the genuine confluence of the critique of mass society offered by the youth culture and the rapidly transforming corporate world.[67]

The 1960s look far different after Frank's demonstration of "the enthusiasm of ordinary suburban America for cultural revolution" and of how corporations kindled that enthusiasm.[68] In Frank's telling, the boundaries between the mainstream culture and the counterculture, Madison Avenue and the Haight-Ashbury, were so fluid that it is hard to specify when, or how, or even if the counterculture was truly oppositional. By extension, the integrity of the movement's resistance was threatened not only by the possibility that radicals would unwittingly reproduce what was evil or ugly in their society; their apparent rebellion could be disconcertingly or embarrassingly close to the values celebrated by "progressive" forces within the cultural mainstream.

If the use of countercultural themes and images in advertising once seemed manipulative or galling, we should now be long past any sense of scandal. Since the 1960s, rebellion has become *the* dominant cultural value in America, in which nearly everybody claims to participate, no matter how normal or complacent their lives. In what Frank terms "liberation marketing," advertisers routinely stage the showdown between conformity and individuality, power and resistance, by presenting their products as signifiers of youthful vitality and originality that defy the homogeneity and superficiality of mass society. Sprite's "Taste is everything. Image is nothing" campaign and The Body Shop's line of beauty products called "Activist" are conspicuous examples of this contrived liberation from what corporations themselves construct as the foil of corporate tyranny. The paradox of this kind of advertising is that it urges you to express yourself and feel like a nonconforming individual within constraints, and on a set of terms, established by the corporations themselves, whose ultimate goal is that you buy their products. This tension is well expressed—even laid bare—in a superbly executed 1999 Gap TV commercial in which a camera runs by a hip, multicultural group of young people all wearing vests. As the camera passes, each person sings a few lines of a song, thus making the music his or her own. The ad concludes with the slogan, "Everybody in Vests." The ad suggests that the Gap both recognizes and celebrates the individuality and diversity of its customers; therefore, they need not feel that their uniqueness is threatened by all wearing the same thing—vests. In this clever way, outward or superficial conformity becomes a sign of substantive diversity, on which the Gap intends to capitalize.

The Frankian universe, which is choked with such messages, appears a more pernicious, because more perfect, form of totalitarianism. No longer do we inhabit, as Marcuse theorized, a "one-dimensional" society that tries to liquidate and neutralize whatever resistance does exist. Ours is a superficially two-dimensional society—in truth a closed system—in which resistance is both produced by and contained within the logic and language of the market itself.

In such a system, the chances for meaningful resistance, let alone revolution, appear bleak. Aging baby boomers don't help the odds. Once the great bearers of rebellion, boomers now sit at or near the command and control centers of dominant culture, and are the demographic group that drives the contemporary consumer economy. Speaking to what they perceive as boomers' quotidian wants and deepest desires, advertisers continually restage the symbolic killing of the long-dead father in an empty drama of rebellion. A recent ad for a sports utility vehicle (SUV) typifies this strategy. In the ad, a gigantic, suited bald man—a cartoonish version of the archetypal 1950s father—drives signs into the ground commanding "Stop" and "Do Not Enter" in wildly exaggerated gestures of disapproval. The figurative son (or daughter) darts through his legs and around the signs in a giddy romp of adolescent defiance. In such scenes, the 1960s generation—drawn to SUVs more to protect their children than to go on off-road adventures—lays claim to the same rebellious spirit of its youth, despite its now domesticated existence. Its rebellion, however, is now expressed through owning an SUV, conspicuous consumption and the environment be damned![69]

Jacoby, defining again the Zeitgeist of the late 1990s, announced, "We have entered the era of acquiescence, in which we build our lives, families and careers with little expectation the future will diverge from the present."[70] Yet for many this acquiescence reflects neither resignation nor malaise, but a choice. The Marcusean maxim of the early 1960s seems again to hold, suggesting that our world has once more revolved ("number ten? number ten?") without quite changing. When people perceive the times as good and access to the good life is reasonably broad, people want a future that is little different from the present.

IX

The recognition of the need for radical change is not, as Marcuse noted, sufficient to produce such change. But neither does its seeming impossibility mean that it is not still desirable or necessary from a moral and political standpoint. Despite continued prosperity, relatively low unemployment, political stability, and apparent widespread satisfaction with the status quo, the times remain, in the words used by Daniel Berrigan thirty years ago to indict his era, "inexpressibly evil."[71] There are in the United States millions for whom the prospects of a career, a stable family, and a life lived to its potential are severely hindered or made outright impossible by poverty, racism, disease, illiteracy, violence, crime, the criminal justice system, addiction, and hopelessness. These conditions are largely preventable, but our society, by virtue of a complex choice, decides not to prevent them. Within a Marcusean calculus, which judges a society against its capacity for improving the circumstances of life, the United States is underachieving, woefully or even criminally so. And there are millions of people, members of the 1960s generation among them, who are outraged by this failure and who work to promote social justice. Indeed, the times are also "inexhaustibly good"—as Berrigan said as well of his era—"solaced by the courage and hope of many."[72] In this light, Jacoby's portrait of universal acquiescence is a grossly deceptive one, based on the false assumptions that nearly everyone lives in at least middle-class comfort and that no one feels the urgent need for change. To the contrary, no sooner did Jacoby declare the end of utopia than a vibrant and highly visible movement came into being that questions in radical ways the fundamental justice of the global economy and political order and the ability of the American system to serve even remotely the interests of all of its people, especially the poor.

This is not to say that the masses in the United States are for the most part suffering, certainly not compared to most times in U.S. history. Any plan for radical change based on the expectation of growing and pervasive economic misery is likely to fail.[73] Nor does renewed activism mean that a major upheaval is brewing or that the values of freedom and equality are winning. These observations do provide, however, a starting point for assessing the chance for alternatives to the current order and for reviving something of the utopian spirit. Another of Marcuse's assertions helps to orient these tasks. Marcuse insisted that critical theory, whose mandate is to develop a rationale for and an image of liberating change, must be rooted in an understanding of "actual tendencies."[74] The vision of the future, in short, must be based on the realities of the present.

Though the times have changed significantly, one compelling continuity exists between the challenges of the 1960s and those of today. In response to foreign conflicts like Vietnam and under the rubric of anti-imperialism, U.S. activists interrogated global power relationships, chiefly that between First World prosperity and Third World poverty. In the name of solidarity, they participated in a transnational culture of resistance that sought to transcend boundaries of race, class, and nation through opposition to a common enemy. Though anti-imperialism has virtually disappeared as a critical stance and a political movement, aspects of its spirit have survived in efforts to organize against the inequities of the new global economy—a task that has quickly become the closest thing to a consensus agenda for the Left worldwide. Zizek, from his cosmopolitan perspective, recently proclaimed, "The way to fight the capitalist New World Order is . . . by focusing on the only serious question today: how to build *transnational* political movements and institutions strong enough to constrain seriously the unlimited rule of capital."[75]

The protests against the World Trade Organization (WTO) in Seattle, against the World Bank and International Monetary Fund in Washington, D.C., and in countless cities throughout the world against institutions implicated in the global spread of capitalism indicate that this movement is already taking shape. A *New York Times* op-ed piece on the WTO demonstrations described the emerging anticorporate activism as "the most internationally minded, globally linked movement the world has ever seen."[76] The breadth of the movement is equally impressive, as environmentalists, labor union members and other workers, the urban poor, advocates of international human rights, students, anarchists, and assorted rebels find common cause—whatever the diversity of ideologies and disagreements over tactics—in opposing the current reign of multinational corporations and the institutions that protect their power. The politics of

"We Shall Overcome," "Redeem the Times," and, at the far edges, "Smash Capitalism" are making a comeback, prompting numerous comparisons between the new activism and that of the 1960s.

However bold some of today's anticapitalist rhetoric, the de facto goal of the new activists seems more to constrain than somehow "overthrow" capitalism. Such an ambition may reflect the withering of true utopianism; more likely, it is a valid concession to reality that, given capitalism's current strength and the paucity of well-developed and compelling alternatives, shares still in idealism. Either way, it has served as a catalyst for renewed activism and the deepening of the sense, once integral to anti-imperialism, that true justice must be global justice. How much momentum this movement may develop is impossible to predict. Its promise lies in its robust vision of justice, its stress on solidarity, and its commonsense understanding of the need for a fundamental redistribution of power domestically and abroad.

Basing a vision of the future on qualities of the present means also building on strengths. From the standpoint of progressive or radical politics in the United States, strength lies in diversity—of races, ethnicities, cultures, and experiences. The last several decades have witnessed the emergence of new political actors; tremendous cultural initiative from marginalized and disempowered groups; unprecedented insight into how race, class, gender, and sexuality combine in systems of power; awareness of the inadequacies and exclusions of traditional paradigms of emancipation; and calls for coalition politics as a way to organize around shared interests while affirming differences. This multicultural energy need not be dismissed as simply a new expression of pluralism—an ideology that, though long a part of America's official cultural mission, has failed to make society truly tolerant or ensure equality among groups. Nor should one, like Jacoby, blame the decline of utopian thinking in the past several decades on academics who have allegedly rejected their proper role as "public intellectuals" speaking out on behalf of universal truths and instead have concentrated on enhancing their careers by peddling often impenetrable theories of power, resistance, and the virtues of multiculturalism.[77] Overwhelmingly large structural forces—not a handful of postmodern thinkers purportedly operating in bad faith—are responsible for weakening utopianism and the belief in "truth" in the modern West.

The task, then, is to develop the transformative potential of multiculturalism as a means for addressing identity-based oppression, economic injustice, and the way the two reinforce each another. More specifically, the challenge is to combine a politics of recognition—which stresses the need for mutual respect between individuals and groups, and seeks to eliminate prejudice, scapegoating, and other forms of objectification—and a politics of redistribution—with seeks to redivide not simply wealth but the means to produce social wealth.[78] No force of historical or structural necessity dictates that a movement devoted to this complex challenge will grow or succeed; the shape of the future remains, in the last instance, a choice. To recognize this and take responsibility for choices, individual and collective, may be the best way to seize the meaning and participate in the legacy of the 1960s.

X

More than 150 years ago, Karl Marx penned in his eleventh Thesis on Feuerbach what has served since as a guiding maxim for reformers, radicals, and revolutionaries world-wide: that while philosophers have interpreted the world, the point is to change it.[79] This message has special relevance for an era in which the utopian imagination and the project of radical change, which long seemed near extinction, are showing again small signs of life. Chiefly, it functions as a reminder that one cannot *think* a society out of acquiescence, apathy, or malaise. Resurrecting utopianism, as a new generation of activists are discovering, entails liberating once again the imagination; for this, study of 1960s radicalism may provide inspiration and guidance, as well as insight into what to avoid. But it requires, more fundamentally, a renewed commitment to collective *action,* through which we define the boundaries separating the possible from the impossible, dream and desire from delusion. Whether we will forever dwell in the cold universe of "Revolution 9," where worlds revolve without truly changing, or whether we will realize the spirit of Thesis Eleven, can be decided only in practice. In flashes the Beatles, despite their artful cynicism, shed some happy light on the kind of effort that is demanded, the values that must guide us, and the form our actions must take: "One, two, three, four, can I have a little more? Five, six, seven, eight, nine, ten, I love you. All together now!"

Notes

1. Kirkpatrick Sale, *SDS* (New York: Random House, 1973), 457.

2. Jean-Paul Sartre, "France: Masses, Spontaneity, Party" in *Between Existentialism and Marxism*, trans. John Mathews (New York: Pantheon, 1974), 125.

3. "Eyes on the Prize, Part 2," videotape 7.

4. Thomas Powers, *Diana: The Making of a Terrorist* (Boston: Houghton Mifflin, 1971), 118.

5. Sale, *SDS*, 457.

6. Jack Whalen and Richard Flacks, *Beyond the Barricades: The Sixties Generation Grows Up* (Philadelphia: Temple University Press, 1989), 79, 73.

7. By one estimate, there were as many as 2,800 political bombings between January 1969 and early April 1970, the period when the "revolutionary 1960s" reached their crest. Sale, *SDS*, 632.

8. Christopher Hitchens, "The Children of '68," *Vanity Fair,* June 1998, 94.

9. The first page of the spread advertising the minivan shows a picture of the globe, over which is superimposed the text: "It was a revolutionary machine that broke new ground in technology. Since 1983 it has continually moved the world forward." *People Magazine,* 15–22 March 1999.

10. I use the term "New Left" to refer to the primarily white, middle-class movement of students and youth that was an important facet of 1960s radicalism. "The movement" is a broader term that includes the civil rights and black power struggles, as well as segments of the antiwar movement. Much of what this essay argues about revolution pertains to both the New Left and the movement as a whole, though my analysis is geared most strongly to the New Left. During the 1960s themselves and in the historiography of the era, terms like the "New Left" and "the

movement" are not used with any great specificity or consistency. My own use of the terms is not meant to imply any rigid division or segmentation of a protest culture whose internal boundaries were in fact very fluid.

11. Doug Rossinow reorients 1960s historiography in this way in *The Politics of Authenticity: Liberalism, Christianity, and the New Left in America* (New York: Columbia University Press, 1998).

12. Herbert Marcuse, *One-Dimensional Man: Studies in the Ideology of Advanced Industrial Society* (Boston: Beacon Press, 1964), x.

13. Ibid., ix.

14. Ibid.

15. Ibid., xv.

16. Ibid., 256.

17. Ibid., 254.

18. Quoted in Todd Gitlin, *The Sixties: Years of Hope, Days of Rage* (New York: Bantam Books, 1987), 177–78, 184.

19. Scott Braley, interview by author, 7 Feb. 1999.

20. David Caute, *The Year of the Barricades: A Journey through 1968* (New York: Harper and Row, 1988), 148–49.

21. The shootings of students at Kent State and Jackson State Universities were still months off, permitting this description of the violence at San Francisco State. William H. Orrick Jr., *College in Crisis: A Report to the National Commission on the Causes and Prevention of Violence* (Nashville: Aurora Publishers, 1969), 3. By the end of 1969 there had been at the college over seven hundred arrests, at least eighty injuries to students and thirty-two to police, and nearly a dozen bombs planted on campus.

22. Bill Ayers, interview by author, 15 March 1995.

23. Gitlin, *The Sixties,* 287.

24. "On Solidarity—The Communes," flier, 1968, Social Protest Collection, University of California at Berkeley.

25. "The Reminiscences of Jeff Jones," 24 Oct. 1984, Columbia Oral History Project, Columbia University, Butler Library, 64. The "Weathermen" emerged as a faction in SDS in the summer of 1969, shortly before SDS dissolved. It advocated militant action and then "armed struggle," which it pursued starting in the winter of 1970, when the group went underground. The Weathermen initially had around five hundred adherents, though only a hundred or so members made the transition underground. The group was most active in the early 1970s, by which point it had changed its name to the "Weather Underground." The Weather Underground bombed mostly symbols of state power and corporate buildings in response to specific instances of state violence. It committed roughly two dozen bombings before it disbanded in 1976.

26. Louis Althusser, "Ideology and Ideological State Apparatuses" in *Lenin and Philosophy and Other Essays*, trans. Ben Brewster (New York: Monthly Review Press, 1971), 127–86.

27. A reliable sense of how many people engaged in political violence in the sixties and early seventies eludes us, both because there are no comprehensive statistics and because violence can be defined in different ways. Sale asserts that "violence took place on a larger scale—in terms of the number of instances, their geographical spread, and the damage caused—than anything before in this century." As many as 1 million people, by his estimate, participated in violence in the form of "rioting, trashing, assaults on buildings, and confrontations with police" (634–35). In a special issue on "Guerrilla Warfare in the United States," *Scanlan's* magazine recorded close to

five hundred acts of arson or bombings of government, corporate, police, military, and university targets in the first six months of 1970 (Jan. 1971, 1:8). Others contend that violence occurred on a small scale and at the hands of a small few. Dan Georgakas asserts that "violent tactics were a distinctly minority activity" within the movement, but received inordinate media attention (Dan Georgakas, "Armed Struggle," in *Encyclopedia of the American Left,* ed. Mary Jo Buhle, Paul Buhle, Dan Georgakas [Urbana: University of Illinois Press, 1992], 57). By his estimate, the "number of people who participated in armed struggle numbered in the low hundreds" (62). This number, in light of the figures provided by *Scanlan's* and Sale, seems implausibly low. At the same time, Sale's estimate of one million is highly misleading because it includes people who engaged in petty acts of violence such as trashing property in street demonstrations. The number of people who committed more serious acts, like bombings, conceived as part of a "revolutionary armed struggle" strategy, was vastly smaller. On New Left militancy, see Dave Dellinger, *More Power than We Know: The People's Movement towards Democracy* (New York: Anchor Press, 1975).

28. Robin Palmer, interview by author, 14 Nov. 1994.

29. *Ann Arbor Argus,* 31 Dec. 1969, 3. Jeff Jones made this statement at the height of the Weathermen's most militant phase, when the group was prone to extreme hyperbole.

30. "The Reminiscences of David Gilbert," 17 Jan. 1985, Columbia Oral History Project, Columbia University, Butler Library, 346.

31. The speech was given at an anniversary gathering of the left-wing newspaper *The Guardian.* It was printed as "Marcuse on the Left" in the *RAG,* 26 Nov.–6 Dec. 1969.

32. This is the conclusion of Sale, Gitlin, and James Miller, *"Democracy Is in the Streets": From Port Huron to the Siege of Chicago* (New York: Simon and Schuster, 1987).

33. "Reminiscences of David Gilbert," 158.

34. For many, this proved a temporary experiment in altering one's class identity driven by a largely antiquated ideology. Yet those who stuck with their commitment to labor organizing beyond the 1960s and early 1970s helped preserve a progressive streak in American organized labor during a time of declining union strength. Their experience and their impact on American labor remain largely unrecorded and need further research.

35. Naomi Jaffe, interview by author, 13 Oct. 1995.

36. France's Régis Debray, *Revolution in the Revolution?* (New York: Grove Press, 1967), and Che Guevara, in scattered writings, interpreted the Cuban revolution this way.

37. *Guardian,* 18 Oct. 1969, 14.

38. "Marcuse on the Left."

39. Herbert Marcuse, *An Essay on Liberation* (Boston: Beacon Press, 1969), 72.

40. *Rat,* vol. 1, no. 26, 8. Rubin was probably referring to Che Guevara's ideal of the "New Socialist Man."

41. Quoted in Jonah Raskin, *For the Hell of It: The Life and Times of Abbie Hoffman* (Berkeley: University of California Press, 1996), 188.

42. *The Berkeley Tribe,* 12–19 Dec. 1969.

43. Susan Stern, *With the Weatherman: The Journey of a Revolutionary Woman* (Garden City, N.Y.: Doubleday, 1976), 205. The meeting was run by the Weathermen and was only nominally an SDS event. By the winter of 1970 the organization was in disarray, and few rank-and-file SDSers wanted to affiliate with the Weathermen. Referring to the Manson Gang's Tate–La Bianca murders of a few months earlier, in which the murderers stuck a fork in one of their victims, a Weatherleader proclaimed, "Dig it; first they killed those pigs, then they ate dinner in the room

with them, then they even shoved a fork into pig Tate's stomach. Wild!" Quoted in Dellinger, *More Power than We Know*, 152. The Weathermen soon grew to regret the comment and to distance themselves from the politics it implied.

44. This is a strong theme in Morgan's early writings, developed in *The Demon Lover* (New York: Norton, 1988).

45. Daniel Berrigan, "Letter to the Weathermen," in *The Eloquence of Protest: Voices of the 70s*, ed. Harrison Salisbury (Boston: Houghton Mifflin, 1972), 15–16. Berrigan was underground to avoid serving his sentence for destroying draft cards in Catonsville, Maryland, in 1968.

46. Kenneth Kenniston, "The Agony of the Counterculture," in Salisbury, *The Eloquence of Protest*, 219, 220.

47. Others interpreted the song very differently. Charles Manson, who built his cosmology on idiosyncratic understandings of biblical scripture and Beatles' lyrics, saw "Revolution 9" as a complement to the Bible's "Revelations 9." Both texts, he felt, foretold an imminent race war that would plunge American society into chaos, from which the Manson Gang would emerge as a kind of holy elect. See Vincent Bugliosi (with Curt Gentry), *Helter Skelter: The True Story of the Manson Murders* (New York: Norton, 1974), esp. 321–31.

48. Kenniston, "The Agony of the Counterculture," 224.

49. *Ann Arbor Argus*, 24 May–9 June 1969, 11. The statement was made by the White Panthers, a radical group from Detroit that flirted with violence.

50. On 6 March 1970 three Weathermen blew themselves up in a New York City townhouse while making bombs intended for use at an army dance in New Jersey. Thereafter, the group attacked property only.

51. Whalen and Flacks, *Beyond the Barricades*, 75.

52. Ibid., 117.

53. Ibid., 116–17.

54. On the murder of Hampton, ordered by the FBI, see Churchill Ward, "'To Disrupt, Discredit, and Destroy': The FBI's Secret War against the Black Panther Party," in *Liberation, Imagination, and the Black Panther Party: A New Look at the Panthers and Their Legacy* (New York: Routledge, 2001), 106–7.

55. Palmer, interview.

56. Braley, interview.

57. Eldridge Cleaver, "Requiem for Nonviolence," in *Post-Prison Writings and Speeches*, ed. Robert Sheer (New York: Random House, 1969), 76.

58. *The Berkeley Tribe*, 16–23 Oct. 1970, 7.

59. Ibid., 26 June–3 July 1970, 3.

60. Ibid., 10–17 April 1970.

61. Russell Jacoby, *The End of Utopia: Politics and Culture in an Age of Apathy* (New York: Basic Books, 1999), xi.

62. Jean-Francois Lyotard, *The Postmodern Condition: A Report on the Status of Knowledge*, trans. Geoff Bennington and Brian Massumi (Minnesota: University of Minnesota Press, 1993), 112.

63. Slavoj Zizek, *The Sublime Object of Ideology* (London: Verso, 1993), 5.

64. Jacoby, *The End of Utopia*, 6.

65. Thomas Frank, *The Conquest of Cool: Business Culture, Counterculture, and the Rise of Hip Consumerism* (Chicago: University of Chicago Press, 1997), 7–8.

66. Ibid., 9.

67. This point of Frank's is certainly counterintuitive and probably an overstatement. Frank argues it, however, with great vigor. For example, he shows that, in their own right, people in the corporate world in the 1960s "deplored conformity, distrusted routine, and encouraged resistance to established power" (9). He also documents the extent to which the counterculture was already a highly commercialized phenomenon and how thoroughly its language and style and those of the advertising world interpenetrated. Even so, it is hard to fully accept what Frank appears at times to think: that in no way and at no point did the counterculture represent a true alternative to the ideology, sensibility, and habits of the mainstream society.

68. Frank, *The Conquest of Cool,* 13.

69. The portrayal of SUVs, despite the notorious hazards they present to the environment and to other cars, as emblems of freedom tinged with 1960s hedonism is common. Nissan's TV ad for one of its SUVs, the Xterra, shows the vehicle tearing happily through rugged terrain interspersed with footage of surfing and snowboarding, sports that connote freedom and youthful abandon.

70. Jacoby, *The End of Utopia,* xi.

71. Daniel Berrigan, *The Trial of the Catonsville 9* (Boston: Beacon Press, 1972), 95.

72. Ibid.

73. Radicals once asserted that industrialization would drive the masses into the arms of revolution; now some predict, probably with equal futility, that "globalization" will necessarily spur a global revolt of newly dispossessed masses.

74. Marcuse, *One-Dimensional Man,* xi. According to Marcuse, this accountability is what gave critical theory its "objectivity." By extension, he felt that critical theory was morally credible and politically useful only if it spoke to actual qualities and trends within a given society.

75. Slavoj Zizek, "Against the Double Blackmail," *The Nation,* 24 June 1999, 22.

76. Naomi Klein, "Rebels in Search of Rules," *New York Times,* 3 Dec. 1999.

77. This is an insistent theme of *The End of Utopia.* One senses that Jacoby, rather than mourn and try to work through the apparent loss of the utopian imagination, partly transforms his grief into derision of other thinkers, including those one might expect him to affirm.

78. Nancy Fraser frames this challenge in "From Redistribution to Recognition? Dilemmas of Justice in a 'Post-Socialist' Age," in Nancy Fraser, *Justus Interruptus: Critical Reflections on the "Post-Socialist" Condition* (New York: Routledge, 1996).

79. Karl Marx, "Theses on Feuerbach," in *The Marx-Engels Reader,* ed. Robert Tucker (New York: Norton, 1978), 145.

CHAPTER 12

Letting Go: Revisiting the New Left's Demise

Doug Rossinow

How did the New Left end? This may, at first glance, seem a trivial question. Surely it is more important that we explore the main concerns and activities of this radical movement during its heyday. Indeed, this is exactly what the past twenty years' worth of writing on the subject has done. In addition, historians in the 1980s and 1990s have focused a great deal of attention on the question of the New Left's beginnings. It seems that the "silent generation" of the 1950s was not so silent or complacent after all, and several writers have combed that decade carefully in order to find the seeds of dissent sown prior to 1960.[1] For those sympathetic to the Left, as most historians of the New Left are, this is a happy task.

How dismal, in comparison, it now seems to map out the collapse of Students for a Democratic Society (SDS) in 1969, to revisit those nasty days of RYM and PLP (Revolutionary Youth Movement and Progressive Labor party), when the Left seemed intent on self-destruction. Early historians of SDS, like Kirkpatrick Sale and Irwin Unger, concentrated much of their energy on just this grisly business.[2] But later works suggested that further analysis of the dissolution of SDS, and of the movement it so imperfectly embodied, was unnecessary and uninteresting. If everyone agrees about the ending of the New Left's story, then perhaps it is logical to think that we have nothing left to learn about the matter.

Yet it is not so simple. Most scholars of the New Left by now agree that this movement included far more than SDS. While Sale and Unger seemed to equate SDS with the New Left, recent works have reasserted the primacy and breadth of the New Left *as a social movement*. Andrew Hunt's insistence on including Vietnam Veterans against the War (VVAW) in the New Left is perhaps the most striking move in this direction, and a welcome one.[3] The New Left was a messy agglomeration of national and local groups and initiatives. Many of these groups associated themselves with SDS, but a large number did not. Many radical initiatives did not cohere as organizations of any kind, and most that did (including many SDS chapters) paid little attention to the niceties of membership. The New Left gleefully ignored organizational structure. Certainly by mid-decade, its members thought of it as a mass movement, and rare was the New Left activist who thought an accurate organizational flow chart was the path to the mass heart. By the time SDS broke apart in 1969, the New Left seemed big enough to live without it.

Indeed, the radical movement continued to exist after 1969, when SDS ceased to function effectively on both the national and the local levels. This is seen most easily by examining leftist activism at the local level. The national narrative of the New Left essentially ends with the Weathermen's "days of rage" in 1969. There is simply not much to say about national left-wing activity in the following years, save for the inconsequential pronunciamentos that Weathermen occasionally issued from the underground, and the unsuccessful efforts of a small number of leftists to create an updated version of national SDS in the New American Movement (NAM). In Austin, Texas, one of the biggest SDS chapters in the country, based at the University of Texas at Austin (UT), seemed almost to vanish into thin air during the 1968–69 school year, reflecting larger developments. Yet the radical movement culture in Austin actually became bigger and more vibrant in the years between 1969 and 1973.

In the fall of 1968 SDS chapter meetings at UT drew hundreds, yet by the conclusion of the fall 1969 semester, the chapter was gone. It felt the withering hand of a very small Friends of Progressive Labor (FPL) group, which succeeded magnificently in turning away the large numbers of young people who, during and just after the wrenching events of the 1968 election campaign, looked to SDS for leadership. FPL members promoted a "Worker-Student Alliance" but did little if any organizing along these lines. Politically inexperienced students, new to the SDS chapter, perhaps unsure of their exact commitments, probably desired a program aimed more at antiwar efforts; since they did not stay in the organization, this is difficult to say for certain.

In Austin there was no Weatherman faction to compete with FPL for organizational control, although some in the SDS chapter there were sympathetic to the Weathermen. To use a pugilistic metaphor, there was no brawl here; instead, FPL was left alone in the ring, jabbing and cutting into the air and eventually exhausting itself, like a fighter "punching himself out." As early as the end of 1968, one UT student who had gravitated to SDS became disillusioned, finding it "dysfunctional," and left the group. In 1970 this student was elected president of the university's student government on an avowedly radical, left-wing program. This seemed like a watershed for radical student politics locally. Ironically, it had nothing whatever to do with SDS, even though SDS had pioneered the practice of running radical candidates for student government offices at UT.[4]

The story of the SDS national convention in Chicago in July 1969, from which the opposition to PL seceded and formed the Weathermen, is a familiar one. Less well known is the story of the last national council meeting of national SDS, which occurred in March of the same year, in Austin. It suffices to quote Kirkpatrick Sale's characterization of the meeting: "contentious and unpleasant."[5] The reaction of the local Austin delegates, who were hosting the national council, is instructive. Favoring an emphasis on local autonomy within the national structure, they felt they had no home in the factionalized gathering. Discouraged by both of the two major factions, some of the local radicals actually organized a small walkout. While PL and RYM debated whether the industrial working class or a hoped-for coalition of Vietnamese and African Americans were the real vanguard of the impending revolution, the Texas New Left activists wanted a politics that put them and their concerns front and center. As one longtime Austin SDS activist put it, "'Other'-oriented politics" held no appeal for him. "My basic beliefs haven't changed that much since I first joined SDS," he averred, but the national organization clearly had changed. Whether one views such local sentiment as backward or refreshingly clearheaded, it was indeed out of step with developments in SDS at the national level. The Austin chapter was sufficiently torn that in the aftermath of the July convention it officially declared itself affiliated with both PL's and Weatherman's versions of SDS. Perhaps it was too uninterested by that time to side wholeheartedly with either; this double affiliation was simply a prelude to the chapter's disintegration. The story of SDS's decline and fall seems more poignant at the local level than the national, since the aspirants to national leadership of SDS at this time made themselves forever unlikable.[6]

The loss of SDS was certainly of deep significance to the New Left. SDS had offered a focus for national left-wing attention, a center stage on which national debates over leftist strategy could occur. The possibilities for debate over the proper direction for the American Left thus suffered injury, contributing to the confusion of radicals in the early 1970s. After SDS no longer existed as a national group, it became gradually more difficult for left-wing activists to see each other, and themselves, as members of a coherent national movement. For most of the 1960s, New Left radicals, even when they sharply disagreed, had felt committed to each other and to trying to work together. SDS was the symbol and the vehicle for this cooperation. After 1969, when leftists disagreed about important matters, they were far more likely than before simply to go their separate ways. The organization's demise thus played an important role in the ultimate decline of the movement. Yet this decline was a two-stage process. First SDS cracked and vanished; then, within another five years, the New Left as a social movement scattered to the winds. This in itself suggests that we need to revisit the death of the New Left, and to revise the story's ending so that it accords with our broadened understanding of the New Left and the place of SDS within it.

One measure of the confusion, and indeed the pain, of the immediate post-SDS years for at least some radicals is the difficulty that many people had in coming to terms with the very fact of the New Left's decline. Some, like James O'Brien and Paul Buhle, readily acknowledged the movement's death; they both published obituaries for the New Left in 1972. In their view, with the decline of the ideal of participatory democracy and the atavistic appearance of ersatz Old Left sectarianism among radicals, the New Left as they had come to know it no longer existed; it was, as O'Brien said, "history." Even earlier, in 1969, Carl Oglesby called the 1960s "ready for the dustbin," reflecting his own disappointment in the direction the New Left had taken. He meant his gesture of closure to be descriptive as well as prescriptive.[7]

Yet others continued for years to protest that the New Left had not expired after all. In fact, those who, well after 1969, detected more life yet in the movement were legion. They were generally grassroots activists who saw lively local left-wing coalitions become larger than ever at exactly this time. It is arguable that Oglesby, as a figure of national prominence and a former president of SDS, saw the New Left's demise because he took a top-down view of matters; for him, perhaps, SDS *was* the New Left. Furthermore, many women on the Left, engaged in the project of building a radical feminist movement during the post-1969 years even as they remained engaged in anti-imperialist and other left-wing activism, found this last period of the New Left the most radical and exciting of all. As some historians have asked, why should we not celebrate, rather than lament, developments on the Left around 1970? Certainly the New Left's story was not over at that time, and the suspicion lingers in some quarters that those who did not care for the "decentering" of the New Left wished to close the door, mentally, on the radical movement.[8]

In Austin there was a veritable multitude of people who in 1969 remained deeply interested in left-wing activism of the kind that, until quite recently, had gone forward under the standard of SDS. In their view it was SDS, not they, that had defected from the cause of the New Left. There is no reason to think this was not the case all over the United States. Such people devoted themselves in the following years to anti-imperialist work, women's liberation activity, and the development and maintenance of hip counter-institutions of a stunning variety. Indeed, it was in the post-SDS years that the New Left—always working in an uneasy but productive relationship to the hippie counterculture—built a full-fledged movement culture. In a place like Austin, leftists began to express a self-conscious, at times wry, awareness that they were enacting an ideal they long had held dear of an alternative, dissident way of life. One local wit asked playfully in 1972, "What can I tell you about Austin? This town, this community is so organic people will turn to compost before your very eyes."[9]

It was in the years between 1969 and 1973 that, in many locales around the country, young (and not-so-young) people could, if they wished, almost entirely avoid the majority of the American population uninfluenced by political and cultural radicalism. In the early 1970s radicals most fully lived the lives they long had hoped for, especially if they were in the right places. They almost lived in another country, an alternative America, filled with people of similar commitments and affinities. During these brief years this was, despite the conservative shadows falling over the U.S. political system, fundamentally a hopeful movement culture, seemingly complete unto itself and harboring an aspiration that it might one day overwhelm the mainstream "straight" culture. This alternative America did not, as things turned out, last very long. But while it lasted it was real, and it should not be forgotten. This was the New Left's last phase.

In part because of the tensions that existed within the New Left during its last years, in certain quarters it was—and it has remained—politically charged to talk about the movement's death. Some simply declined to discuss the matter at all during the crucial years of the early 1970s, when the New Left continued during the interval between dispersal and dissolution. This initial reluctance imparted a measure of confusion to some historical accounts of this movement. Although, as already noted, some of the New Left's earliest chroniclers argued unambiguously that the New Left had died in 1969, other historians disagreed. As late as 1973 John Patrick Diggins said merely that the New Left was "presently at a critical juncture in its uncertain career," a comment fascinating for its intellectual uneasiness, coming as it did from a historian not generally known for his hesitant judgment.[10]

Later historians added to the confusion. In the 1980s George Katsiaficas was quite certain the New Left had never ended, since in his view it was in essence a Hegelian spirit rather than a social movement, and as such could not have its existence proved or disproved through empirical examination of its political history.[11] Indeed, the spirit and the political commitments of the New Left were kept alive by a relatively small number of hardy souls throughout the 1970s, 1980s, and 1990s. But this is invariably the case with defunct political movements; there are always surviving believers. An ideology, even with a few remaining caretakers, is not the same as a movement.

In the 1990s Terry H. Anderson occupied an interpretive middle ground. He cited the comment of Richard Flacks, an early SDS leader, around 1970, that "The New Left no longer exists." Flacks clearly had a perspective similar to that of Oglesby and Buhle. At the same time, although Anderson clearly thought there was some basis for this view, he went on to discuss at great length the "second wave" of the 1960s generation, the extensive political and cultural dissent that flowered after the events of 1968 and 1969.[12] And indeed there was a "second wave" of radicalism. To Anderson, however, the New Left in itself was not that important. He saw it as merely one part, and perhaps a fairly small part, of a much broader "movement toward a new America" whose political complexion was far less radical than that of the New Left. If we agree with Anderson and view the New Left as one component of this broader reformist wave, then we might say that the New Left lived on past the early 1970s. Yet the price for retrospectively lengthening the New Left's life span in this way is to sacrifice the distinctive, and distinctively radical, ideology of the New Left. By following Anderson's logic we see a hint of the political ambiguity involved in efforts to read the New Left into contemporary history.

Although not all historians agree about when, how, or even whether the New Left came to an end, a great many recent left-wing commentators agreed that there was no cohesive American Left in the 1990s—which suggests that the New Left did come to an end at some point. If this is the case, then perhaps we can work backward in time from the present, eventually arriving at a point where the New Left seems suddenly present. Martin Duberman, in a blistering 1996 review of Michael Tomasky's book *Left for Dead,* agreed with Tomasky's argument that, in Duberman's paraphrase, "No substantial or unified left exists today. Instead there are disconnected shards."[13] But Duberman evaluated the reasons for this very differently from Tomasky. Todd Gitlin anticipated Tomasky when he wrote in *The Sixties,* "The vision of One Big Movement dissolved into—or, optimists would say, became realized in—distinct interest groups."[14] Duber-

man clearly tended to the "optimistic" side on this question. His review was largely devoted to rebutting Tomasky's contention that "progressives" (to use Tomasky's term,
whose very capaciousness underlines the problem of defining a continuing leftist project in the United States) needed to trim their sails. Yet Duberman's description of the
change after 1969 was essentially the same as Gitlin's. Although questions of evaluation
and interpretation persist, there has been little disagreement on the facts. Indeed, there
has been even more agreement about how to interpret these facts than the customary
polemics of the Left might at first suggest. Duberman sharply criticized those, like
Tomasky and Gitlin, who seemed to call for a fresh embrace of Enlightenment concepts
such as universalism and progress. The gist of Duberman's rebuttal was that we cannot
go back to the left-wing past and we should not wish to if we could. Yet his comment
about "disconnected shards" betrayed an unmistakably elegiac sentiment.

In the mid-1990s there were still more sanguine observers, like Robin D. G. Kelley,
who suggested that this picture of a Left disintegrating in the 1970s into "disconnected
shards" was just empirically wrong. Kelley, like Duberman, heavily criticized the "neo-
Enlightenment" leftist perspective that Gitlin and Tomasky articulated. In fact, he directed his criticism mainly at the prescriptive aspect of the neo-Enlightenment argument. Kelley contended that the declension of the Left from some universalist moral
peak in the mid-1960s was a myth. But this empirical issue was a minor theme in his
discussion. He suggested that even if this change had occurred, he would see no reason
to go back to a neo-Enlightenment project. Thus there is genuine and unambiguous disagreement within the contemporary American Left about the values and vision that a
Left ought to uphold. The central point at issue here, however, is the empirical one:
whether a political change, in any significant way similar to that which Gitlin lamented
and which Duberman acknowledged ambivalently, really occurred in the post-1969
years. Did the American New Left ever really die? Even Kelley, in speaking of "hopeful
signs of movement" on the left and asserting that "radical renewal might actually be on
the horizon," conceded much of this point.[15]

While we can agree that the movement outlived SDS, we should also be able to agree
that the New Left certainly did come to an end. Even if it lacked a unifying organizational framework, the New Left as a social movement, with a self-consciousness of itself as such—as, in its members' rather presumptuous phrase, "the movement"—lin-
gered into the early 1970s all over the United States. In these last years of its existence,
the New Left was largely a white, anti-imperialist, anticapitalist movement with a
strong neoanarchist bent and a very prominent feminist component. This movement's
existence did not end with a bang, but it did end. Certainly there is room for reasonable
argument about where to place that endpoint. January 1973, when the Vietnam War officially ended for the United States, and when the U.S. Supreme Court handed down the
Roe v. Wade decision, is as good a terminus as we can establish. A collective self-consciousness is not so easy a thing to trace into oblivion, but after a certain point it simply is no longer in evidence.

There is little point in debating further whether anything has changed in the shape of
the American Left since the New Left, as a social movement, died. Clearly a momen-

tous change has occurred, yet the question of exactly how to characterize this change remains contested. Was Duberman correct in saying that there is no American Left? Duberman himself seemed to be of two minds even on this point. In the same review, he referred to "the multicultural left," what Henry Louis Gates in 1990 dubbed "the cultural left." Duberman made clear that, in his view, this cultural Left ought to be viewed as the New Left's legatee.[16] John Patrick Diggins, in the recently updated and expanded version of his 1973 book *The American Left in the Twentieth Century*, also argued that out of the "shards" of the New Left there had taken shape by the 1980s the fourth American Left of the twentieth century, primarily within American universities. Unlike Duberman, Diggins tends to think that this academic Left had abandoned the beliefs and goals historically attributed to the Left.[17] Whichever of these contrary views one holds, it is clear that if there indeed has been a cohesive Left in the United States in the last quarter of the twentieth century, it is the fourth American Left of the century—not simply a continuation of the New Left of the 1960s.

What is the shape of left-wing radicalism in twentieth-century America? Has the comforting pattern of rise, decline, and rebirth truly extended to century's end? The question *Is there an American Left?* should encourage us to place the radicalism of the 1960s within a broader historical perspective. The peculiar ending to the story of the New Left is a key to understanding how this movement fits into this larger picture. Upon reflection, it appears that the distinctive ending of the New Left is one of its outstanding features as a twentieth-century American radical movement. Yet the distinguishing quality of its endgame is rarely noted.

Although historians argue over whether there has been another left-wing movement in the United States since the 1960s, they agree that there were three distinct Lefts in the first seven decades of twentieth-century America. These were the "lyrical left" of the century's first two decades, that is, the radicalism of the Industrial Workers of the World (IWW), Eugene Debs, and *The Masses;* the "Old Left," dominated by the Communist party, whose heyday came in the 1930s; and the New Left of the 1960s. Links of personnel and sentiment tied these different eras of radicalism to one another. But despite such intergenerational points of contact, it is widely accepted that sharp historical divisions separated these distinct radical movements. This sense of clear change within the history of the Left has been produced in part by the intellectual, cultural, and political differences of emphasis among these three movements. But the sense of change is also based on the clear perception that each of these Lefts was a social and political movement, and that in each of the gaps separating them, the old movement went away. Both the Old Left and the New Left were new movements that arose to challenge the prevailing political and social formations of their times; neither was simply the old movement regrouping.

To say this is merely to state the rather prosaic point that the lyrical Left and the Old Left each clearly came to an end. No one seriously disputes this. There is little reason to think that left-wing historians are generally unwilling to admit that left-wing movements end. Whence the distinctive treatment of the New Left in this regard? A large part of the explanation can be found in the relatively dramatic ways in which the lyrical Left and the Old Left came to their ends: Each was repressed by means of outright state action. Government at all levels took steps to identify, harass, and persecute those who had taken part in these two social movements (and, in the bargain, many others whose radicalism was questionable or nonexistent also were harmed). In the case of the lyrical Left, the repression was more violent, and the government received strong support from vigilantes in its antiradical efforts. On the other hand, Ellen Schrecker, assembling a wealth of evidence in support of her conclusion, calls the second red scare "the most widespread and longest lasting wave of political repression in American history."[18]

The details of these two red scares are extremely well known to historians, although the second one, often called simply "McCarthyism," remains far more familiar to the American public. Thousands were arrested and imprisoned during and just after World War I for resisting the war or for belonging to radical organizations, and many were maltreated and even tortured. In 1919–20, the IWW was virtually crushed by the government, and this group's members faced yet greater danger from private citizens who formed themselves into lynch mobs looking for radical labor organizers and free-speech activists. Hundreds of members of the immigrant-dominated Left were simply put on a boat and deported to Russia.[19] In the late 1940s and early 1950s, McCarthyite repression against the Old Left was less violent but still extremely effective. Schrecker estimates that perhaps ten thousand Americans lost their jobs because of their political affiliations, activities, and beliefs.[20] The leaders of the Communist Party were tried, convicted, and jailed, under the Smith Act, for having held these positions. In both the first and second red scares, the main organizations of the Left were simply destroyed, and the left-wing agenda was rendered politically illegitimate, dangerous to uphold. The American Left was forced underground.[21]

In the late 1960s and the 1970s, the situation was different. Much has been made, and rightly, of the FBI's COINTELPROs (Counter Intelligence Programs), which infiltrated many radical groups in these years and wreaked havoc through the use of agents provocateurs.[22] My point is not that no repression was visited upon the New Left. But it is important to arrive at an accurate understanding of the extent, purpose, and effects of this coercion. One indication of the limited nature of the coercion directed against the New Left is the difference between the experiences of white and black radicals during these years. Both local police and the FBI suppressed the Black Panther Party, the most notorious example of police violence being the 1969 assassinations of Fred Hampton and Mark Clark in Chicago. The violence used against the American Indian movement was also terrible.[23] However, these groups did not associate themselves with the category of the "New Left" but identified themselves primarily as agents of racial liberation. It was their militance as leaders of subaltern racial minorities, not their leftist politics, that bought them so much trouble.

There can be little question that nonwhite radicals received far harsher treatment than white leftists did. The only white radicals killed by law enforcement officers during the entire era were the four students gunned down at Kent State in 1970. Little-known incidents in Texas, a state quite inhospitable to both leftist radicalism and countercultural activity, support this distinction. In 1970 Carl Hampton, a black activist, was shot and killed by Houston police officers who fired on him from atop a building. While a white radical, George Vizard, was murdered in Austin in 1966, provoking suspicions of assassination and conspiracy, there is little reason to think that either local law enforcement or any organized vigilante group had a hand in his death. In 1967 policemen fired enough bullets into buildings at Texas Southern University—a historically black school and a center for militant black political activity—to make the campus look like a war zone. Nothing like this ever happened in Austin, where white radicals made UT the biggest New Left hotbed in the South. Perhaps the best publicized case of a police vendetta against a political activist in the state was that of Lee Otis Johnson, a radical black organizer in Houston and Austin, who received a thirty-year sentence in 1968 for handing a marijuana cigarette to an undercover policeman. Johnson served seven years in prison. The only comparable case in the state involving a white radical was the persecution of Stoney Burns, editor of the underground newspaper *Dallas Notes*. The Dallas police arrested him several times, to no avail, until they finally succeeded in convicting him of possession of one-twentieth of one ounce of marijuana, which resulted, as with Johnson, in years of jail time.[24]

All this may seem to prove the case for the existence of a government campaign of repression against both white and black radicals. Indeed, at times, white leftists, like African American militants, found themselves the objects both of government coercion and of violent attacks by fellow Americans outraged by political and cultural dissent. But white leftists still had less to fear from agencies of government in this era than black radicals did. The main exception to this rule was the GI antiwar movement, a branch of radical activity whose members were completely at the mercy of the military authorities.[25] On the other hand, white radicals possibly had more to fear from citizens acting in a private capacity than they did from the police, and perhaps were more vulnerable to vigilante attacks than were black radicals. The countercultural accoutrements that New Left radicals shared with hippies—especially long hair on men—routinely provoked harassment and violence by some white men against others, sometimes rather serious violence. Given the persistence of de facto racial segregation, African American activists may have had a bigger margin of safety, among other private citizens with whom they had routine contact, than did white activists, whose fellow whites were not at all likely to support or admire radical dissent.

In any case, the New Left as a movement was not the target of a systematic program, violent or otherwise, aimed at its eradication. In general, the harassment, persecution, and violence that New Left activists experienced seemed to reflect a rather low level of coordination, both among different levels of government and between public and private sources of antiradical sentiment. A comprehensive effort to suppress the Left might still have emanated from the FBI. But even this traditional nemesis was frustrated in its efforts.

J. Edgar Hoover's FBI made the organized New Left an official COINTELPRO target; Hoover took this action in 1968, after the student takeover of buildings at Columbia University.[26] By this time, however, SDS was breaking up. Hoover had devoted extraordinary resources to his decades-long campaign against the Communist Party USA (CP), even to the point where he had enough agents working inside the CP that he considered organizing a factional coup to take over the organization. He had been preoccupied with the CP long after it became an insignificant political entity; and to a great extent he applied this model of observation and infiltration to the New Left (just as he applied it to the Socialist Workers Party). But just as the New Left COINTELPRO was getting started, SDS was losing its leadership role in the larger radical movement. Hoover needed a well-organized left-wing party or organization of national scope in order to apply his model, and in following this path in the years after 1968, he really missed the boat. The FBI's agents provocateurs, like those of local police forces' "red squads," could induce self-destructive and unpopular behavior on the part of sectarian leftist groups; Hoover's men could harass individual leftists and make their lives miserable. But it is difficult to see how a COINTELPRO could destroy a movement that, for the most part, did not fit the FBI's template for left-wing radicalism. If we agree that the New Left went far beyond SDS, it becomes harder to credit the FBI with a central role in its downfall.[27]

Furthermore, radicals and others who opposed the Vietnam War faced plenty of hostility, but nothing like the pervasive harassment and violence that dissenters from World War I confronted. Under both the Johnson and the Nixon administrations, outspoken opponents of the government's war policy were very likely to receive unfriendly attention from the national police and surveillance apparatus, and were the most likely of all activists to appear on the radar screens of top federal officials. The most celebrated political trials of the late 1960s, such as that of the Chicago Eight, stemmed directly from antiwar agitation rather than from radical activity per se. Several of these eight defendants, for example, had been prominent radical agitators for years, but they were tried in federal court only when accused of conspiring to organize the large antiwar demonstrations that occurred outside the Democratic National Convention in Chicago in 1968. They and the movements they helped lead paid a price for this persecution. Yet the defendants won acquittal on the conspiracy charge, and higher courts effectively nullified their other convictions, including numerous contempt citations, by the end of 1973. These activists were never incarcerated for any extended period of time.[28] The Smith Act defendants, by contrast, saw their convictions upheld by the U.S. Supreme Court and went to prison for several years, an interval during which the communist movement withered, before a somewhat altered Court reconsidered their cases.[29] The prosecutorial hand of the government lay heavily upon some leaders of the movement against the Vietnam War, but it was far gentler than what earlier leftists had felt in the World War I era and during the McCarthy years. In addition, although antiwar protesters were routinely harassed and often physically assaulted by pro-war counterdemonstrators on college campuses and elsewhere, antiwar organizers did not routinely have to fear for their very lives during the Vietnam War, unlike their predecessors during World War I.

In contrast to the second red scare, government investigations in the late 1960s and 1970s rarely and with slight effect probed the politics of American citizens to uncover incriminating leftist affiliations. This was the case, perhaps, because such affiliations would not have proved incriminating at all, as they had during the 1950s. The youth demonstrations against the House Un-American Activities Committee (HUAC) in San Francisco in 1960, and the ensuing outrage over the police brutality visited upon these protesters, struck a great blow against HUAC's credibility as an instrument of fear. The documentary film that captured this clash, *Operation Abolition,* was widely seen on university campuses in the following years and did more to inspire derision and opposition to the committee than to shore up support for HUAC's mission, as had been the filmmakers' intention. By 1966 Jerry Rubin ridiculed HUAC's inability to intimidate citizens any more. Subpoenaed to appear before the committee, Rubin arrived dressed as a Continental Army soldier and gleefully admitted his revolutionary intentions. As Stephen Whitfield tells the story, Abbie Hoffman wore a shirt with an American flag motif when appearing before the committee, enraging spectators; he then proceeded to tear off his shirt, revealing a Cuban flag painted on his skin.[30]

The spirit of conformity that McCarthyites had established in the 1950s had come to be seen as the quintessential feature of the mainstream culture that the nation's young were rebelling against. By the late 1960s HUAC was not simply scorned; its mission of policing American citizens' politics seemed beneath contempt, an object of mockery. Furthermore, HUAC in its heyday had used blacklisting as its major tool for extracting obeisance. In the years of economic growth and affluence that followed, when radicals rejected careerism and celebrated voluntary poverty, the authorities could not hope to achieve their goals by threatening the middle-class lifestyle or social status of dissidents. In an era when the raised middle finger became a symbol of political and cultural dissent, government officials certainly could not hope to curb dissent by threatening to undermine radicals' sense of "respectability."

For the second half of the twentieth century, the pattern of repression visited upon left-wing movements was one of decreasing severity. Arguably this trend holds true for the entire century, since the first red scare was more violent than any since; but that point is debatable, given the efficacy of the repressive measures involved in the second red scare. Perhaps this pattern of diminishing brutality should give heart to those who believe that our society has gradually become a more tolerant one.

The matter is, of course, not so simple. Many historians have come to agree that in the earlier decades of the twentieth century, much more so than later, the United States as a society actually faced a wider array of real choices about the political, social, and economic direction the country might take. There are plenty of explanations for this gradual narrowing of the scope of political discussion and choice. For our purposes it is perhaps sufficient to note merely that political tolerance does not in itself make for a vigorous, pluralistic political culture. There are even, we might say, different kinds of tolerance, as well as different degrees. In the 1960s Herbert Marcuse theorized that tolerance can actually prove more repressive than coercion in its effects.[31] In spite of the virtually universal derision with which this idea was met, there remains at least a germ of truth in Marcuse's argument. The legitimacy not only of leftist ideas but of liberalism as well declined precipitously in the years following 1973 or so, and it had not made a comeback by the century's end. But the most important reasons for this have nothing to do with coercion.

The characteristic beliefs, commitments, and ideals—both social and personal—of the New Left have lived on, in the hearts and minds of a good many Americans, in the years since the New Left as a movement ended. Some commentators may yet manifest confusion about this matter. But historians of recent America, and particularly of radicalism and of social movements, ought to clarify this distinction—between the New Left as a political outlook and the New Left as a social movement—in order to dispel any remaining uncertainty about the chronology of the 1960s endgame. Possibly the ambiguity and disagreement on this subject arise because the end of the New Left does not follow the pattern of earlier incarnations of the American Left. The strength and breadth of the New Left as a social movement, which recent historical work has appreciated anew, insured that the New Left's denouement was somewhat different, somewhat novel. A political movement that sought to enact participatory democracy could frustrate some of the best laid plans of presidents and policemen.

Notes

Acknowledgments: This essay has its origins in a paper delivered at the annual meeting of the Organization of American Historians in Toronto, Ontario, in 1999. I wish to thank all those who participated in this session for their comments.

1. See especially Todd Gitlin, *The Sixties: Years of Hope, Days of Rage* (New York: Bantam Books, 1987), chap. 1; Van Gosse, *Where the Boys Are: Cuba, Cold War America, and the Making of a New Left* (London: Verso, 1993); and Maurice Isserman, *"If I Had a Hammer . . .": The Death of the Old Left and the Birth of the New Left* (New York: Basic Books, 1987). Doug Rossinow, *The Politics of Authenticity: Liberalism, Christianity, and the New Left in America* (New York: Columbia University Press, 1998), chaps. 1–4, also discusses these matters.

2. Kirkpatrick Sale, *SDS* (New York: Random House, 1973); Irwin Unger, *The Movement: A History of the American New Left, 1959–1972* (New York: Dodd, Mead, 1974).

3. Andrew E. Hunt, *The Turning: A History of Vietnam Veterans against the War* (New York: New York University Press, 1999). Also see Hunt's essay in this volume.

4. See Rossinow, *The Politics of Authenticity*, 203–4. The student was Jeff Jones (no relation to Weatherman Jeff Jones).

5. Sale, *SDS*, 537.

6. Rossinow, *The Politics of Authenticity*, 205–6.

7. James O'Brien, "Beyond Reminiscence: The New Left as History," *Radical America* 6 (July–Aug. 1972); Paul Buhle, "The Eclipse of the New Left: Some Notes," *Radical America* 6 (July–Aug. 1972); Carl Oglesby, "Notes on a Decade Ready for the Dustbin," *Liberation* 14 (Aug.–Sept. 1969).

8. Winifred Breines has been most clear on this point. See Winifred Breines, "Whose New Left?" *Journal of American History* 75 (1988), 528–45. Also see Alice Echols, "'We Gotta Get Out of This Place': Notes toward a Remapping of the Sixties," *Socialist Review* 22 (Apr.–June 1992), 9–33. Rossinow, *The Politics of Authenticity*, chap. 8, documents the persistence of leftist activism among radical feminists in the post-1968 period.

9. Rossinow, *The Politics of Authenticity*, 291.

10. John Patrick Diggins, *The American Left in the Twentieth Century* (New York: Harcourt Brace Jovanovich, 1973), 195. This comment, rather uncertain and hesitant itself, seemed at odds with Diggins's preceding discussion of the various factors in the New Left's dissolution over the previous five years; see 176–86.

11. George Katsiaficas, *The Imagination of the New Left: A Global Analysis of 1968* (Boston: South End Press, 1987).

12. Terry H. Anderson, *The Movement and the Sixties: Protest in America from Greensboro to Wounded Knee* (New York: Oxford University Press, 1995), 290.

13. Martin Duberman, "Bring Back the Enlightenment," review of Michael Tomasky, *Left for Dead: The Life, Death, and Possible Resurrection of Progressive Politics in America* (New York: Free Press, 1996), *The Nation* (1 July 1996), 25.

14. Gitlin, *The Sixties*, 422.

15. Robin D. G. Kelley, "Identity Politics and Class Struggle," *New Politics* 6 (winter 1997), 1 (electronic version available at <http://www.wilpaterson.edu/~newpol.issue22/kelley22.htm>). This is a vigorous and extensive rejoinder to Tomasky and Gitlin.

16. Duberman, "Bring Back the Enlightenment"; Henry Louis Gates Jr., "The Master's Pieces: On Canon Formation and the African-American Tradition," *South Atlantic Quarterly* 89 (winter 1990): 89. Also see the response to Gates (and others) by Richard Rorty, "Two Cheers for the Cultural Left," *South Atlantic Quarterly* 89 (winter 1990): 227–34.

17. John Patrick Diggins, *The Rise and Fall of the American Left* (New York: Norton, 1992), 279–98. The new title, of course, expresses Diggins's own ambivalence on this point.

18. Ellen Schrecker, *Many Are the Crimes: McCarthyism in America* (Boston: Little, Brown, 1998), x. Schrecker summarizes the devastating and remarkably pervasive effects of McCarthyism on U.S. political culture in chap. 10.

19. Two-hundred forty-nine were deported via the *Buford* in December 1919. Five-hundred ninety-one others were deported in 1920 and 1921. About five thousand arrest warrants, intended to lead to deportation, were drawn up in late 1919 and early 1920; about three thousand of them were used. Robert K. Murray, *Red Scare: A Study of National Hysteria, 1919–1920* (Minneapolis: University of Minnesota Press, 1955), 206–9, 251. On the deportations generally see William Preston Jr., *Aliens and Dissenters: Federal Suppression of Radicals, 1903–1933* (Cambridge: Harvard University Press, 1963), 181–207. Helen C. Camp notes that Preston counts only twenty-seven Wobblies deported by the U.S. government in these years (assuming, I think, that none was aboard the *Buford*), but she argues that this number is too low. Compare Preston, *Aliens and Dissenters*, 206 and Helen C. Camp, *Iron in Her Soul: Elizabeth Gurley Flynn and the American Left* (Pullman: Washington State University Press, 1995), 92.

20. Ellen Schrecker, *The Age of McCarthyism: A Brief History with Documents* (New York: St. Martin's Press, 1994), 92.

21. Richard Flacks, *Making History: The American Left and the American Mind* (New York: Columbia University Press, 1988), argues that these underground avenues have been the American Left's strongest means of influencing American culture and society.

22. See Ward Churchill and Jim Vander Wall, *The COINTELPRO Papers: Documents from the FBI's Secret Wars against Dissent in the United States* (Boston: South End Press, 1990).

23. See David Farber, *The Age of Great Dreams: America in the 1960s* (New York: Hill and Wang, 1994), 207–9, on violence directed at (and by) the Black Panthers.

24. Rossinow, *The Politics of Authenticity*, 175–76, 200, 180.

25. Ibid., 231–32.

26. Churchill and Vander Wall, *The COINTELPRO Papers*, 176. I should note than Churchill and Vander Wall take a very different view, arguing that the FBI deserves a great deal of the credit for the death of the New Left. See esp. 165–230.

27. Athan Theoharis, *Spying on Americans: Political Surveillance from Hoover to the Huston Plan* (Philadelphia: Temple University Press, 1978), 57, notes that top FBI personnel were aware of the difficulties that the peculiar nature of the New Left presented to the bureau's surveillance and disruption techniques. Yet the FBI still had difficulty changing to meet this challenge. Still, we should note those adjustments the bureau did make. In 1971 J. Edgar Hoover altered the FBI's criteria for listing individuals on an index of those to be interned during national emergencies (a contingency plan that the FBI had developed and used since 1939, and whose existence became widely known only in the 1970s). According to these new criteria, "Membership in 'old line revolutionary organizations' no longer need be established; bureau investigations could henceforth concentrate on the 'new breed of subversive individual.'" Ibid., 61–62.

28. See Marty Jezer, *Abbie Hoffman: American Rebel* (New Brunswick: Rutgers University Press, 1992), 208–9; and J. Anthony Lukas, *The Barnyard Epithet and Other Obscenities: Notes on the Chicago Conspiracy Trial* (New York: Harper and Row, 1970).

29. In 1950 the U.S. Supreme Court upheld the Smith Act convictions in the *Dennis* case; Chief Justice Fred Vinson's decision explicitly cited international affairs and national security (rather than the law and factual statements about the defendants' actions) as the basis for this decision (Schrecker, *Many Are the Crimes*, 199–200). Only in 1956 and 1957 did a set of Supreme Court decisions narrow and effectively cripple the Smith Act as a tool of political repression. The convictions of the Chicago Seven (Bobby Seale having been severed from the case), for having crossed state lines with intent to riot, in addition to their contempt citations, never reached this level of the federal judiciary, so weak was the perceived case against them and so outrageous Judge Julius Hoffman's courtroom conduct.

30. Stephen Whitfield, *The Culture of the Cold War*, 2d ed. (Baltimore: Johns Hopkins University Press, 1996), 125; Gitlin, *The Sixties*, 233. Jezer, *Abbie Hoffman*, 113, 186. Jezer does not mention a Cuban flag on Hoffman's skin in his discussion of the flag-shirt incident.

31. Herbert Marcuse, "Repressive Tolerance," in Robert Paul Wolff, Barrington Moore Jr., and Herbert Marcuse, *A Critique of Pure Tolerance* (Boston: Beacon Press, 1965).

Afterword

About the Contributors

AFTERWORD

How Sweet It Wasn't: The Scholars and the CIA

Paul Buhle

What accounts for the often derided irrationality of the New Left, its stubborn unwillingness to place itself on the side of modest reformers and thereby to pilot liberalism's glory epoch past troubles encountered along the way? The image of the bright and brimming America of the dawning 1960s, full of promise that young radicals would build up further and then devastate with their shenanigans (borderline homosexual "spoiled brats who posed as revolutionaries while being subsidized by their parents," in the phrasing of a *New York Times* writer),[1] remains a liberal publicist's vision, half-endorsed by the memoirs of early movement leaders and reiterated by successive generations of interpreters.[2] As the writers in this volume suggest, it is arguably the largest and least challenged generalization about the radical politics of the 1960s.

The argument has long been made, and continues to be made, against the young. Those sincere Democrats and liberal academics were needlessly alienated, their dreams and constructive plans for a more just America lost, thanks to the terrorization of the campus and political life at large—not by National Guardsmen or cops, omnipresent FBI informers or administrators determined to placate the regents, but by antiwar demonstrations, by the (largely nonviolent) occupations of campus buildings, and by the sympathy that young people expressed for the Vietnamese under fire and for the parallel African American uprisings—surprisingly mild after centuries of slavery and oppression. More than thirty years since 1970 and twenty years since Ronald Reagan's election as president, the sins of 1960s radicals somehow seem to outweigh any mistakes that the nation committed abroad or on the home front.

The retrospective vindication of America's policy in Vietnam continues to present a hard sell. But the notion that students had the right to take action against the universities' collaboration in Cold War projects against Third World populations—most specifically high-tech wars and neocolonial economic programs aimed against little nations—

is often described as an intolerable affront to true academic freedom. Thus at Stanford University, locus of the Hoover Institute, that cerebral inaugurator of the Reagan Revolution, something so apparently democratic as the students' insistence on voting for their own representatives to a campus-wide committee in 1967 assessing the research university's basic purposes (rather than accepting the ones hand-picked by the administration), continues to be shown as proof beyond doubt of the terrible unreason of the young. How could prestigious administrators seriously be asked to discuss openly, let alone impede, the flow of corporate and intelligence dollars that had so transformed campus life and the sources of campus politics since the 1940s?[3]

The question is rhetorical, the possibility that undergraduates, graduates, and their professorial allies (guilty, as Irving Howe put it without irony, of "whoring with the students") might actually be defending the purposes of the university against corruption and takeover not even worthy of consideration. And so the monologue continues in the halls of respectable opinion, conservatives and a large swath of liberals firmly united against nostalgic memories of presumptuous young people and dangerously unsettled times.

Today's educational reform movements, such as unionization of teaching assistants or regularization of jobs for desperately underpaid adjuncts—changes earnestly sought from below and just as ferociously resisted from above—continue to raise the same basic issues of prerogative. (So does the student movement against corporate globalization, in which demonstrators have recently been invited to present "alternative" views —but not to take part in the decision-making process.) Whether by technocratic administrators or by professors horrified at the return of building occupations and the prospect of graduate students bargaining collectively, campus propriety has once more been defined as acceptance of the existing order. That order itself, meanwhile, continues to be defined, increasingly so, by direct corporate intervention and conservative foundations along with the high-flying entrepreneurial profs. In a circle-the-wagons narrative that once more depicts students as the howling redskins in the delicate ecology of higher learning, today's embattled innovators of modern education soldier bravely onward, awaiting perhaps the bugle call of the cavalry (read: a better job) or at least the dean of students with disciplinary threats in hand.

The seemingly endless hue and cry against the 1960s student movement has in recent years been amplified by accounts pointedly sympathetic to the moderate versions of social democracy that—like the technocratic liberalism of university officials—reveal the perverseness of anyone who would think of sabotaging historic moments of such great promise. In a reclamation of 1950s "Lib-Lab" themes by philosopher Richard Rorty, for instance, the labor movement under George Meany had nearly delivered unto American society "the world's first classless society"—and then that darned Vietnam War came along.

Everything might still have come out all right, and the campus youngsters would have found their (subordinate) place within the grand coalition. But there was something deeply wrong with the young radicals. Traumatically for the whole destiny of the nation (and perhaps the world), the foulmouthed students spitting at Vietnam veterans "lost the respect and the sympathy of union members," thus "unthinkingly destroy[ing] an alliance that was central to American leftist politics."[4] The audience listening to Rorty's ruminations at the Columbia University labor-student teach-in of 1996 booed the speaker roundly, and with good reason: He had come to attack student activism on its own grounds and to defend past labor thuggery, when one might have expected him to congratulate the labor reformers who had overturned the machine and successfully attracted today's college students. But these claims, so characteristic of Rorty's widely read essays and interviews in recent years, nevertheless deserve close attention. We might properly call them the summa of horror narratives about the student movements of the 1960s.

First in the list of Rorty's bizarre claims is surely the idealism attributed to the deeply corrupt and energetically gay-baiting Meany (he told reporters that New York's McGovern delegates were "a bunch of fairies"), who dedicated a large part of his career precisely to uprooting "leftist politics" within the labor movement. Like other labor leaders of the time (with precious few exceptions), Meany viewed the war in Vietnam as the great test of American will, and would not have despised students any less if they had conducted their protests like perfect ladies and gentlemen. From a historical standpoint, Rorty also conveniently ignores the nature of Meany's rule of the AFL-CIO (1955–89), which was characterized by the sharp division of distant, obscenely paid union officials from an increasingly and understandably disillusioned union membership. Further, in pointing to the horrible student radicals "spitting at Vietnam veterans," Rorty determinedly joined the familiar antistudent mythmaking of the 1960s. As other scholars have convincingly demonstrated, this grave insult never actually took place and was just one more invention of rightward drifting (Democratic as well as Republican) editorialists for the credulous, obviously including the philosopher himself.[5] But the defeat of liberalism from 1968 onward had to be somebody's fault, and if liberals were innocent and no communist conspiracy could be discovered, then, for Rorty at any rate, the New Left and its assorted allies must be to blame.

Behind Rorty's blatantly inaccurate account can be found the most basic sources of disconnection between the New Left, its left-wing predecessors, and the hopes for a wider set of alliances than the circumstances of the 1960s permitted. Since at least the mid-1930s and arguably long before, the participation of organized labor has been crucial to the strength and also the tilt of any liberal coalition. Indeed, the very first PAC was created by the Congress of Industrial Organizations in order to offset corporate donations to the Republicans and to intensify working-class support for Franklin Roosevelt. One of the chief triumphs of Harry Truman's Cold War democracy lay in housebreaking the unions: Purged of those elements most aggressive in community mobilization, they became what Truman's supporters wanted—a safely top-heavy special interest group mobilized not for controversial strikes or organizing drives but for political lobbying at election time. Communists in particular were targeted by FBI agents and congressional investigating committees, by organizations of labor's Catholic conservatives, by local red squads, and by the tabloids. But others who resisted the bureaucratization of labor were swept away almost as efficiently.

The process was never completed, especially at middle and lower levels, and it is important to our story to recall that thousands of unionists supported the civil rights movement, just as thousands protested the war in Vietnam, opposed environmental degradation, and were sympathetic to women and homosexuals. These were exactly the union members who offered experience and advice to the younger activists who finally overthrew the labor oligarchy in 1995. Different choices might have been made long before, and in this one interpretive detail of the 1960s Rorty is correct—but from the wrong side of the potential coalition. To imagine the 1960s AFL-CIO joining up with peace demonstrators, feminists, gay activists, environmentalists, and black, brown, red, or yellow liberationists is truly to imagine a different outcome of the decade, certainly for labor and the Left, perhaps for the United States and the suffering world. That this happy prospect didn't materialize had absolutely nothing to do with students' language or their inappropriate behavior.

If the crisis of liberal intellectual life during the later 1960s opened up American thought to fresh and threatening ideas, making the university a vastly more interesting place, labor's solidly bureaucratic institutions prevented a parallel breakdown of order and effectively blocked assorted progressive movements, including the New Left, from mobilizing labor on a massive scale. The rebellious working-class constituency so visible in the GI antiwar mobilization (and so often invisible among the younger, dope-smoking, antiwar union members)—emphatically including emboldened minority and women members and Vietnam vets—was never allowed to reach its student counterparts. There lies the real tragedy of the epoch.

The subsequent "rainbow" coalition that sections of labor, militant minorities, women's liberationists, environmentalists, and students sought to construct during later decades, with limited and but sometimes impressive electoral success, thereby lacked a crucial element. Today's campus activists, reawakened to the importance of labor issues on a global scale, could have played a crucial role had they been present thirty years ago, when young radicals had more energy and more bodies to contribute to labor causes than they would for the rest of the century. The "Teamsters and Turtles" coalition at the anti-WTO protests in Seattle in 1999, and the subsequent protests against the World Bank and the International Monetary Fund, which included a significant labor contingent, further dramatize how dangerous this alliance would have been to the corporate agenda in the 1960s. There was nothing that George Meany would not have done, and little that he did not do—protecting unions against affirmative action, sabotaging the 1963 March on Washington, attacking gay and women's liberation—to stop such a potential coalition in its tracks.

We have far to go in understanding the connected systems of power underlying intellectual life and the labor movement. But the changes in labor leadership since 1995 and the accompanying "retirement" of intelligence operatives from the labor movement's global apparatus may allow fresh insights into the sources of left-of-center disunity.[6] And recent revelations of collusion between leading American intellectuals and the heavily funded projects of intelligence agencies offer especially valuable sources for further discussion.[7]

At the risk of overloading the conceptual agenda, one more piece of argument is crucial here. Consumerism and popular culture, it has been persuasively argued, were the real victors of the twentieth century. In the popular formulation, America's establishment intellectuals so despised both communism and television that they were thoroughly flummoxed when television overcame communism in Eastern Europe and bid fair to do so elsewhere. These militantly highbrow Cold War liberals had utterly disdained mass culture since the 1930s, by that means defining their avant-garde status. Their counterparts, the communist-connected denizens of the Popular Front, had meanwhile been crucially implicated in large zones of popular culture as actors, directors, writers, singers, musicians, and audience, sometimes right through the 1960s, from Aaron Copland and Pete Seeger to Arthur Miller and Martin Ritt. The New Left, who had virtually no understanding of these contrasted or warring histories, and whose counterculture was far from folksy Popular Frontism, nevertheless looked suspiciously pop, at least to the suspicious-minded liberal savants.

So the framework was set for misunderstanding—unless it was not misunderstanding at all. Taken together, additional fresh sources provide a crucial context for reinterpreting the skepticism of the young 1960s radicals and their subsequent scholarly allies toward presumed betters—entirely apart from the stimulating effects of LSD and premarital sex. New Leftists have their own history, now being filled in at last. But they also had an opposition whose considerable strengths beyond the power of ideas we are only beginning to understand. The notions of denial and deniability, not unfamiliar but rarely used in public since the Iran-Contra scandals, reopen fascinating terms for the adventures of respectables in assorted off-the-books projects, operating in purported defense of open society and the freedoms that the campus movements have so frequently been charged with endangering.[8]

The self-confidence that once lay behind liberalism's framework can be usefully traced to the 1950s and early 1960s climate of seemingly successful institution building, to the theories and the self-interpreted political role of the intellectuals themselves. The optimistic sense that the major issues of American society had been settled, and that a kind of meritocratic elite had emerged to fulfill post–New Deal visions, underlay the liberal and institutional labor shock at the appearance of the New Left. The larger meaning of the clash had, in my view, quite as much impact as the actual events of the 1960s upon the apparent collapse of liberalism into the more conservative consensus of the 1980s–90s. The horrors of Vietnam merely dramatized the workings of bipartisan U.S. policy in many parts of the Third World; the appearance of assorted racial liberation movements underlined larger issues of the society, as the women's movement (and later the gay movement) revealed the impossibility of continuing to live by existing norms.

By accepting many of the conservative positions of earlier decades, by ruling out serious redistribution of power, and by loyally supporting the arms race and the military-industrial economy, establishment liberals came to believe that they had achieved a sort of hegemony, or at least a proper balance with the Right. The Eisenhower years were dull but far from unsatisfying to labor leaders and up-and-coming intellectuals. The

Kennedy victory of 1960 promised nirvana, their eagerly awaited moment in the sun. They continued a jolly public battle with conservatives, each side careful—in those days of congenial congressional politics—not to go too far. The Goldwater campaign of 1964 threw liberals into a momentary panic. But any serious challenge from the Left to the post–New Deal liberal worldview of that day, especially a Left that could not be derided as communist and thereby driven from public life, was likely to inspire an intellectual and institutional Armageddon.

Liberals may have deceived themselves about American democracy and its global role, as a recent sympathetic reinterpretation suggests.[9] But the most prestigious and influential among them were far more than willing victims. A moment after cursing the New Left's irreverent attitude toward accepted symbols of propriety, Richard Rorty once more hailed the days when "academics like Daniel Bell, Arthur Schlesinger, Jr. and John Kenneth Galbraith worked side by side with labor leaders like Walter Reuther and A. Philip Randolph."[10] Side by side, indeed: All but Galbraith and Randolph in this short list were working in covertly funded CIA-based operations, and the brave old black crusader himself was en route to becoming one of the CIA's favorite labor assets, along with Bayard Rustin, during their respective declining years.[11]

Why should we care about the sources of their funds and connections now that (since the dawn of the Reagan years) conservative foundations openly sponsor all sorts of projects and successfully back candidates for Republican cabinets? The answer is deceptively simple: because utmost secrecy was deemed so vital by the participants themselves and their government handlers.[12] Thomas Braden, the CIA's most candid official, put it this way to a sympathetic interviewer, describing Meany's flat-footed denials in 1967 of agency operations within labor: "For Meany to have admitted CIA money would have absolutely ruined the AFL. . . . Meany also would have been regarded as an absolute scoundrel by his closest European allies." Fortunately, Braden concluded, Meany "had the persona to carry this off."[13]

So, obviously, did intellectuals around the British-based *Encounter* and its U.S. counterparts, the *New Leader, Partisan Review,* and *The Public Interest,* each of these journals of opinion institutionally supported and one (*The Public Interest*) actually launched with heavy CIA participation. A. H. Raskin and Sidney Hertzberg of the *New York Times,* Elliot Cohen of *Commentary,* Max Ascoli of the *Reporter,* art critic Clement Greenberg, novelists James T. Farrell and Saul Bellow, poet Delmore Schwartz, academics Arthur Schlesinger Jr., Walter Laquer, Edward Shils, Sidney Hook, David Riesman, Daniel Bell, Nathan Glazer, Lionel and Diana Trilling, political operatives like Irving Kristol and future Americans for Democratic Action (ADA) leader John Roche—not to mention European luminaries Isaiah Berlin, Raymond Aron, and Iganzio Silone—were only the most prominent among dozens who occupied considerable status as figures in the CIA's pet Congress for Cultural Freedom and its U.S. counterpart, the American Committee for Cultural Freedom (ACCF).[14] Altogether, it looks a great deal like the enthroned intellectual elite of an age, rule-makers and gatekeepers for what troubled campus observers called the "Silent Generation" but others more acidly dubbed the "Silenced Generation."

For thirty years secret intelligence outlets dispensed large quantities of cash, arranged sumptuous global junkets, offered participants highly useful personal connections and heightened reputations. As Jason Epstein of the *New York Review of Books* observed in 1967, this constituted altogether a carefully programmed alternative to the supposed intellectual free market, an institutionalized "system of values" of personal advancement based on quiet allegiance. It is fair to say that nothing later managed by the right-wing Olin or Scaife Foundations, the Hoover Institution, or Rupert Murdoch has had the public credibility or liberal panache of the original game. For that matter, the transition from intelligence funds to conservative corporate funds was, strictly speaking, a continuation of the original process, and it was watched over by some of the same leading personalities, especially Irving Kristol. The original personalities faded and the Cold War ended eventually, but the influence—and the celebration—of the luminaries continues on and on, sometimes now as a family enterprise, through highly placed sons and sons-in-law, mostly conservatives but some (like Rorty himself) true-to-the-Cold War liberals.[15]

Of all the figures cited so far, Arthur Schlesinger Jr. was the most influential player. As the first volume of his memoirs suggests, he gained his political identity within the Office of Strategic Services (OSS) during the Second World War. An odd venue that included numerous left-wingers (including philosopher Herbert Marcuse and future film noir master Abraham Lincoln Polonsky), the OSS subtly shifted direction during the last years of war, turning against partisans who risked their lives behind enemy lines while extending sympathy and assistance to anticommunists, like the Vichy French officials who happened to be fascist collaborators at the time but also saw the end of the Axis coming.[16] The CIA, officially born in the Truman years, was already operating much as it would later, with some of its liberal operatives and allies firmly in place.

Schlesinger, designated by *Life* magazine in 1946 a foremost "expert" on American communism, set out to drive Cold War opponents from unions and liberal organizations, foreshadowing U.S. global policy in the postwar years by urging expanded armed forces during peacetime, military intervention abroad, and even the tactical use of atomic weapons if necessary. He was, Frances Stonor Sanders notes, a major "source, consultant (if not a paid one), a friend, a trusted colleague to [top CIA staffers] Frank Wisner, Allen Dulles and Cord Meyer. He corresponded with all of them, over more than two decades. . . . He was even helping the CIA get coverage for the themes it wanted airing" in mainstream newspapers and magazines.[17] With his advice and guidance, the CIA brought the Congress for Cultural Freedom into prominence.

Schlesinger's grand political polemic, *The Vital Center* (1949), laid out the technocratic justification for these moves. He condemned society's "sentimentalists, the utopians, the wailers," that is to say, the old-fashioned radicals, destined to be cast aside by "the politicians, the administrators, the doers."[18] This was, in a nutshell, the central notion of Cold War liberalism. Postindustrial society, more liberal than conservative in its origins, had its origins in the operations of universities and institutes then sprouting up on all sides, with government funding on a scale previously unimaginable. Liberal sentiment, moving away from the 1930s–40s era of labor radicalism, was perhaps naturally inclined to view the technocratic energy of the new liberal middle class as the driving force of the change.

The leading thinkers and functionaries had thus effectively, and with a significance hardly appreciated or even acknowledged in those years, taken crucial issues of income distribution off the table. The unwanted legacy of the 1930s and the Popular Front had apparently been conquered in the United States, save for a discredited fringe of intellectuals, labor, and African American activists cast out of the mainstream. But in ravaged Europe and even more in the emerging nations, threats of unruliness remained, including in the realm of culture, where veterans of the Resistance still had prestige and used it to urge some kind of diplomatic neutralism between the great powers, and eventually a postcapitalist order.[19] America would therefore need to lead the world—as the intellectuals led the nation—meanwhile substituting the expansion of "social services" for class resentment and the threat of class warfare.

This perspective, perfected more completely in the multiversity and the armed forces than in most branches of government and the less flexible corporate apparatus, swept more under the rug than economic inequality. The prospects for all-out nuclear war continued to rise steadily with the arms race, the threat of doomsday scenarios nearly realized in the 1960–61 crises over Berlin and Cuba.[20] But the fault could nearly always be displaced outward. If the most important early role of the Congress for Cultural Freedom (CCF) was the ardent support for the CIA's blood-drenched overthrow of the Guatemalan agrarian-reform Arbenz regime in 1953, its intellectuals were hard at work in the Kennedy years, rationalizing an aggressive "New Frontier" foreign policy involving assassinations and coups, along with the usual economic and political pressures on other nations. To do otherwise, as doubting professors and freelance radicals were often reminded, would undercut the social engineering projects on the home front.

Meanwhile, America's global empire remained the fundamental basis for winning the loyalty of the world's population. In real life, if not in liberal theory, the modest advances toward racial integration at home, continuously hailed as proof positive of good intentions and steady progress, barely affected the rising trajectory of inner-city poverty except to redefine it, in Moynihanesque terms, as no fault of the liberal power elite.[21] With the blessing of social science the government shifted the resources of hard-pressed cities to subsidize the infrastructure of emerging (largely whites-only) suburbs by underlining the hopelessness of those left behind.[22]

These developments were not, until the outbreak of ghetto uprisings, viewed as especially troubling. The most sophisticated social observers had practically abolished the old discourse on democracy in any case. As the redistribution of wealth had been discredited as policy, so was any large-scale redistribution of power from an elite to "the people." Yale sociologist Robert Dahl frankly concluded in *Who Governs?*—one of the landmark studies of the day—that actual majority rule did not and probably could not work in America, but something nearly as good had already been set in place. The "rule of minorities" exerting their influence on electoral politics ensured inclusion of all the important interests, including ethnic blocs and, of course, local business. Democracy could not be reasonably expected to do more.[23]

John Kenneth Galbraith added that the power of property was fast being overtaken by the power of the corporate officeholder in any case, so that the very meaning of profits had been transformed into future holdings. These claims echoed the arguments of Daniel Bell and others that America had already entered the era of "mixed economy," and that bad old capitalism had given way to a more benevolent, results-oriented mixture of corporate leaders and skilled specialists (including a cooperative stratum of labor leaders) together ushering in a well-functioning society and a proper model for the world.

This is not to say that the politics of "abundance" lacked critics. Behind the combination of optimism and irony in Galbraith's *The Affluent Society* (1958) could be felt a moral uncertainty about the effects of automation. More acute or pessimistic observers, unable to predict a vastly expanding service economy of low-wage jobs, accurately painted grim visions of vanishing well-paid industrial work. The impending crisis of too much "leisure" suggested untold psychological disorientation in the twenty-five- or even fifteen-hour work week to which the masses could allegedly look forward. Mass culture, feeding off the power of the media and the tastelessness of the average consumer, would swallow both art and culture. This was hardly what the optimistic savants had in mind.[24]

The defense of high culture indeed highlighted the cultural legacy of the 1950s, whose leading post–Popular Front and pre–New Left nemesis could be summed up in a single word (coined by Daniel Bell's friend Irving Howe): "conformism." Bell had complained to ACCF leaders in 1952 that "the drift toward conformity is observable in all cultural areas." He was careful, however, not to blame either business or government as such; "bureaucratic stupidity," a modern state of mind, was the most likely culprit.[25] A *sine qua non* for intellectual independence from mass society, the idea of conformity quickly gained totemic influence through works like David Riesman's *The Lonely Crowd* (1950), and just as quickly wore thin through the over-popularization of psychological themes in middlebrow fiction, films, and television. The fretting about suburban-style sameness was the precursor of an almost unbounded rage at youthful tastes and behavior.[26]

In the climate of curiously muted social criticism, the constrained ambivalence of Bell's *The End of Ideology* (1960) was greeted as one of the most provocative works of the era. A collection of Bell's essays portraying a noncapitalist or postcapitalist order in which the classic conditions of the market no longer existed, it also suggested somewhat ominously that if social problems were deeply moral in character, technocrats could not hope to solve them.[27]

In its title as well as its contents, *The End of Ideology* ironically secured Bell's reputation as a 1950s-style thinker unsettled, if not actually disproved, by subsequent developments. At the first glimpse of the emerging, increasingly rebellious popular culture of young people, Bell and his colleagues found an anti-solution, a very devil in the flesh. By undermining authority, weakening the posture of the West against the still dangerous communist ideologies, by unbalancing stable relations between parents and children, likewise between men and women, the proto–New Left infected the society with something as bad as Marxism, perhaps even worse for an otherwise stable and capitalistic America.

If the civil rights movement had little impact on Bell's theories, the peace movement and above all the campus restlessness was to all but a repentant few of the CCF/ACCF intellectuals the very proof of mass irrationality. Bell granted that liberalism at large offered no emotionally satisfying solution to the problem of alienation. But as Schlesinger, during the 1940s, had described the American communist as neurotic and psychologically unstable, Bell saw in the new rebel an anomic and potentially destructive individual seeking self-definition in a modernity that denied real purposefulness to radicalism. In this caricature, as much as in Vietnam or the black urban rebellions, lay the truest sources of Cold War liberals' quest for revenge against New Leftists.

And yet, as the 1960s dawned, the assorted problems at hand could be cheerfully debated, no more worrying than the annoyance of rock 'n' roll on the radio. The newer Cold War, jump-started by the Cuban events, served as a major stimulant for a public wearying of the arms race and warned by outgoing president Dwight Eisenhower of an ominous "military-industrial complex." With experts ready to take over the reins of the Kennedy administration, economic paradigms rooted in classical liberal faith and empowered at the highest levels made a dramatic comeback from the complex and tedious welfare economics of the age. Or rather, one economic paradigm was used to explain the increased suffering around the world and the potentially universal solutions already realized by the American genius.

The increasingly evident and dangerous condition of global poverty prompted liberal and conservative intellectuals alike to seize upon "development" as the solution to remaining global dilemmas. Walt Whitman Rostow, a convert from youthful Marxism to a ferocious conservatism and a key policy advisor to the Kennedy administration, set out the issues clearly. The right kind of societies reached the "take-off stage" of sustained growth while the wrong kind never did. Which were the right kind? Apart from their agreement with U.S. aims, they were middle-class societies with an effective state policy. When first written, Rostow's theories offered a complementary parallel to Bell's; within a decade or so, Rostow's argument would be almost indistinguishable from Milton Friedman's supposed free-market (but actually government-subsidized) solutions, and Rostow himself recognized as one of the great Republican hawks on Vietnam.[28]

The deeper conceptual problems in Rostow's view barely reached the surface of discussion and were thrust down again as alien and heretical. Could predominantly agricultural societies with large forests "grow" indefinitely without irremediable harm to ecological diversity, and where did that issue lie within "growth" calculus? Could any society escape poverty while remaining a supplier of natural resources to the developed world, buying manufactured goods (or making them only on a sweatshop-export basis) that precluded the development of a sustained home market? Could a stable middle class prosper when a peasantry, driven off the countryside by agricultural modernization, huddled impoverished at the margins of overcrowded cities?

As the era's most prestigious sociologists approached this evident difficulty, they predicted that the benign workings of the market would wear down the constricting kinship ties and promise a happier, more productive individualism in the era ahead. In this light, the U.S. presence in Vietnam was applauded early on as a long awaited "modernizing" force operating to free Vietnamese from their backward social relations, even as dissidents disappeared and bombs increasingly fell upon their villages. If the ACCF's liberals had better solutions for the global problems and the cruelties vastly expanded by U.S. military presence, none were forthcoming. Vietnam offered a marker because the Vietnamese successfully resisted, but the longer-range problems of class society, especially ecological ones, found no convincing answers here. Nor were they answered—or even asked—in the free-trade visions of 1950s liberalism's successor, the neoliberal Clinton regime of the 1990s.

The infamous crash of CIA cultural policies at the White House Festival of the Arts in 1965, where invited guest Dwight Macdonald shocked fellow dignitaries by passing around a petition denouncing U.S. policy in Southeast Asia, preceded the unraveling of CCF funding secrets and has tended to make liberal intellectuals seem vastly more rebellious than their previous record would suggest. In fact, their worldview was in extreme crisis.

The cities had begun to slip out of control of the planners and visionary technocrats even before the universities slipped out of the control of University of California chancellor Clark Kerr, then admired as the liberal savant of higher education. Along with the university, the liberal intellectuals seemed to be losing their native and long-favored urban domain to an enemy mainly dark-skinned and increasingly dangerous.[29] Their successful recovery from diminished reputation and self-confidence would only be achieved in time, and by then prove maddeningly incomplete. Long before they had become senior scholars on the edge of retirement or beyond, railing against the plague of "political correctness" around them, the Cold War ancients had experienced the anxiety of campus opposition and the humiliation of lost intellectual celebrity.

The perks and the high-stakes plans certainly continued, not only for themselves but for younger writers and scholars whose work they approved. And here their influence definitely continued to count. By the early 1960s, a beginning flood of perhaps a thousand volumes began to flow through selected presses, in some cases actually written by unacknowledged CIA staffers, in other cases simply subsidized as amenable to CIA positions. These senior scholars occupied some of the highest-paid academic chairs afforded by corporate contributions, with political protégés as their known successors. Their children, to the manor born, would become movers and shakers in the world of conservative journalism and punditry.

All this must have been gratifying, and yet it was hardly what they had expected earlier. Bernard Levin, who attended a sort of reunion of CIA operatives and friends in 1992, with Irving Kristol, Gertrude Himmelfarb, Edward Shils, and others in attendance, observed nostalgically that "having a great enemy had been almost as good as having a great friend and . . . arguably better. A friend was a friend, but a good adversary was a vocation."[30] No outsider could have put it more cogently.

Howard Brick argues in their defense that leading "systems theorists" of the 1950s and early 1960s (he generously resists connecting their ideas with their CIA involvements), admittedly notable as leading attackers of the New Left, had nevertheless in some cases pioneered the "postindustrial" theories taken over by the early New Left and had actually set the stage for the shift of radical argument from class economics to culture.[31] This is a provocative suggestion but hardly a persuasive one, and not only because the New Left was demonized as soon as it turned to the forbidden question of what price global populations (and ecology) paid for the West's abundance.

Contributors to this volume have argued, to the contrary, that the moral and spiritual background of the civil rights movement and the rejection of bureaucratic political models East and West prompted the practice and dream of participatory democracy, with all its weaknesses. The New Left's critique of liberalism, they have argued, also led to intractable difficulties in a society that allotted resources and media approval only to mainstream liberals and conservatives. The faulty or at least highly unproductive projection of "co-optation" as the chief tactic of "the system" to forestall and prevent sweeping change undoubtedly foreshadowed its opposite, the vanguard notion of early global victory over empire.

Perhaps there really was a "conscience liberalism" the whole time, misunderstood and precipitously discarded by the young. But from the good George McGovern (who never supported campus peaceniks before 1970) to the morally shaky Robert Kennedy, with his dark past in McCarthyism, it was so uncertain of itself, so compromised by alliances with the worst of corporate liberalism, that it failed utterly to provide young people with an alternative until the crucial moment had passed and the New Left fell in upon itself. The denouement was a profound tragedy, and there is plenty of blame to go around. But the young folks have carried more than their share of it for too long now. What remains to be analyzed, beyond the scope of this or any single study of the 1960s, is how the defection of the liberals to the causes of the weapons economy, neocolonialism, and highbrow culture negatively shaped and distorted the campus movements. Part of the problem is one of counter-history or parallel universes: We know that if organized labor had embraced the new social movements, they would have become a much larger, much more powerful social force. Organized or unorganized liberal intellectuals, on campus and off, would surely not have had as much grassroots impact. But if they, whatever their past moral compromises, had taken the lead in demanding the removal of all war-making and human rights–violating connections from campus, and done so in the name of real educational purposes, we may be sure that students would have recognized and even honored that leadership.

We stretch counter-history to the realm of fantasy to imagine George Meany promoting the cause of feminism or gay liberation. It is impossible to imagine Arthur Schlesinger Jr. or even Irving Howe hoisting the red banners in a student-faculty strike, entering the college president's office to open the file cabinets full of dark secrets of dirty deals—or using the pages of *Fortune* magazine and the *New York Times* to apologize for U.S. brutality across Asia, Africa, and Latin America, and to demand, long before 1970, an immediate withdrawal of the U.S. forces pouring hell upon little Vietnam.

The great majority of the CCF and ACCF intellectuals, from Sidney Hook and Diana Trilling to William Phillips (and for that matter Elia Kazan), never seem to have given an inch to the young, accurately trusting that in the long run, greater resources and influence would win back for their side at least the most eagerly opportunity-seeking segment of the Best and the Brightest. But there were exceptions, or partial exceptions, like Dwight Macdonald and Mary McCarthy (still rather angrier at Lillian Hellman than at the Pentagon), who perhaps raised in us wider but false hopes—and for that reason our disappointment in them is greater than the savants probably ever imagined it could be. Not that we idealized them as they evidently wished to be idealized. But as intellectuals and scholars ourselves, we self-consciously inherited their sometimes-radical history, along with the collective legacy of Tom Paine, the Transcendentalists, the Abolitionists, Walt Whitman, Ash Can artists, Village bohemians, Margaret Sanger, Socialists, Wobblies, Popular Fronters and Trotskyites, Woody Guthrie, Orson Welles, and all the rest. We wanted to meet them as equals, which was surely not too much to ask. At their near-last historical moment, amply protected by tenure as well as reputation, they might have joined us against the campus administrators and eager-to-punish professors. No one was asking them to take LSD, or to enjoy the Beatles, or even to wash the dishes at home, necessarily. Just to be on our side against the really bad guys.

Alas, even by 1965 it was way too late. The fall of the Berlin Wall on the day after its construction and a sudden end to the Cold War would probably not have made any great difference—we would naturally have been against corporate globalization, as our young successors are today, and they logically in favor of technocratic solutions, ecology an afterthought. The contrasts of generation, and ways of looking at power and prestige, were already too great. The liberal intellectuals' day had come within the mainstream when we happened along to spoil their fun.

Ironically, for the many of us who proceeded from disillusionment with the Russian betrayals of socialism and the hokiness of the Popular Front model, eager to find better roots among the further-left histories, it was the ex-communist old-timers who were self-effacing about their own past failures and illusions, and eager to assist in teaching hands-on organizing, campus by campus or neighborhood by neighborhood. That unexpected rapprochement matches our contemporary experience. On the campus, as we teachers search for useable artifacts, 1950s literary criticism leaves students cold and Abstract Expressionism bores, but Woody Guthrie, *Salt of the Earth,* and the *Port Huron Statement* touch generation after generation, along with Beat literature and the anti-globalist Indie bands.

We look back today in wonder that as revelations about CIA practices emerged in 1967, and scandal enveloped some of the most prestigious and influential liberals in American society, the absence of shock or embarrassment was nearly deafening. At almost the same moment, a strategic sequel went right to the heart of the whole contemporary liberal dilemma. According to the historian of the ADA, when Arthur Schlesinger Jr. pressured Vice President Hubert Humphrey to appoint new experts to run the

Vietnam War, Humphrey (who determinedly believed that the Chinese guided the National Liberation Front) snapped, "Arthur, these are your guys. You were in the White House when they took over. Don't blame them on us."[32] Let that little bit of unintentional eloquence stand for the unresolved problems between the generations.

Notes

1. Brent Staples, "Blaming Nixon," *New York Times Book Review,* 16 Jan. 2000.

2. Perhaps no writer more than Todd Gitlin has at once celebrated his own early status as a leader and bemoaned what happened to an out-of-control, younger New Left. *The Sixties: Years of Hope, Days of Rage* (New York: Bantam Books, 1987) is the classic account, to which have been added various ex-radical memoirs of pure vitriol. It is fair to say that the more sympathetic accounts about local activities have never received similar attention.

3. George Packer, *Blood of the Liberals* (New York: Farrar, Straus & Giroux, 2000), 229–30. Packer earns our sympathy: His father, the Stanford administration's voice on the issue, suffered a stroke after a few years of campus stress. Still, even that tragedy can hardly justify Stanford's ardent protection of its own considerable debt to military and intelligence contractors.

4. Richard Rorty, "The People's Flag Is Deepest Red," in *Audacious Democracy,* ed. Steven Fraser and Joshua B. Freeman (New York: Mariner Books, 1997), 61.

5. See Jerry Lembcke, *The Spitting Image: Myth, Memory and the Legacy of Vietnam* (New York: New York University Press, 1998).

6. The South Bay (San Francisco) Labor Council issued a historic resolution (25 Sept. 2000) called "It's Time to Clear the Air about AFL-CIO Policy Abroad!" noting a *Labor Studies Journal* (summer 2000) documentation of AFL-CIO collaboration with Henry Kissinger, the CIA, and the Rockefeller interests in overthrowing the elected Allende government of Chile in 1972. Regrettably, the new AFL-CIO leadership has backed away from opening up its files on assorted illegal activities and human rights violations involving some of its most prominent past figures, from Meany to Lane Kirkland and Albert Shanker. See "AFL-CIO Caught in Cold-War Time Warp," *The Labor Educator,* June/July 2001.

7. Frances Stonor Saunders, *The Cultural Cold War: The CIA In the World of Arts and Letters* (New York: New Press, 2000), has broken the main new ground here. Other studies, including my own *Taking Care of Business: Samuel Gompers, George Meany, Lane Kirkland and the Tragedy of American Business* (New York: Monthly Review Press, 1999), have essentially brought scattered sources together.

8. A distinctly different argument was made by Christopher Lasch in "The Cultural Cold War: A Short History of the Congress of Cultural Freedom," reprinted from the *New York Review of Books* in *The Agony of the American Left* (New York: Knopf, 1969), 61–114.

9. See Maurice Isserman and Michael Kazin, *America Divided: The Civil War of the 1960s* (New York: Oxford University Press, 1999) for a vivid example.

10. Rorty, "The People's Flag," 62. An earlier, collective version of Rorty's wronged-liberalism thesis was recorded in a *Commentary* statement in 1970 when those disillusioned (in Nathan Glazer's phrase "deradicalized") by the movement stated their defense of American society against its criticisms—although to call them "deradicalized" was quite an exaggeration for the vast majority of the cases. These included such old CCF/ACCF hands as Glazer himself, and future CIA assets such as Rustin, Carl Gershman, Penn Kemble and Elliott Abrams, and also such

Reagan era conservative notables as Michael Novack and Diane Ravitch. Inasmuch as not one of them had *ever* opposed the Vietnam War on principle and most of them had already engaged in assaults on the campus antiwar movement, their conversion was understandably viewed with contemporary skepticism. Others signing on included veteran CCFers Kristol, Seymour Martin Lipset, Walt Laqueur, Daniel Bell, Jean Kirkpatrick, and Theodore Draper (see William Gid Powers, *Not without Honor: The History of American Anticommunism* [New York: Free Press, 1992], 342). Thanks to Daniel Bell for permission to look at the papers of the American Committee for Cultural Freedom at Tamiment Library, New York University (hereafter ACCF Papers).

11. See Paul Buhle, *Taking Care of Business,* chap. 4, 204–27.

12. Thus executive Sol Stein wrote to the Rockefeller Foundation on 3 Dec. 1953, "We do not derive any financial support, whatsoever, from the government," a staggering deception (ACCF Papers). Did the officers of the Rockefeller know better when they turned down the ACCF? We can only suspect.

13. Quoted from an interview of Braden by Ben Rathbun in *The Point Man: Irving Brown and the Deadly Post-1945 Struggle for Europe and Africa* (Montreaux: Minerva Press, 1996), 121.

14. Among others formally connected with the CCF/ACCF as the "American Committee" were Daniel Aaron, Jacques Barzun, Bruno Bettelheim, David Dubinsky, Max Eastman, Richard Hofstadter, Ferdinand Lundberg, Allen Nevins, Philip Rahv, George Schuyler, John Steinbeck, Peter Viereck, Robert Warshow, Thornton Wilder, Karl Wittfogel, Bertram D. Wolfe and, James Rorty, Richard Rorty's father. Schlesigner served as a vice chair, along with Reinhold Neibuhr and others, with Sidney Hook as chair and William Phillips of the CCF-subsidized *Partisan Review* as cultural secretary. While a small handful of these and other American Committee members later repudiated the CIA connections and opposed the Vietnam War, the anti-campus peace movement rhetoric turned out by the majority would fill a large and vituperative volume. Not one of them seems to have urged the withdrawal of the United States from Vietnam—at least not before 1970.

15. William Kristol is editor of the *National Standard,* John Podhoretz a leading figure at the *New York Post,* and Elliott Abrams (son-in-law of Norman Podhoretz), convicted of lying to Congress about Contra funding during the 1980s, is now senior director of the National Security Council's Office for Democracy, Human Rights, and International Operations in the Bush administration. The ACCF Papers contain much further valuable confirming information of an intimate nature here, including David Riesman's note recalling proudly his youthful participation in the New York state brief against CCNY instructor Morris U. Schappes in 1940 as part of the first campus red scare of post-1920 days. Sensitive sections of the collection remain closed.

16. James Strodes, *Allen Dulles: Master of Spies* (Washington, D.C.: Regnery, 1999), 416.

17. Saunders, *The Cultural Cold War,* 379. Schlesinger admits to none of this in *A Life in the Twentieth Century: The Innocent Years* (New York: Houghton Mifflin, 2000), perhaps saving the darker truths for a subsequent volume of memoirs.

18. Arthur Schlesinger Jr., *The Vital Center* (Boston: Little, Brown, 1949), 159.

19. Thus Hans Kohn, at an executive committee meeting of the ACCF in April 1955: "Communism is not a danger in the U.S. but it is a danger in the intellectual community" (ACCF Papers).

20. On Moynihan's role, see Eric Chester, *Covert Network: Progressives, the International Rescue Committee and the CIA* (Armonk, N.Y.: M. E. Sharpe, 1995), 213.

21. The ACCF executive previewed this interpretation by insisting that African Americans convicted of capital crimes in the South were perforce guilty, inasmuch as they had received constitutionally proper jury trials (ACCF executive on the conviction of "Negroes in Martinsville,"

a major civil rights case of the moment, telegram to Paris office of CCF, 28 Feb 1951, ACCF Papers).

22. By contrast, the flattened definition of women's role and status during the postwar era had hardly seemed problematic to liberals even by the end of the 1950s. Women's status in the CCF and ACCF more than underlined this general rule: With the rarest exceptions, it was only as wives, girlfriends, and hostesses that they appeared and influenced events, and the rage against feminism by CCF/ACCF veterans was unsurpassed by any other political passion in the era to follow. Nonwhites, for their part, could scarcely be found among the collaborating intellectuals, apart from the conservative George Schuyler.

23. Robert Dahl, *Who Governs? Democracy and Power in an American City* (New Haven: Yale University Press, 1961), a volume widely assigned in undergraduate political science, sociology, and even history courses during the early to middle 1960s.

24. John Kenneth Galbraith, *The Affluent Society* (Boston: Houghton Mifflin, 1958). See Stonor Saunders's informative and amusing chapter on the campaign for Abstract Expressionism and, especially, the chosen favorites of Clement Greenberg, "Yanqui Doodles," in *The Cultural Cold War,* 252–78. ACCF executive committee minutes for 19 March 1952, reveal Greenberg furiously conspiring against an Artists' Equity that he considered to be "Fellow Travelers," thus holdouts against his own artistic tastes and suitable for purging from the judges of art shows (ACCF Papers).

25. Bell at executive committee meeting, 3 March 1952, ACCF Papers.

26. Riesman himself in the mid-1960s defended corporations as the true centers of intellectual freedom, in contrast to universities, their climate obviously threatened by young people who pointedly refused to follow the straight-and-narrow path to successful corporate careers, in a hectic correspondence with his old friend, former Marxist Richard Hofstadter (Hofstadter Papers, Columbia University, esp. Riesman to Hofstadter, 7 Dec. 1964).

27. Daniel Bell, *The End of Ideology: On the Exhaustion of Political Ideas in the Fifties* (Glencoe, Ill.: The Free Press, 1960).

28. Howard Brick, *Age of Contradiction* (New York: Twayne, 1998), chap. 3, esp. 44–52.

29. As Nelson Lichtenstein has observed, their "social policy debacle symbolizes the failure of New Deal statecraft to renew its ideological and political mandate at one of the most propitious moments of the postwar era, the golden hour of early 1960s liberalism" (Lichtenstein, "Vanishing Jobs in a Racialized America," *Radical History Review* 78 [fall, 2000]: 179).

30. Isaiah Berlin pleaded with fellow operatives, apparently with great success, *not* to reveal in memoirs what might prove deeply embarrassing to all and to none more than himself. Levin quoted in Saunders, *The Cultural Cold War,* 421.

31. Brick, *The Age of Contradiction,* 55.

32. Quoted in Steve Gillon, *Politics and Vision: The ADA and American Liberalism, 1947–1985* (New York: Oxford University Press, 1987), 198. The ADA, whose inner workings might be described as a public face for CCF/ACCF power-wielding, never recovered.

About the Contributors

PAUL BUHLE is a lecturer in American civilization at Brown University. He was founding editor of *Radical America*, the preeminent journal of the New Left, and he is author or editor of twenty-four books on American radicalism, labor, and popular culture, including (with Mari Jo Buhle and Dan Georgakas) *Encyclopedia of the American Left* (1999).

DAVID COCHRAN teaches at John A. Logan Community College in Carterville, Illinois. He is the author of *American Noir: Underground Writers and Filmmakers of the Postwar Era* (2000).

MICHAEL S. FOLEY is an assistant professor of history at the College of Staten Island, City University of New York. The University of North Carolina Press will publish his forthcoming book on the draft resistance movement during the Vietnam War.

JENNIFER FROST is an associate professor of history at Northern Colorado University and author of *"An Interracial Movement of the Poor": Community Organizing and the New Left in the 1960s* (2001).

ANDREW HUNT is an associate professor of history at the University of Waterloo in Waterloo, Canada. His book *The Turning: A History of Vietnam Veterans against the War* (2001) was picked by *Choice*, the journal of the American Library Association, as a book of the year in 2001. He is currently writing a biography of David Dellinger.

IAN LEKUS is a Ph.D. candidate in history at Duke University, where he is finishing his dissertation, "Queer and Present Dangers: Homosexuality and American Antiwar Activism, 1964–1973."

PETER B. LEVY is an associate professor of history at York College in York, Pennsylvania. His publications include *Let Freedom Ring: A Documentary History of the Modern Civil Rights Movement* (1992), *The New Left and Labor in the 1960s* (1994), and *America in the Sixties: Right, Left, and Center: A Documentary History* (1998).

ROBBIE LIEBERMAN is professor of history at Southern Illinois University–Carbondale. She is author of *"My Song Is My Weapon": People's Songs, American Communism, and the Politics of Culture, 1930-1950* (1989) and *The Strangest Dream: Communism, Anticommunism, and the U.S. Peace Movement, 1945-1963* (2000). She is currently working on an oral history of Midwestern student radicals in the 1960s.

KEVIN MATTSON is associate professor of history at Ohio University. He is author of *Intellectuals in Action: The Origins of the New Left and Radical Liberalism, 1945-1970* (2002) and *Creating a Democratic Public: The Struggle for Urban Participatory Democracy during the Progressive Era* (1998). He has also coedited *Democracy's Moment: Reforming the American Political System for the Twenty-first Century* (2002).

DAVID MCBRIDE is an editor for Routledge Press in New York City. He received his Ph.D. in American history from UCLA, and his dissertation examined the counterculture in 1960s Los Angeles.

JOHN MCMILLIAN teaches history and literature at Harvard University. He has published articles and review essays in *Radical History Review, Rethinking History,* and *American Quarterly,* and he is coeditor (with Timothy Patrick McCarthy) of *The Radical Reader: A Documentary Anthology of the American Radical Tradition* (2003). He is currently writing a social history of the New Left.

GREGG L. MICHEL is assistant professor of history at the University of Texas at San Antonio. His dissertation, "'We'll Take Our Stand': The Southern Student Organizing Committee and the Radicalization of White Southern Students, 1964-1969," will be published by Palgrave/St. Martin's Press.

FRANCESCA POLLETTA is associate professor of sociology at Columbia University. She is author of *Freedom Is an Endless Meeting: Democracy in American Social Movements* (forthcoming) and coeditor of *Passionate Politics: Emotions and Social Movements* (forthcoming).

DOUG ROSSINOW is assistant professor and chair of the history department at Metropolitan State University, Minneapolis. He is the author of *The Politics of Authenticity: Liberalism, Christianity, and the New Left in America* (1998), as well as numerous articles, and is working on a book entitled *The Vital Margin: Interpreting "Progressive" Politics in Modern America.*

JEREMY VARON is an assistant professor of history at Drew University. He is the author of *"Shadowboxing the Apocalypse": Political Violence, Utopia, and Terror in the American and West German New Left* (forthcoming). He has published essays in *New German Critique* and is a contributor to *Public Affairs: Politics in the Age of Scandal* (2003).